MW00987597

Most Fortunate
UNFORTUNATES

"How Noble Its Arches," from 1909 Annual Report. Courtesy of JCRS.

Most Fortunate
UNFORTUNATES

THE JEWISH ORPHANS' HOME
OF NEW ORLEANS

MARLENE TRESTMAN

For Randy Smith
I'm honored to
share the story of

LOUISIANA STATE UNIVERSITY PRESS
BATON ROUGE

Isidore Newman School!
all best wishes
marlene Trestman
10·25·2023

Published with the assistance of the V. Ray Cardozier Fund and the
Mike and Ayan Rubin Endowment for the Study of Civil Rights and Social Justice

Published by Louisiana State University Press
lsupress.org

Manufactured in the United States of America
First printing

Designer: Barbara Neely Bourgoyne
Typeface: Whitman
Printer and binder: Sheridan Books

Jacket photograph: Home children, 1909. Courtesy of Jewish Children's Regional Service.

Library of Congress Cataloging-in-Publication Data
Names: Trestman, Marlene, 1956– author.
Title: Most fortunate unfortunates : the Jewish Orphans' Home of New Orleans /
    Marlene Trestman.
Description: Baton Rouge : Louisiana State University Press, [2023] |
    Includes bibliographical references and index.
Identifiers: LCCN 2023004009 (print) | LCCN 2023004010 (ebook) | ISBN 978-0-
    8071-7290-2 (cloth) | ISBN 978-0-8071-8088-4 (pdf) | ISBN 978-0-8071-8087-7 (epub)
Subjects: LCSH: Home for Jewish Widows and Orphans (New Orleans, La.)—History. |
    Isidore Newman School—History. | Jewish orphanages—Louisiana—New Orleans—
    History—19th century. | Jewish orphanages—Louisiana—New Orleans—History—
    20th century. | Children—Institutional care—United States—History—20th century.
Classification: LCC HV995.N42 N498 2023 (print) | LCC HV995.N42 (ebook) |
    DDC 362.73/2—dc23/eng/20230720
LC record available at https://lccn.loc.gov/2023004009
LC ebook record available at https://lccn.loc.gov/2023004010

To my husband,

HENRY D. KAHN

and

In memory of my parents,

MAE SCHWEDELSON TRESTMAN
September 4, 1912–January 7, 1968

and

ANCHEL TRESTMAN
June 23, 1893–March 28, 1965

You shall not mistreat any widow or orphan.
If you do mistreat them, I will surely hear their cry.

—EXODUS 22:23

In this dread uncertainty of life and fortune, who is there among this community . . . who can say that this Institution is not for him and his?

—BENJAMIN FRANKLIN JONAS,
future U.S. senator, at the dedication of the Home for
Jewish Widows and Orphans, January 8, 1856

Fortunate Unfortunates. That's what we were—we kids who were raised in the Jewish Children's Home in New Orleans.

—LOUIS PETERS, Home alumnus (1925–1932), May 1980

CONTENTS

Illustrations follow page 124.

PREFACE AND
ACKNOWLEDGMENTS

I am well acquainted with the imposing red brick structure that once stood in uptown New Orleans at the intersection of St. Charles and Jefferson avenues, on the downtown river side. I knew it as the Jewish Community Center, or JCC, a two-story building whose deteriorating third floor and grand ornamental towers had been removed a decade earlier. The JCC occupied the former Jewish Children's Home and provided office space to the Home's successor, today known as the Jewish Children's Regional Service (JCRS). Before the entire structure was torn down in 1964 to make way for the JCC's current building, I frequented the former orphanage to attend day camp and ballet classes and to meet with JCRS social workers assigned to my case. Like many "half-orphans" and other dependent children who once lived in the Home, my mother struggled alone to raise my brother and me in the St. Thomas Public Housing Project; my father, a Russian immigrant who once owned a pharmacy on Dryades Street, was confined to the state mental hospital in Jackson, Louisiana, for years before he died in 1965.

Less than three years later, when I was eleven, my mother died from breast cancer. My brother and I, now "full orphans," were declared wards of the state. I am keenly aware—had the Home remained open for about two more decades—that I would have lived there. Instead, having earlier ended institutional childcare, JCRS oversaw my foster care in the home of an extraordinarily loving family that to this day I consider my own. Moreover, I may be the only Jewish orphan who, after the Home closed, was admitted to Isidore Newman School pursuant to a 1946 agreement that the school would continue to educate "any qualified child who shall now or at any time hereafter be a ward" of the Home. For these lifechanging opportunities, including scholarships to Camp Barney Medintz and Goucher College, and lifelong Newman School friends, I consider myself a "most fortunate unfortunate."

The years I spent researching the life of Bessie Margolin—one of the Home's (and Newman's) most acclaimed alumni and the subject of my first book, *Fair Labor Lawyer*—deepened my curiosity about the orphanage. What was it like to grow up in the Home? How did those experiences change over time? Did those kids, too, feel they were fortunate unfortunates? This book is my effort to answer those questions and others. This book is also the story of an institution born from the vision and commitment of men and women who gave their time and money to ensure that the neediest Jews of New Orleans and the mid-South were sheltered until they were deemed capable of supporting themselves or their families regained the ability to care for them.

I am grateful to the following people who made this book possible:

Project funders: American Jewish Archives, Dallas Jewish Historical Society, Texas Jewish Historical Society, and Southern Jewish Historical Society.

Readers: Mark Bauman, Jonathan Sarna, Scott Langston, Reena Sigman Friedman, Irwin Lachoff, Louis Y. Fishman, and Catherine Cahn Kahn.

Other historians, researchers, archivists, and genealogists: Wendy L. Besmann, Caroline Light, Hollace Weiner, Gary P. Zola, Jean H. Baker, Bobbie Malone, Ellen Barnett Cleary, Florence Jumonville, Richard Campanella, Genie McCloskey, Adrien Genet, Audrey Kariel, Susan Thomas, Wayne Carp, Jennifer Light, Walter Stern, Janet Cook, Dale Rosengarten, Barry Stiefel, John Kennedy, Victoria Fisch, Brian Thompson, Bart Wallet, Jacquelynn Weiss, Cynthia Johnson Hebert, and Joseph Yranski; the staffs of American Jewish Archives, Tulane University Libraries Special Collections, Louisiana State Museum, Institute for Southern Jewish Life, New Orleans Public Library—Louisiana Division, and New Orleans Notarial Archives; and fellow members of "'Hear Their Cry': Understanding the Jewish Orphan Experience," a scholars' working group serendipitously convened from 2019 to 2021 by Amy Traver and Susan Jacobowitz under the auspices of the Center for Jewish History.

Technical wizards: Developmental editor Heather Lundine, transcriptionist Theresa DuBois, and indexer Scott Smiley.

Cheering squads: Ned Goldberg, Mark Rubin, and Jewish Children's Regional Service; Biographers International Organization "Group Biography" working group; the pandemic-born "Fridays with Goucher Friends" Zoom group; and my wonderful family.

Beloved New Orleans hosts: Ann Thorpe Thompson and the late Shaw Thompson.

Finally, this book's bibliography identifies many, many people who generously shared with me their own or family members' experiences of growing up or working in the Home. I hope that in my selection of people, stories, and photographs to include in this book, by necessity a tiny fraction of all that I have come to know, I do no injustice. In addition to materials beautifully exhibited at the Museum of the Southern Jewish Experience in New Orleans and previously published in my newsletters, I invite readers to explore appendices, stories, and images in an *Online Supplement* to this book at marlenetrestman.com.

Most Fortunate
UNFORTUNATES

INTRODUCTION

In the nineteenth and into the twentieth centuries, before government assumed responsibility for supporting indigent families, orphanages were common across the country. Although the total number of children reared in America's orphanages is unknown, in 1900, more than 1,000 orphanages operated throughout the nation (including 20 Jewish orphanages) where nearly 100,000 children resided.[1] Mostly private and often run by religious organizations, these institutions—whether known as orphanages, asylums, or homes—served a crucial role by protecting, sheltering, and educating children who lacked family or friends able and willing to care for them. Conditions in orphanages varied widely, largely determined by the community support they received, although regimentation and harsh discipline characterized most of them, especially before 1900. As childcare methods and philosophies evolved with pressure from progressive reformers and the emergence of professional social workers, orphanages became more humane, ultimately yielding to the priority of keeping families intact wherever possible and, when not, placing children in private foster homes.

The Home for Jewish Widows and Orphans in New Orleans ("the Home") offers a window into the history of institutional childcare in America, generally, with particular focus on Jewish orphanages across the country and orphanages in New Orleans. When its doors opened on February 1, 1856, the Home became the nation's first building designed and erected to house Jewish orphans. It was not, however, the first American organization to address those needs. South Carolina's Hebrew Orphan Society, founded in 1801, holds that distinction. Nor was the Home the first American Jewish orphanage, a title held by Philadelphia's Jewish Foster Home, which opened in rented quarters six months before its New Orleans counterpart.[2] Instead, staking the

Home's finely parsed claim as the country's first purpose-built Jewish orphanage conveys the permanence and purposefulness intended by its founders. At a time when fatal epidemics and the needs of poor immigrant coreligionists overwhelmed New Orleans's existing Jewish benevolent societies, building an orphanage from the ground up demonstrated the founders' unmistakable commitment to addressing of the needs of vulnerable Jews. And in a city where the predominant religious groups had long before established such asylums, the Home entitled New Orleans's Jewry to assert equal standing.

The Home was unique in other ways, driven as much by its leaders' obedience to the biblical commandment to care for widows and orphans as by their conformance to the norms of their adoptive city. No other Jewish orphanage was built by founders while enslaving Black persons (including children) or lost the service of officers banished for refusing to pledge loyalty to the Union during the city's federal occupation after the Civil War. Nor did any other Jewish orphanage officially celebrate its anniversary on a secular holiday, as did the Home by choosing January 8 to honor its longevity, the day in 1815 when General Andrew Jackson defeated the British in the Battle of New Orleans. Moreover, by opening the Isidore Newman School in 1904, the Home was the only American orphanage of any religious affiliation to establish and maintain a coed, secular school that admitted outside children (albeit then only white children) whose parents paid tuition.[3]

The Home, which sheltered a total of 1,623 children and 24 adult women, also cast a relatively wide geographic footprint. Until 1930, when the Pauline Stern Wolff Home opened in Houston, it was the only Jewish orphanage located within the seven mid-South states of B'nai B'rith's District 7 (Louisiana, Texas, Alabama, Arkansas, Mississippi, Tennessee, and Oklahoma) and served as the primary orphanage for those states' Jewish children.[4] After an average stay of seven years, the Home discharged its children to no fewer than twenty-eight states, sending more than half of its wards to a different community from which they were admitted. These former wards often relocated before settling and raising families. Descendants of alumni span the nation.

The Home thus contributed to the identity of Jewish communities in and beyond New Orleans. While ensuring that the mid-South's neediest Jewish children were reared within the faith, the Home also enabled its donors and volunteers to demonstrate their Judaism through philanthropy and humanitarianism without requiring them to join a synagogue or adhere to religious traditions. Moreover, with its prominent buildings (in two locations), regular public events, and the visibility of its children in frequent and overwhelmingly favorable news accounts and official reports, the Home served as a cultural broker, making an indelible and positive impression about Jews on the greater New Orleans community and beyond.

Compared to Jewish orphanages in other parts of the country, the Home had a relatively small population. Even at its largest enrollment of 173 (which occurred only briefly during 1915), the Home's population was dwarfed by those of New York's Hebrew Orphan Asylum and Cleveland's Jewish Orphan Asylum (CJOA), which respectively reached peak occupancies of 1,755 in 1916 and 600 in 1906, and whose respective cumulative populations reached 18,000 (between 1860 and 1941) and more than 3,000 (between 1868 and 1917).[5] Nonetheless, given the relatively small size of New Orleans's Jewish community compared to those of New York and Cleveland (in 1918, for instance, Jews constituted 2 percent of New Orleans's population, compared to 26 and 13 percent in the much larger cities of New York and Cleveland, respectively), the Home assumed greater significance in its locale.[6] Despite its importance, and the relatively large number of books and memoirs about orphans and other orphanages, this is the first complete history of the Home.[7]

Throughout most of its existence, the Home's relatively small population enabled its benefactors to provide more than subsistence in terms of food, clothing, medical care, furnishings, recreation, and education. While most alumni described their childhoods with only or largely positive sentiments, others expressed sadness or bitterness about a policy or practice, such as the regimented schedule and discipline, or from seemingly unfair or disparate treatment, such as wrongly being accused of misconduct. Yet, considering the lack of viable alternatives amid tragic or desperate family circumstances, the vast majority of alumni expressed gratitude for the care and opportunities the Home provided and the strong bonds they forged with fellow residents and staff.

Overall, the Home's investment in its wards paid off. Hundreds of alumni lived lives of significant accomplishment in medicine, law, engineering, business, social work, and teaching. Four alumni, Isadore Moritz, Edgar Goldberg, Jake H. (Batkowski) Butler, and Joe Samuels, who were discharged from the Home between 1894 and 1934, founded or took over newspapers in Texas.[8] David Stifft, who lived in the Home from 1874 to 1882, cofounded the Minneapolis Society of American Magicians and became a celebrated magician.[9] Sam Rosenthal, who spent a decade in the Home before his discharge in 1918, served forty-six years as mayor of Rolling Fork, Mississippi, which named its municipal building in his honor.[10] As brothers Sam and Emanuel Pulitzer were building what became Wemco, Inc., one of the world's largest neckwear manufacturers, Rogers Perlis gained recognition throughout Louisiana as a clothing retailer who turned a crawfish into a popular sportswear logo.[11] Memphis-born Joe Bihari, who lived in the Home from 1931 to 1943, earned a place in the Blues Hall of Fame in 2006 for his contributions as a pioneering music producer who recorded the likes of B. B. King and Etta James.[12] Most alumnae married and nurtured families, while some also supported family businesses, taught, became nurses or social workers, or volunteered in their communities. Leah Hoodman Goot, a refugee of the Russian pogroms who lived in the Home from 1883 to 1887, founded Hadassah's San Antonio chapter, served as the organization's Texas president, and was celebrated for her work with the Youth Aliyah project which relocated thousands of orphaned children to Israel.[13] A few alumnae defied gender barriers and pursued professions. Bessie Margolin, who lived in the Home from 1913 to 1925, championed workers' rights at the U.S. Supreme Court as associate solicitor of labor.[14] Hilda Crystal White, who lived in the Home from 1920 to 1928, authored several books, including *Wild Decembers,* a biography of fictional orphan Jane Eyre, which was inspired by Hilda's childhood.[15]

Not all alumni became goodwill ambassadors for the Home. After his 1862 expulsion for "utter want of subordination," Morris Mengis went on to a life of alleged arson, gambling, commercial bankruptcy, and high-profile litigation, including his million-dollar verdict in 1904 arising from an ill-fated business deal with several railroad tycoons.[16] Norman Mayer, who lived in the Home from 1923 to 1933, captured national headlines in 1982 when he held nine tourists hostage in the Washington Monument in a misguided effort to ban nuclear weapons. Although no one else was injured, Mayer lost his own life to police sharpshooters after falsely claiming that his truck was loaded with explosives.[17]

Nor is the Home's record unblemished, even when judged by contemporaneous standards. In 1865, the Orleans Parish Grand Jury, which inspected the city's charitable institutions, found the Home "badly managed" with conditions "evinc[ing] a want of care."[18] The "Golden City," the Home's heralded program of self-governance that prevailed from 1909 through 1925, was later condemned for entrusting youngsters to the authority and occasional tyranny of older peers.[19] Beginning in 1925, the Home faced questions about the potential harm from sending its children to Newman School where, mixed with scions of the city's middle and upper classes, they might be subject to "snobbery and class prejudice."[20] The Home also withstood scandal. In 1886, the board fired its superintendent for "gross immoral conduct towards a female inmate of the Home."[21]

Moreover, the Home—as a congregate child-care institution—had its detractors. By the early twentieth century, the Home's board began steadfastly resisting calls from professionals in the evolving field of social work to reject institutional childcare and move toward foster care in those cases when families could not be kept intact. Instead, Home managers addressed such criticism by making the institution as "homelike" as possible, such as by transforming the "barracks-style" dormitory wings into small uniquely furnished bedrooms, and disbanding insular activities to integrate the children into the community's clubs and Reform congregations. The Home achieved remarkable success in becoming, as the *Times-Picayune* reported in 1930, "the institution that is not an institution."[22]

By 1939, as New Deal programs enabled poor, single parents to retain their children, only sixty-three children remained in the Home. Even if the board had been inclined to keep the institution open—something the cavernous structure's high fixed costs made economically unfeasible—the sudden death of longtime superintendent "Uncle Harry" Ginsburg in June 1946 cemented its inevitable decision to close the Home. Since then, the successor organization today known as the Jewish Children's Regional Service (JCRS) has provided funding and other nonresidential services for Jewish children and their families in what it calls its "Modern Era." This is the story of the ninety-one years that came before the Modern Era, when the physical structure of the Home embodied the organization's mission and the modernity of its time.

chapter one

A PERMANENT HOME
1853–1856

In the summer of 1853, Babette Baer Schwartz became a widow at thirty-five. The pregnant mother of three young children, however, had little opportunity to dwell on the death of her husband, Benjamin.[1] Nor was her plight unusual. Benjamin was one of eight thousand New Orleanians who died of yellow fever that summer, an estimated death rate of one in every twelve to fifteen residents.[2] New Orleans's Jewish community alone lost one hundred members, including Benjamin, to the disease that year.[3] This was the nation's single most fatal epidemic of the disease whose cause—the bite of an infected *Aedes aegypti* mosquito—was not discovered for another half-century.[4]

All summer long, bells tolled incessantly as cemeteries hosted back-to-back interments and unbroken funeral processions crowded the roads. Carriages and omnibuses followed wagons and hospital carts piled high with coffins. The crude wooden boxes awaited the attention of overwhelmed gravediggers, giving rise to the morbid expression that the dead might need to dig their own graves.[5] On the day Benjamin died, 191 yellow fever victims were buried among the city's dozen cemeteries. The horror did not peak, however, until August 22— "Black Day"—when more than 254 people succumbed to the disease.[6]

Beyond the commotion in and around the cemeteries, Babette and her children could not escape the bone-shaking blasts from cannons stationed across the city, a futile experiment to rid New Orleans's hot and humid air of noxious and supposedly fatal effluvia.[7] Equally unavoidable, acrid fumes, eerie glow, and dense columns of smoke rose from barrels of burning tar in another pointless attempt to purify the atmosphere of the "bad air" mistakenly believed to carry the disease.[8] Meanwhile, stores were shuttered as the city's usual carnival-like sounds of shoppers, vendors, and entertainers were silenced by illness, death, and fear.[9]

No record remains of the progression of Benjamin's illness or whether he endured any of the prevailing ineffective and often toxic treatments. Yellow fever's gruesome and debilitating symptoms, including jaundice and internal bleeding, earned it over one hundred nicknames in five languages, such as "Saffron Scourge," "Maladie du Diable," and "Black Vomit." It was also known as "the Stranger's Disease" because newcomers to New Orleans, whether from other states or foreign shores, lived in greatest peril.[10] "Unacclimated," the name given to newcomers, reflected a science that eluded understanding; natives of New Orleans and other locales where yellow fever remained endemic often had previously and unknowingly experienced a mild case from a mosquito bite that had conferred immunity. People just understood that the plague most closely haunted immigrants and newcomers, especially the poor, who caught the blame for spreading the disease.[11]

The entire Schwartz family remained unacclimated, although only Benjamin perished. He and Babette had traveled to America from Bavaria with their two girls, Hannah and Sarah, shortly before their son Lazar was born in Woodville, Mississippi, in 1852, and had resettled in New Orleans when the epidemic hit. Like many other recent immigrants, the Schwartzes had no way to escape the city before Benjamin fell ill, nor nearby relatives to provide support after he died. Babette lacked means to care for her three toddlers, or for twins Regina and Wolff, who were born four months after their father's death.[12]

During the same period that Benjamin Schwartz died from yellow fever, James Koppel Gutheim survived the disease. In 1843, the twenty-six-year-old son and grandson of Talmudic scholars sailed to America from Westphalia, Germany, where he studied under the province's chief rabbi. He first lived in New York, where he gained fluency in English while working as a bookkeeper and correspondent for a Jewish monthly journal. In 1846, although he was not ordained, he launched his rabbinical career in Cincinnati. As one of only five Jewish ministers in America with full command of the English language, he earned a reputation as a compelling pulpit speaker. In 1850, Gutheim answered the advertisement of New Orleans's oldest Hebrew congregation, Gates of Mercy, which sought an English-speaking leader. Gutheim exceeded their requirements.[13] In 1853, while tending to the city's sick and dying, he contracted yellow fever.[14] Once recovered, Gutheim dedicated himself to caring for New Orleans's neediest Jews, including Babette and her children.

NEW ORLEANS—THE SOUTH'S QUEEN AND NECROPOLIS

The Schwartzes and Gutheim came to New Orleans when it reigned as the "Queen of the South." Cotton was "king" of the economy, sweetened by the rich returns of sugar plantations, all fueled by enslaved labor. Businesspeople seeking prosperity and immigrants seeking a better life swelled the city's population to 160,000 by 1860, an increase of more than 50,000 over the preceding decade.[15] The nation's fifth largest city by population, New Orleans rivaled New York as America's busiest port.[16]

New Orleans also was the most international and ethnically mixed city in the nation. It represented a unique and vibrant mélange of populations of not only German, French, Irish, Creole, Spanish, Haitian, Cuban, Native American, and free people of color, but also, as one visitor of the time remarked, "nearly all possible mixed varieties of these and no doubt some other breeds of mankind."[17] Antebellum New Orleans, too, was the nation's largest market of enslaved Blacks, who constituted 15 percent of the population.[18]

Despite the entertainment, arts, and architecture that flourished from its ethnic diversity, the Crescent City was also one of America's dirtiest and most dangerous places. Pre–Civil War New Orleans had the highest mortality rate of any city in the country.[19] Sitting below sea level on the Mississippi River and near the Gulf of Mexico, the city faced heightened danger from hurricanes and floods.[20] Cotton bales, warehouses, and ships along the levee commonly ignited into raging fires.[21] Cypress cisterns captured drinking water, while gutters and canals provided sewerage and drainage. Staggering death rates—from both endemics (such as consumption and typhoid fever) and epidemics (such as yellow fever, cholera, and smallpox) earned New Orleans its reputation as the "Necropolis of the South."[22]

Amid this complex terrain, Jews carved an important place for themselves. Even before the Louisiana Purchase ended the French Catholic "Code Noir," which decreed the expulsion of Jews and declared Roman Catholicism as the region's official religion, the drive for financial opportunity beckoned Jews to New Orleans by the mid-1700s.[23] By the time the Schwartzes and Gutheim arrived, New Orleans's Jewish population numbered somewhere between one thousand and two thousand, the largest in the South.[24] Despite the relative ease of assimilating and marrying out of the faith, by then the Jewish community established three congregations. Like the proverbial Jew who described the second of two synagogues he built while shipwrecked on a desert island as the one he would "never set foot in," New Orleans Jews built houses of worship to accommodate distinct geographic and cultural roots along with varying prayer traditions and social status.[25]

The Sephardic traditions of Jews of Spanish and Portuguese descent, including those who hailed from the Netherlands and Caribbean, differed from the Ashkenazi traditions brought by Jews from the German states, France, and Eastern Europe. Although the beliefs and practices of Sephardim (such as separating men and women during prayer) tended to align with Ashkenazim's Orthodox rituals, Sephardim and Ashkenazim follow different customs for naming children, speak distinct Hebrew dialects, eat different traditional foods, chant different prayer melodies, and even worship from differently shaped Torah scrolls.[26] Sephardim, having historically achieved higher educational and professional status, which enabled them to integrate more readily into the surrounding secular culture as a result of their crypto-Jewish status and practices, generally considered themselves superior to Ashkenazim. Similarly, in turn, Ashkenazim from the German states, who readily adopted modern customs of Reform Judaism, generally regarded themselves as superior to their Eastern European brethren, who largely observed Orthodox traditions.[27]

These patterns played out in New Orleans. Congregation Gates of Mercy was founded in 1827 to follow Sephardic rites, but by 1842 began adopting Ashkenazi traditions of Jews arriving from Alsace and the German states. Three years later, seeking to regain Sephardic tradition while distancing themselves socially from German newcomers, some Gates of Mercy congregants founded Congregation Dispersed of Judah, and in 1849 lured the Reverend Gutheim away from Gates of Mercy. In 1850, newly arriving Alsatians and Germans, primarily small shopkeepers and river workers who lacked the affluence or social standing of their coreligionists at Gates of Mercy, formed Congregation Gates of Prayer in Lafayette City, an upriver suburb that New Orleans annexed four years later.[28] Benjamin Schwartz's burial in Gates of Prayer's cemetery suggests his modest social standing, if not the epidemic's exigencies.

CARING FOR THEIR OWN

Many adult Jewish yellow fever victims served as their family's primary breadwinner or caregiver, leaving their grieving families destitute. This inordinately beset newcomers without nearby relatives, like Babette and her children. By the time Benjamin died, several Jewish charitable organizations in the New

Orleans area assisted needy fellow Jews, including the Hebrew Benevolent Association (HBA), founded in 1844; its auxiliary Ladies Hebrew Benevolent Association (LHBA), founded in 1847; and the Jewish Benevolent Society of Lafayette, founded in 1849.[29] Typical of Jewish charities elsewhere in the country, such as the nation's oldest Jewish benevolent societies in Charleston, South Carolina (founded in 1784) and New York (1822), these groups aided coreligionists in times of crisis by supplying food, money, shelter, medical care, and Jewish burials.

In New Orleans, which lacked a municipal welfare system, charitable associations founded to care for "their own" were not limited to Jews.[30] Nationality-based groups included the Portuguese Benevolent Association and the Saint Andrew Society for Indigent Scotchmen.[31] Profession-based groups included the Mechanics' Society and the Barkeeper's Benevolent Association.[32] The Howard Association, New Orleans's largest private nonsectarian charitable organization, which was founded in 1837 in response to a cholera outbreak, ministered to the poor of all religions and ethnicities during epidemics. By 1853, in addition to serving their religious benevolent societies, New Orleans Jews ranked among the Howard Association's active members.[33]

The political imperative for Jewish self-reliance in the United States dates to 1655, when the Dutch West India Company expressly conditioned the settlement of colonial Jews on the requirement that their poor not burden the Christian community.[34] In New Orleans, prior to 1803, the Code Noir also threatened Jews with expulsion, making it dangerous to seek help beyond their small community. Powerful intrinsic forces applied as well. The Torah commands no fewer than thirty-six times that Jews must protect orphans and widows or face God's wrath.[35] Whatever its root cause—threat of expulsion, biblical mandate, fear of losing their young to another faith, or the fear that failure to provide for needy brethren would stir antisemitism—Jews took care of each other. By the 1850s, New Orleans's gentile majority had noticed. "Although members of the Hebrew Association rarely call upon their Christian fellow citizens for contributions in aid of charities," wrote the *Picayune*'s editor, "we believe they are, many of them, amongst the most constant and liberal supporters of benevolent enterprises. They take care of their own poor—who has ever seen a Jew beggar?—and render aid to the needy of other religions."[36]

New Orleans's Jews were painfully sensitive to even the appearance that their children would be sheltered out of the faith. "We have been requested to state," ran a correction in the *Picayune* in 1853, "that the statement that several Hebrew children, left orphans by the late epidemic, had been placed temporarily in the Howard asylums, is erroneous. No Hebrew children have been in [the] charge of the Howard Association, all who needed assistance or protection having, as usual, been taken promptly in charge by the Hebrew Benevolent Association."[37]

By December 1853, after five months of death and chaos, all yellow fever victims had either recovered or died. Across the city, as hundreds of orphans quickly outnumbered volunteer guardians and paid infant nurses, the Howard Association donated more than $30,000 to care for additional children in existing orphanages and established temporary asylums which were rapidly filled with forty to seventy children each in every district.[38] Yet, great as the calamity had been, the HBA recorded neither the need nor the desire to create a Jewish asylum.[39]

As soon as the city recovered from the 1853 epidemic, the yellow scourge returned the next summer and carried off nearly twenty-five hundred additional victims. Although the 1854 epidemic claimed far fewer lives than were lost the year before, statistics provided little consolation to victims and their families, again including many Jews.[40] Babette and Sarah Ehrman, sisters from Alsace, ages eleven and nine, had arrived in New Orleans with their aunt in the fall of 1854. After only a few weeks, their aunt died of yellow fever, leaving Babette and Sarah to fend for themselves.[41]

Still reeling from the prior year, HBA's resources proved insufficient to care for Jewish yellow fever victims and their families. HBA's small, rented quarters were inadequate for untold numbers of occupants forced to cook, eat, sleep, and wash in a single space.[42] "The burdens and difficulties which were besetting [HBA] on all sides would, unless relieved in some practical manner, wreck it," HBA secretary Joseph Magner wrote years later. Thus, the idea emerged to create a separate organization to provide long-term support for Jewish widows and orphans.[43]

In the city where Ursuline nuns established the nation's first orphanage in 1726, the tradition of caring for children in religious asylums was deeply rooted. By 1854, at least nine New Orleans orphanages existed, operated by Catholic, Protestant, and other religious groups.[44] But no Jewish orphan asylum building existed anywhere in the country. The absence was not due to lack of need or awareness. By this time, South Carolina's Hebrew Orphan Society, established in 1801, was providing relief to orphans and other needy children by paying for their care in private homes and providing schooling.[45] In 1850, influential educator Rebecca Gratz and *Occident* editor and minister of her congregation Rev. Isaac Leeser publicly called for a "foster home" for poor Jewish children in Philadelphia, a goal toward which serious progress was first made five years later.[46] In 1852, New York's Jewish newspaper, *Asmonean*, announced philanthropist Sampson Simson's bold (and unsuccessful) plans to establish a "Jews' Asylum for Widows and Orphans" in that city.[47]

When the 1853 epidemic hit New Orleans, six years had passed since the last yellow fever outbreak. Thus, when the 1853 scourge ended, the city had little reason to expect, much less prepare for, a recurrence the following year. Or perhaps, notwithstanding the plight of Babette Schwartz and her children and others like them, the HBA did not think that the small number of Jewish orphans and widows who continued to seek its support warranted the creation of an asylum. Whatever the reason, New Orleans Jews did not call for the creation of a Jewish asylum until November 1854, after the epidemic had once again ravaged the city.

If New Orleans's Jews had wanted to build an asylum after the 1853 epidemic, they failed to seize an exquisite opportunity. Gershom Kursheedt, the Virginia-born grandson of America's first native (and non-ordained) Jewish minister, enjoyed a personal relationship with Judah Touro, a Rhode Island–born Jew, son of the minister of Newport's synagogue, and New Orleans's wealthiest citizen. On January 6, 1854, Touro executed a will distributing his estate of more than a half million dollars (roughly $17.6 million in 2022) to charitable organizations. Kursheedt played a role in this historic act of philanthropy by exerting his influence to increase the number of Jewish beneficiaries.[48] In addition to the nearly $200,000 Touro bequeathed to support existing synagogues and other Jewish institutions, including $5,000 for HBA, Touro left money to support eight non-Jewish orphanages in New Orleans and Boston. Yet, even with Kursheedt lobbying his dying friend to fund Jewish causes, Touro left no money to create a Jewish orphanage in New Orleans or anywhere else. His will did create other institutions, leaving $80,000 to establish a New Orleans Alms House for "the prevention of mendicity." Touro's use of his will to establish an alms house and to support existing non-Jewish orphanages, coupled with his gift to HBA—and Kursheedt's knowledge of the city's needs from his dual roles as treasurer of HBA and Howard Association—strongly suggest that Touro and Kursheedt believed HBA would suffice to address the needs of any Jewish widows and orphans left in the wake of the 1853 epidemic. Touro died on January 18, 1854, six months before yellow fever returned.[49]

A MASS MEETING OF ISRAELITES

In November 1854, after the epidemic abated and lacking a benefactor to fund the orphanage they now desired, HBA president Joseph Simon, vice president Gutheim, and secretary Joseph Magner convened a "mass meeting of the Israelites of the city" at the Masonic Hall on St. Charles Avenue.[50] After a robust discussion of what Magner described as "many divergent opinions," the group elected the relevantly knowledgeable Kursheedt to chair an executive committee charged with reporting back in a week with "the most feasible plans" to move forward.[51]

If the divergent opinions voiced at the mass meeting reflected the cultural differences that two years earlier prompted Kursheedt and other Sephardic traditionalists to break away from Gates of Mercy to form Dispersed of Judah, they did not impede progress. In New York, in contrast, the cultural chasm between Orthodox Sephardim and Reform German Ashkenazim, and their respective charitable institutions—which erupted in a "Tammany-style brawl" at a joint dinner in 1858 over wearing *yarmulkes,* the traditional skullcaps— delayed the creation of that city's Hebrew Orphan Asylum until 1860.[52] Nor were New Orleans's Jews swayed by the idea recently advanced by Cincinnati's influential Isaac M. Wise that coreligionists from St. Louis, New Orleans, and Louisville should unite to create a central orphanage to both spare New Orleans the expense of supporting the institution alone and locate it in a more agreeable "northern climate."[53]

Kursheedt's executive committee met weekly for the next three months. By March 1, 1855, they formed themselves into the Association for the Relief of Jewish Widows and Orphans.[54] Seventeen men signed the charter that declared the organization's purpose: "To establish a Home or Asylum, in the City of New Orleans, to receive under its care, and support indigent Hebrew Widows; also to receive, foster, provide for, maintain and instruct Jewish orphans and half-orphans of both sexes."[55]

Later that month, one dozen new members joined the incorporators at a meeting in Masonic Hall where they elected officers and directors.[56] Kursheedt, the likely choice for president given his leadership thus far, declined nomination; he was obliged to accompany Sir Moses Montefiore to Jerusalem to carry out one of Judah Touro's bequests.[57] The attendees nevertheless elected a board with the experience and gravitas to place the new association on firm footing. As president, they chose thirty-two-year-old Meyer M. Simpson, who within eight years of moving from his native Charleston, South Carolina, had established himself in New Orleans as a stock and exchange broker and an active member of HBA's relief committee.[58] As first vice president, they elected London-born Isaac Hart, a shirt manufacturer who came to New Orleans in 1839 and had demonstrated leadership as an HBA fundraiser and officer of Congregation Gates of Mercy.[59] As second vice president, they enlisted Henry M. Hyams, a wealthy lawyer and planter who later that year was elected Louisiana state senator, a position he held before winning election as lieutenant governor in 1859. Hyams was born and lived in Charleston before being lured to New Orleans by his famous cousin, Judah P. Benjamin, who served in both houses of the Louisiana legislature before winning election to the U.S. Senate in 1852.[60] Aptly chosen as secretary and treasurer, respectively, were newspaper publisher and notary Joseph Cohn and Daniel Goodman, an agent for a dry goods wholesaler and treasurer of his Masonic lodge.[61] The board ratified the new association's constitution, memorializing the forces that compelled the asylum's creation and their perceptions of the women and children they pledged to serve:

> Within the compass of humanity there is nothing which touches more powerfully the heart of the true philanthropist, than the destitute, forlorn condition of the poor Widow and Orphan. Bereft of their natural protector, exposed to the merciless buffetings of a selfish world—the one, with the finer sensibilities of her sex, cramped in her exertions to secure a maintenance—the other, with powers and capacity yet undeveloped, tossed about by the fierce waves of privation and hunger, and unguided impulse—they present the strongest claims to the sympathies of the good and benevolent. No charity, therefore, can be better applied than that which has for its object the amelioration of the condition of the Widow and Orphan.

> . . . .

> In view of the increase of the Jewish population, and the too often fatal acclimating ordeal through which so many have to pass, an institution for the relief of Jewish widows and orphans has become a serious want. The existing Jewish Charities, seconded by the private liberality of benevolent individuals, have been found insufficient to meet all demands. True, therefore, to the spirit in-

culcated by a Holy Religion, and inherited through a long line of ancestors, the Association for the Relief of Hebrew Widows and Orphans has been founded.[62]

From their first meeting in late March 1855, which President Simpson convened at his Prytania Street residence, the board dedicated itself to three priorities. It took over the cases of widows and orphans that HBA had been supporting with stipends until the Home was ready to admit them. It also selected a building site, architect, and contractor, and negotiated the necessary contracts. Above all, to finance its endeavors, the board recruited members, which the constitution limited to "Israelites" who paid twelve dollars per year, and donations from Jews and gentiles alike.[63]

THE FOUNDERS

The roughly thirty men who participated in the Home's founding included New Orleans's most prosperous and influential Jews of the time, but in 1855 they were neither as prosperous nor influential as they became over the next few decades. Uniting from different backgrounds the world over, they contributed diverse experiences and perspectives to the task of building a Jewish orphanage. None were native to New Orleans—at least sixteen were foreign-born—and thus shared the status of outsiders seeking acceptance. Ranging in age from twenty-seven to fifty-four, only one had come to the city as a child. Of the foreign-born men, half had already adapted to American life elsewhere. They held occupations including merchants of books and jewelry, wholesalers of hats and produce, brokers, bankers, lawyers, and legislators. Some merchant founders enjoyed steady success after starting out as peddlers, while a few others already reestablished businesses gone bankrupt. At the same time, the founders shared relationships and experiences that drew them together. Nearly all had previously participated in Jewish benevolent organizations, most commonly HBA's epidemic relief efforts. Further cementing ties among them, in addition to founders who shared foreign places of birth, at least three founders previously lived in Mobile, Alabama, while four founders earlier lived in Charleston, South Carolina, where they or a prior generation engaged in common religious, business, or benevolent activities, including Charleston's Hebrew Orphan Society.[64] Several founders were also related by blood or marriage.[65]

Most Jews in antebellum New Orleans chose not to affiliate with a congregation either due to assimilation and indifference to religion or the economic necessity to work on the Jewish Sabbath.[66] In contrast, most Home founders connected themselves to a Jewish house of worship, somewhat spanning the congregational divide. Although Gates of Prayer's financially modest members were not represented among the founders or initial donors, the Home drew support from congregants of Gates of Mercy and Dispersed of Judah alike.[67] It probably also drew support from wealthier unaffiliated Jews. While in Charleston, as a member of the Reformed Society of Israelites, Henry Hyams had supported the first organized attempt to reform Jewish liturgy in North America. The Reformed Society sought to make the Sephardic congregation's ritual more accessible by adding English translations and shortening services.[68] Founder and Amsterdam native Benjamin DaSilva, before coming in 1849 to New Orleans where he served as Dispersed of Judah's sexton, had displeased his Ashkenazi congregation in Mobile, Alabama, with his Sephardic reading style.[69] Avoiding any religious or cultural differences that may have existed among them, the founders included only two provisions in the founding documents that addressed the religious observances to be followed in the Home. Bylaw XIII simply stated, "The culinary department of the 'Home' shall be conducted upon strictly Jewish principles and practice." Bylaw XIV provided, "The inmates of the 'Home' shall be required to attend the Synagogue on Sabbaths and Festivals." The founders did not specify a congregation.[70]

The founders shared a commitment to the Home, many of them serving the institution throughout their lives. For the next decade, Meyer Simpson continued as president, succeeded by founders George Jonas, a London-born banker who served from 1865 to 1869, and Joseph Simon, from 1878 to 1882. Gutheim served as first vice president for all but six of the Home's first thirty years, ending with his death in 1886.[71] Founders Simon, Magner, and Marks witnessed the Home's fiftieth anniversary in 1905, each capping five decades of service to the institution.[72]

Despite their dedication to caring for Jewish widows and orphans, some founders' actions reflected the moral failings of their time and place. While establishing the Home, at least fourteen founders enslaved a total of ninety-two men, women, and children. The number of persons each founder enslaved ranged from one by director Lambert B. Cain, a native of France who then imported dry goods, to fifty-four by vice president Henry Hyams. Although Hyams kept forty of these persons on two plantations outside the city, other enslaving founders did not own any real estate. Typical of urban merchants, the persons enslaved by Gershom Kursheedt (two) and Manuel Goldsmith (three) were maintained in rented quarters as house servants.[73] Perhaps most incongruous is the founders' enslavement of children. Founders Joseph Marks, George Jonas, Joseph Simon, and Abraham Haber enslaved a total of twelve children, three to ten years old. Haber placed the following ad in the *Picayune* several times over the summer of 1853, offering a hundred-dollar reward for the return of Esther, whom he referred to as "my negro woman," and her daughter Maria: "The woman is about 40 years of age, of mulatto color, has bad teeth, and delicate looking; speaks English and is about 5 feet 4 or 5 inches high; her daughter is a handsome griffe, about 9 years old, 3 feet 4 inches high, she is very lively and intelligent."[74]

The large size of the reward (more than many then offered for "runaway" enslaved women and children) and the detailed descriptions suggest both Esther's and Maria's importance to Haber and his familiarity with their appearance and Maria's personality. "A handsome, very lively, and intelligent 9-year-old girl" are words Haber could have used to describe an orphan in need of the Home's protection, or his nine-year-old daughter, Josephine.[75] And yet, Haber failed or refused to appreciate the moral dissonance of enslaving human beings including children while lavishing his time and treasures on the Home's children as his own.

It is difficult to reconcile that these otherwise charitable individuals, many of whom treasured philanthropy as an essential characteristic of American freedom, enjoyed their prosperity on the backs of humans in bondage. It is particularly difficult to reconcile that Jews, whose history had been defined by persecution on account of their purportedly immutable characteristics, were willing to assume the role of persecutor. Slavery was central to the city's economy, and even founders who did not actually enslave other humans nonetheless profited from the scheme, whether as merchants of goods produced or used by enslaved labor, bankers who invested in plantations and their output, notaries and lawyers who collected fees for transactions involving enslaved persons, or simply as recipients of city services funded by taxes assessed on enslavers for their "property." In a paid advertisement in Cohen's *New Orleans Directory for 1855*, for example, one retailer of oil cloth garments boasted that his plantation customers witnessed "great change for the better in the general health of their slaves" who could continue to "work in the field instead of peopling the hospital." And when enslaved persons did get sick or injured, medical providers such as Touro Infirmary, which was founded in 1852 as the Hebrew Hospital of New Orleans, profited ("Slaves $1 per day") by bringing them back to full strength so that owners received full value in the field or at auction.[76]

Jews in the antebellum South did not wrestle with such ethical concerns. Being Jewish played no discernible role in the relationship of Jews to slavery. Instead, they used slavery as a means to acclimate themselves to their environment and to be accepted as equals by their fellow white citizens. Whether or not a Jew enslaved a Black person was only a matter of finances and social status. Moreover, these Jewish enslavers did not risk local disapproval.[77] With only two known exceptions, Jewish thought leaders in the Old South did not question the justice of slavery. And even those two abolitionists carried little weight in antebellum New Orleans: Moses Elias Levy of Florida successfully kept the antislavery views he expressed in England "out of public in the U.S.," while Rabbi David Einhorn, who did not reach America until 1855, fled north from his Baltimore pulpit in 1861 to escape the mob angered by his abolitionist preaching.[78] Reverend Gutheim, on the other hand, five years before fleeing federally occupied New Orleans for refusing to pledge loyalty to the Union in 1863, married the daughter of Mobile's prominent Jewish auctioneer, who sold enslaved persons alongside lots of boots and brandy.[79]

Despite efforts to fit in, New Orleans's Jews, including Home founders, often were perceived first as Jews. In charitable and social affairs, local news accounts of Jewish activities were overwhelmingly philosemitic, such as the *Daily Delta*'s praise in 1854, "Our Israelitish population is no less distinguished for the benevolence and liberality of their hearts, than for their intelligence and enterprise," or the *Picayune*'s observation in 1853 that "some of the most beautiful women of the city" and "some of the greatest heiresses" attended a charity ball hosted by "descendants of the Children of Israel."[80]

Candid comments, however, recorded by local correspondents of the R. G. Dun & Company ("Dun") commercial credit reporting firm, the precursor to Dun & Bradstreet, reveal the precarious position some Home founders occupied in New Orleans's business world precisely because they were Jews. These reports, which Dun's paid subscribers used to assess customers' creditworthiness, captured each business's nature, duration, and worth as well as the owners' character and reputation.[81] Nine of fifteen Home founders evaluated between 1848 and 1855 were explicitly identified by their religion. "Jews," wrote a Dun correspondent about Abraham Haber and his dry goods business partner, before adding, "Another party says they are not honest."[82] A later report, which dubbed Haber a "blackleg," meaning swindler, added, "They are all Germans and were poor drovers and ragpickers at home. . . . They are all now rich and do a large business, they are not honest and will cheat any man if they have a chance."[83]

While praising founder Isaac Hart's shirt business as having a "large stock and fine location," a Dun correspondent regarded Hart less favorably: "Rankly Israelitish in his tendencies. Has made money, a cunning prospering Jew [who] would swear to any lie."[84] Founder Moritz Stiewel, who owned a dry goods store before opening a jewelry store, received the following harsh appraisal: "A Jew, reputation is not very good. Has been in the city 12 or 15 years and is supposed he will prove tricky if he gets opportunity."[85]

Other Home founders identified as Jews nonetheless were deemed creditworthy, albeit dressed in benign antisemitism. Leopold Klopman and his wife's brother, who together owned a wholesale dry goods firm, were dubbed "Creoles of Jerusalem" who were "shrewd and persevering men." Two years later, they were deemed "Israelites (of the better order)."[86] Founding secretary Joseph Cohn, besides being a printer and publisher of a local German-language newspaper, was also a notary public, a legal officer under Louisiana's civil law who drafts, authenticates, and archives private agreements. "Regarded as an honest, upright man," wrote a Dun correspondent, followed by the next year's remark, that Cohn "must have made an extra good year with his notary office as he has charge of all Jewish failures that occurred this year."[87]

"Owning slaves," in the callous vernacular of the time, was deemed by Dun correspondents as an attribute of creditworthiness equal to owning land. The report for founder Manuel Goldsmith, who then sold men's furnishings, noted that his assets, including "R[eal] E[state] and negroes," favorably exceeded his liabilities.[88] Similarly, Abraham Haber, notwithstanding his religion and reputation for unreliability, was favorably regarded for owning assets including his "Negroes, 6m$."[89]

Dun correspondents reserved their praise for the most successful founders who were also highly assimilated, whether from their American birth or non-Jewish business partners. Home incorporator Benjamin Florance, another South Carolina native who moved to New Orleans in 1830, was an agent for the U.S. Life Insurance Annuity and Trust Company of Philadelphia. Without noting Florance's religion, the Dun clerk reported, "The affairs of this office are well-managed and they are doing a fair business."[90] London-born George Jonas, who owned a cotton broker business with non-Jewish partners, and whose wife

Rosalie Block was a second-generation Virginian, received the following accolades without mention of religion: "Gentlemen, honest and undoubted, and fine businessmen," and "One of the best houses in the City; good for any amount."[91]

LAYING THE CORNERSTONE

In summer 1855, yellow fever returned to the city for the third year in a row. By the time it ended, at least sixty-three "unacclimated Israelites" had been buried in the city's Hebrew burying grounds.[92] The latest epidemic heightened the urgency for the Home's completion. "The Widows' and Orphans' Home Society have already seventeen widows and orphans in [their] charge," reported *The Occident,* to which it added by postscript the latest news that "one newly born infant and seven other infants just deprived of their parents had to be taken charge of."[93]

By August, in response to the exigency, the board was ready to lay the cornerstone for its new building. It had selected a site on the southwest corner of Jackson and Chippewa streets. The neighborhood, just two miles upriver from the French Quarter, was now part of New Orleans, the result of the burgeoning city's annexation of the municipality of Lafayette only four years earlier.[94] The board appreciated the site's "quiet and well-regulated" location, accessible by the Lafayette Railroad's mule- or horse-drawn omnibuses (which looked like stagecoaches but required no advance booking) that frequently ran along Jackson from today's St. Charles Avenue to the Mississippi River.[95] For six months, the board had raised funds and garnered support for its endeavor with singular focus.

Facing an increasing number of applicants, the board considered but ultimately rejected amending the constitution to limit admissions to full orphans. Instead, it recommitted itself to accommodating all unfortunate Jews who needed the Home's services. Babette Schwartz and her five children were among the first applicants the board considered. Resolving to admit them as soon as the Home opened, the board agreed until then to pay the Schwartzes a stipend of seventy-five dollars per month.[96] After consulting LHBA, the board also placed nine-month-old Henry Kaufman, whose mother died of yellow fever in July 1855 and whose father's whereabouts were unknown, with a trusted woman in the community who agreed to care for the baby for twenty dollars per month until the Home opened.[97] Esther and Rachel Carillion, whom the board accepted as beneficiaries in May 1855, were temporarily being cared for in Mandeville, Louisiana, a summer retreat from the city's heat and yellow fever on Lake Pontchartrain's North Shore. After being assured that the caregiver to whom it entrusted the girls' well-being was paying "every attention," the board appropriated ten dollars to buy them shoes and clothing "of which they stand sadly in need."[98]

On January 8, 1856, two hundred men and women gathered to dedicate the completed building. The crowd, representing nearly 10 percent of New Orleans's Jewish population as well as a respectable number of gentile well-wishers and supporters, had braved the dreary day's bone-chilling mist and the city's treacherously muddy streets.[99]

Rising three stories in stuccoed brick, the handsome symmetrical building was designed by William A. Freret, the twenty-three-year-old son of the city's former mayor, who was launching a career that would lead him to become the United States' supervising architect.[100] The Home's "somewhat ornamental" facade, with its small but neatly columned portico, was in keeping with the solemn purpose carved into the prominent cement plaque, in both English and Hebrew, viewed as occult by local eyes.[101]

THE HOME FOR JEWISH WIDOWS AND ORPHANS

If Freret had wanted models for creating an orphanage, he could have looked to the Poydras Female Orphan Asylum on Camp Street or St. Elizabeth's Asylum for young women on Magazine Street, designed by architects Lewis Reynolds and Henry Howard, respectively, or to any other of the city's non-Jewish orphanages.[102] As for a Jewish orphanage, however, he had no ready template; "the Home"—as the orphanage already was known—was the first such structure to be erected in this country.[103] Its creation signaled a bold new achievement: the Jews of New Orleans had the resources and passion to care for their neediest women and children around the clock, every day of the year, and to prepare them to become the "architects" of their own fortune in New Orleans and in life.

The handsome structure was first captured on film by noted photographer Theodore Lilienthal, who included the bold image—shot from an unusual frontal vantage to highlight its symmetry—in his portfolio for the 1867 Paris

Exhibition, which was presented to Emperor Napoleon III.[104] Designed for maximum ventilation and natural illumination, priorities for a congregate dwelling, the Home boasted tall ceilings on every floor, numerous, large windows, and several wide, interior hallways.[105]

On the day of the dedication ceremony, the Home's first floor remained unencumbered by the furniture and supplies that would occupy it before the first residents arrived the following month. Eager guests filled every seat that temporarily crowded the large dining room, before spilling over to stand in the adjoining rooms and hallway where they could hear, if not see, the proceedings. After Professor Michel Hoffner's orchestra opened the program with a soothing Haydn andante, Gutheim recited Psalm 146, praising God for protecting orphans and widows, and then recited the *Shehechiyanu,* the Hebrew blessing that thanks God for "preserving us alive, sustaining us, and allowing us to reach this season."[106] Traditionally chanted upon building or buying a new house, the prayer fosters appreciation for the otherwise fleeting nature of a rare achievement.[107] Considering the three successive years of yellow fever they had survived, the prayers evoked special meaning.

The orator of the day was Benjamin Franklin Jonas, the twenty-two-year-old nephew of founder George Jonas and rising star junior law partner of founder and state senator–elect Henry Hyams. After imparting lessons of ancient Jewish history, Jonas stressed that Jews not only support "their own unfortunate" but contribute equally to the burdens born by all citizens. Jonas also used the occasion to reassure all that the Jews of New Orleans were prepared to honor and defend the laws and customs of their adopted city. If afforded civil and religious rights, continued Jonas who twenty-three years later became the third Jew elected to the U.S. Senate, "the Israelite is a faithful and devoted citizen of the land which has afforded him an asylum and a home."[108]

Even the date of the Home's dedication underscored the founders' intent to honor their adopted community. January 8, which coincided with the building's actual completion, was a public holiday that commemorated General Andrew Jackson's 1815 victory over the British in the Battle of New Orleans.[109] For New Orleanians, whose state joined the Union in 1812 and thus had played no role in America's Revolutionary War, celebrating Jackson's triumph helped diffuse remaining skepticism about their allegiance to the nation.[110] The Home's board, too, used the day to assuage any concerns about Jewish allegiance. As Jonas noted, it was fitting for the Home's board, "feeling a deep interest in the welfare and prosperity of their city, and in the historic glory of their country," to celebrate their orphanage on a day "when patriotic memories are aroused throughout the land."[111]

Delighted with the response to holding the Home's dedication on January 8, the board permanently claimed the date to celebrate the association's anniversary. Although the constitution originally set the celebration during "Hannuckah," the eight-day festival that commemorates the rededication of Jerusalem's Second Temple, the board never followed that religious timeline.[112] Instead, it seized the popular January 8 holiday, which long rivaled July 4 as a local and national display of patriotism, to offer a yearly reminder of Jewish allegiance to the city and country. Even in 1864, the board proceeded with its January 8 celebration despite the date's coincidence with Asara B'Tevet, a day on which Orthodox Jews commemorate the Babylonian siege of Jerusalem with mourning and fasting.[113] Although other Jewish orphanages also organized annual celebrations to generate goodwill and funding sometimes on a Jewish holiday, the Home was the only one known to officially adopt a secular event to commemorate its longevity and endear itself to its host community.[114]

Following the example Jonas set in his dedication speech, future Home anniversary orators frequently highlighted the loyalty of Jews to their adopted city and nation, linking their philanthropy with freedom and sometimes employing a social concept of race to assert a beneficial place for themselves in society.[115] In 1859, Eleazar Block noted how "peculiarly fitting and appropriate that Israelites" should identify "their pride and their glory [with] a country which was first among nations to open to our persecuted and down-trodden race their arms of brotherhood."[116] "The sun of the glorious Eighth of January," pronounced Gutheim as he began his 1861 oration, "warms our hearts with patriotic fervor."[117] In speeches, children's performances, and decorations, the Home's anniversary events—which took place on or as close as possible to January 8—continued to echo these themes of Jewish loyalty and patriotism well into the next century.[118]

As with Jonas and Block, the board began choosing high-profile, accomplished professionals as orators from its earliest years, including founder and assistant city attorney David Cohen Labatt, and founder Lionel L. Levy, also a lawyer.[119] Beyond elevating the community's awareness of ancient Jewish history and current events, these orators represented the success that Jews had achieved in secular society while retaining their commitment to Jewish institutions. New Orleans had made this possible. There were no legal impediments to Jews holding public office—unlike those which North Carolina and

New Hampshire imposed until 1868 and 1877—and the gentile community willingly accepted Jews who matched their own wealth and position as members of Masonic lodges and charitable organizations, and on civic and business boards of all kinds.[120] As historian Bertram Korn concluded, there was probably less prejudice against Jews in New Orleans in the antebellum period than in any other important city in the country."[121]

In New Orleans, establishing the Home fulfilled an important rite of passage for its Jewish citizens. With a staggering death rate and lacking a public welfare system, the "Necropolis of the South" had long hosted orphanages established and maintained by other major religions. "We are happy to see," New Orleans's *Daily Crescent* favorably remarked, "that our Jewish citizens have erected an asylum which shall entitle them to an equal standing with those of other religions."[122] Although the Home's founders included the city's most affluent and influential Jews, they were still perceived first as Jews, for better and worse. From its beginning, the Home represented a unified Jewish effort to obey the biblical mandate to care for widows and orphans while ensuring that needy coreligionists would not become a burden on gentiles. It provided its founders and supporters a prominent venue to make a positive impression about Jews in and beyond New Orleans.

The board had envisioned a Home that would be as "enduring as time." Despite the growing number of parentless children and widows, the board had quickly rejected the expedient option of renting a house, "resolving not to hazard success by an imprudent experiment." Aware that it would achieve nothing without the necessary funds, the board instead viewed erecting an orphanage from the ground up as the "best means of inspiring confidence" among donors to secure "a speedy augmentation of means."[123] The board proved correct, as the Home became the physical embodiment of its mission. And once the Home was built, despite occasionally voting to briefly support a widow or an infant outside the Home, the changing roster of members who comprised the board continued into the next century, never seriously considering whether its wards could or should be placed into the care of private homes, as opposed to the institution they built.

chapter two

FIRST YEARS
1856–1861

Having established the Home, the board turned its attention to the business of running an orphanage. Common to childcare institutions elsewhere, prevailing norms regarding gender-determined roles in society and ideals of preparing children for adulthood shaped decisions over daily affairs: who would manage and how. Deciding who was entitled to receive the institution's benefits was not only driven by the plight of families with no other recourse but also, for a Jewish orphanage, struck at the core of religious identity and perpetuation.

FOUNDING WOMEN

The pleasant weather on February 1, 1856, a welcome change from the dreary cold of the past few weeks, heralded a fresh start for Babette Schwartz and her five children. Throughout the city, ice melted in gutters while people shut dampers on parlor stoves and threw doors and windows wide open.[1] So, too, the doors of the Home—*their home*—finally opened. Over the past seven months, Babette had depended on the board's stipend to sustain her family.

Matron Ann DePass welcomed the Schwartz family and the Home's seven other inmates, the term commonly used for resident beneficiaries of charitable asylums. In choosing this forty-year-old widow from New York, the board fulfilled what President Meyer Simpson declared its most delicate responsibility to date: selecting a "Lady in all respects worthy and competent" to perform the duties of matron. "It is upon the administration of this office above all others that the ultimate success and future usefulness of our institution depend." DePass demonstrated her competence, if not also her assertiveness, from the start. The board acceded to her demands of fifty dollars per month, thereby doubling its initial salary offer, and twenty dollars in advance.[2]

Entrusted with the institution's "domestic economy," DePass endured the Home's growing pains. Her tenure, which ended as Louisiana seceded from the Union in 1861, roughly coincided with the Home's admission of its one hundredth inmate. During that time, the Home experienced other milestones: the advent of the elaborate anniversary celebrations, the first marriages of its girls, the return of yellow fever, and the first discharges and deaths of its inmates.

In choosing DePass, the board overlooked the incongruity of selecting a widow to run an institution whose constitution declared that a woman who lost her husband was incapable of caring for herself. Despite the matron's leadership role, the board tightly controlled her activities. Although it expressed no reservations about DePass's personal ability to manage the Home, at least not at the outset, the board's close oversight of its matrons was not unlike the role some of these men played in LHBA. Notwithstanding LHBA's female president and its ability to deliver services and raise money, the group had enlisted men to post public notices and manage fundraising balls.[3] Although LHBA was not unique among southern Jewish women's organizations in relying on men to conduct external activities, it could have followed local non-Jewish models.[4] In New Orleans, for example, Protestant women had founded and run the Poydras Female Orphan Asylum for a half century, overcoming Louisiana laws that prevented women from executing binding contracts.[5] LHBA, however, did not assert this authority.

Unlike the Poydras Asylum and Philadelphia's Jewish Foster Home, whose first two decades were driven by women, men always dominated the Home in New Orleans.[6] Although the Home's charter offered dues-paying membership to "all Israelites" and "persons," women were excluded as members in their own right until 1914.[7] Before then, the bylaws treated "wives of members" as nonvoting honorary members who were eligible for election by the board as volunteer honorary matrons. The honorary matrons, in turn, reported to a volunteer directress, whom the board also selected and supervised.

Despite their ineligibility for full membership, New Orleans's Jewish women were actively involved in establishing the Home. Although the board recorded few details about their contributions, monetary donations by women were welcomed and considerable. LHBA, for instance, donated $1,000 for the Home's founding, which compared to the $2,000 gift from the HBA was a remarkably large amount considering the gender disparity in earning capacities and control over family finances.[8] Within a year, honorary matrons contributed an additional \$450 in donations they solicited from a total of sixty-one women.[9]

Further, despite their titles, honorary matrons did not hold merely symbolic positions. They oversaw the matron, inspecting the Home on assigned visiting days. Honorary matrons also brought their experience in charitable endeavors, particularly from LHBA. The board selected LHBA president Miriam Jung Haber, wife of founder Abraham Haber, to serve as its first directress. The forty-two-year-old Bavarian-born mother of eight led the honorary matrons until her death in 1866. Rosalie Block Jonas served as LHBA vice president. The wife of founder George Jonas, Rosalie was the eldest daughter of scholar Eleazar Block, considered the first Jewish lawyer in St. Louis.[10] From the board's perspective, the limited sphere of authority it gave members' wives (all but two of the fifteen original honorary matrons were married to a board member or founder) was consistent with traditional views on childrearing and the ideal of "virtuous womanhood" that allowed women to play visible roles managing orphanages and other charitable institutions.[11]

In the Home's early years, when children were educated within the orphanage, women also shared teaching responsibilities.[12] Reverend Gutheim taught Hebrew and religion for the first seven years.[13] Unburdened by European traditions that limited the role of teaching to men, the board hired young, single, Jewish women to instruct the children in spelling, arithmetic, and other primary secular subjects in the first-floor classroom.[14] After two women left the post following brief stints, the board hired Frances Hart, who for the next two years proved herself "well qualified as teacher, kind and attentive to the children."[15] When Frances resigned to marry in 1859, the board hired her sister Julia, who taught the Home's children until 1875.[16] As was the case with LHBA, women working as nurturers and teachers bent gender boundaries without breaking them.

THE HOME'S "WIDOWS"

For the first two months, Babette Schwartz was the Home's only adult inmate. By mid-April, the board admitted Carolina Wohl, a native of the Saxe-Weimar German state, and her two children, followed by Bavarian-born Jacobina Weil, her three-year-old son Salomon, and Kate Kirkham, a sixty-five-year-old Dutch "spinster," as unmarried women were known, increasing the Home's population to twenty. Although bedrooms for families were of "respectable size" and a welcome relief from the streets or shelters, long-term residence in the Home nevertheless proved challenging for adult women and mothers with children. They were now supervised by the matron, whose job was to maintain order by enforcing rules fixed by the board regarding meals, clothing, bedtime, and behavior.[17] Initial relief and tranquility gave way as the growing number of adult residents tested the limits of their freedom.

Little imagination is required to envision a scenario—whether slight or serious—that triggered tension between Babette Schwartz, for example, and Matron DePass. In July 1856, the board met to address Schwartz's alleged "insubordination." Revealing a concern for maintaining an orderly image in the community, DePass complained that Schwartz spoke to her in "abusive" and "quarrelsome" language that was loud enough to attract the attention of neighbors and passersby. After considering the matter, without recording specifics, the board reprimanded Schwartz for refusing to conform to the Home's rules.[18] For a year, Schwarz gave no further cause for complaint.

Over the next three decades, a total of twenty-four adult women lived in the Home. Although they were called "widows," the group also included several elderly women, like Kate Kirkham, who had never married. Ranging in age from twenty-five to ninety-one, the women's stays varied in length from a few months to a decade. At least twenty-one were born overseas, including the German states, Poland, Holland, France, and Jamaica, and were likely accustomed to a wide range of norms. Twelve women were admitted with a total of twenty-nine children, including Esther Bensaken Marks and her three grandchildren. Through most of 1857, eight adult women resided in the Home, the largest number ever to live there at one time. Compared to the more than five hundred children who lived in the Home during the same three decades, the widows sparked a disproportionately large number of controversies. Founder Joseph Magner diplomatically described the problem, which persisted until 1880, when the board, by charter amendment, ended the practice: "It had been found incompatible with the discipline of the Home," wrote Magner, "of caring for these old ladies there—old age and extreme youth engendering discomfort to the former, and interfering sadly with the enjoyment of the latter."[19] The board discharged the last widow in 1885.[20] Until at least 1922, the board occasionally granted stipends for destitute women under age sixty and housed those over age sixty at Touro Infirmary, which then ran a home for the aged.[21]

THE MATRON'S TURBULENT TENURE

As challenging as life in the Home's early years was for its widows, it proved equally difficult for the matron. During the Home's first five years, five women occupied the post. Assisted by a resident teacher and a visiting physician, the matron was responsible for ensuring the residents' health and well-being, maintaining daily records of the Home's activities (which were not preserved), and overseeing other Home staff, including a gardener, cook, and custodian.[22] Although the board's supplies committee, in consultation with the honorary matrons, secured all items purchased or donated, the matron was entrusted with their inventory and distribution. Clothing, in particular, demanded her careful attention. Matron DePass described yards of red, brown, and bleached calico cloth, that were ready for sewing into dresses, shirts, and undergarments, while a bolt of "crash," a sturdy linen fabric, awaited fabrication into draperies and bed linens.[23] DePass also asked from the board cradles, chairs, and wash kettles "for the convenience of the inmates." For sixty-five-year-old Kate Kirkham, "who suffers greatly from debility," DePass also requested "light food, also a bottle of porter [beer] daily." At the same time, she expected residents to contribute their efforts to support the Home.[24] To this end, DePass arranged for the widows and older girls to earn money for the Home by sewing for stores and private customers. Noting that these efforts also provided useful training for the inmates, the board endorsed DePass's plan.[25] Typical of other nineteenth-century orphanages, industry of wards for both income and training remained a regular feature of Home life for the next three decades.

Before the first year ended, DePass drew complaints regarding her "arbitrary" methods of discipline, including "unkind treatment" especially toward the younger children. Even after warning her "not to resort to corporal punishment on any occasion," the board discovered that she had brandished a "cowhide," or a braided leather strap, on three-year-old Salomon Weil, leaving marks on his body that were visible a week later.[26] After considering her discharge, the board tabled the matter without explanation, thus retaining DePass as matron.[27] Two months later, the board revisited the issue. Leah Hyams Bensadon, who had admitted her three daughters to the Home following her husband's death, reported that she had learned from an anonymous source that DePass had used the cowhide to punish her eight-year-old daughter, Mary. When confronted, DePass conceded only having "administered a slight correction to the child." The board again discussed DePass's dismissal, but Bensadon refused to reveal her informant, leaving the board unable to take further action.[28] The board was not alone in its equivocation over physical discipline. As early as 1852, the Orleans Parish School Board expressly prohibited corporal punishment but withheld sanctions against a teacher who used it in response to a student's "want of respect" and "insults."[29]

In February 1857, DePass sanguinely summarized her first year. As she reported to the board, she had managed the Home "with all the system and discipline that could be observed." Her only infraction was allowing one inmate to briefly leave the premises contrary to the board's orders, which she promised "shall not occur again."[30] Despite their earlier concerns, board members expressed overall satisfaction with DePass's performance. "She has done all in her power," reasoned one, "considering the infancy of the institution in arranging everything as near our wishes as could be expected under the circumstances."[31] Two weeks later, President Simpson publicly praised DePass, reporting that her work earned the board's "universal satisfaction." Revealing only that her maintenance of discipline had tested the board's "forbearance and sagacity," Simpson gave no details of the serious allegations. Instead he reassured members, donors, and the broader community that the Home was now on sound footing.[32]

Two months later, despite her explicit pledge, DePass had again permitted an inmate to leave the premises without the president's consent.[33] A unanimous board had ruled on her first infraction that, absent such permission, children were prohibited from leaving the premises, with or without their mothers, and that any further infringement of the rules would be cause for termination.[34] Faced with DePass's further infringement, the board terminated her. In DePass's place, the board hired both Mrs. DeYoung as matron to manage the Home and her husband as "Superintendent," although his duties were limited to overseeing collections and other administrative tasks.[35]

The board quickly learned that discipline problems were not limited to DePass. Within a month, Matron DeYoung complained that Babette Schwartz had been "unruly," creating a disturbance by "treating the Matron with contempt." After calling Schwartz to appear, President Simpson threatened expulsion if she violated the rules again.[36] For the next several months, DeYoung complained about other adult inmates. In August, Esther Marks, without permission, worked outside the Home and had allowed her grandchildren to leave the premises. In September, Sarah Duke had purchased a cowhide and "threatened to lay it on the Superintendent," which the board found "highly improper and disgraceful."[37] Later the same month, Babette Schwartz narrowly escaped expulsion for "refractory conduct" by promising, yet again, to obey the rules.[38] The board grew impatient with the overall lack of discipline, at first casting blame solely upon the Home's adult inmates but later changed course. By fall 1857, the board relieved DeYoung of her duties and hired Jennie Goldstein in her place.[39]

Largely private institutions, orphan asylums experienced little or no government oversight even into the early twentieth century.[40] For New Orleans's orphanages, government involvement consisted of inspections and cursory reports by the Orleans Parish Grand Jury, a group of court-appointed citizens with no particular expertise in childcare. In June 1858, after Matron Goldstein served eight uneventful months, the grand jury issued its first disparaging findings about the Home. "The building is very good and requires no repairs; general appearance good, *but not remarkably clean.*"[41] It mattered little to the board that the Home's shortcoming paled by comparison to the grand jury's finding that the inmates at the Boys' House of Refuge had been subjected to abusive discipline (for which its superintendent was criminally prosecuted), or that the nearby Orphan Boys' Asylum was "in a wretched condition," with its boys "not kept as clean or as well clothed as they should be." Until now, prior grand juries had only praised the Home, including calling it "an excellent institution, in every respect" in 1856 and a "credit to the benevolence of this city" in April 1858.[42] Although the board did not record reasons for terminating Goldstein in October 1858, the unfavorable grand jury report three months earlier reasonably appears to be a factor.[43] Published in the press, the grand jury's reports reflected the community's perception of the Home and the Jewish community that sustained it.

Publicity about shortcomings in cleanliness was not the Home's only challenge during Matron Goldstein's tenure. That same summer, yellow fever returned, the city's first major outbreak since 1855. The epidemic took its first victims in mid-June, and its severity was evident by early August. Describing the fever as "very vicious" and "out of control," one New Orleanian wrote in his diary, "[I]t is everywhere!—In the houses of the rich and the houses of the poor."[44] Despite repeated warnings in the newspapers, unacclimated newcomers arrived in a steady stream, "furnishing fresh food to the destroyer."[45] By mid-November, after the summer's prime mosquito-breeding conditions relented, the epidemic had claimed 4,855 lives, nearly 3 percent of the city's population.[46] The Jewish community, now large enough to establish a fourth house of worship, was proportionately stricken. According to the Jewish press, "more than 100 Israelites had been interred by the four congregations."[47]

Yellow fever took a swift and heavy toll on the Home. By early October 1858, the board admitted nine children who had lost parents to the epidemic. The outbreak only renewed the sting of the grand jury's finding. Questions about the Home's cleanliness, at a time when yellow fever was still largely associated with the squalor of poor immigrants, could only stir unwanted prejudice and jeopardize the Home's occasional requests to the state legislature for funding. Having dismissed Goldstein, the board reconsidered former matron DePass. Despite her repeated transgressions, she had overcome the challenges of opening and running the Home during the epidemic three years earlier. The board rehired DePass on the express condition that she "strictly conform" to the Home's rules and abide by the instructions of the board and honorary matrons.[48]

For the next two years, DePass fulfilled her responsibilities as the population mushroomed: forty-two inmates were admitted during and immediately after the 1858 epidemic, more than doubling the Home's total admissions since opening. To DePass's credit, the grand jury lauded the Home in 1859 as "excellent."[49] By November 1860, however, the honorary matrons complained about the "mismanagement of the interior economy of the Home," and urged the board's "energetic action."[50] Whatever deficiencies the honorary matrons identified, the board deemed them sufficient to replace DePass once again. In finding a new matron, the board expressed for the first time its desire "if possible to obtain the services of a Jewess."[51] The board left no clue whether DePass, DeYoung, or Goldstein were Jewish or had been married to Jews, and thus leaves uncertain whether the remark represented a change in practice or a dearth of Jewish women they believed qualified for the role.

DETERMINING ELIGIBILITY

Admission to the Home was a relatively straightforward process. In accordance with the bylaws, an application and relief committee investigated and reported "upon the merits of every application." The committee's recommendations, which the board rarely rejected, were overwhelmingly in favor of admission. Of thirty applications the board considered between May 1855 and May 1858, it granted all but three.[52] The Home's constitution imposed few restrictions. "Indigent Hebrew widows" and "Jewish Orphans and Half-Orphans of both sexes" were the only official criteria for admission. The board also made financial need a requirement for the admission of children. Reflecting the exigencies of the time, two years passed before the board first explicitly rejected an applicant for failing to establish need. In declining to admit the infant, the board noted, "the father being able to support it."[53]

Nor did the founders restrict admission by nativity or residence, a fact that founder Joseph Magner later attributed to his peers' "most liberal spirit, . . . though they well knew that the burdens resting upon our Jewish citizens, in pursuance of this policy, would be heavily increased."[54] As early as 1858, when yellow fever hit Mobile, Alabama, the board approved the creation of an auxiliary admissions committee there. By year's end, the board granted the Mobile committee's request to admit three Hartman siblings, ranging in age from two to ten, whose parents had died in the epidemic.[55] Support for the Home also spread, and by 1862, fifteen citizens of Mobile paid the required dues to join the association as members.[56]

By 1868, the board rejected requests to admit children from St. Louis and Memphis, establishing a principle of not admitting children from too far a distance, *unless* a sufficient number of dues-paying members could be enlisted to support an auxiliary committee, as was done in Mobile.[57] Although neither St. Louis nor Memphis rose to the challenge, by 1873, Jewish communities in Montgomery, Alabama, and Galveston, Texas, established auxiliary committees. Over the next two years, twenty-three children were admitted from those two cities and surrounding areas, generating important new sources of revenue from dues and donations.[58]

The problem with admitting a child from out of state, in the absence of a responsible auxiliary committee, was demonstrated as early as December 1856. The board admitted a fourteen-year-old half orphan boy, at the request of Julius Eckman, the first rabbi of San Francisco, where no Jewish orphanage existed until 1871. The board likely yielded to this admission out of respect for Eckman and because Home founder David Labatt's father was president of his synagogue. The rabbi earlier had officiated in Mobile, New Orleans, and Charleston before assuming the post (which Gutheim had declined) in California.[59] Although the board was prepared to discharge the boy in 1859, distance and difficulties in communication prevented his discharge until 1861, when his father traveled from California to retrieve him.[60]

Over the next few years, as occupancy rose and discipline wavered, the board also addressed the issue of age limits, another matter on which the constitution was silent. In October 1857, with a population of twenty-five children and six widows, the board briefly considered denying admission to half orphans under the age of five and widows under the age of forty-five. Despite concerns that the growing population would exceed capacity, and the added difficulties of caring for very young children, the board continued to liberally treat age in admissions. In 1858, following the death of his wife, Anshel Posner entrusted his three children, including two-month-old Hannah, to the Home and in 1859 the board admitted twenty-eight-year-old widow Jeanette Goldstein (no known relation to the matron) with her three children, Nathan, Sarah, and Marx.[61] Not until the twentieth century did the board restrict admission to children old enough to walk and under the age of twelve, but even then it continued to waive the maximum age limit when compassion dictated. This distinguished the Home from other Jewish orphanages, including the Cleveland Jewish Orphan Asylum and New York's Hebrew Orphan Asylum, both of which enforced a minimum admission age of five.[62] While high mortality rates and added costs of providing infant nurses dissuaded other orphanages from admitting very young children, the board accepted these challenges.[63] Over its history, although the average age at admission was seven, and half fell between the ages of five and ten, about 8 percent of Home residents were two years or younger.[64]

Like other orphanages, the board imposed no limit on the number of children it admitted from one family, which presented a significant issue at a time when many families were large. The vast majority (83 percent) of the Home's 1,623 children were admitted with at least 1 sibling. These 488 sibling groups ranged in number from 2 children, including 14 sets of twins, to the 9 Block siblings. Immigrants from Alsace, the Block parents died from yellow fever in 1858; the children ranged in age from eighteen-year-old Sarah down to two-year-old Bertha.[65] The need to admit large family groups continued into the next century. Following the deaths of their wives, Joseph Tannenbaum and Abraham Beerman each admitted their six youngest children in 1918 and 1924, respectively.[66] Over its years, the Home admitted a total of 24 family groups with 5 or more siblings. In this way, the Home continued to keep siblings relatively intact, a feature that was generally unavailable in adoption or private family placements.

Determining eligibility for admission for full or half orphans was relatively simple when the death of one or both parents could be ascertained. Yet children proposed for admission often presented myriad parental situations and conditions, such as desertion or incapacity due to physical or mental infirmity. In 1866, the board admitted the child of "an abandoned woman" because "we regard the child as a half-orphan."[67] Similarly, in 1874, the board admitted Julia Miller's seven-year-old son, Solomon; his father, although presumed to be alive, had not been heard from in years.[68] And yet, the board occasionally rejected children whose misfortune was created by the desertion, but not death, of a parent, almost always the father.[69] In the absence of recorded reasons, the board's rejections suggest an intent to strictly (albeit inconsistently) adhere to the constitution, while its admissions in these cases suggest that it yielded to compassion.

There is no evidence that the board's occasional refusal to admit children of truant fathers stemmed from general disdain for abandoned mothers. Although little is known about attitudes toward the plight of Jewish women deserted by their husbands in America during the nineteenth century, by the early twentieth century efforts to assist these women ("agunot") were well organized and documented.[70] The board's adherence to its constitutional mandate to exclude children of some deserted mothers more likely stemmed instead from fear of inviting false claims by desperate parents. This explains the board's approach in 1889 when it admitted Julia Levy Block's four children after her absent husband was presumed dead. The board required "three reputable gentlemen" of Block's remote Louisiana parish to guarantee they would promptly notify the board and withdraw the children "should the father ever turn up."[71] The children lived in the Home much of the next decade, the father having never reappeared, affirming either the soundness of the board's safeguard or the difficulty of its enforcement.

Yet, despite the constitution's express limitation to full orphans and half orphans, which the board did not amend until 1924, on other occasions the board treated children *as if* they were orphans. In 1873, it admitted a two-year-old boy whose parents were "mutes and also invalids."[72] In 1882, on the same day the board declined to admit a woman and her child because they were "neither widow nor orphan," it admitted another mother's three children on the grounds that their father was insane.[73] In 1889, the board admitted Emile Szafir's four children from Austin, Texas, on grounds that his wife, Johanna, was an invalid.[74] She died three years later while the children remained in the Home.[75] Given the era's greatly diminished life expectancy for persons with physical disabilities and the shocking conditions and high death rates for patients in mental asylums, especially in Louisiana, it is not surprising that the board sometimes treated the children of parents with these conditions as orphans.[76]

In January 1857, the board first grappled with whether a child was Jewish. Mrs. Aaron, a gentile widow, applied to admit her three children following the death of her Jewish husband. Her sons had been circumcised, and she had complied with her husband's wishes to raise his children as Jews. For guidance, the board turned to Reverend Gutheim, who served as secretary, chair of its education and discipline committee, and resident Jewish scholar. As minister of Congregation Dispersed of Judah, Gutheim then identified as Orthodox although his distinctly liberal leanings later led him to champion moderate Reform Judaism. In New Orleans, where Jewish marriages to gentiles had long been sufficiently common to require loosening rules governing eligibility for synagogue membership and burial in Jewish cemeteries, Gutheim was well versed in the subject.[77] Provided the children of an interfaith marriage had completed all formalities prescribed for conversion, he opined, the applicable Jewish law was "clear and positive" on their acceptance as Jews: "However averse we are to a system of proselyte making and however circumspect in inquiring into the purity of the motives of those who voluntarily offer themselves to become Jews, we are not permitted to reject those who come under the operation of our law and whom both the dictates of humanity and sound policy bid as to protect." For these reasons, Gutheim recommended "that the applicants be admitted and the necessary formalities be executed to make them full converts to Judaism.[78] Although the Aaron children never entered the Home, Gutheim's analysis established the liberal precedent the board followed into the next century.[79]

At the same time, given the history of forced conversions of Jews to Christianity dating to the Middle Ages, children who risked being raised outside the Jewish faith if not admitted to the Home garnered the board's special attention. In 1859, following the death of his gentile wife, Jacob Bernard sought to admit his three sons. Noting the father's distress, including his fear that his sons would not be raised as Jews, the board admitted the boys pending Gutheim's determination of their religion.[80] Bernard, a native of Bohemia, lived in St. Louis, where he married his wife and raised the boys. Aware of her impending death, Bernard's wife requested that he raise the boys as Jews. After she died, her parents hid the boys in St. Louis's Roman Catholic asylum. Jacob managed to regain custody and, fearing further action by his in-laws, took his sons to New Orleans. Aided by members of the Polish Congregation Temime Derech, the newest of New Orleans's synagogues, Jacob had his sons circumcised.[81] The board accepted Gutheim's recommendation, in which he relied on the precedent of the Aaron children, and admitted the Bernard boys.

The board's fear that the boys might be raised out of the Jewish faith was heightened by incidents far and near. A few months earlier, in a highly publicized case, Pope Pius IX had ordered the abduction of six-year-old Edgardo Mortara from his Jewish parents in Bologna, Italy. Citing the canonical prohibition against Jews raising Christians, the papal police seized and kept the boy on the word of the family's Christian servant who, claiming the boy faced impending death from illness, had reportedly baptized him.[82] The international outrage quickly reached New Orleans, where the city's synagogues formed a joint protest committee with Gutheim as chair and Meyer Simpson as secretary.[83]

In December 1858, while Gutheim and Simpson protested the Mortara boy's abduction, the plight of little Alice Levy came before the board. It unanimously voted to admit the eighteen-month-old baby to honor her Jewish mother's dying wishes. A nurse taking care of Alice, however, claiming emotional attachment, kept the baby for months before enlisting the aid of a Mrs. Capdeville, a charitable Catholic woman of no known relation to the nurse or the baby. Believing the nurse's story that the baby had been abandoned, Mrs. Capdeville planned to baptize the child. Apparently perceiving a sense of duty, Capdeville initially refused the Home's demand for custody but later apologetically relented when President Simpson called upon her to surrender the child. By January, Alice Levy was delivered to the Home.[84]

Although Alice's arrival at the Home seemed to mark the end of the matter, the Mortara controversy kept her story alive for several months. In mid-March, after the baby was already in the Home, the board received an inquiry from the French consul, who belatedly got involved at the request of the grandmother of the baby, whose parents were French. President Simpson responded with a full statement of the case, to which he added, "It is a source of peculiar gratification to the Israelites of this country, to witness at this juncture, the prompt intervention of your Government in a case so similar to that of the Italian child Mortara, for whose parents there seems to be no prospect of relief."[85] Simpson was correct. Despite international outrage, the boy was raised as a Catholic and became a priest.[86]

Simpson proudly recounted the entire Alice Levy affair in his 1859 annual report, which *The Occident* reprinted, appending his correspondence with the French consul. The *Israelite* also reprinted the letters, under the headline, "No

Mortara Case." The secular press, too, spread the news, contrasting the Home's swift success in taking custody of baby Alice with the hopeless case of Edgardo Mortara. "Another Mortara Case with a More Honorable Termination," reported the *New York Times* in May. The next month, the *San Francisco Bulletin* published Simpson's letter to the French consul under the heading, "A Mortara Case at New Orleans—French Intervention." Internationally, an account of the Alice Levy affair made its way later the same year into a Peruvian treatise and Germany's monthly journal on the "history and science of Judaism."[87]

"By advertising the case," concluded historian Mark Bauman, "the association was giving credit to the French government and, thus, further admonishing the Papal authorities by placing their actions in contrast."[88] At the same time, the Home's board, as leaders of New Orleans's Jewish community, demonstrated that they could effectively intervene even with foreign governments and that their cause was important to other Jews and the broader population. Within just four years after its founding, the Home was fulfilling its mission to protect needy Jewish orphans and its success was being celebrated on an international and interfaith stage.

Other examples exist of the board's sensitivity to Jewish children being reared by non-Jews. For example, when the board suspected in 1857 that a Jewish boy had been placed in the House of Refuge, a municipal institution for juvenile delinquents, it promptly charged a committee to investigate and retrieve the boy, if true.[89] At the same time, the board's reputation for preventing Jewish children from being sheltered out of the faith invited desperate applicants. In 1868, for example, Frida Posner told the board that, having been abandoned by her husband in New York, she was unable to support her child and, if the board refused to admit her son, "she would make the necessary application at a Christian asylum." Gutheim urged the board to deny the application, noting that Posner could have placed her child in a Jewish asylum in New York and suggested it defray her expenses to return there. After concluding that yielding to the threat would invite "constant applications of this kind," the board unanimously voted to reject Posner's application.[90]

In determining applications for admission, the Home's leaders faced competing goals. On the one hand, they wanted neither to lose a child to another faith nor tarnish Jews' reputation for taking care of their own. In support of the Louisiana legislature's 1856 appropriation of $6,000 to the Home, one gentile legislator noted that Jews as a class "were rarely found asking alms, they were in the habit of taking care of themselves."[91] Despite the legislator's prediction that the Home's request "was their first and last asking," over the next two decades the Home received additional appropriations totaling more than $10,000 from the state, over and above its per capita share of the city's annual disbursements for support of orphans, apparently without besmirching the self-sufficient reputation of Jews.[92] On the other hand, the pressures to deny admission partly stemmed from not wanting to improperly claim a child of another faith. As reflected in Gutheim's recommendation to admit the Aaron children, the Jewish aversion to proselytizing dated back to the Roman Empire's prohibition against conversion to Judaism (or for Jews to seek converts) under penalty of death. The aversion was heightened by threats of losing Jewish children to another faith through forced conversions.[93] Finally, in deciding applications for admission, the board also faced practical constraints: the Home's limited physical and financial capacity.

The Home's constitution also was silent on the subject of children with disabilities, an issue the board encountered in its earliest days. In September 1855, before the Home opened, widower Samuel Kalisher applied for the admission of his five-year-old daughter, Emily, whom he described as "paralyzed and half-blind." After consulting its physician, the board admitted Emily, who remained in the Home for five years, ultimately with a nurse dedicated to her exclusive care. During the last two years of her stay, the board found itself unable to help "this unfortunate creature" and feared her time in the Home was tending to "confirm the state of her idiocy." It repeatedly requested that Kalisher move his daughter to an asylum "more beneficial to a child in her condition" and in 1860 transferred Emily to the State Insane Asylum at Jackson, Louisiana. Six months later, the board learned she had died and arranged to remove her body to a Jewish cemetery."[94] In 1864, the board again considered admitting a person with a physical disability. This time it declined to admit Adele Levy, whom it described only as a "blind young lady."[95]

The board's minutes reveal few instances in which it knowingly admitted children with special needs, whether serious physical impairments, developmental disabilities, serious learning disabilities, or emotional or behavioral disorders. "Our Home is a home for normal children," the Home's newsletter directly stated in 1933, before adding the factors it considered in determining a child's normalcy: "his physical condition, his emotional condition, his degree of cooperation, and other influences."[96] When such conditions became evident after admission, the board transferred the children to another institution, such as the Vineland Training School, which opened in 1888 as the

New Jersey Home for the Care and Education of Feebleminded Children. The Home's exclusion of children with significant physical or other disabilities typified the policies of orphanages and society at large.[97] In 1928, however, the board admitted eleven-year-old Maurice Garb from San Antonio, Texas, who two years earlier had lost an arm in an accident. A strong student and gifted athlete, Garb became captain of his varsity football team and a speaker at his graduation, before entering Tulane, where he made the dean's list.[98] The board's decision to admit and retain the talented boy confirms its aversion to admitting children who required special accommodation or attention.

DISCHARGE

The discharge of orphans demanded as much, if not more, time and attention as applications for admission. Although it set no hard and fast rules, the board was mindful of the Home's limited physical space and resources. Absent a parent or relative willing and able to assume care, a child's discharge generally required self-sufficiency. This was determined by age and maturity, or, especially in the Home's early years, a suitable employer or apprenticeship for boys and a respectable husband for girls. Adoption provided another, albeit limited, circumstance for discharge.

In December 1856, Hannah Amanda Bensadon, whose sister Matron De-Pass allegedly punished with the cowhide, was the first child discharged by the board. Less than nine months after her admission, the board returned the ten-year-old girl to her mother's care.[99] Although Hannah's stay was far shorter than for most children admitted, returning to a parent or other relative provided the most common basis for discharge, reflecting the board's interest in reuniting children with their families, whenever possible. That Hannah's two younger sisters remained in the Home for two more years was also common. Many widowed parents were able to resume care for some but not all of their children, especially when they were old enough to contribute to the household by performing chores or earning income. In 1857, the board discharged four other children to a parent or relative.[100] This was typical of the first five years of the Home's operation: of thirty-four children whose discharge circumstances are known, twenty-nine were returned to a surviving parent. Additionally, the three eldest Block sisters were discharged after a short stay because, at ages eighteen to twenty, they informed the board they intended to provide for themselves.[101] Over the Home's ninety-one years, the board returned more than 70 percent of its children to a parent, adult sibling, or other close relative.[102]

The practice of reuniting children with their families was followed by other Jewish orphanages elsewhere in the country and by Catholic and Protestant orphanages in New Orleans who also saw their role in temporarily caring for needy, parentless children. The Home and other orphanages that sought family reunification remained unswayed by some later nineteenth-century social reformers. New York's Charles Loring Brace and Minnesota's Public School at Owatonna, for example, advocated permanently separating indigent urban youngsters from their natural families and placing them on farms, presumably for a healthier environment and opportunity—without ties to their religious roots.[103]

"RESPECTABLY SETTLED IN LIFE"

Well into the twentieth century, the board viewed marriage among the best ways to secure the future of its female wards. This was, of course, in keeping with gender norms of the nineteenth and early twentieth centuries in New Orleans and elsewhere in the country and across the Atlantic. With most professions reserved for men, young, single women faced few job opportunities without a family business or the funds to start one.[104] Those who secured employment in domestic service or the "needle trades" could expect room and board or subsistence wages at best.[105] Even women who became teachers, a well-regarded position for educated single women, were expected to hold their posts only until they found a husband. "Respectably settled in life," boasted President Simpson about the Home's first young women to wed. Their marriages, he said, provided "bright testimony of the glorious results achieved by our Institution, and the high estimation in which it is held by the community."[106]

Twelve-year-old Esther Carillion and her younger sister, Rachel, the first children taken into the Home's care, were the orphan daughters of Rabbi Benjamin Cohen Carillion, who earlier served a congregation in Jamaica, and the former Rebecca Levy, who worked as a dressmaker upon the family's arrival in New Orleans in 1849. Although the circumstances of his and his wife's deaths are undocumented, Rabbi Carillion's difficult tenure in Jamaica left him unable to secure a pulpit in New Orleans. An 1850 census described the Jewish clergyman as "insane."[107]

In 1859, at age sixteen, having completed her studies, Esther performed housework in the Home for which she earned six dollars per month.[108] She also captured the heart of Herman Gilbert. Seeking the board's permission to marry its charge, the thirty-one-year-old house painter wrote that he was capable of supporting Esther and pledged to make her happy.[109] Recognizing the decision's importance as precedent for other female inmates, the board acceded to Gilbert's request.[110] In addition, on Matron DePass's recommendation, the board appropriated one hundred dollars to provide Esther with a proper wedding trousseau.[111] The practice of providing funds when Home girls married was institutionalized in 1900, courtesy of a fund endowed by Simon Gumbel, a prosperous merchant who served as the Home's treasurer for fourteen years.[112] The gift to Esther was the board's first generous act of its kind, consistent with marriage then being the most desirable outcome in life for a young woman.

Five months later, the board dispensed with its regular meeting to celebrate the happy occasion. The Reverend Gutheim officiated "in a solemn manner and according to the forms and rite of the Holy Jewish Religion in presence of the Board of Officers, Board of Honorary Matrons and large concourse of friends of the respective parties."[113] Although Esther left no account of her views about marrying Gilbert, they remained married for four decades until his death, when he was eulogized as "industrious, honest, and generous." She bore him thirteen children.[114]

As content as the board appeared to be with Esther's marriage, Gutheim nevertheless warned that secret courtships, as Esther and Herman must have had, were a "serious impropriety" that needed to be addressed. It was the matron's duty, asserted Gutheim, to prevent clandestine romances before it was too late to object. Gutheim urged that engagements required the board's thorough review as guardians and that they had been fortunate thus far as there had been "no disgraceful results."[115] Especially in the South, a single woman who defied the deeply inculcated values of purity and chastity through improper behavior imperiled her social respectability and chances for marriage.[116] The consequences for the Home and its board, who pledged to guard its wards from "temptation and vice," would be dire.[117] Gutheim may have also been concerned about Home girls marrying non-Jews. Although interfaith marriage by Jews was common in New Orleans, there is some evidence that Jewish women who married out of the faith were treated less favorably than Jewish men who did the same.[118]

The marriage of Sarah Ehrman, however, posed no such concerns for the board. Three years after her admission, the board first attempted to secure Sarah's future in 1859 when she was thirteen by discharging her to Mr. H. Frank, presumably as a domestic worker. The next month, however, the board readmitted Sarah after Frank advised that he could "keep her no longer owing to her insubordination."[119] In 1861, Jacob Bernard, the St. Louis widower whose three boys were admitted two years earlier when Gutheim deemed them Jewish, expressed his desire to marry Sarah and reclaim his sons. Jacob had regained sufficient financial stability to contribute to his children's support in the Home, a practice the board and other orphanages encouraged to provide income and to keep a surviving parent or relative connected to a child even if lacking the means to resume full custody.[120] Viewing this as "an honorable settlement in life" for Sarah while at the same time reducing by five the Home's growing enrollment, the board discharged Sarah to marry Jacob, who took with them his three sons and Sarah's sister, Babette.[121]

For boys who could not be discharged to a family member, the board sought jobs and apprenticeships, usually by age thirteen or fourteen. In 1861, for example, J. Hockersmith Jr., of Southern Mills & Co., agreed to employ fourteen-year-old Morris Mengis, paying him wages of ten dollars per month, and find him board and lodging with a family.[122] In 1862, Isaac Berkhoff, age fourteen, whose parents had died from yellow fever in 1858, and Manuel Bergman, age thirteen, who lived with his mother in the Home, were discharged as apprentices, with wages plus board and lodging, in Mr. Hans's crockery store and A. Schwab's apothecary store, respectively.[123] Consistent with general norms regarding young men's transition to adulthood and the practices of other orphanages at the time, the board considered placing boys of this age with reputable employers as a desirable way to ensure their productive and self-sufficient futures—if those placements lasted.[124]

Just as Isaac and Manuel were settling into their new situations, Morris returned to the Home and to the board's attention. Born in Bayou Sara, Louisiana, Morris and his London-born sister Sarah had been admitted on the Home's first day at ages seven and eleven by their widowed stepfather. Now, Morris's promising apprenticeship in the mill had ended, and the board considered removing him from the Home. "Through his utter want of subordination," Morris was "entirely beyond the control of the Matron or the Committee on Education & Discipline," reported committee member Joseph Magner, who called for the boy's immediate removal. After debating its choices, the board summoned Morris and told him he was to be placed in another apprenticeship, with a strict thirty-day probationary period. President Simpson admonished him to behave in his new position to avoid "any severer measures in the future," threatening to enlist him in the Navy, which was then permitted at age thirteen with parental consent, or send him to the House of Refuge, the city asylum for juvenile offenders.[125] Within two weeks, the board discharged Morris to Mr. J. Lucas, a jeweler, who promised to teach Morris the business and "treat him as a son in all respects."[126] The Home never heard from Morris again.

Just how long Morris worked as a jeweler's apprentice is unknown. When he died at age seventy-three in 1921, his obituary—which appeared in newspapers across the country—reported that he had served as a drummer in the Confederate Army before moving to Boston, Baltimore, and finally, New York, where he spent the bulk of his life and died.[127] Although articles and obituaries detailed Morris's colorful and controversial life story—as newspaper owner, litigious railroad investor, bankrupted hotel owner, inventor, and thoroughbred horse owner, they did not mention his years as an orphanage inmate. At least one account, however, noted his passion for fine jewelry.[128]

While marriage, employment, and maturity frequently led to discharges, the board entertained little more than a dozen instances of adoption over ninety years. The board's earliest references to "adoption" likely were not actually the legally sanctioned relationships that are common today but instead "free placements" in which the adopting family promised to treat the child as their own, but may not have bestowed the right to inheritance. As a general matter, adoption—the notion that adults should be able to become the legal parents of a child who was not their biological offspring—did not become widespread in the United States until the twentieth century.[129] In Louisiana through the Home's first decade, adoption required a special legislative grant, a burdensome process at best. Even after 1865, when Louisiana enacted its first law generally authorizing adoption, most Home children had at least one parent living, from whom consent would have been required.[130]

Henry Kaufman was the first of the relatively few children the board discharged for what it called "adoption." In December 1854, after giving birth to Henry in Louisville, Kentucky, his German-born mother, Sophie, traveled to New Orleans. In July 1855, she contracted yellow fever and died.[131] By August, nine-month-old Henry's plight came to the attention of the board, which paid for his care by a nurse in the community until the Home opened.[132] In 1858, shortly after Henry turned three, French Quarter grocery-store owner Henry Ber and

Matilda Gottschaux Ber petitioned the board to adopt the boy. After vetting the childless couple, the board consented, "provided the [Bers] bind themselves in writing to properly treat and educate said orphan and recognize at all times the guardianship of the board over the same."[133] Whether they failed to obtain the legislative permission to adopt him or simply honored the boy's birthright, the Bers did not change their son's last name; instead they called him Henry Ber Kaufman, making their last name the boy's middle name. Henry lived happily and comfortably after his adoption, never returning to the board's agenda.[134]

Three years passed after Henry left the Home before the board discharged a second child for what it called "adoption." The board entrusted five-year-old Begala Levy, a full orphan, to Mr. B. Finkle and his wife, with the proviso that they "take the requisite steps to adopt her fully in due course of the laws."[135] A year later, the board learned that the Finkles had traveled to Europe, leaving Begala with Finkle's brother and niece. The board was ready to retrieve her, but relented upon determining that she was being well cared for and upon hearing from Begala's "own mouth her affection for the niece of Mr. Finkle and that it would be painful for her to leave her adopted home."[136]

The small number of children adopted from the Home appears consistent with the experience of other New Orleans orphanages and other Jewish orphanages elsewhere, including New York, Cleveland, and Philadelphia. Not only was the process lengthy and arduous in the mid-nineteenth century, but even in later years continued to be a reasonable option only for full orphans or abandoned children young enough to adjust to an adoptive home, categories which comprised a small percentage of children in orphanages.[137]

THE HOME'S FIFTH ANNIVERSARY—JANUARY 1861

Over its first five years, the Home proved its value. Since opening, the Home had admitted eighty-six children and fourteen adult women. Owing to discharges, the Home now held seventy inmates, or in Gutheim's words, "the number of souls which Jacob brought down with him to Egypt."[138] The Home had welcomed natives of not only Louisiana, but also of sister states, Alabama, Mississippi, Tennessee, South Carolina, Missouri, Ohio, and New York, as well as foreign countries of Poland, Germany, France, Belgium, Holland, England, the West Indies, and Canada. At the fifth anniversary celebration, Gutheim proclaimed, "Our Home is no longer an experiment, but a fact."[139]

The Home's children, too, played a key role in these anniversary events.

They were prominently seated for all to observe their neat and appropriate attire, and their apparent good health and happiness.[140] In 1864, the children began the annual tradition of taking the stage to recite poetry or short essays, give musical or theatrical performances, or stage elaborate tableaux.[141] More than seventy years passed before childcare professionals considered the exploitive nature of displaying needy children publicly, and seventy-nine years before the board abandoned the practice. Until then children's performances constituted a central and popular feature of each Home anniversary, memorialized by detailed press accounts that lauded and identified the young performers by name.[142]

First and foremost, the anniversary celebrations had become the single largest source of the Home's annual income. Gutheim, for instance, used his anniversary oration in 1861 to urge his listeners to give—over and above their usual donations—to create an endowment to sustain the Home, transforming it into a monument "more enduring than bronze."[143] Other fundraising activities, too, enabled the Home to endear itself to New Orleans's lively social and cultural scene, such as the May 1858 vocal and instrumental concert at the Odd Fellows Hall, featuring "morceaux from the compositions of Rossini, Weber, and Meyerbeer" for which more than seven hundred people paid $1.50 per ticket.[144] While crucial for the Home's tight budget, these occasional efforts never matched the funds raised at the anniversary celebrations. In 1859, for instance, when the event committee unapologetically combed the crowd for donations and cajoled generous bids while auctioning the inmates' handicrafts, they raised $5,000.[145] The community took note of the Home's success in raising funds at its anniversaries. Years later, Bishop J. N. Galleher sought to inspire similar generosity for the Protestant Episcopal Children's Home. Pointing to the "fine" Jewish orphanage across Jackson Avenue, he told his congregants that each year "the children of the elder children of God gather together and in three hours a year's maintenance is provided."[146]

Over its first five years, the Home had transformed from experiment to reality. Unlike other orphanages that were founded or run by women, men dominated the Home's formal governance. While constrained by Victorian gender norms of the mid-nineteenth century, women nevertheless played crucial roles in the Home's fundraising and operation, as evidenced by its volunteer honorary matrons and paid female matron and teachers. Together, these men and women placed the new Home on sound footing to care for needy Jews and prevent them from becoming public burdens while seeking community acceptance and maintaining the asylum's public image. Like the Schwartz family and the city, the Home, its board, and its managers had overcome a wide range of trials, not the least of which was serving a growing population. But the Home and New Orleans were about to face even bigger challenges.

chapter three

CIVIL WAR AND FEDERAL OCCUPATION 1861–1868

Although the Civil War turned thousands of American children into orphans and half orphans, the Home experienced the years during and shortly after the tragic rebellion in other ways.[1] In addition to financial hardship, encroachment of liberties, and the return of yellow fever, all of which affected the entire city, the period was marked for the Home, as a Jewish institution, by leaders who invoked the Bible to uphold the laws and customs of its adoptive community, including slavery.

SECESSION AND ITS AFTERMATH

The last Saturday in January 1861 was cold, windy, and gray. Suddenly, at half-past noon, the city began to reverberate. Cannon blasts punctuated the steady ringing of fire-alarm bells. This was not a useless attempt to rid the air of pestilence as in 1853, but rather an announcement: Louisiana had seceded from the Union.[2] The state earlier had strongly opposed secession, a position held by many New Orleanians with personal or commercial ties to the North. But these attitudes swiftly reversed with the presidential election of Republican Abraham Lincoln, which many southerners viewed as a declaration of northern hostility.[3] "The people of Louisiana were unwilling to endanger their liberties and property by submission to the despotism of a single tyrant," explained one state secession official. Instead, they sought "to preserve the blessings of African slavery."[4] These changed views also found support in New Orleans, including within the Home's board.

To Home president Meyer Simpson, a slave owner and cotton broker, news of secession was neither surprising nor unwelcome.[5] Earlier that month, he publicly invited "all true friends of the South" to a meeting of the Southern Rights Association to call for secession and the creation of a "confederated government" of southern states.[6] A month before that, he signed a letter with thirty other prominent New Orleanians calling for the publication of Dr. Benjamin Morgan Palmer's fiery Thanksgiving sermon, in which the Presbyterian theologian preached that it was the South's duty "to conserve and to perpetuate the institution of domestic slavery as now existing."[7] It is less clear, however, whether Simpson or any other Confederate was prepared for the consequences that soon flowed from dissolving all ties with the United States of America. Within a week, recounted one city resident, "Everything financially, politically, and socially, is resolved into an aggregate of utter incertitude."[8]

Three months later, U.S. troops broke through the Confederate barrier on the Mississippi River and took control of the city. Although neither battle nor physical damage occurred, New Orleans was nonetheless under siege. After Commodore (and later Admiral) David G. Farragut captured the city, Major General Benjamin F. Butler controlled the occupation, aided by some 100,000 Union soldiers under his command. They established their headquarters just two miles downriver from the Home in the unfinished U.S. Custom House on Canal Street, the city's largest government building. Over the next few years, the Union Army used the same building to imprison Confederate soldiers, reportedly as many as 2,000 at one time.[9]

Home board member Philip Sartorious, a young merchant from rural Louisiana, was in New Orleans when it fell. He recalled the "almost indescribable" scene of Confederate merchants and troops in a frenzy to avoid Union seizure of their possessions. "Bales of cotton were cut open and set on fire," he wrote, while "hoodlums threw balls and shells overboard."[10] According to historian Robert Rosen, "The streets were packed with people fleeing. The Jewish community reacted as other New Orleans citizens did—with shock, anger, disbelief, and disdain."[11] When the city fell to the Union, Clara Solomon was a sixteen-year-old girl from a prosperous family who attended Reverend Gutheim's Dispersed of Judah Congregation. Clara wrote, "A gloom envelopes our dearly-beloved city. My breaking heart but aches the more. . . . Oh! Never shall I forget the 25th of Apr. 1862."[12] Outrage intensified when "Beast" Butler, as angry locals quickly dubbed the Union Army's commanding officer, executed a man for destroying a Union flag flying over the federal mint. Like many New

Orleanians, Clara decried the death sentence, writing, "It is atrocious & oh! God, help us to revenge it."[13] Despite Clara's and other's disdain, the hanging served Butler's goal of stifling further rebellion.[14]

The Union had ample reason to target New Orleans. With the sixth largest population in the country, it was the biggest Confederate city by far, whose strategically crucial port supplied the rebel forces by linking the Mississippi River and the Gulf of Mexico. Union occupation of New Orleans remains historic for another reason. Other than New York under British occupation during most of the Revolutionary War, it is the only large American city ever to undergo a lengthy wartime occupation by an "enemy" military force; the fact that people on both sides were American renders the situation all the more remarkable.[15]

By the time the city fell to the Union, other Home leaders besides President Simpson aired Confederate sympathies. In April 1861, an editorial in New York's *Jewish Messenger* urged readers "to be loyal to the Union, which protects them," and "not be backward in realizing the duty that is incumbent upon them to rally as one man for the Union and Constitution."[16] In a heated rejoinder, Gutheim, joined by Simpson and six other Home leaders, accused the editor of echoing the "Abolitionist press" by insulting the citizens of nearly half the states of the former union. The Home's leaders decried the editorial, titled "Stand by the Flag," because the Union's "once glorious flag [had already been] dishonored and metamorphosed into an emblem of the most atrocious military despotism that was ever wielded to crush our popular liberty, solely and completely by Northern fanaticism." It was the new Confederate flag, born from the pursuit of justice and liberty, they wrote, that deserved honor and respect.[17] In solidarity, Benjamin DaSilva, the sexton for Gutheim's congregation and the Home's assistant secretary, resigned his post as the *Jewish Messenger*'s New Orleans sales agent.[18] These and other southern Jewish men—immigrant and American-born alike, from peddlers and storekeepers to wealthy enslavers—were deeply committed to the Confederacy and its customs because it was the homeland that gave them freedom and financial opportunity.[19]

Even the Home's 1862 anniversary celebration took a decidedly pro-Confederate stance. The board had invited Reverend Bernard Illowy, Gates of Mercy's new spiritual leader, to deliver the oration. After acknowledging the wisdom of celebrating the Home's anniversary on "that glorious day" when Andrew Jackson triumphed over foreign enemies, Illowy castigated the North for its antisemitism and xenophobia. "Our glorious Confederacy," contrasted

Illowy, made no distinction "between him who comes from distant shores and him whose ancestors were born in the land," regardless of language or religion. "Whoever seeks protection may place himself under our flag and he will be protected."[20] Ignoring the inhuman treatment the Confederacy inflicted on thousands of enslaved persons, Illowy was correct that the antebellum South was far more hospitable to Jews than the North.[21] In this regard, Illowy likened to the Confederacy the Home's liberality in sheltering needy Jewish widows and orphans without regard to nationality or whether their Jewish tradition was Orthodox or Reform.[22]

That Illowy used the Home's 1862 anniversary to rally Confederate support was not unexpected. Just one year earlier, Illowy, then Baltimore's leading Orthodox clergyman, publicly defended slavery. He pointed to the biblical examples of Moses and Ezra, who condemned enslavement of Jews yet accepted the enslavement of others, as "irrefutable proofs that we have no right to exercise violence against the institutions of other states or countries, even if religious feelings and philanthropic sentiments bid us disapprove of them." Illowy condemned abolitionists who "under the color of religion . . . have thrown the country into a general state of confusion." He openly sympathized with secessionists, asking, "Who can blame our brethren of the South for seceding from a society whose government cannot, or will not, protect the property rights and privileges of a great portion of the Union?" Illowy's remarks that day resonated with Gates of Mercy's congregants, whether they only agreed that Jews must abide by the laws and customs of their community or also supported slavery. Tripling his Baltimore salary, the congregation hired Illowy as their new spiritual leader.[23]

Home leaders supported the Confederacy with more than words. They funded and volunteered for the Confederate war effort. In October 1861, Gutheim and fellow board member Joseph H. Marks, a wholesale grocer, joined forces with Mayor John T. Monroe to feed Lieutenant Colonel Edmonston's Confederate battalion.[24] Directress Miriam Haber, too, aided the cause, donating twenty-four pairs of woolen socks to the Confederate company, the Florance Guard.[25] In turn, the Florance Guard honored the financial backing it received from its namesake, Home founder Benjamin Florance.[26]

Once the Confederacy's commercial core, New Orleans transformed into an economic ghost town under Union occupation. Shops, offices, and warehouses were locked and dark, leaving many unemployed to roam the streets or gather at the levee to survey the Union fleet.[27] The upheaval engulfing the city also brought new challenges in running the Home. Two days after the city's capture, the board instructed Gutheim, who alternated as treasurer and secretary, to withdraw all bank deposits to prevent confiscation by Union forces.[28] The Home's financial statements reported the balance on hand in both "current" and "uncurrent" funds, reflecting the fact that Confederate money, an unbacked promissory note that offered the illusion of payment six months after the war, was then worth about 60 cents on the dollar and continued to depreciate as the Union prohibited its commercial use.[29]

While chaos swirled outside, the Home continued to care for its wards. The board met every two weeks as usual throughout the war. In mid-February 1861, Hannah Noel of New York accepted the board's offer to serve as matron, replacing Ann DePass. The board allowed Noel's mother to also live in the Home and approved funds for the women's traveling expenses, provided that they leave for New Orleans as soon as possible.[30] If the women worried about moving to the new Confederate States of America, they left behind no account. By April 7, Noel assumed her post overseeing the Home's sixty inmates.[31]

As they did across the South, secession and the ensuing war stressed the Home's finances and dampened support from the community, whose attention and funds were diverted to more pressing needs. Only thirty-four of the Home's three hundred members attended the 1861 annual meeting, representing less than half of the prior year's attendance.[32] To cut costs, the board postponed printing its annual report for more than a year. It dismissed the gardener and directed Noel to institute "such reforms in the economy of the Home" as necessary under "the pressure of the times."[33] These pressures, however, did not impair the board's engagement in its charges' welfare. After a meeting that month, the board assembled the children in the dining room, where Simpson reviewed each child's conduct, praising or admonishing as warranted.[34]

Although the Home remained financially stable, the result of frugality with money previously raised, the war had constrained the Home's donors, and, as Simpson noted, "the prices of all the necessaries of life have reached an unprecedented height."[35] By the end of the year, the board reduced all staff wages, cut the matron's personal spending, and gratefully accepted Assistant Secretary DaSilva's offer to forego his salary.[36]

The children and widows also felt the pinch. In the summer of 1862, the board authorized the honorary matrons to secure only articles "absolutely required."[37] By fall, in view of the approaching High Holy Days, when one's best clothing is expected, Miriam Haber received the board's permission to address the inmates' "want of shoes."[38] For more than two years butcher Samuel Levy continued to furnish the Home with beef at 8 cents per pound, a huge favor considering the rate for meat had spiked to 40 cents per pound across the city. By fall of 1862, however, 15 cents per pound was now the lowest price Levy could offer the Home.[39] Notwithstanding these difficulties, a commission appointed by Union General Edward Canby in 1865 to examine the needs of the city's charitable institutions reported, "The Jewish community have sustained the poor of their own persuasion in a much better condition than any other denomination in the city." While it found that other asylums lacked food and clothing and required repairs to their buildings, the commission reported that the wants of the Home were "comparatively few" but like others had "suffered in the amounts subscribed for their support." Accordingly, to supplement what the Home could purchase, the commission recommended issuing the Jewish orphanage 130 barrels of coal, thirty-two blankets, and a dozen sheets for the winter, along with four barrels of flour monthly, which was less than it recommended to meet the dire needs of the city's other orphanages.[40]

Despite the Home's relatively few material deficiencies, the people who lived in and ran the Home were not immune from the negative sentiments that most New Orleanians held during the Union occupation. As one historian described the atmosphere, "There was just enough deprivation, discouragement, and constraint on personal liberty, to create a general sense of bitterness."[41] The sense of bitterness that beset occupied New Orleans also beset some Home benefactors who defied Union authority. Despite General Butler's infamous "Woman Order" that condemned women who disrespected his troops as prostitutes, Laurel Smith Hyams, wife of Home founder and Lieutenant Governor Henry M. Hyams, fled the city after fatally shooting a Union soldier who demanded her compliance.[42] Rowena Florance, founder Benjamin Florance's nineteen-year-old daughter, was arrested for concealing the swords of an absconding Confederate general.[43]

Within the Home, as well, residents chafed under authority. In 1862, after a year without discord, Matron Noel lodged her first complaint about a widow, reporting that Julia Hyman had been disobedient despite "frequent remonstrations and advice." After reviewing her alleged offenses, the board permitted Hyman to leave the Home three times per week to find a new residence and employment.[44] Whatever difficulties a poor widow with children faced before the war, times were even tougher during the federal occupation. With so many Union troops needing lodging, affordable housing became scarce and all goods were expensive.[45] Despite the challenges, Hyman managed to secure other accommodations, taking her sons Manuel and Abraham with her.[46] A year later, however, Hyman asked the board to readmit her boys. Finding the widow "in great distress," the board acceded and also permitted Manuel to attend the school Rabbi Illowy conducted.[47] The boys remained in the Home until discharged to their mother five years later.[48]

Babette Schwartz had initially managed to avoid Matron Noel's displeasure, but that also changed in October 1862. Noel sought the board's "relief and guidance" regarding the widow's "bad and rebellious conduct."[49] In May 1865, after Schwartz risked expulsion on three more occasions for reportedly disrespecting Matron Noel, her seventeen-year-old daughter Sarah was discharged to an uncle. Before the end of the year, Babette left the Home with her fifteen-year-old daughter, Hannah, after more than nine years in residence.[50] Her son Lazar and his twin siblings Wolf and Regina stayed on, receiving education and support until Babette withdrew them in 1869.[51] Lazar, then sixteen, wrote a letter of gratitude: "I ask myself the question will I ever be able to repay you. I will try my very best in after years to approach it as near as possible. . . . I thank you a thousand times for the kindness you have shown to me."[52]

The Schwartzes went on to lead productive lives in or near New Orleans. Babette, who never remarried, joined LHBA and watched her children grow up, marry, and raise families of their own. Lazar, owner of a dry goods store on Magazine Street, became president of Congregation Gates of Prayer, which built its synagogue across the street from the Home. In 1905, Babette died at age eighty-seven, joining her husband, Benjamin, in the Jewish cemetery on Joseph Street, where he had been buried for five decades.[53] That the Schwartzes enjoyed apparent success after leaving the Home, where Babette and her older children had struggled to conform to its rules, illustrates the conflict inherent in institutional life: the ideal of beneficence versus the reality of dependency.

Throughout the city, like the rest of the South, the Civil War produced many widows and orphans, prompting the creation of additional orphanages.[54] By 1863, concern for the loss of coreligionists' lives and its impact on their families prompted the call for a Jewish orphanage in the Midwest to care for orphans of Jewish Civil War soldiers. This proposal led to the creation of the Cleveland Jewish Orphans' Asylum, which opened in 1868.[55] Surprisingly, despite an estimated two thousand Jewish Confederate servicemen (in addition to more than eight thousand Jews in the Union Army), the Home's board was not similarly besieged with applications during the early years of the conflict.[56]

Nor did it ever record a single war-related admission. Though it approved several eligible applicants, the board admitted only one widow with her two sons in 1861, no inmates in 1862, and two children in 1863.[57] Since opening, the Home had never admitted so few individuals per year and would not again until 1934. Even in 1864, when the board admitted fourteen children, ten of them were later reclaimed by their fathers.[58]

LOSS OF LEADERSHIP

The Home's greatest challenge during the Civil War came not from economic woes but rather from losing leaders who refused to accede to Union authority. In September 1862, before leaving New Orleans, General Butler issued Order No. 76, which required all adult residents who failed to swear allegiance to the United States to declare themselves enemies of the government, resulting in confiscation of their property and expulsion from the city.[59] Many men and women took the oath, whether willingly or as a bitter pill, rather than lose their homes, livelihoods, and personal belongings. Even those who delayed taking the oath in hope of a Confederate victory relented when the situation grew hopeless.[60] The Home did not suffer the consequences of Butler's order until his replacement, General Nathaniel Banks, began to enforce the oaths in earnest by rounding up the refusers.

Four important Home leaders persisted in defying the Union. Joseph Marks, a board member since the Home's founding, was the first to formally resign in March 1863.[61] The grocery wholesaler who had resided in New Orleans since the early 1850s returned to his native Columbia, South Carolina, and lived there until General William T. Sherman's Union Army burned his property. Marks then retreated to New York where he successfully managed a branch of his former business. He did not return to New Orleans until 1880.[62] Although he, too, refused to sign the oath and left New Orleans, President Simpson never resigned. After attending the board's May 3, 1863, meeting, the minutes for the rest of Simpson's term simply note his absence. Vice President George Jonas served as acting president, noting in the 1864 annual report that Simpson was "in a foreign land."[63]

At the same time, Gutheim, his wife, Emily, and their young son left New Orleans for Mobile, Alabama, where Emily's father was an auctioneer and community leader. Gutheim refused to betray what he considered the cause of right and justice. "Circumstances over which I have no control," as he described his fate to the board, "compel me to take this step."[64] He also wrote a letter to a friend, in which he shared personal details: "Day after tomorrow I shall leave . . . by order of the military authorities. All those who have refused to take the oath of allegiance to the Dictator of Washington are ordered beyond the lines—that is, into Dixie. I am of that number. Nearly the whole of my congregation are similarly situated." In exile, as spiritual leader of Congregation Kahl Montgomery, Gutheim continued to deliver sermons supporting the Confederacy.[65] When Alabama governor Thomas H. Watts issued a proclamation in 1864 asking the "Christian people" of the state to pray for the Confederacy, Gutheim objected only because the official had not addressed himself to citizens of all religions.[66]

Joseph Magner, the youngest Home founder and dutiful board secretary, also withheld his loyalty from the Union. The Hamburg native, now a commercial agent, had served in the Confederate Army, fighting in the Battles of Chickamauga, Stonebridge, and Murfreesboro.[67] On May 13, 1863, Magner submitted his resignation to the board, enclosing ninety dollars in Confederate bills and pledging, "Wherever my destiny may carry me, I shall never cease to look with interest upon the Institution, which has become our noblest pride."[68] Years later, he described his departure from New Orleans: "Indeed, the evil day had come. The effect of the war between the States showed its traces everywhere. But a kind Providence watched over our Home, and inspired its friends and supporters to the noblest efforts in the midst of the fearful ordeal through which they were passing."[69]

These Home leaders were not alone in leaving the city. Albeit a fraction of the total inhabitants under Butler's command, an estimated four thousand "registered enemies" fled rather than swear the oath.[70] Enough Jews had left the city that it seemed, as one New Orleans Jew wrote, like "almost the entire Jewish population daily leave."[71] The *American Israelite* reported that "over seven-eighths of the members of the Portuguese congregation and their Hasan, Rev. Mr. Gutheim with them, have emigrated as registered enemies to various parts of the confederacy."[72] That eleven of fifteen board members, including enslavers George Jonas and Abraham Haber, remained in the city and attended the board's biweekly meetings, is therefore noteworthy.[73] Presumably they pledged loyalty to the Union, but whether they did so because they experienced an awakening about either slavery or federal sovereignty, or like some other New Orleanians simply did not want their considerable possessions confiscated, remains unknown.[74]

Whatever the Home's children and widows felt about federal occupation, they too left no record. Discretion had to be used regarding anti-Union views, even by children. If made public, both the organization and the offender were accountable. The Orleans Parish Grand Jury for May 1863, albeit silent about the Home, included an ominous report about another nearby orphanage. "We found sentiments of a treasonable character to the [Union] Government expressed by the children of this institution, and we recommend that immediate measures be taken to correct these sentiments."[75] The consequences the orphanage faced are unknown, but the Union imposed penalties for disloyal conduct on other civilians. Having found a man guilty of preventing a child from singing "The Star-Spangled Banner" (and rewarding another child for singing the Confederate "Bonnie Blue Flag"), the city's federal provisional court imposed a sizeable fine for the "reprehensible" conduct.[76] In the public schools, two boys were expelled for refusing to sing at the 1864 inauguration of the state's first Union governor. Even in the private schools, which General Banks considered "treasonable nurseries," teachers received stiff fines for allowing students to draw rebel flags.[77]

In April 1865, General Robert E. Lee surrendered the last major Confederate Army to Ulysses S. Grant at Appomattox Courthouse. Over the next two days, the New Orleans press spread the word. One editorial described the situation, "We have arrived at the summit of the mountain and the promised land of peace is before us. The crisis has now been passed, and well they say in Washington, that the war is near its end."[78]

In these waning days of the war, the Home's attention was quickly diverted to other matters. The same newspapers that broadcast the war's end now carried a report that struck a blow to the heart of the institution. The grand jury issued the Home's first negative report in seven years and its most damning. "We found this Asylum badly managed, the children disorderly and the building dirty and miserably kept," the grand jury asserted. "Everything about the premises evinces a want of care and neglect, that in consideration of the object of the institution is absolutely criminal."[79] Two days later, as newly elected president George Jonas convened a special meeting to investigate the matter, the *Times-Democrat* published a zealous defense of the Home. While denying any connection to the Home's board, the anonymous author decried the grand jury's "scandalous assertions" as utterly false. "You say the building is dirty and miserably kept. I defy any one of your cloister cells, dens or mansions, to come up to it in order and cleanliness."[80]

The author accused the grand jury of reserving its praise for the city's Catholic asylums, not finding "one single fault" in any of the asylums run by "the brothers and sisters, who you extol with all your might," while spewing all of its "venom on the Jewish Home." The Home's anonymous defender went on to write that the grand jurors would have "done well in the times of Ferdinand and Isabella," referring to Spain's banishment of Jews during the Inquisition, but they had no place in this country which protected "the Jew and the Gentile, all alike."[81]

The board, however, issued no public protest to the grand jury's charges. Instead, it reminded the matron and inmates of two Home rules. The first, which suggests a concern that Home children had wandered off premises, was to reiterate that inmates were prohibited from leaving without first obtaining the president's permission. Second, the board reiterated its 1858 directive that the children "be uniformly dressed in and outside the Home."[82] Unlike its swift removal of Matron DePass in response to the undesirable conditions it found in 1861, the board issued no reprimand to Noel. To the contrary, in its next annual report, the board announced its "undiminished confidence" in her management of the Home.[83]

Their continued support for Noel and relatively minor corrective responses to the grand jury's report suggest that the Home's leaders believed the serious accusations were unfounded. The board's corrections also reflect a desire to maintain a positive public image. Even if they agreed that the grand jury had been driven by antisemitism, the Home's leaders depended on the community's good will for the institution's continued success and, reasonably fearful of arousing more negative attention, chose not to confront the discrimination. Apart from keeping Home children out of school when the schedule occasionally conflicted with a Jewish holiday, the board left no record of having requested a religious accommodation from any secular authority.[84] Whereas the board's public protests over Edgardo Mortara's forced baptism had been directed toward Rome, even appearing to accuse fellow New Orleanians of antisemitism would have hit too close to home.

In July 1865, Gutheim returned from his exile, resumed his board duties, and returned to the pulpit at Dispersed of Judah, albeit briefly.[85] He found his synagogue virtually empty, since many members had also fled the city rather than take the Union oath. Others who remained in the city, known for its religious laxity, had become less observant of Jewish traditions, with many having married out of the faith. Rabbi Illowy had recently resigned from Gates of Mercy, having fallen into disfavor with the increasingly Reform congregation for his insistence on Orthodox rituals. After the High Holidays, Gutheim accepted a loftier position to minister at Gates of Mercy, the city's largest congregation.[86]

By 1866, life in New Orleans began to return to something like normal. Business had revived, and the population had increased. Wharves were rebuilt, and longshoremen returned to work at increased wages. Although the Crescent City never lacked amusements or pastimes during occupation, in February, for the first time since the war started, the Mystic Krewe of Comus resumed what was then the city's only organized Mardi Gras parade and a ball.[87] At the Home's annual meeting that year, President Jonas happily reported that the "blessings of peace have been conferred upon us." The Home's anniversary two months earlier, which Jonas boasted had been attended "by the largest number of Israelites ever assembled together in this City," yielded $8,000. He thanked the members and donors who supported the Home throughout the war "when almost every other similar institution in the city was destitute, and in a measure, reduced to beggary."[88]

Even during the war, the board continued to seek opportunities for inmates to start lives outside the Home. In February 1864, Marx and Sarah Goldstein left the Home in the care of their mother, Jeanette, and their older brother Nathan. The board had admitted the family in December 1859, following the death of Jeanette's husband, Ezekiel, from typhoid fever. The Polish family came to the Home from Amite County, Mississippi, where they had settled upon their recent arrival from England. Nathan, who was no more than eight years old when his father died, demonstrated an unusually strong spirit. He accompanied his father's coffin on a horse-drawn cart all the way to New Orleans for burial. By 1862, precocious Nathan had endeared himself to Gutheim, who personally supervised the twelve-year-old's continued studies during summer recess and enrolled him in a "good writing school" to improve his penmanship.[89]

Gutheim's efforts to educate Nathan paid off. In January 1864, a local merchant offered to employ Nathan, promising to provide for him and pay him wages.[90] Although the board approved, Nathan's mother had other plans. Two weeks later, acknowledging Jeanette's desire "to engage in business," the board discharged her with Nathan, leaving Sarah and Marx in the Home's continued care, and appropriated fifty dollars for her support. Jeannette and Nathan opened a retail stall in the French Quarter.[91] Despite its oft-repeated descriptions of lonely widows rendered helpless without their late husbands' protection, the board sanguinely supported Jeanette's entrepreneurial plan.[92]

By the time Gutheim returned to the board, Jeanette and Nathan were successful enough to reclaim Sarah and Marx. Nathan, fourteen years old, in a lengthy letter that demonstrated his fine penmanship, thanked the board for the care he and his family had received. He closed his letter by pledging that the Home "will never be forgotten."[93]

Nathan later moved to Greenville, Mississippi, where he was welcomed into the merchandising enterprise of Morris Weiss, who later became Nathan's father-in-law and business partner. Over his long life, Nathan became an investor and officer in nearly all of Greenville's banks, insurance companies, and its cotton exchange. A respected civic leader, Goldstein faithfully served on the city council and school board, and led the town's board of supervisors. He helped organize Greenville's Hebrew Union Temple, serving as its president for fifty-five years. In 1929, the Jewish fraternal order of B'nai B'rith honored Nathan's record-breaking attendance at fifty-four of fifty-six annual conventions.[94]

True to his word, Nathan never forgot the Home. By 1873, he donated twenty-five dollars and within two years became a regular member of the association.[95] Goldstein was elected vice president of the Home's alumni organization in 1893 and within a decade was elected to the Home's board, the first alumnus to achieve that distinction.[96] He attended every anniversary celebration with a sizable check in hand, encouraging fellow alumni to do the same. Before his death in 1937, Nathan left money to his children with a list of requested recipients—topping the list was the Home.[97]

Although Nathan Goldstein stands out as one of the Home's most accomplished alumni, especially from its early years, and his mother, Jeanette, may be the only woman the board helped start a business, much of their story is typical of Home residents. They had turned to the Home during crisis and left to rejoin family or when they achieved self-sufficiency. Other alumni also received help upon leaving the Home from Jewish merchants in the region. Apart from the size of Nathan's donations, his show of gratitude was not unique, as evidenced by the dozens of letters thankful alumni wrote to the board and their later service to the institution and to their communities.

RECONSTRUCTION

While President Jonas welcomed the "blessings of peace," the end of the Civil War also marked the beginning of Reconstruction, which created new tensions and challenges. In New Orleans, racial conflicts erupted as embittered and defeated former Confederates stubbornly resisted the changes that came with the end of slavery and granting rights to newly emancipated Blacks. In June 1866 the city's mayor incited the massacre of two hundred Black Union war veterans who sought voting rights, and in April 1867 a massive protest forced the city to abolish its racially segregated "star car" streetcar system.[98]

The end of the Civil War was also marked by yellow fever's return. Although the last federal troops did not leave Louisiana for another decade, the state board of health returned to civilian control in 1866. The next summer, without the incentives of bayonet and military arrest to enforce sanitation and quarantine (which unknowingly inhibited the mosquito-borne disease), the scourge returned to the city, taking more than 3,000 lives from a population of 190,000.[99] "How sad to think," lamented one local journalist, "laboring for months as we have pertinaciously to recover from political adversities, that the trying ordeal of a terrible plague as we are now suffering from should be inflicted upon us."[100]

The epidemic's impact on the Home was extreme, a bitter reminder of the events that brought the orphanage into being. By March 1868, the Home admitted fifty-four children, the largest number of yearly admissions since its founding. Even with twenty discharges, and two deaths, the Home's population had risen to eighty-six, its largest to date. Every room was filled while in some instances three and four children shared a bed. After rejecting exorbitant bids to construct a new and larger building, the board instead decided to erect an addition to the existing building.[101]

The large population, reported President Jonas, was testing the Home's capacity "to its fullest extent," but it was not the only problem. Jonas sought a solution to "separate the sexes; a necessity which was not provided for at our organization, but which is now found to be indispensable."[102] With twenty-four boys and girls between the ages of twelve and seventeen closely residing under one roof in a city where public schools were separated by gender, the board apparently felt no need to explain the urgency of the delicate situation.[103] Until a solution could be found, the board denied several requests for admission, instead offering financial assistance to support the children outside the Home. The board also identified and pressed capable parents and relatives to withdraw their children.[104] In July 1868, work began to convert the first-floor schoolroom into sleeping quarters. The Home's across-the-street neighbor, Gates of Prayer, provided its synagogue basement as a classroom for Hebrew lessons and for the secular studies of children too young to attend public school.[105]

Although until now the board had expressed only satisfaction with Matron Noel, in fall 1868, notwithstanding recent favorable grand jury reports, an internal review disclosed a laxity of discipline, the building's neglectful appearance, and the matron's inability to properly discharge her duties. The board decided the solution was not just to dismiss Noel but to abolish the primary post of matron altogether. The board called upon Michel Heymann, a man whose name had been favorably mentioned as a candidate for a new position, superintendent, responsible for the Home's operation and management.[106] Heymann assumed the post on October 1, 1868.

The board's summary dismissal of Noel was disrespectful and demeaning, but not inconsistent with the sexist standards of the day. It coincided with the selection of a male superintendent to run Cleveland's Jewish Orphan Asylum, which opened in September 1868, and followed the same practice New York's Hebrew Orphan Asylum had instituted from its 1860 opening.[107] As Jonas unapologetically explained, when the Home's population reached ninety-six, it became evident that "a more rigid and systematic control was necessary than it was possible for any lady to exercise."[108] Surely, Noel, who controlled neither the number of inmates nor the construction budget, was blameless for the overcrowding. Calling it a resignation did not change the fact that the board gave Noel little choice in the matter. When invited to remain as housekeeper or in another role subordinate to Heymann, Noel declined.[109]

DEALING WITH DEATH

Before Matron Noel's tenure abruptly ended in the fall of 1868, she faced the Home's first and only accidental death of an inmate. Hetty Hartman, who had resided there for a decade, died. Despite explicit instructions to walk straight to school, the fourteen-year-old stopped along the way to visit her older sister, who had been discharged a few months earlier.[110] While warming herself by the flames of a stove, Hetty's clothing caught fire, a common occurrence at a time when expansive, cinch-waisted skirts were in fashion.[111] Despite the efforts of the Home's physician, the girl died the next morning with Reverend Gutheim at her side.[112]

Hetty Hartman's tragic death led the board to secure plots in Gates of Mercy's cemetery for "burying the Home's dead."[113] Despite the medical care the Home provided its children by some of the city's most highly respected physicians and at Touro Infirmary, the Home would need those plots. Over its history, thirty-two children died while under the Home's care, the last in 1903. Outbreaks of measles, yellow fever, influenza, and scarlet fever accounted for half of these deaths. Although the Home's overall childhood mortality rate was slightly higher than experienced in Jewish orphanages in New York and Philadelphia, it was comparable to other orphanages in New Orleans.[114]

Two factors help explain the discrepancy: the greater prevalence of diseases along the lower Mississippi and the admittance of younger children. Sixteen of the Home's decedents were five years or younger, including seven infants. Other Jewish orphanages, including those in New York and Philadelphia, enforced a minimum admission age precisely because, as late as 1900, with no understanding of "germ theory," one in four American children did not reach their fifth birthday.[115] Among American asylums in the late nineteenth century, one historian reported that a stunning death rate of over 90 percent for children under three was "not uncommon."[116] Despite these odds, the board persisted in admitting needy infants and very young children into the next century.

CHANGE IN LEADERSHIP

The Home underwent a dramatic shift in leadership. Heymann's replacement of Noel represented more than a change in staffing. Going forward, except for rare and brief interim occasions, a male superintendent oversaw the institution. At the same time, having declined reelection, George Jonas was replaced by Isaac Scherck, the first Home president who had not taken part in its founding. Any institutional memory Scherck lacked could be filled by Jonas and founding member Abraham Haber, who served as his vice presidents. A Prussian immigrant who left his business in Summit, Mississippi, when the Civil War broke out, Scherck served in the Confederate Army as captain of the McNair Rifles and then as assistant commissary chief with the rank of major. Arriving in New Orleans after the war, Scherck quickly established himself as a cotton factor and commission merchant. In 1866, he married Esther Marks, daughter of Home founder Joseph H. Marks, in a ceremony Gutheim officiated. Scherck went on to serve as Home president for nearly a decade, before winning acclaim for directing the city's rations in the yellow fever epidemic of 1878.[117]

The honorary matrons, too, experienced turnover. Caroline Beer Klopman succeeded Miriam Haber, who had died in 1866 after serving as directress since the Home's founding.[118] A formidable woman who held the post until

1874, Klopman a decade earlier had divorced her husband, Home founder Leopold Klopman, who remained on the Home's membership roster until his death.[119] At a time when divorce was rare, and Jewish divorces even rarer, the board's willingness to elect a woman who had divorced a founder and current member appears unusually broadminded, especially in contrast to its summary dismissal of Noel.[120] The board may have been impressed by Caroline's financial independence, a result of her divorce decree under Louisiana law that awarded her half of the marital assets plus $400.[121]

In the summer of 1868, news quickly spread that Gutheim planned to leave New Orleans for New York to become reader at Temple Emanu-El, a large Reform congregation whose members included many of the wealthiest and most influential Jews in the country. Gutheim also may have been enticed by the prospect of succeeding the incumbent spiritual leader.[122] His congregants entreated him to stay at Gates of Mercy, where he had only begun to implement reforms in worship and practice—such as use of an organ, mixed-gender choir, and English prayer—that had been or were being adopted by congregations elsewhere in the United States as means to add decorum and to ease acceptance and acculturation within their gentile communities.[123] More than a hundred non-Jewish New Orleanians also urged him to reconsider, calling his departure "not merely an irreparable loss to your church and people but a calamity to this city and state."[124]

In equally dramatic pleas, the Home's board praised Gutheim as "one of the strongest pillars of the several charitable and religious societies" and considered his departure "a threatening convulsion which may send their future usefulness asunder."[125] Despite the plaintive missives, on November 1, 1868, Gutheim resigned from the board. Having dedicated himself to the Home from its inception, he promised to "ever watch its interests and prosperity with the deepest solicitude."[126] Gutheim proved true to his word.

When the Civil War presented the choice, the Home's board pledged loyalty to its adoptive Southland, which had granted them civic and social standing along with prosperity. Eschewing the choice of quiet acquiescence in the matter, board members publicly advocated for the Confederacy and the institution of slavery. Top officers temporarily abandoned their orphanage duties while in exile.

Although the Civil War and the city's occupation by federal troops strained the Home's finances, the institution and its supporters emerged from the war mostly unscathed. As with the rest of New Orleans, the Reconstruction era was a time of change and tumult for the Home. Faced with increased public scrutiny, complete turnover in leadership and management, and the admission of many more inmates, the Home entered a new phase.

chapter four

A SERIES OF
SUPERINTENDENTS
1868–1886

As American readers of the second half of the nineteenth century embraced fictional orphans and half orphans, such as Cosette of Victor Hugo's *Les Miserables* (1862) and Mark Twain's *Tom Sawyer* (1876) and *Huck Finn* (1884), their real-life counterparts were also capturing the nation's attention. Communities worried about increasing numbers of parentless children and street urchins, whether a result of the Civil War or rising immigration, whose presence and plight were heightened by a reduced demand for unskilled child labor brought on by industrialization.[1] Between 1860 and 1890, nearly five hundred new orphanages emerged across the country. To ensure their orphans would not be lost to another faith, Protestants and Catholics seemed to compete, as each decade one religious group built more orphanages than the other.[2] To care for Jewish orphans, the fraternal order of B'nai B'rith sought to establish regional orphanages across the country. The seven-state partnership B'nai B'rith struck with the Home brought more children and resources, spurring physical expansion and new efforts in education and job training under the watch of four superintendents.

SUPERINTENDENT MICHEL HEYMANN
AND MATRON VALENTINE EISENMANN HEYMANN
1868–1870

On October 1, 1868, the cool weather ushered in more than a new season. It marked Michel Heymann's start as superintendent. The board expected more from a male superintendent, and Heymann did not disappoint. Unlike the matrons, whose untold lives before and after their tenures reflected the era's scant opportunities and disregard for women's stories, Heymann's life was deemed noteworthy. Born in 1837 in Alsace, young Michel set out for neighboring Strasbourg, where he spent his days studying and nights working to support himself. Although originally destined for the rabbinate, by age seventeen Heymann had launched his career in teaching. Over the next decade, he taught in Damascus for the Alliance Israélite Universelle, which supported Jewish rights and education, and continued teaching upon his return to France.[3]

Heymann's blue eyes peered over an aquiline nose and small mouth, accentuating his fair, oval face and chestnut-colored hair.[4] In 1864, he married a fellow Alsatian, Valentine Eisenmann, with whom he sailed to America two years later.[5] The couple made their way to New Orleans, where he secured work teaching at the Hebrew Educational Society, New Orleans's first Jewish day school.[6] The society, which Gutheim and other board members founded in 1866 to educate Jewish children, also admitted white non-Jewish pupils.[7] The timing of the school's creation also may have reflected the Jewish community's participation in the city's broader white opposition to the integration that occurred during Reconstruction. From 1864 to 1877, when one-third of the city's public schools were racially mixed (making it perhaps the country's most integrated school system), the number of New Orleans's private schools also climbed dramatically.[8]

During his two-year tenure at the society, Heymann acquainted himself with Home board members and their work at the orphanage. The $2,000 per year the Home offered the Heymanns was also a likely enticement to assume the new role.[9] In exchange, Michel became the Home's superintendent, Hebrew teacher, and assistant secretary to the boards of both the Home and the honorary matrons, while Valentine, as Matron, tended to housekeeping matters. This arrangement, which included room and board, was particularly timely for the Heymanns as Valentine was pregnant with their first child, Eugenie, who was born ten days after they arrived at the Home.[10]

Heymann immersed himself in the new job, making recommendations at the board's next meeting about the children's clothing, education, and vocal music. Heymann also quickly learned that he was not immune to the disciplinary challenges that his female predecessors had confronted. Within two months, he sought the board's guidance on the punishment of certain boys. Although the identities and details of the culprits and their offenses are unknown, the infractions prompted the board to mete out stiff penalties: "solitary confinement & that they should be fed upon bread and water."[11] As harsh as this sounds, the boys were spared the whip that Heymann's counterparts often wielded at the Cleveland Jewish Orphan Asylum or in many other non-Jewish orphanages at the time.[12]

Unlike the matrons, the board entrusted Heymann with the children's secular and religious education. Previously, for their secular studies, the older children attended nearby public schools, and "those too small" were taught in the Home. Gutheim and other spiritual leaders taught Hebrew and religion classes.[13] By January 1869, however, noting only "the impropriety of sending the children at present to the public schools," the board directed that all Home children be taught exclusively within the Home.[14]

Heymann set rules for the Home's school, which convened weekdays from 9:00 to 11:30 a.m. and from 12:00 to 2:00 p.m. He made sure that teacher Julia Hart oversaw the children's entry "without confusion or unnecessary noise," and dismissed them "in the utmost good order." He supervised Hart's adherence to a curriculum approved by the board and ensured that she recorded the children's class rank and behavior and kept an inventory of books and supplies.[15]

Heymann managed to win the board's favor despite tough circumstances. He arrived to face a population that exceeded capacity and, beginning in May 1869, spent the rest of his tenure maintaining order despite the noise, dust, and other disruptions of the three-story addition and remodeling project.[16] In November 1869, while construction continued, Heymann unexpectedly submitted his resignation. At the board's urging, he stayed until the renovation was complete. He was the first manager the board regretted losing, as evidenced by the large, engraved silver loving cup they presented him along with their wishes "that his retirement from the superintendency will not abate his interest in the Home."[17]

Heymann likely was considering his growing family. In March 1870, Valentine gave birth to their second child, Leon.[18] The demands of caring for eighty-eight children and two widows under their charge while raising their two small children provided ample reason to change lifestyle. Making matters more difficult, in the spring of 1869, just before Heymann submitted his resignation, two of the Home's young charges, three-year-old Fanny Goldstein and two-year-old Mayer Block, died during the city's measles outbreak.[19] In

January 1870, while Valentine was still pregnant with her second child, the Home admitted newborn Rachel Block, Mayer's younger sister. The baby, who entered the Home in sickly condition, languished for several months despite medical care, and died one week after Heymann insisted the board accept his resignation.[20] For parents of a toddler and a newborn, the emotional difficulties of heading a facility in which three children died or were dying in the span of a year may have proved too much. However, as the board had hoped, Michel Heymann's interest in the Home did not abate.

SUPERINTENDENT LEVI SHOENBERG
AND MATRON MARY SHOENBERG, 1870–1879

Levi and Mary Shoenberg, natives of Germany, assumed their posts as superintendent and matron in August 1870.[21] Although nothing is known of their prior work, the Shoenbergs were well received by the community. Thirty-nine-year-old Levi was described as "courteous, gentlemanly, and kind looking." Mary Shoenberg, age twenty-six, presented as "a sweet and affable lady" who shared "the beauty . . . of [Sir Walter] Scott's Rebecca," *Ivanhoe*'s fictional Jewess who was believed to be modeled after Rebecca Gratz, the founder of Philadelphia's Jewish orphanage.[22]

From the start, Levi Shoenberg's tenure benefited from the Home's expanded and remodeled facilities. With a new wing, described as airy and clean, the Home now separated the sexes, and offered the boys "a fine swimming bath which conduces greatly to their health." Notwithstanding a reporter's exaggerated claim that the enlarged building could house "some two hundred children," the Home easily accommodated its current population of eighty-six children and two widows with room for growth.[23] By the end of the Shoenbergs' first year, the board publicly praised the couple for the Home's "excellent sanitary condition" and the children's good discipline and appearance.[24] The children's strong academic records throughout Shoenberg's tenure also pleased the board. In March 1871, having earlier decided without explanation to return all but the youngest children to the public schools, President Scherck touted that nine Home children had earned top grades, while all received "very creditable marks for behavior and progress" in their studies.[25]

Gutheim returned to New Orleans in November 1872. His time in New York had not gone as he had hoped. The senior rabbi had not retired, thwarting

Gutheim's chances for promotion. But he also missed his beloved New Orleans, where he, too, had been missed. During his absence, Temple Sinai, the city's first congregation founded on Reform principles, had been established primarily by members of Gates of Mercy, including Home leaders, who sought a more conveniently located house of worship without the traditional strictures that limited acculturation, such as constraints on food, dress, and religious ritual. The new congregation chose Gutheim as its first spiritual leader. The Home's board welcomed him back, as well, and in March 1873 elected him first vice president. Gutheim faithfully served Temple Sinai and the Home in those roles until his death in 1886.[26]

B'NAI B'RITH

By 1874, the Home's population included an increasing number of children referred by the auxiliary committees in Mobile and Montgomery, Alabama, and Galveston, Texas. Having thus already expanded the Home's reach and donor base, the board was intrigued by the proposition Mayer Ulman of Memphis, Tennessee, presented the following year. Representing the newly established southern district of the International Order of B'nai B'rith, Ulman offered to pursue a formal relationship with the Home which promised an even greater source of funding.[27]

Founded in New York City in 1843 by mostly German Jewish immigrants, the fraternal organization B'nai B'rith ("Sons of the Covenant") had since attained a national presence through the creation of lodges in and beyond the state of New York. B'nai B'rith's goal, largely driven by Reform Jews, sought to connect coreligionists and provide them with social services. The order's lodges were organized into districts, and by 1874, after a series of reorganizations, a new seventh district emerged with headquarters in Memphis. The new district, comprising Texas, Tennessee, Mississippi, Arkansas, Oklahoma, Alabama, Louisiana, and the Florida Panhandle, sought to expand the order across the South and with it the fraternity's insurance system. Previously, these southern states had been part of the much larger and more northern District 2, which in 1868 had founded the Cleveland Jewish Orphan Asylum (CJOA). As Ulman proposed, the new District 7 sought a refuge for its Jewish orphans closer to their homes. B'nai B'rith's earlier attempts to partner with Jewish orphanages in New York, Baltimore, and San Francisco had failed, due to the New York institution's refusal to admit all needy Jewish orphans of the district (and not just those who lived in New York City or whose fathers belonged to the order or a congregation) and to the Baltimore and San Francisco institutions' refusal to relinquish board seats to the order's delegates.[28]

Such concerns, however, did not deter the Home's board. Selecting the January 1875 anniversary celebration as an opportune occasion to explore Ulman's proposal, the board treated the delegates like visiting royalty.[29] When they arrived in a caravan of carriages, the orchestra, on cue, struck up a lively march.[30] As customary for these annual celebrations, an immense tent covered the Home's yard to accommodate what one reporter described as a "very large and brilliant" crowd filled with the city's "best merchants" and their families. Flowers adorned a platform, erected to seat B'nai B'rith's delegates with the Home's board. In addition to their healthy and happy appearance, the children's well-rehearsed orations and performances, including several original compositions, now regular anniversary features, offered an entertaining demonstration of the Home's attention to its wards.[31] B'nai B'rith's delegates also witnessed the community's outpouring of affection for the Home and its children, culminating in a grand banquet, also a regular anniversary feature, at which Mary Shoenberg and the honorary matrons donned aprons and served special foods and treats donated by dozens of well-wishers.[32] Rivalling anything they had seen at CJOA, the celebration supplied any reassurance the delegates needed to advance their partnership proposal.

By March, the parties struck a deal that lasted seven decades. B'nai B'rith gave the Home a portion ($2 at first) of each District 7 member's annual dues, the same rate they gave to CJOA. In return, the Home admitted eligible children the district's lodges recommended. To oversee its investment, B'nai B'rith received eight of twenty seats on the Home's board.[33]

The partnership's consequences for the Home proved swift and significant. For the first year, the Home received $3,298 from B'nai B'rith's dues, in addition to lodge members' voluntary contributions, which together greatly surpassed the $2,139 the Home collected in dues from its other 374 members.[34] By 1922, B'nai B'rith contributed $15,000 annually to the operation of the Home, still a larger source of income than the $13,533 it collected from association members' dues.[35] With B'nai B'rith's funding, of course, came additional children. The Home's population increased, as did the proportion of children from outside Louisiana. In just one year, the Home's out-of-state enrollment increased from

28 percent to 35 percent, including the Home's first children from Huntsville, Alabama; Okolona and Natchez, Mississippi; Camden, Arkansas; and Dallas, Texas.[36] In 1916, 85 percent of children living in the Home (141 of 166) had been admitted from outside the state. Over the Home's history, approximately 900 (70 percent) of 1,300 children for whom information is available were admitted from out of state. Texas provided the largest number of out-of-state children, 394.[37]

Ralph Beerman was one of those Texas children. Admitted in 1924 with five siblings by their widowed father, Ralph years later vividly recalled his five-hundred-mile journey to the Home from West, a small town north of Waco. Accompanied by a B'nai B'rith volunteer, Ralph boarded the Pullman car, his first time on a train, and his initial objections to being sent to the Home gave way to a thirst for adventure. On the first evening of the two-night trip, after watching wide-eyed as the porter converted seats into beds, Ralph climbed into his berth, "almost too excited to sleep." The next day, after enjoying "a good breakfast" in the dining car, the train—"constantly shifting back and forth, stopping at every stop"—eventually pulled into Houston's "big grey railyard." The second morning, the train halted again, this time to cross the Mississippi River. In heavy fog, Ralph gazed with fascination as men loaded the train onto a huge barge. Soon, while sirens blared, Ralph felt the train floating on water. After what seemed a long time, the barge and its mammoth cargo reached the other side of the river, where workers reassembled the train cars for the last leg of the trip. Despite the hardship that prompted the journey, for Ralph and his siblings, whose worldview had been limited to West's few small buildings, the sight of the big city of New Orleans was thrilling. "We were enjoying every minute of it!" recalled the remarkably upbeat Beerman.[38]

Compared to their local peers, the greatest challenge for out-of-state children was the difficulty in maintaining family ties. Like many other parents living at a great distance from the Home, Abraham Beerman managed to visit his six children only once during his children's six-year stay.[39] Despite the emotional toll this estrangement must have taken, anecdotal information suggests that children from both groups won comparable recognition for academic achievement and shared the spotlight in the Home's public events. Among early out-of-state admittees, Addie Bernhold from Helena, Arkansas (admitted in 1877), and Hannah Frishman from Natchez, Mississippi (admitted in 1881), excelled in school and secured positions as assistant teachers in the Home.[40] At the Home's 1884 anniversary performance, for example, where managers presumably reserved solo parts for exemplary wards, Elias Weisenfeld of Greenville, Mississippi, and Jacob Smith of Galveston, Texas, shared the stage—and the favorable press coverage—with local children Ida Barnett and Meyer Alexander.[41] Among current wards and alumni the board selected as principal anniversary orators between 1895 and 1899, four of five had been admitted from out of state.[42] In terms of success after discharge, Isaac Hochwald's story suggests that out-of-state children suffered little disadvantage compared to their local counterparts. Admitted from Galveston, Texas, in 1874 after the death of his parents, "Ike" was discharged four years later to Lionel Kahn, a bachelor, who took the savvy boy into his heart and into his thriving railroad supply business in Marshall, Texas. After Kahn's death, Hochwald continued to grow the business and brought the Rotary Club to Marshall. He served for two decades on the local school board, was founding president of Marshall's Moses Montefiore Congregation, and earned the moniker "Father of East Texas Baseball" for his work organizing the professional sport in the area. He also never forgot the Home, contributing regularly to its support and even attending the hundredth anniversary in 1955 as the Home's oldest living alumnus at age eighty-nine.[43]

LIVING AND LEARNING IN THE HOME

With at least one hundred children on hand and more expected, the Home again required expansion. President Scherck proposed another enlargement to provide additional residential space and to "establish in our Home workshops which will better fit the inmates for active and useful life when we discharge them."[44] The influx of cash from B'nai B'rith enabled the board to purchase the adjacent residence on Jackson Street and an unimproved lot behind the Home. In addition to greatly expanding facilities for sleeping, dining, classrooms, and outdoor play, the newly acquired structure and renovations added a workshop where a carpenter taught boys to build and repair objects and furniture to use in the Home and to sell for income.[45] The self-sustaining workshop focused on boys "about 14 years of age," reflecting the board's willingness to retain older children. The enterprise demonstrated its value at the next anniversary when items crafted by the boys, including a desk, footstool, and armoire, raised forty-five dollars at auction.[46]

The board also sought to secure the future of its girls. Two years earlier, the board withdrew its eight oldest girls from the public high school, having decided "useful employment within or outside the Home" was preferable to their continued education.[47] Upon reconsideration, the board now permitted girls who showed "more than ordinary talent" to graduate from the public high school. In Pauline Ellman's case, the board not only allowed her to graduate but also hired her to teach the youngest children in the Home's school. Ellman, who held the position for two years before leaving to marry, paved the way for hiring other "exceptional" Home girls to teach and assist the superintendent. Like their peers at other orphanages, older girls of ordinary talent, however, continued to be taught housekeeping not otherwise done by the Home's cooks and washwomen, as well as plain sewing to clothe the children and fancy work to raise money for the Home.[48]

A typical day in the Home during the Shoenbergs' tenure, like most institutions of the time, featured the ringing of bells to signal activities.[49] The children rose at 5:30 a.m. before answering roll call at 6:00 a.m. After chores and breakfast, they began school at 9:00. When the older children returned from school, dinner was served as the main meal of the day. After studies, more chores, and playtime, a bell again summoned the children for a light supper. They stood by the dining room's long benches and tables as the superintendent led mealtime prayers, and then "at a given signal, all wheeled around and faced the board," where tea and milk were served with white bread. At 9:00 p.m., the lights were put out for bedtime. On Friday evenings and Saturday mornings, the superintendent led the children in Sabbath prayers.[50] Despite the regimentation, the Home's childcare won praise. In 1878, one reporter described "the home-like, cheerful look upon [the children's] bright young faces" while the next year another remarked that passersby "hear the merry ripple of laughing which ever comes from within."[51]

The Home was well equipped and furnished, evidencing the community's ongoing support. During Shoenberg's time, this included a new upright piano in a walnut cabinet, a gift from Louis Grunewald, a German immigrant who founded Grunewald's Hall and Music Store. In 1878, this musician expressed his delight with the Home's "admirable system" of management by donating an "instrument to inspire musical scholars with any degree of ambition to practicing on same."[52] By 1879, the Home was among the city's earliest adopters of the telephone, invented just three years earlier, which enabled it to summon Dr. Frederick Loeber, the first physician in New Orleans to also own the device.[53]

THE SHOENBERGS' LAST YEARS

In March 1877, after serving nearly seven years, Levi Shoenberg tendered his resignation.[54] Before leaving the Home, the board granted his request to take two-year-old Ida Levy, a Home ward, into his care.[55] For the childless Shoenbergs, becoming parents provided a sweet ending to their tenure, and a bright beginning for the toddler. Ida entered the Home in August 1875 as an infant following the drowning deaths of her parents, Moses Levy, a peddler, and his wife, Rosa.[56] As Shoenberg recounted the event, he was awakened at midnight by the sexton of the Rampart Street synagogue, who placed the baby in his arms.[57] Since then, Mary Shoenberg cared for the child at the Home.[58]

The Shoenbergs stayed away for less than a year. Their replacements, the Lewisohns, did not last long.[59] Levi Shoenberg was amenable to returning and willingly withdrew his recent application for a higher-paying position at CJOA.[60] By May, the Shoenbergs returned to the Home with little Ida in tow.

Two months after the Shoenbergs returned, yellow fever again struck the Crescent City. From mid-July to mid-November of 1878, New Orleans suffered its worst scourge since the 1850s. One in five fled the city, and more than four thousand lost their lives.[61] Founder Joseph Simon, who had recently succeeded Scherck as president, instituted "every necessary precaution," including a strict quarantine.[62] Despite these steps and the best available medical care, nearly one-third of the Home's 113 children contracted the disease. Although nearly all recovered, 3 of the Home's youngest children perished.[63] Before the epidemic ended, it took another life at the Home. Matron Mary Shoenberg died on October 21, 1878.[64]

The next morning, Gutheim conducted the funeral.[65] On her headstone, Levi Shoenberg carved a loving tribute. "When from the dreaded pestilence in terror men were flying, she stayed in God her confidence to aid the sick and dying."[66] She had been "a true mother to the orphans," resolved the board in its matron's memory, "guiding them with a gentle hand, a loving heart and intelligent devotion."[67] The local press, too, praised her courtesy and worthy character, which had endeared her to the children she mothered and the community.[68] Alumna Sarah Adler Rosenfelder praised Mary Shoenberg for giving her "the constant care which fond parents bestow upon their blood children."[69]

Levi Shoenberg attempted to resume his duties assisted by alumna Pauline Ellman, who had been working as the Home's teacher. By February 1879, however, Shoenberg resigned, which President Simon explained as a "consequence of his bereavement."[70] After returning to Chicago, Shoenberg remarried. His daughter, Ida, stayed in Chicago, where she married and had two children. She died in 1947 at age seventy-two.[71] Years later, Ida's daughter traveled to New Orleans to visit the grave of her grandmother, Matron Mary Shoenberg.[72]

SUPERINTENDENT NATHAN J. BUNZEL AND MATRON REGINA COHEN BUNZEL, 1879–1883

In February 1879, the board elected Nathan and Regina Bunzel of Little Rock, Arkansas, as the Home's new superintendent and matron.[73] A native of Bohemia, Nathan in 1869 married German immigrant Regina Cohen in New York City, before moving to Little Rock, where Nathan ran a retail business with Regina's brother.[74] The board's decision to pay the Bunzels $200 per year less than the Shoenbergs and Heymanns suggests that fifty-nine-year-old Nathan had little, if any, experience teaching or running an asylum.

By all accounts, the Bunzels fulfilled their duties admirably. Reports in the Jewish and the secular press lauded the Home as "scrupulously clean, neat and tidy," while crediting the Bunzels for creating "a general air of cheerfulness."[75] The most distressing events during their tenure were a complaint from Mr. Cortissez, the assistant superintendent, that Mr. Bunzel had treated him rudely, and vandalism committed by a "gang of hoodlums" from the Jackson Street ferry landing. The board quickly dispensed with Bunzel's alleged rudeness, clarifying the men's division of labor, while several older Home boys proudly organized themselves to alert the police of any further wrongdoing.[76]

In March 1882, Joseph Simon declined renomination after four years as president. Edwin Israel Kursheedt was elevated to the post. A nephew of Home founder Gershom Kursheedt and board secretary for the past twelve years, Edwin Kursheedt, a stonework merchant, pledged to fulfill his duty "faithfully and well." With Gutheim and Abraham Haber reelected as first and second vice presidents, the new president was surrounded by experienced Home leaders. Colonel Kursheedt, as he was often known in deference to his Confederate Army service, said he was rewarded "every time he entered the Home, and saw the winning smiles and outstretched arms of the orphans."[77]

In summer of 1883, Superintendent Bunzel submitted his resignation.[78] He and his wife later moved to St. Louis, where they managed the Jewish Home for Aged and Infirm.[79] As at the Home, the Bunzels won acclaim in St. Louis for "devot[ing] all their time to minister to the cares and wants of the inmates."[80]

The Bunzels had joined a growing class of Jewish and non-Jewish professionals who often moved between organizations in the nascent field of social work.[81]

SUPERINTENDENT SIMON L. WEIL AND
MATRON JENNIE PECK WEIL, 1883–1886

By August 25, 1883, news had spread that Simon L. Weil and his wife, the former Jennie Peck, accepted appointment as superintendent and matron of the Home. Weil, a thirty-one-year-old native of Bohemia, for the past four years had served as spiritual leader of Woodville, Mississippi's Congregation Beth Israel.[82] He also traveled around and beyond Mississippi, teaching, lecturing, and performing marriages.[83] The *Pointe Coupée Banner* of New Roads, Louisiana, described Weil as a "very agreeable gentleman" who had won the community's respect.[84]

Weil also impressed the Home's board, which had recently announced plans to strengthen the education of the youngest children. Weil had taught in St. Louis's public schools, where by 1875 he served as principal. He later worked in the public schools of Chicago, where he met and married Jennie in 1878, before moving to Mississippi where he ran Woodville's Hebrew Educational Society.[85]

Simon Weil quickly became engaged in Home activities. Weeks after arriving, he led Rosh Hashanah services at Congregation Gates of Prayer, presumably with the Home's children in tow.[86] He even composed a song, "Our Home, how good, how fair," which he and teacher Hattie Conn led the children in singing at the 1884 anniversary.[87]

After three years of accolades and positive reports, Superintendent Weil's tenure abruptly ended in scandal. Lena F., a fifteen-year-old inmate, reported that Weil had sexually assaulted her or, as one paper described it, had "criminally approached" her. Lena's precise accusation is unknown as she left no account and the mores of the time compelled the use of ambiguous euphemisms. Kursheedt officially decried Weil's "gross immoral conduct" while Gutheim used the phrases "secret crime" and "deplorable occurrence." The editor of the *Jewish Free Press* refrained "for obvious reasons" from printing the "revolting evidence."[88]

In early February 1885, Lena's uncle, having been apprised of the situation by his niece, arrived at the Home and confronted Weil with Lena's accusations. The girl, too, bravely lodged her complaint against the superintendent in the presence of his wife, who summoned Kursheedt. In his account, Kursheedt wrote, "I said to [Weil] that I had heard of it, and if it were true he could not remain here one minute, and asked him if he knew what the result would be. He replied, 'Yes, the gallows.'" After dismissing all others from the room, Kursheedt questioned Lena in the presence of a fellow director and "satisfied myself as to the truth of the charges." When Jennie Weil returned to the room, Kursheedt continued, "there was quite a scene." Kursheedt demanded that Weil immediately submit his resignation, a demand to which Weil acceded. After agreeing to take charge of the Home, Jennie Weil offered parting words to her husband, "Simon, if you are guilty, go; if not, remain." He fled the state.[89]

Within days of Weil's termination, news of the assault appeared in papers across the county.[90] "Shocking Crimes in an Orphans' Home," reported the *St. Louis Globe-Democrat*, while the *New York Times* revealed "A Jewish Rabbi's Crime" arising from his "foul treatment" of a fifteen-year-old girl in his charge, claiming that this was "the first time in the history of Judaism in Louisiana that such a charge had been made upon a spiritual leader of the people." The story had already changed with several papers reporting that Weil had fled the city before the girl's relative could confront him and at least one paper claiming that with nearly seventy girls living in the Home, "at least eight of the young girls have been ruined."[91] Considering "the delicate matters involved," the *Daily Picayune* cautiously advised it would "wait for an official promulgation of the facts in the case."[92] The next day, however, the same paper relented to the demand for news, reporting, "The greatest indignation prevails amongst the people of the Hebrew faith in this community, and should Weil ever be brought to justice here his most inveterate prosecutors will be his co-religionists."[93]

The horrific incident came at a particularly sensitive juncture. The Home's occupancy had reached a record high of 146 inmates, once again greatly exceeding the building's capacity. Although the board initially considered expanding the current facility for a third time, it had since announced plans to erect a larger building in a new location.[94] A shameful scandal could only jeopardize crucial fundraising efforts that were already underway. And yet, even by today's standards and especially by the standards of the 1880s, the Home's board demonstrated remarkable candor in publicly reporting the incident and, to a certain extent, fairness. Within days after the abuse, the board prepared an announcement of Weil's discharge for "gross immoral conduct" which it distributed to the city newspapers and the national Jewish press. At the same time, Kursheedt appointed Gutheim to chair a committee to investigate Weil's management of the Home throughout his three-year tenure.[95] Moreover, Kursheedt and the board made clear they believed the superintendent's fifteen-year-old female accuser.

However, despite Kursheedt's and the board's obvious sympathy for Lena's plight, they expressed their concern inconsistently, succumbing to prevailing Victorian attitudes toward victims of sexual assault, including minors. When a reporter inquired months after the event, Kursheedt protectively demurred, "It would be equally wrong to review the affair on her account, innocent as she is, and was."[96] At the same time, without any expression of regret or contradiction, and likely believing they were acting in Lena's and the Home's best interests, Kursheedt and the board had already discharged the girl to the care of her brother in Port Gibson, Mississippi.[97] What, if anything, Lena understood or was told about her discharge is unknown. The committee charged with investigating the assault also expressed an inconsistent tone. While it found Weil's crime "deplorable," the committee also seemed to be questioning the character of his victim or other potential victims. After examining Lena's fellow inmates, the committee found "but one inmate was involved, who is now discharged from the Home, that all the remaining inmates are pure and innocent, and as regards morality and chastity, our Home is in as excellent a condition as can be desired."[98] Succumbing to conventional norms of female sexual virtue, the board and its committee presumably were prepared to discharge any other "involved" inmate, further victimizing Weil's victims by depriving them of the Home's services and care.

In the face of rumors about Jennie Weil and members of the board, the substance of which was not identified, Gutheim's committee also found these to be "unfounded exaggerations, erroneous deductions, or false statements of facts."[99] Kursheedt ordered that the committee's report be distributed to all lodges of B'nai B'rith District 7 and to the Conference of Southern Rabbis, which Gutheim had founded a year earlier to promote professional fellowship among Southern Jewish clergy on issues of religion and congregational practice.[100] Kursheedt also resolved to prosecute criminally any person or persons who propagated or spread scandalous reports that would damage the Home's good character and standing.[101]

Lena's discharge was not the last news of her. In April, Lena's uncle requested her readmission. The board rejected the request, informing the uncle that it was "unwilling to take any further responsibility" on Lena's behalf but that "members of the Board individually might do all in their power to aid her in getting a situation."[102] The board's response and the language of its committee's report suggest that it believed sending Lena away was the only way to ensure the Home's "morality and chastity," because her defilement—albeit through no fault on her part—had nonetheless stolen her "purity and innocence," and her continued presence would only impose a corrupting influence on others.[103] Although its offer of informal assistance suggests it appreciated that Lena's discharge had caused her further harm, the board expressed no concern that sending her away and rejecting her readmission discouraged other children from reporting abuse.

Nor would justice be meted out to Weil by the legal system. Kursheedt expressed his regret that "there is no law in the statutes of this State by which the offender could be punished."[104] "There is no law against seduction in Louisiana," reported the *Daily Picayune* about Weil's offense, in an apparent and confusing reference to the common law cause of action for damages that could be brought in other states against a man who induced a women to consent to sexual relations through persuasion and the promise to marry, "and no punishment under the law was meted out to him."[105] No mention was made of prosecuting Weil for rape, likely reflecting the onerous legal requirements to prove violence and resistance.[106] Moreover, Lena was fifteen whereas Louisiana's legal age of consent was then twelve, a shockingly young age by today's standards. Another decade passed before the state recognized the crime of statutory rape.[107] Weil apparently was not aware of his immunity from prosecution when he fled, believing he was destined for the gallows.

Jennie Weil's steady management enabled the Home to carry on as smoothly as possible in the wake of her husband's transgressions. By early May, despite earning the board's praise, she submitted her resignation but agreed to stay on until it hired her replacement.[108] Although Jennie Weil had performed commendably, and at least one board member considered a male superintendent unnecessary, the board already had publicly committed to hiring a man for the job.[109]

GUTHEIM'S DEATH

One month later, a new tragedy hit with little warning. On June 11, 1886, the Rev. James K. Gutheim, the "High Priest of Southern Judaism," died after a short illness.[110] Jewish mercantile houses shuttered; in Baton Rouge the legislature adjourned, and in New Orleans courts and municipal buildings closed.[111]

Among his eulogists, in an unusual if not unprecedented occurrence in a Jewish funeral, was his friend Rev. Benjamin Morgan Palmer, pastor of New Orleans's First Presbyterian Church, with whom he had long collaborated to advance their shared ideals: religious freedom and participation, the importance of family life, and—albeit by having earlier defined the "nation" as the Confederacy—national unity and patriotism.[112] With Louisiana's governor and the city's mayor among the pallbearers, and a cortege stretching an estimated two miles long, the funeral was hailed as "the greatest demonstration of respect ever shown to a Jew in the United States."[113] The next day, thousands of people "representing every creed and every nationality—people of every class of society," assembled to honor Gutheim.[114] He was a "model citizen," lamented the *Times-Democrat*, "which men of every creed may well emulate."[115]

Gutheim had staunchly defended the Confederacy and its tenets of white supremacy, founded the Hebrew Educational Society, which in effect if not also in intent avoided Reconstruction's integrated education, and, while serving on New Orleans first post-Reconstruction public school board, voted with the majority to segregate public schools. In so doing, he believed that he was pursuing national loyalty and unity, as well as benevolence and religious freedom. He accepted that the Confederacy lost the Civil War but praised the resulting "better mutual understanding" that was spreading between the North and South, which he hoped would lead to "loyalty to the Constitution, attachment to the Union, and the zeal for establishing the fundamental rights of liberty." Despite or because of these beliefs, Gutheim was respected across the South.[116] Among the many mourners at his funeral were not only the Ladies Confederate Benevolent Association—whose later success in erecting a Confederate monument was largely credited to Gutheim's wife, Emily—but also reportedly some thirty Black ministers who came as a group to mourn the minister and civic leader.[117]

While a loss to the entire community, Gutheim's death pierced the Home deeply. Spanning three decades, save for his two absences from the city, Gutheim acted as a driving force in the governance of the Home since its inception. He was the Home's authority on Jewish law and Hebrew education. At the same time, he never shied away from immersing himself in the lives of individual children, from admission to discharge. As described by one Home ward, Gutheim had "looked forward with great joy to Thursday and 'Shabbas,'" the two days each week he regularly visited the Home while most board members visited only once weekly. "How eagerly did he grasp each hand and give each one a kind word! . . . All who had been bereft of a father found another in him."[118]

Gutheim had raised large sums of money for a new building he never saw. He had begun the search for a new superintendent but did not live long enough to see who would be hired. He had shepherded the Home's investigation of the ugly Weil affair, and just ten days before he died had written his final words on it, trying to stem a reporter's queries by insisting the board was "loath to revive the horrible scandal which has nearly died out, and leave the wicked man to his fate."[119] Proclaiming him "Father to the Fatherless," the board issued resolutions in Gutheim's memory: "In the progress of the human race there have developed from time to time extraordinary men who, by dint of their goodness, nobility of soul and energy, directed by lofty aims, have elevated their fellow men above the plane of selfish action and, by example and exhortation, encouraged them to deeds of love and charity. Such a man, pure, good, and noble, was James K. Gutheim."[120]

THE SEARCH FOR SUPERINTENDENT CONTINUES

By mid-July, Jennie Weil was still in charge, and the board had made little progress in finding a new superintendent. Late one evening, perhaps emboldened by his freedom from criminal liability, Simon Weil reappeared at the Home. According to one news account, he rang the bell, rousing Jennie from sleep. She told him that she wanted nothing to do with him and intended to sue for divorce. After her threats and entreaties, he left the premises.[121]

Distressed by Simon Weil's unwelcome return, and the renewed unfavorable press attention, the board requested that Jennie Weil withdraw from the Home.[122] It issued ardent resolutions honoring her service and vouching for her character.[123] Within days, after saying goodbye to the children, she left New Orleans for her parents' home in Chicago. Her only misdeed, opined the press, was being married to her husband.[124] A year later, on allegations of "infidelity and outrageous and criminal conduct," the Illinois court granted Jennie Weil's requests for divorce on grounds of adultery and the right to resume her name, Jennie H. Peck.[125] Simon Weil returned to Missouri, where he got a job as a railroad draftsman and remarried but had no children. He never resumed a position of trust involving the care of youth.[126]

Left without a superintendent or matron, the board temporarily engaged eighteen-year-old Carrie Housman, representing the first time it entrusted an alumnus with running the Home.[127] Within two weeks, the board replaced Carrie with a person of greater maturity, selecting Adelaide Jones Hyams of Mobile, Alabama, to serve as matron until it could hire a male superintendent. Whatever Hyams lacked in experience, she compensated in provenance. She was the sister of Gutheim's wife, Emily, who was then serving as an honorary matron.[128]

For Carrie Housman, too, all worked out. Having endeared herself to the outgoing matron, the board approved Carrie's discharge to Jennie Weil and appropriated twenty-five dollars for travel expenses to Chicago.[129] Carrie was born in Tennessee, and her admission to the Home at age two was almost as noteworthy as her discharge. "This case being a peculiar one," read the board's March 1870 minutes, "the mother being in a dying condition and her husband having left her." In one of its humanitarian exceptions to its constitutional charge to admit only orphans and half orphans, the board approved Carrie's admission.[130] The breach was short-lived however, since Carrie's mother died three months later.[131]

By August, President Kursheedt had grown frustrated in his efforts to find a new superintendent. After more than six months, he was "puzzled to know who to get." As early as February 19, 1886, when the *American Israelite* reported that the board had discharged Weil for "gross, immoral conduct," it also advertised the position: "Wanted! Superintendent and Matron for the Jewish Orphans' Home in New Orleans. Persons applying for these positions must be fully qualified for the responsible duties devolving upon them and be able to furnish the best of reference as to character."[132]

LAYING THE CORNERSTONE ON ST. CHARLES AVENUE

On Thanksgiving Day 1886, the board proudly laid a cornerstone with Masonic honors for the grand new building that would run the full block of St. Charles Avenue between Leontine Street and today's Jefferson Avenue. The timing was fitting, in symbol and practice. The day was both a national day of gratitude and a weekday holiday that allowed more than one thousand people to attend the event. It was also thirty-two years to the day after the "mass meeting of Israelites" addressed the plight of Jewish orphans left in the wake of the city's yellow fever epidemics of 1853 and 1854.[133]

Isaac L. Leucht, now New Orleans's senior Jewish spiritual leader, chaired the Home's celebration committee. Born in Hesse, Germany, in 1844, Leucht first came to New Orleans in 1868 to serve as cantor at Gates of Mercy, quickly becoming its minister when Gutheim left for New York. When Gutheim returned to New Orleans in 1872 to become the spiritual leader of Temple Sinai, Leucht joined him there as cantor. In 1879, Leucht returned to Gates of Mercy when both its minister and cantor died from yellow fever. Two years later, when Gates of Mercy merged with Dispersed of Judah, Leucht served as minister to the resulting congregation, which became known as Touro Synagogue, in honor of their earlier shared benefactor Judah Touro. For the next thirty-three years, Touro Synagogue flourished under Leucht's leadership and support for Reform Judaism.[134]

Although Leucht's direct involvement with the Home began in 1870 when he delivered the anniversary celebration's opening prayer, the new building project had captured his interest. By 1885, he committed himself to raising construction funds, taking a leave of absence from Touro Synagogue to join Gutheim in canvassing the region.[135] He organized the children of his congregation's religious school to help pay for the cornerstone. Leucht also envisioned the new structure as a means to serving its children in a bold, new way. Specifically, in January 1886 he urged the board to address "the necessity of opening a school for industrial pursuits in the new building." It took years, however, before the board considered the idea. In the meantime, he filled the void in the Home's governance left by Gutheim's death. By March 1887, Leucht won election as first vice president and assumed the chair of the education committee.[136]

The opening prayer at the cornerstone ceremony was given by Rabbi Max Samfield of Memphis, Tennessee, Gutheim's successor as president of the Conference of Southern Rabbis, which was aiding the Home's ongoing fundraising efforts for the new building. As the printed program advised, less than half of the projected $90,000 construction costs had been raised. To stir emotions and open purse strings, the orator of the day was Leo Napoleon Levi, an impressive young lawyer from Galveston, Texas, and the incoming president of B'nai B'rith District 7, who by the end of the century would lead the national order.[137] Embedded into the marble cornerstone, a lead time capsule held important documents, such as Gutheim's address at the laying of the original Home's cornerstone in 1855. It also contained two dozen rare coins from around the world, all donated by Isidore Newman and his son, Jacob K. Newman, foreshadowing the family's future largesse toward the Home.[138]

MICHEL HEYMANN RETURNS

After months of searching, the name of former superintendent Michel Heymann emerged for consideration to fill the post. For the past sixteen years, Heymann had been living in Jeanerette, a small, agricultural town in southwestern Louisiana, today about a two-hour drive from New Orleans. Heymann had gone into business and became active in various civic and community affairs, such as helping to found a B'nai B'rith lodge in New Iberia and serving as secretary and treasurer to the Iberia Immigration Society, which connected the parish's planters with recent immigrants in need of work.[139] Heymann's experiences in public welfare and fundraising and his prior successful stint as superintendent ultimately made him an irresistible candidate for that position once again.[140] In April 1887, the board hired the Heymanns and requested that the couple take charge as early as practicable.[141] Preparations were soon underway for the move to the new building.

Just as he had been the first superintendent in the Jackson Street building, Heymann would soon be the first superintendent in the Home's new building on St. Charles Avenue. Between his resignation in 1870 and return in 1886, the Home had twice expanded, but the facilities nevertheless proved insufficient to accommodate the current population—50 percent larger than when he left—reflecting the new obligation to serve B'nai B'rith's expansive region. In January 1886, Rabbi Jacob Voorsanger of Houston served as the Home's first anniversary orator who resided outside of New Orleans. "The entire South is enlisted in your grand and good work," he asserted, further noting that the "new and splendid" Home would serve as "evidence of the deepest religiousness on the part of our Southern Hebrews."[142] Thus, with the backing of the region, the board had redoubled its energies on a new building. It soon set its sights on another bold goal.

chapter five

A NEW HOME AND THE DREAM OF A NEW SCHOOL
1887–1903

By the time the children moved to the new building, Home leaders' views of their mission had shifted dramatically. In early years, they spoke of their sacred duty to shelter, sustain, and console friendless orphans. As Superintendent Michel Heymann, looking back over his career, put it, "In former times, the idea of protecting poor children against hunger and want has been considered the only necessary object of associations—the present, and not the future, was the main point in view."[1] Now nearing the final decade of the nineteenth century, Home leaders and alumni urged the institution to prepare its wards to succeed in life. Over the next sixteen years, impeded by competing demands for time and money, and naysayers, what started as a call for an industrial training school annexed to the Home for only its wards emerged in a bolder and unprecedented form: a physically separate school that offered a superior, coed, secular education for its wards alongside children from the community, regardless of religion, whose parents could afford to pay tuition.

On September 1, 1887, just two weeks before Rosh Hashanah, moving day had finally arrived. By mid-morning the old building on Jackson was deserted. One hundred forty children, under the watchful eye of Superintendent Heymann and his wife, Matron Valentine Eisenmann Heymann, a cadre of teachers, staff, board members, and honorary matrons arrived on foot and in carriages at the new Home.[2]

86

Barely three miles apart, more than distance separated the two locations. The original neighborhood was mostly working-class, and owed its nickname, the Irish Channel, to the largest group of immigrants who settled there in the early nineteenth century. Now the Home would be in the "new uptown," where the city had spread into neighboring suburbs and former plantations. It was less than a mile from the newly renamed Audubon Park, three hundred acres of urban green space where only three years earlier the city hosted the World's Industrial and Cotton Centennial to showcase a "New South" that was focused on progress and commerce.[3] The neighborhood attracted wealthier, older, more Germanic, acculturated, and highly influential Jews—such as those who now populated the Home's board. These "St. Charles Avenue Jews" greatly outnumbered their working-class, Eastern European–immigrant coreligionists, the "Dryades Street Jews," who lived within walking distance of their downtown Orthodox synagogues. Whether drawn to St. Charles Avenue or Dryades Street, Jews remained numerical minorities in New Orleans.[4]

St. Charles Avenue was and remains one of the city's most beautiful thoroughfares.[5] Under a canopy of live oaks, horse- and mule-drawn streetcars clopped along the "neutral ground" that divided the wide two-way street.[6] Noted architect Thomas Sully's design, competitively selected, ensured that the Home honored the neighboring mansions, including the Queen Anne–style residence he recently built for himself.[7] In Romanesque style, the main building's facade featured a large portico supported by columned arches, three dozen tall arched windows, and three ornamental towers. Comprising four connected buildings that formed a hollow square with wide wooden galleries overlooking the interior courtyard, every room of the Home could be reached without leaving the shelter of the roof. The other three buildings—two dormitory wings and a rear building for dining, cooking, and laundry—each consisted of two stories and a ground-level basement. The Home, with its gracious front lawn, occupied the entire block, some two hundred feet wide and six hundred feet deep, dwarfing the original asylum.[8] And yet, the new orphanage did not seem out of place in a city that took pride in its charitable and educational institutions. The Protestant Home for Destitute Orphan Boys sat two short blocks away and, notwithstanding the strong racial divide of the time, the Home's next-door neighbor, New Orleans University, a private Black college, had broken ground on its new four-story building.[9]

The community held the Home and its benefactors in high regard, heralding the Home as a "Magnificent Monument to Hebrew Benevolence" and a

"Model Institution."[10] Passersby admired the new building and its finely sculptured fountain that depicted a child shouldering a vase from which a plume of water sprayed into the air. The "Mite Society," a group of Jewish children organized by Emily Jones Gutheim, the Rabbi's widow, donated the fountain, a seemingly extravagant ornament for an orphanage.[11]

The large size and divided configuration of the new Home accommodated its fluctuating population, even when enrollment briefly peaked at 173 children in 1915.[12] These features also ensured a separation of the sexes, a common priority at orphanages into the next century.[13] In addition to the nursery for the infants, older boys and girls separately occupied the two long dormitory wings that paralleled Leontine Street and today's Jefferson Avenue, respectively. Each of the four rectangular dormitory rooms (two in each wing) held as many as forty iron-frame beds in two rows. Tall windows fitted with shades flanked both sides of each dormitory room. The sparse sleeping quarters, with lofty ceilings and bare wood floors, were orderly, clean, well lit, and well ventilated—essential features for congregate childcare throughout the nineteenth century.[14] Further ensuring the gender divide, an iron fence divided the playground. At mealtime as well, boys and girls ate separately at long tables on opposite sides of the spacious dining room.[15]

The basement (the ground floor in below-sea-level New Orleans) of each dormitory wing was paved with asphalt to provide a covered play area in bad weather. Each basement also featured a swimming bath—one for boys and another for girls—big enough to hold a dozen bathers at once. Not only important for protecting the children's health, the swimming baths offered amusement, an opportunity to learn to swim, and a way to cool off in the hot and humid summers.[16] To bolster the children's health and general well-being, in addition to swings and basic playground equipment, the board installed a gymnastics apparatus and hired a physical education instructor to lead the children in calisthenics.[17] At a time when organized exercise was not yet common in public schools, the board showcased the children's ruddy complexions as they performed synchronized drills with dumbbells and Indian clubs at the anniversary celebrations.[18] On the second floor of the main building overlooking the entrance stood the infirmary where Dr. Loeber, the Home's principal physician, and a team of visiting doctors and dentists minded the children's medical needs. Children with serious conditions or requiring surgery continued to be sent to nearby Touro Infirmary, where founding Home board member Joseph Magner now served as director and later as superintendent.[19]

With the move to St. Charles Avenue also came a change in public school. Those old enough, ages seven or eight, now attended McDonogh Public School No. 14, a primary and grammar school just four short blocks away. Like their former public school, McDonogh No. 14 admitted only white children, consistent with other New Orleans public schools, which had been segregated since 1877 via local fiat.[20] The city's post–Civil War racially integrated public schools had gradually disappeared after Reconstruction as state legislators passed laws intended to maintain white supremacy. In a dramatic backlash to Louisiana's 1868 constitutional prohibition of racially segregated schools, the state's constitution of 1879 permitted segregated public education until the constitution of 1898 made it mandatory.[21] In the late nineteenth century, many Jewish orphanages in the United States sent their children to public schools, most often citing the importance of outside socialization to foster good American citizens.[22] Whether in institutional or public schools, however, orphanage children generally received more education than their community peers. This was especially true in New Orleans, where education did not become compulsory until 1910, when only about half of school-age youth were enrolled in schools.[23]

To ensure that Home children completed their homework, the board designated in the new building a study room equipped with a big horseshoe table, allowing Heymann and his assistants to easily supervise. Still years before the city opened a public library, the new Home also contained a children's library. A pet project of Rabbi Leucht, the Home's library soon boasted more than 500 books, almost all donated, ranging from *The Works of Voltaire* and *The History of the Jews* to Dickens's *Oliver Twist*.[24]

Across the hall, drawing considerable praise, was the Home's new kindergarten, an educational innovation which was gaining traction in national circles and only recently had been introduced in New Orleans.[25] Although the Home had first launched a kindergarten in the old building three years earlier when it hired a teacher from one of the city's first such private schools, the program blossomed in its new quarters.[26] The kindergarten movement was founded by German educator Friedrich Froebel and carried to America by his immigrant disciples during the 1850s, first taking root in the Midwest. The idea, radical and experimental at the time, held that early education for children between ages three and six was an extension of mothering, and provided a means to impart to immigrant and other poor mothers the values that advocates of the Progressive movement deemed essential for citizenship and self-sufficiency. Rejecting memorization and drills, then typical instruction methods, the kindergarten movement preached that children should be encouraged to develop by engaging the world around them through play and mental curiosity.[27] In New Orleans, as in many other American cities before public school systems fully incorporated kindergartens, the early work of preparing children to attend first grade was conducted privately for the well-to-do or by charitable "free kindergartens" for poor children.[28] Less than three years after a private kindergarten opened in the city, the display of a model kindergarten at New Orleans's Centennial Exposition in 1885 greatly increased awareness of the movement throughout the South and spurred the city school board to establish kindergartens in primary schools.[29] By 1902, six free kindergartens operated in New Orleans in addition to kindergartens in all public primary schools.[30]

Occupying a generous space (forty-three by twenty-four feet), the Home's kindergarten included an upright piano and child-size tables and chairs. Following Froebel's pedagogical principles to prompt learning through organized play, a large painted circle brightened the wood floor, dissected into triangles of primary colors. Motivational maxims and kindergarten truths, such as "Children are like tiny flowers" and "All growth must come from voluntary action of the child himself" adorned the walls in pleasant colors.[31] The Home's kindergarten not only prepared its children for public school but also, because the city's public normal school did not provide training for kindergarten teachers until 1895, served as one of the city's earliest training facilities for its older girls and other women in the community who wanted to become "Kindergartners," as kindergarten teachers were known.[32]

Michel Heymann was naturally drawn to the concept, having admired in his youth the *salle de'asile*, the French nursery schools that offered rooms of "asylum" for small children whose mothers lacked time or knowledge to engage their curiosity and intellect. "Children always attracted me," Heymann wrote, "and to raise them properly seemed to me a great privilege; hence I tried to become a friend of the kindergartners—I hope with success—and the happiest moments of my life have been spent in their midst."[33] Heymann's exposure to kindergartens across the country and around the world increased his pride in the Home's "children's garden." While attending an international conference in Paris in 1905, Heymann was pressed for his opinion of a kindergarten built by the renowned Rothschild banking family. "Frankly, if you'll visit New Orleans," he proudly replied, "we can show a kindergarten from which you can learn some points."[34]

Unlike the first building, which had no purpose-built space for prayer, the new Home featured a synagogue. Located in the main building, the diminutive house of worship was lined with rows of polished wood pews which faced the ark that held the Torah, oriented east toward Jerusalem, as tradition dictates.[35] In this space, later decorated with Star of David–patterned stained-glass windows, Heymann led the children in worship on Sabbath and the Jewish holidays. The Home's synagogue also welcomed alumni and community members who brought their children. With sermons crafted by Heymann and his successors for their young audiences, the Home became the first New Orleans "congregation" to offer a children's service.[36] Until he retired in 1908, Heymann taught the children biblical history, Hebrew reading, and translations of prayers, assigning such texts as the *Union Hebrew Reader* and Frederick Desola Mendes's *Jewish Chronology* in 1891. Like other Reform Jewish orphanages of the time, Heymann sought to ensure that no child left the institution without reading and understanding at least the most important prayers in Hebrew.[37]

THE NEED FOR A TRAINING SCHOOL

In March 1888, after six years as president and fifteen prior years as secretary, Edwin Kursheedt declined renomination. In his stead, the members elected Henry Newman, who had served on the board for a decade. Born in Germany, Newman had immigrated to New Orleans with his family and founded a cotton-brokerage firm with his younger brother, Charles. Their older brother, financier Isidore Newman, had just assumed leadership of the association's new board of trustees, created to manage the endowment.[38] Only a few months into his term, Henry Newman contracted an illness, for which he sought treatment in Europe. During his year-long absence, First Vice President Isaac Leucht stepped in as acting president while continuing to head the education committee.

In February 1889, Leucht revisited the Home's need for an industrial training school, a proposal he first advanced three years earlier, but which the board had quickly tabled.[39] Since then, capping Leucht's service as founding secretary of the Louisiana Educational Society, the governor appointed him to the state board of education, establishing his authority in the field while connecting him to the state's top educators and trends in teaching.[40] Other Jewish orphanages had already embarked on industrial programs, including the CJOA, which had opened a shoemaking shop, and New York's Hebrew

Orphan Asylum, which cofounded the Hebrew Technical Institute.[41] With the board's approval to conduct a preliminary study, Leucht declared in that year's annual report, "The best legacy we can give these children, is a sound body and a fair education." Reflecting contemporary gender norms that emphasized domestic work as fitting employment for young women while on their way to marriage, Leucht first addressed the situation of the Home's girls. "It has often been claimed," said Leucht, "that our girls when discharged from our care are not well fitted for the practical side of life; that too much attention was paid to school advancement and not sufficient scope allowed to home education." Leucht underscored the wisdom of the board's longstanding policy (which was consistent with the treatment of girls in the nearby Poydras Home) to take all but the most academically proficient girls above the age of fourteen out of school, where domestic science was not taught, and place them under the matron's supervision to perform housework to prepare them to run a household, whether their own or for an employer until marriage.[42]

"Gentlemen," said Leucht to the all-male membership, "this is a step in the right direction, but it does not cover the case. I am strongly of the opinion that in the near future something must be done, enabling our boys to enter a useful career as mechanics, and this blessed end can only be reached by an industrial school." Leucht urged that the most sacred aim of this institution transcended simply feeding, clothing, and sheltering its wards to "fit them for life and its struggles."[43]

For Home girls, however, this meant little change. Upon his return, President Henry Newman endorsed the Home's continued "practical education" of most older girls by Matron Heymann in household duties to prepare them for domestic employment or "for the responsibilities which as housewives must in due course fall to their lot."[44] This approach carried over into the next century. "It is not our intention to rear professional cooks," reported the board in 1900, "but we shall attempt, however, that our girls leaving the Home must be fitted to prepare a palatable meal for a modest household."[45] Similarly that same year, when the board launched a "sewing school" run by the honorary matrons, the goal was not to train professional seamstresses, but rather teach the basics of household repair and needlework.[46] To enable girls to be self-supporting in domestic work until marriage and prepare them for their roles as wives and mothers was standard at orphanages at the time.[47]

Initially fearing that a training school for the boys would entail significant additional attention and money, a year later President Newman deemed it a "necessity" to establish an "industrial school in order that our boys may acquire a trade which would fit them for other occupations in life besides following mercantile pursuits," reflecting a desire to avoid the centuries-old stereotype of the Jew.[48] In September 1891, to explore the school's feasibility, the board retained Gabriel Bamberger, a nationally recognized educator and one of America's earliest proponents of the pedagogical field of "manual training" which originated in Germany.[49] He ran the Jewish Training School, a manual training school in Chicago's Eastern European immigrant ghetto for children whose language and cultural differences were not being addressed by the public schools.[50] The movement for manual training, a balance of classical academic learning with hands-on training in various crafts, launched in America in the late 1870s to remedy secondary education's inability to respond to the needs of an urban-industrial society. Rooted in the same concepts of Friedrich Froebel's kindergarten and seen by a growing number of educators as its logical extension, manual training in America, which generally emphasized a liberal education conducive to college preparation, flourished for three decades before being superseded by the vocational education movement, which emphasized the development of marketable occupational skills.[51]

Creative work with objects, as Bamberger explained to the board, enhanced the learning of traditional subjects. Distinct from "industrial training," whose goal is met by teaching competency in a trade, "manual training" intended to supplement and advance the academic curriculum though a broader, creative process of making and doing with the hands. Even the generally accepted term "manual training" inadequately conveyed the principles it promoted; the more precise term, "manumental training," which explicitly conveyed the intended connection of hand, heart, and brain, simply never caught on in educational vernacular.[52]

Within two months, Bamberger submitted an "elaborate report & plan of formation of a Training and Industrial School" to the board.[53] Perhaps overwhelmed by the projected cost or complexity of Bamberger's plan, the board voted at least temporarily to "abandon" the proposal for a manual training school.[54] The decision cannot be explained by any diminution in the Home's need to better prepare its wards. To the contrary, many Home wards faced an uncertain future and were in apparent need of such training. Max Hyman had been admitted at age three from Memphis, Tennessee. Now fourteen, Max was readmitted in June 1891 just one month after an unsuccessful discharge to work for a local merchant. Six months later, having failed to find an appropriate training school for the boy, the board decided to retain Max in the Home to assist the gardener and stableman under Heymann's supervision in the hopes of better preparing him for life outside the Home.[55]

Home ward Lena Phelps's uncertain future also worried the board. In 1884, at age nine, Buenos Aires–born Lena entered the Home with three of her four younger siblings following the death of their father. In 1885, their mother died from malarial fever, prompting the admission of their baby brother. The Home's registry, which contained brief, undated comments about the behavior and intellect of some children, noted for Lena, "intelligence fair, temperament wild."[56] Over several years, the board placed Lena into a series of ill-fated domestic posts. In 1888, the board discharged fourteen-year-old Lena to Jonas Wolf, a merchant in Ouachita City, Louisiana. One month later, the board granted Wolf's unexplained request to return the girl, provided he pay her traveling expenses. After two more years in the Home, the board discharged Lena to Morris Jacobs, a Poydras Street clothing merchant. By 1893, Lena went to work as a house girl for Jennie Berkson, the wife of the board's second vice president. As Berkson soon complained to the Home, "The girl gives no satisfaction."[57] Little could the board foresee that Lena would years later defy their limited expectations and gender conventions. After enrolling in commercial courses, Lena became a successful accountant and notary public, deferring marriage until age fifty, after which she continued to use her last name professionally.[58]

In 1892, Gabe Kahn was elected president, replacing Henry Newman at the end of his second two-year term.[59] Kahn had already served two years as the board's second vice president and three years as president of B'nai B'rith's District 7. Born in the Germany states in 1832, Kahn left behind his humble beginnings and arrived in Louisiana at age twenty, reportedly "full of hope and determination to win his way to success." He worked in country stores around the state and, after serving in the Confederate Army, settled in New Orleans, where he became a dealer in waste cotton, a lucrative pursuit known as the "cotton pickery business," which he later turned over to his sons and grandsons.[60]

Kahn actively participated in the same philanthropic associations that drew Leucht and Heymann, exposing him to progressive ideas, such as what Heymann called "practical sociology" to improve society through educational and institutional approaches, not the least of which were kindergarten and

manual training. By 1896, for example, Kahn became a director of New Orleans's Charity Organization Society, a voluntary association of charitable
managers and funders to coordinate services to the poor, of which Heymann
was founding secretary. When Heymann headed the society's campaign to
lobby the Louisiana legislature to create a state charities board, Kahn signed
Heymann's petition.[61]

In March 1893, perhaps inspired by his humble beginnings, Kahn expressed
the hope that the board had reached "the beginning of a new era . . . to enable
our children to adapt themselves for a higher range of occupation than common drudgery work, and which constituted a bar to their progress in life."[62]
Kahn found a fellow champion for a school in Heymann. Coinciding with
his growing involvement and leadership in educational and other charitable
organizations, locally and nationally, Heymann had become an ardent and
vocal proponent of the need to teach trades to the Home's children. He chas-
tised members, donors, the general public, and the press who read the board's
annual report, writing: "We take a small baby, feed him, clothe him, educate
him, until he is 15 years old,—and, all at once, without warning, we tell him,
'Go and look out for yourself.'" Heymann further chided, "And what age needs
more watching for a boy, and more so for a girl, than the age at which we send
them out?" Invoking the authority of his professional affiliations, Heymann
related that child-saving experts with whom he recently conferred at the International Congress of Charities and Correction in Chicago had explored the
best methods to diminish pauperism and crime. "The unanimous conclusion,"
reported Heymann, "was Kindergartens for all at the basis, and a trade for each
child to finish his education." The Home always had a few bright children who
were certain to become professional men or women, noted Heymann, but
the majority will have to do manual work for a living. "Let us make of them
fine mechanics."[63] Over the next eight years in person and in print, Kahn and
Heymann advocated for a training school.[64]

Home alumni added their voices to the call, shedding new light on the
shortcomings of the Home's training and discharge practices for its former
wards. Established in 1890, while wards recently discharged from other Jewish
orphanages were founding similar organizations, the Home's alumni association pledged to support its alma mater and to "assist each other and such as
have been inmates of the 'Home' in times of emergency, distress or necessity."[65] Founding alumni association president Abraham Yarutzky, who after

entering the Home at age ten in 1877 was discharged four years later to his uncle, acknowledged that the Home had afforded him and his contemporaries only "the rudiments of a common school education, a sense of honor, and a knowledge of right and wrong," with the result that "many prosper, while some have fallen by the wayside." By sending its charges out in the world as "architects of their own fortunes," challenged Yarutzky in 1891, who was now married and working as a bookkeeper, the Home provided little guarantee of success unless it also taught the prerequisite skills.[66]

Other successful alumni followed Yarutzky in using the prestigious anniversary platform to call for a school to benefit less fortunate peers. In January 1896, twenty-year-old Max Frishman delivered the address. Discharged in 1893 after thirteen years in the Home, Max worked as a law clerk in New Iberia, Louisiana, with plans to study law.[67] Though grateful that the Home had prepared him to earn a living, Max considered himself one of only "a chosen few." He condemned the Home's "evil and harmful" practice for most other children who reached the age of fifteen years or so, to place a boy with a country merchant or make a girl a servant in a well-to-do family without any special trade or profession. "To the orphan bereft of natural protectors," urged Max for an industrial school, "a head well-filled with knowledge, and the hand well-skilled for work . . . are life itself: with it, he conquers; without it, he will be lost upon the vast ocean world—without compass, without rudder."[68]

Over the next six years, other alumni echoed Max's call for a training school. In 1899, fifteen-year-old Alex Moskowitz followed stockkeeper Jack Bernhold in 1897 and riverboat clerk Ferdinand Henriques in 1898 urging anniversary audiences to help Home inmates who had not been as fortunate in securing positions.[69] As Alex told the crowd, "We know our chances are more slim than those of other children for we are called upon early in life to go out into the world to . . . stand upon our own resources."[70] These alumni orators—and alumnae such as Hannah Frishman and Ida Barnett, who had graduated from high school and normal school and became teachers and principals—were considered "so gifted" that it was relatively easy for them to support themselves in commercial, industrial, or other careers. "But," as Heymann stressed in 1899 as Kahn earlier had done, "the majority of children are destined to make a living by actual manual work; therefore they should be prepared by manual training to make use of their hands intelligently, so as to enable them to make an honest living."[71]

THE HOME'S OVERALL PROGRAM FOR
EDUCATION AND TRAINING

While the pursuit of a training school continued, the Home provided its children other educational and vocational opportunities. Heymann hired academically talented alumnae, such as Addie Bernhold and Lena Barnett, to assist kindergarten teacher Lena Kneffler.[72] Heymann also hired seventeen-year-old Bella Loeb, after nine years in the Home, as a governess for the younger children.[73] For the Home's most promising boys and girls, Heymann encouraged stenography and typewriting, which he viewed as important tools for students who were destined to make a living by means of a trade. Nonetheless, he condemned "promiscuous" teaching of these skills, believing only the "most advanced and intelligent students" could profit from the lessons which should be imparted methodically to ensure accuracy. Reflecting the value of carefully selecting his students in this way, in March 1895, Heymann reported that all his recent stenography graduates had found paying positions, including eight boys who were earning fair salaries with large firms in and outside the city. Within two years, alumnae Hannah Frishman and Annie Rubenstein were teaching two newly formed classes. Heymann was particularly pleased that the Home's courses in this "winged art" did not interfere with the children's studies and required no additional expenditures for outside teachers, whose salaries likely would have exceeded what the Home paid to its alumnae instructors.[74] Appointing qualified wards to staff positions was common among childcare institutions of the time. The practice alleviated personnel shortages in the childcare field, known for its long hours, low salaries, and few opportunities for advancement. Such positions were considered natural vocational choices for young men and women who had been reared in institutions, and some Jewish orphanage directors encouraged their wards to seek such positions as a way of repaying the debt they felt these youngsters owed their benefactors and the Jewish community.[75]

By 1900, a large portion of the ground-level basement of the boys' dormitory had been converted into a workshop, harking back to the Home's original woodworking program. The calisthenics instructor now trained the boys in "Sloyd." Swedish for "handicraft" and closely associated with the principles of Froebel's kindergarten and the manual training movement, the Sloyd educational method used woodworking to build children's intelligence, moral character, and hand-eye skills. Like the earlier workshop, the Home's Sloyd program soon took hold, as evidenced by the attractive toy furniture the boys proudly displayed at the Young Men's Hebrew Association fair in 1900.[76]

By 1898, the Home embarked on another important training venue. The National Farm School, established one year earlier on 122 acres in Doylestown, Pennsylvania, was a four-year agricultural program designed to give Jewish lads training in farming, landscaping, and animal breeding. For Heymann, like other Jewish orphanage managers, sending boys to the National Farm School or similar programs promised a double reward.[77] As envisioned by founder Rabbi Joseph Krauskopf, the experience would prepare them for a career in agriculture as well as help reverse historic discrimination that had prohibited Jews from owning land or belonging to trade guilds, and had transformed them from "a race of shepherds and farmers to merchants." Hoping to relieve Jewish boys of the "drudgery of the counter and of the sweatshops," Heymann embraced Krauskopf's philosophy that farm schools provided an answer to "the Jewish question" and a means to redress antisemitism.[78] In its earliest years, the Farm School awarded scholarships to two promising Home boys, Solomon Pizer and Harry Rich. After graduating and having edited the school's newspaper, Pizer managed a celery farm in Iowa, where he found "happiness and contentment in this ideal form of life."[79] Rich secured a job with the U.S. Department of Agriculture, where he specialized in tobacco cultivation throughout his career.[80] Over its years, the Home sent twelve boys to the National Farm School.[81]

Placing a child with an employer or an educational program did not guarantee success. In 1891, Edward Bernstein became the Home's first student accepted at Hebrew Union College (HUC), which had been established in Cincinnati in 1875 by Rabbi Isaac Mayer Wise, founder of the American Reform movement. Bernstein's success at HUC likely would have led to a career as a rabbi. Instead, he was unable to complete his first semester due to an eye ailment. By the next year, frustrated after the young man squandered opportunities they provided for his upkeep and medical care, the board voted to "have nothing more to do with him."[82] Other Jewish orphanages of the time, including CJOA and New York's Hebrew Orphan Asylum, successfully sent qualified young men for rabbinical training either at the Reform HUC or later at the Conservative movement's Jewish Theological Seminary.[83] Perhaps the board's frustration with Bernstein soured them on this direction. Despite

HUC's offer of scholarships for Jewish orphanage wards, Bernstein was the only boy the Home ever identified for rabbinical studies.

Through the turn of the century, the board continued to take pride in placing its boys whenever possible as apprentices, often enlisting association members' influence in the community. In 1895, for example, the board announced that two boys had been apprenticed with jewelers, one with a tinsmith, and another in a shoe factory.[84] Although the board evaluated homes and situations before making placements, often declining questionable applications to take children, no formal program existed to monitor the children's progress after discharge. The board welcomed anecdotal reports it received, and by 1889 Heymann reported that he had compiled a book of photographs and short biographies intending to follow the children's careers to "see what fate has in store for them."[85] In the century's last decade, the Home discharged 209 children; in addition to 149 children discharged to a parent or relative, 9 whose discharge circumstances are uncertain, and 3 discharged for further education at the Farm School or the normal school for teachers, 49 children (38 boys and 11 girls) entered apprenticeships and jobs. Among the boys' work placements, 7 started jobs as stenographers or clerks, with the rest placed into situations to learn a trade, including florist, baker, shoemaker, jeweler, and druggist. The girls were placed as teachers, nannies, and housekeepers.[86]

Some alumni built strong relationships with their first employers that set them on a steady path in life. In 1888, David Davis, for example, endeared himself to his employer, Capt. Sam Haas, an Alsatian Jew who owned a sugar and cotton plantation in Bayou Chicot, Louisiana. Haas arranged a private tutor for David, who had completed public grammar school while in the Home, and later gave the young man a horse. David rode the horse eight hundred miles to Louisville, Kentucky, to enter and ultimately graduate from Louisville's Medical College.[87] Alphonse Pincus, admitted to the Home in 1899 after his parents died from consumption, was discharged six years later at age fourteen to Sam Kessler, a prosperous Jewish sugar-plantation owner in Belle Rose, Louisiana. For the next decade, Alphonse remained in Belle Rose, where he worked as a grocer.[88] He later returned to New Orleans, where he worked at the D. H. Holmes department store before and after his World War I military service, married, and raised a son.[89]

Assessing the Home's contribution to the long-term welfare of its wards must also consider the importance of reuniting families, which the Home achieved during this time for three times the number of children it placed directly into jobs or apprenticeships. Examples of children returned to their family at the end of the nineteenth century who went on to notable careers included Isadore Moritz, a pioneering newspaperman in the Rio Grande Valley, Joseph Sonnenberg, a well-known member of New Orleans's mounted police, and Adolph D. Henriques, a physician who championed the early use of X-rays in the South and served as a consultant to the U.S. Public Health Service.[90]

LEUCHT TAKES BOLD ACTION

Since Leucht first proposed a training school in 1886, competing priorities had demanded the board's attention and budget. At first, these priorities included discharging the debt on the new Home's construction and negotiating with architect Thomas Sully to remedy the instability of the third floor and roof.[91] Then came the national financial panic of 1893, followed by a four-year depression that tightened donors' purse strings.[92] Later, the board focused on expanding the infirmary after the yellow fever epidemic of 1897 struck 68 Home children, killing 3, and the influenza outbreak of 1898 struck 4 more children, killing 1.[93] Most recently, seeking to avoid the health disaster that had befallen New York's Hebrew Orphan Asylum, where dysentery from faulty drainage had sickened 150 of 850 children before taking the lives of 5 children and the superintendent, the Home's board undertook a costly overhaul of its sanitation, plumbing, and drainage systems.[94] Competing priorities were a given.

Nevertheless, on the eve of the twentieth century, Leucht intensified his efforts for a school. He invited eleven of the South's most prominent rabbis to the 1899 anniversary celebration to witness the Home's good work, understand the need for further training, and then return to their pulpits as spirited ambassadors to raise funds for the Home's school.[95] Seeking to inspire in his fellow clergy "not simply warmth" for the idea of the school "but a conflagration," Leucht carefully executed his plan.[96] Rabbi Max Samfield of Memphis prayed to "make this institution still grander and nobler" while Rabbi Samuel Sale of St. Louis, Missouri, lauded manual training "as one of the most essential elements of all thorough education."[97] After raising the specter that untrained Home wards "thrust upon the cold, pitiless world" might end up in prison, Leucht called upon "the rich men" to give now rather than leave their wealth to charities after they died.[98] Despite the team of southern rabbis who preached the cause of the training school, and the fervid pleas in countless speeches, reports, and resolutions, no donor emerged.

Undaunted, in spring 1902, Leucht convinced his colleagues to again retain the services of Gabriel Bamberger to report on "the feasibility of erecting a 'Manual Training School' on our grounds."[99] In April, more than a decade after he first outlined a plan, Bamberger appeared at a special board meeting where he reviewed the principles and workings of manual training, often referring to his Chicago institution where twenty-five teachers taught an average of seven hundred pupils daily. He explained that manual training developed character, promoted truthfulness by requiring each child to perform work with exactitude, taught forethought because what the hand executed the brain must have planned, and instilled economy by compelling each child to select the necessary material from the stock on hand. Manual training also offered opportunities to discover each child's natural inclinations, enhancing the choice of an appropriate profession. Music, too, was an important part of the program, explained Bamberger, as it "brings about a harmony between the real and the ideal."[100]

Bamberger responded to board members' questions and concerns. One issue proved particularly troublesome: was it advisable to entirely remove the children from public school and educate them exclusively in the manual training school on the Home's grounds? By the end of the meeting, the board *seemed* satisfied that the risk of isolating children from their outside peers was small, reassuring themselves that "the home was not a prison and the children had constant contact with the outer world." After the board gave Bamberger a "rising vote of thanks," a jubilant Leucht told a reporter immediately following the meeting, "I believe that we can safely prognosticate that a manual training school will soon be a fact and not a dream."[101]

Over the next week, the attributes that made the Home's school unique came into being. By grappling with lingering latent concerns that such a school would isolate the Home's children, a dramatically new concept for the Home's school emerged. Leucht, on behalf of the education committee, articulated the following conditions:

1. It shall be conducted in a building separate and distinct from the "Home" building.
2. Pupils from outside the Home shall be admitted without discrimination because of creed.

3. The number of outside pupils and the rules governing their admission shall be fixed from time to time by the Board of Directors; but the number which may be admitted shall be limited only by the capacity of the school, after our own wards are provided for.[102]

Leucht felt confident that these conditions offered Home children the advantages of a manual training education without isolating them from community peers.[103] For every hundred Home children, Leucht proposed that the school admit twenty-five outside "pay scholars" who would be attracted by the school's superior facilities. At $40 per pay pupil, Leucht calculated that the $1,000 total paid in tuition would more than offset the $800 estimated to furnish the one additional teacher required. Moreover, Leucht reasoned that "the payment of a fee and the supervision we will be able to exercise over the children seeking admission will tend to make the scholars of this School superior in many ways to the average in the ordinary public school."[104] The association was in prosperous financial condition, wrote Leucht, and could afford the $6,000 per year Bamberger projected to run the school, especially with funding anticipated from B'nai B'rith and the community. Thus, without any expectation that tuition from outside students would cover total operating expenses but with every expectation that the Home children would benefit from contact with "superior" students whose parents could afford to pay, the board unanimously resolved to build a manual training school.[105]

Immediately after the board adopted the committee's plan, Leucht surprised his fellow board members by producing a letter in which Isidore Newman offered to fund the construction.[106] A native of Bavaria, a penniless Isador Neumond settled in New Orleans in 1853 after his family's first venture into cotton brokerage had failed. Since then, Newman invested in a wide range of successful enterprises—from street-railway lines and department stores to the stock market—always seeking to repay the city that made his fortune possible.[107] After a two-year term as board member in 1874, in addition to the contributions made for many years by his wife, Rebecca Kiefer Newman, as honorary matron, Isidore Newman resumed his direct service to the Home in 1890. Over the next two decades, overseeing the Home's endowments, Newman's investments quadrupled the value of the Home's portfolio.[108] In his brief letter, Newman apprised Leucht of his intentions: "Appreciating your noble efforts for the past ten years to erect a training school for boys and girls, and having read the able and convincing address of Mr. G. Bamberger, I have concluded to offer to you the money requisite to erect such a building, and hope that Providence may spare you to see this building completed and enable the boys and girls of our city to derive the full benefit of your labor."[109]

Leucht, on behalf of the Home, thanked Newman for his gift, which Leucht accepted for the purpose of building a manual training school "for boys and girls *of our Home and* of our city," clarifying the rightful place of the Home children in the new school by adding four words that Newman had not used (*emphasis added*). Leucht also expressed his gratitude for being selected by Newman "as the messenger of your benevolence." Newman's decision to address his letter to Leucht, said the clergyman, "is the proudest sign of recognition and friendship that ever came to me."[110]

Perhaps that same close relationship led the two men to collaborate on the conditions under which the school was founded. Both dated May 3, 1902, without indicating time of day, Newman's letter and Leucht's report raise the question whether Newman's offer prompted Leucht to devise the three conditions in his report, or vice versa. To effectuate Newman's stated desire that "the boys and girls of our city derive the full benefit" of his gift, the school needed to attract children who did not live in the Home. Situating the school outside the orphanage and admitting children regardless of religion, as outlined in Leucht's report, were also effective means to achieve Newman's stated goal.

Simultaneously, despite their inclusive language, neither Newman nor Leucht contemplated opening the school to the city's Black children. Racial segregation in New Orleans and Louisiana was ubiquitous, imposed by social norms and legal mandates in almost every facet of life: on trains and streetcars, in railroad waiting rooms, prisons, mental institutions, marriage, and education.[111] Both men were well aware of racial segregation in public schools. In addition to Leucht's tenure on the state board of education, he and Newman were founding members of the Louisiana Educational Society, created in 1884 to "promote and encourage public education" in the state.[112] Thus, even in the absence of a law prohibiting racial integration in *private* schools, Newman did not need to explicitly exclude Black children for his words to be readily understood that way. Such a specification would have been unusual and unnecessary amid the pervasive segregation and discrimination of the Jim Crow era.

In 1903, the *Times-Picayune* awarded Newman its prestigious Loving Cup, having selected his gift for the nonsectarian manual training school as the "most meritorious public benefaction" during the year. Newman remarked that he had been considering the gift for the "past two or three years," encouraged by his wife Rebecca, his children, and by rabbis in the B'nai B'rith region, who often called to discuss the school's benefits. He gave only two reasons for his final decision. First, he had the money and owed it to the community that enabled him to earn it. "Second, I had the disposition to give it. That was all." Newman, the once-poor Jewish immigrant who had won social and professional acceptance in his adoptive gentile host community, expressed particular pleasure that the school would admit children of all religions. "This, no doubt," said Newman, "will redound to our reputation for liberality, and convince the community that we are not clannish or sectional."[113] Even if Newman had not initiated the requirement for a freestanding and nonsectarian school, he championed it.

On the one occasion Isidore Newman spoke directly about imposing conditions on his gift, he described a single, entirely different condition. "I have concluded to erect an institution to help others, insisting upon but one condition," revealed Newman in 1905, "and that was that music should be taught there for in all my troubles music has been a great consoler."[114] Whatever uncertainty surrounds the role Isidore Newman played in devising the conditions under which his namesake school was founded, there is no doubt about his generosity. When told that $15,000 was needed to construct the school, Newman responded, "You better take $25,000, as a starter, and you will need more than that."[115] He was correct; his initial gift of $25,000 quickly grew to nearly $50,000. And before Newman died in 1909, he had donated to the school an additional $27,000, not including $5,000 his children donated in honor of his seventieth birthday or his last gift, his $10,000 bequest.[116] To this day, Isidore Newman's family has sustained his legacy of philanthropy for the school.[117]

At the 1903 annual meeting, President Kahn happily reported, "A great event has transpired, one fraught with deep import for the future glory of our Institution, and of profound interest for the future destinies and fate of those entrusted to our care. For the idea—and what a great many considered but an ideal, a dream—of a Manual Training School has become a reality!" "Blessed be the true Israelite," added Heymann in prayers for Isidore Newman, "who enables us, through his liberality, to give to the orphans of the seven Southern States, a thorough, practical education to become an honor to the Jews of our country."[118]

By the end of the nineteenth century, some twenty Jewish orphanages had opened around the nation. As noted by historian Reena Sigman Friedman, German Jews who were well established in their communities and assumed responsibility for the needy children of newly arriving East European brethren largely led these orphanages. These so-called "uptown Jews" and their orphanage managers sought to uplift and Americanize their charges through state-of-the-art educational, vocational, and health programs so they could contribute their energies and talents to the American economy and society as honorable Reform Jews.[119]

Friedman's observations apply equally to the Home. Prominently situated in one of the loveliest areas of uptown New Orleans, the grand new building offered its young residents the opportunity to see and be seen by some of the city's wealthiest Jewish and non-Jewish citizens. Like other Jewish orphanages, as well, the Home's board recognized the importance of sending its children to public schools to interact and socialize with community peers, while adding exercise programs, an institutional kindergarten, and training programs that the public schools lacked.

In Jewish orphanages in other parts of the country, kindergartens and manual training schools were already common. However, the Home embraced these educational innovations before they were widely adopted in New Orleans or the South. Moreover, when proposing a secular manual training school outside the institution, the uptown Jews who ran the Home sought a particular group of classmates to uplift and Americanize its wards: tuition-paying students who were "superior in many ways to the average in the ordinary public school." Compared to other Jewish orphanages, the Home's board had set the standard for Americanizing its wards particularly high.

chapter six

ISIDORE NEWMAN
MANUAL TRAINING SCHOOL
1904–1909

In 1904, on the first Monday morning in October, 102 boys and girls walked out of the Home, two by two, neatly and uniformly dressed. The girls wore long-sleeved, knee-length shirtwaist dresses, and the boys sported dark jackets and white shirts with ties, atop knickers for those too young to wear trousers.[1] For the first time since the Home opened on St. Charles Avenue, Superintendent Heymann's wards did not walk three blocks "riverside" to McDonogh School No. 14 where, like other city schools of the time, boys and girls received instruction separately.[2] Today, they headed in the opposite direction, "woodside," to proceed two blocks along today's Jefferson Avenue to their brand-new Isidore Newman Manual Training School, where they would learn together. Over the next five years, as the novel school prospered and expanded, evolving standards of dependent childcare would challenge the institution that founded it.

When the children reached the neat two-story brick-and-marble building, they were joined by 23 classmates from private homes. Twelve had parents who could afford the year's tuition, which averaged $75, or about $2,500 today. Eleven attended without charge, thanks to the board's decision to award a limited number of scholarships to children in the community.[3] The school expanded New Orleans's educational landscape for these and many other children who followed. It added another choice to the list of private schools attended by nearly 40 percent of city schoolchildren, including the offspring of the commercial and civic elite.[4] Newman School also captured the attention of public school leaders. "It is positive," New Orleans school superintendent Warren Easton predicted while discussing the Home's new school, "that manual training for boys will become a feature of public school work in the near future."[5] For now, public school offerings outside of traditional academic courses largely were limited to bookkeeping, mechanical drawing, stenography, and typewriting, and those courses were available only in high schools and, for working boys ages fourteen to eighteen, in night schools.[6]

Reflecting the national attention it drew, James Edwin Addicott, a British-born educator who had directed the manual training department at San Jose, California's State Teachers' College, served as the school's first principal.[7] "I feel perfectly safe in saying," Addicott boasted about Newman School to reporters, "that there is no other school in America engaged wholly in elementary education so amply, thoroughly and superbly equipped as this."[8] Initially limited to grades one through eight, the curriculum for boys and girls included history, science, mathematics, and music, aligned with contemporary gender-based expectations. For girls, the school offered household management, including cooking and food safety; domestic arts, beginning with simple weaving and ending with dressmaking; and fine arts, including drawing and painting. Boys were also offered fine arts, along with mechanical drawing, bent iron work, joining, carving, printing, and lathe work. In addition to classrooms, the school held dedicated rooms for sewing, cooking, pottery, woodworking, forging, and drafting, each outfitted with the latest equipment. The school also offered a well-stocked library, a soon-to-be-furnished assembly hall, and a gymnasium, complete with Roman rings and trapezes, basketball court, and "shower baths" for after exercising.[9] Three years passed, however, before the school had room for a kindergarten.

The board remained committed to the school's nonsectarian instruction and management. It did not seek, and there is no record of, Jewish faculty during the Home's four-decade ownership of the school. Rejecting a proposal to close the school on Jewish holidays, the board instead decided "no pupils of any religious denomination shall lose any marks for non-attendance on their religious holidays."[10] The issue of closing the school on Jewish holidays resurfaced in 1916, when a board member proposed closing the school on the first and last days of Passover. The proposal quickly defeated, his colleagues insisted that it was not only unnecessary due to the attendance policy but also would undermine the founder's desire to operate a nonsectarian school.[11]

Before the first school year ended, the board addressed a different concern. "It is desirable hereafter," wrote education committee chair Leucht, "that the wards, especially the girls, should not all be dressed alike." He expressed concern that wearing the same clothes that signified the children's "positions in life may be mentally depressing" and would prevent them from fitting in with their classmates. The board agreed.[12] At the time, some smaller Jewish orphanages had already begun to individually outfit their children, such as Chicago's Home for Jewish Orphans, with thirty-six wards, but larger orphanages such as CJOA did not abandon uniforms until 1919.[13] For the Home's children, going to their new school with classmates from the community visibly changed their lives.

THE SCHOOL'S DEDICATION AND THE HOME'S GOLDEN JUBILEE

In late December 1904, a dispute with the musicians' union was the last thing Leucht wanted as he finalized details for three simultaneous events to take place within two weeks. As the upcoming year marked fifty years since the Home's founding—its Golden Jubilee—the board chose to dedicate the school the same day. Adding to the excitement and complexity of the arrangements, the Conference of Southern Rabbis, of which Leucht held a leadership position, accepted the board's invitation to hold its annual gathering concurrently. To properly commemorate the events, Leucht enlisted Ferdinand Dunkley, Touro Synagogue's Royal Academy–trained choir director and the school's new music instructor, to lead the choral and orchestral interludes between the prayers and speeches.

After weeks of rehearsals, the union advised that its members would be unable to perform under Dunkley, who was not a union member and refused to join. The nonunion and amateur replacements Dunkley quickly hired, upon fearing reprisal, just as quickly backed out.[14] These exigent circumstances yielded a surprisingly delightful outcome. Eleven-year-old Mike Caplan, a rising cornetist and leader of the Home's band, along with sixteen fellow Home musicians, boys ages ten to fourteen, filled the melodic void.[15] Fortunately, like other Jewish asylums that regarded music as an integral aspect of education and recreation, Heymann and the board three years earlier had recognized that band training could enliven the institution's daily routine.[16] Although individual lessons in singing, piano, violin, and other instruments had long been a part of the Home's program, its brass band was barely two years old. With donations of gleaming instruments from Jacob Kiefer Newman, Isidore's son and a successful banker in his own right, and sharp, military-style uniforms from treasurer Simon Gumbel, the Home's band had been born. Pleased with the young musicians' progress, Heymann also launched a junior division to ensure a pipeline for talent.[17]

At the school's dedication and the Home's Golden Jubilee, the Home band did not disappoint. As President Gabe Kahn later proudly reported, "Our boys supplied the music in a manner that called forth enthusiastic applause, even at the hands of music critics."[18] Perhaps revealing as much hostility to unions as admiration for the boys' performance, the *Times-Democrat* appraised the program as "equally satisfactory" to anything the union musicians could have offered, while the *Picayune* went further, noting that, despite the union's "despotic demands" and refusal to play, "this band of small boys can beat many full-fledged professionals."[19] The Home band not only represented the care and training the Jewish orphanage provided, but also, as students of the Isidore Newman Manual Training School, epitomized the school's founding principle and motto, "Discimus Agere Agendo—We learn to do by doing."[20]

Hours after the school's dedication, the band, the visiting rabbis, and many more people reassembled at the Home's Golden Jubilee at the Athenaeum, the ornate new building of the Young Men's Hebrew Association. Located on St. Charles Avenue at Clio Street, the Athenaeum's large auditorium seated twenty-five hundred people, more than double the capacity of the Home's third-floor anniversary hall.[21] Much as the school's dedication looked to the future of its students, the Golden Jubilee honored the Home's past. Joseph Magner and Joseph Simon, seated among the dignitaries on stage, represented the Home's three surviving founders.[22] After welcoming the crowd, President Kahn lauded the Home's historic half century of childcare, including Superintendent Heymann's "magnificent management and handling of children" over the past eighteen years. In his remarks, former U.S. senator Benjamin Franklin Jonas recalled the oration he delivered at the first building's dedication.[23]

On behalf of B'nai B'rith District 7, President Nat Strauss emphasized the order's unflagging support for the orphanage since 1875. Perhaps wary of rekindling resentment from a debate so heated that the press dubbed it a "battle royale," Strauss made no mention of District 7's decision only a few months earlier to designate the Home as the sole orphanage to receive its money, thus ending its contributions to CJOA.[24] The added advantage of Newman School's training opportunities only increased District 7's enthusiasm for the Home, affirming its decision to defund the Cleveland asylum. That enthusiasm persisted for nearly forty more years before B'nai B'rith District 7 joined others who questioned the benefits Home children received from the school.[25]

Lee K. Frankel, secretary of United Hebrew Charities of New York and a highly regarded professional in the growing field of social work, delivered the keynote address. He discussed the sympathy orphans generated, as evidenced by the nation's Jewish orphanages that together then housed more than 3,500 children. Then, Frankel's remarks took a surprising turn. "If the children under your care have grown up to be responsible men and women and have taken their places in the body politic," which Frankel acknowledged many had done, "it is not due to the fact that they were raised in an institution, but in spite of the fact that they were raised in an institution." Notwithstanding the best intentions of the ablest superintendents and under the most favorable conditions, Frankel charged, "it is manifestly impossible to raise under one roof" the 1,000 children then residing at New York's Hebrew Orphan Asylum or even the 600 children then at CJOA with any likelihood of "normal child development."[26]

If Frankel had limited his criticisms to the nation's largest Jewish orphanages, the audience, especially the board, could have taken comfort in the Home's relatively tiny population of 144 children. Frankel had gone further not only to urge merely improving orphanage conditions but instead to beseech the Home's leaders and supporters to "consider the possibility and the feasibility of returning to their parents, and in particular to their mothers, some of the children who are in your care." Notwithstanding the care and opportunities the Home offered, Frankel insisted, it deprived children of their parents' love and affection and even knowledge of an immigrant parents' language. Although institutions would continue to care for dependent children for whom no other provision can be made, he advocated keeping families intact wherever possible by paying pensions to mothers, the "natural, God-given guardian[s]" of their fatherless children.[27]

Although his criticisms may have stunned most guests, who had come to celebrate their beloved orphanage, Frankel was hardly a lone voice on the subject. While the Home had focused on building a school to prepare its wards for their future, the world of asylums and dependent childcare was evolving. At large gatherings—such as those regularly convened by the interfaith National Conference of Charities and Correction and, beginning in 1900, the National Conference of Jewish Charities—institutional managers, "child-saving" advocates, and other humanitarian workers met to present and debate the latest theories and practices in social welfare.

Superintendent Heymann regularly attended these conferences, serving on committees and actively participating in discussions when he was not a featured speaker.[28] He was already aware of, and had publicly endorsed, efforts to keep children with their families—to the extent possible. A decade earlier, in his annual report to the board, he commended Philadelphia's Jewish Foster Home, which paid some parents and relatives to care for their children.[29] He shared his views on the national stage as well, arguing at the National Conference of Charities and Correction that there should be as few children in institutions as possible, and telling the same group three years later that the majority of dependent childcare advocates recognized the "superiority to institutional life" of placing children in private families.[30] However, lamented Heymann, introducing a system of placing dependent Jewish children in private homes remained, in his view, "impossible."[31] He later explained: "We cannot find proper families for the children. The good families do not want them; and we do not want those who wish to make money out of them. The best way is to keep them ourselves. The only way to place out children is to place them with their mothers, and sometimes that is not very good."[32] Even in Philadelphia, despite success in placing out some of its children, Heymann argued the need for its Jewish orphan asylum had not been eliminated; to the contrary, the Philadelphia institution was still "flourishing."[33]

Leucht, as well, was neither a stranger to these views, nor against them in theory. In a talk at the 1897 Conference of Charities and Correction, he went even further than his superintendent in decrying institutional life: "The orphan's life in an asylum, no matter how beautiful the cage may be—be it of golden wires—is that of an imprisoned bird. . . . The child grows up to do nothing unless a bell rings, unless someone tells him to do something." Although Leucht told the group he was "inclined to try the experiment" of placing children out, there is no indication that such an experiment was ever conducted in the Home.[34] In 1902, at the National Conference of Jewish Charities, just days after Isidore Newman offered to fund the Home's school, Leucht again lamented institutional childcare, but made no mention of placing out children. "At the present moment, there is no better method of rearing orphans than in asylums," Leucht asserted. "And why? Because we do not know anything better."[35]

The sound of a bell continued to signal the regimentation in the Home's "golden cage" into the next century. Twins Joseph and Rudolph Bernstein, who lived in the Home from 1896 to 1906, were among those who described bells ringing throughout the day, telling them when to rise in the morning, report to inspection and school, line up for to meals, and go to bed.[36] Sam Koltun, who lived in the Home from 1905 to 1912, described Heymann as a "humane disciplinarian" who nevertheless strictly imposed a "militaristic system" in which the sparse staff appointed older boys and girls who behaved and did well in school as "monitors" to oversee younger peers.[37] Whether by paid staff or peer monitors, institutional order was sometimes accomplished through harsh practices, even if not always officially acknowledged or condoned. Sybil Bianchini Dehougne, who lived in the Home from 1886 to 1899, told her daughter that bed wetters "were beaten and made to hang the sheets out so that other kids could taunt you." She also resented what she considered the unnatural separation of boys from girls by means of the tall iron fence in the courtyard.[38] Rose Helen Jacobs, who lived in the Home from 1906 to 1914, bitterly recalled having her curly hair shaved off when she was admitted at age six.[39] It mattered little to these children if these and other dehumanizing and emotionally stunting practices were intended to prevent the spread of lice, reduce laundry, and otherwise preserve order—or were common among orphanages of the time, which they were.[40]

In 1903, the Home's board faced an opportunity to place its children with private families. B'nai B'rith's leadership in New York proposed a "National Home Bureau" for Jewish orphans: a central office would act as a clearing-house in concert with the lodges, as liaisons between their communities and institutions, to find and supervise proper private foster homes. A national representative asked the Home to identify children appropriate for place-ment.[41] Concerned that the surviving parent of a half orphan might remarry or otherwise want to later reclaim the child, causing harmful interference or successive changes to the child's environment, the Home's board replied that it would consider placing out only full orphans. B'nai B'rith soon abandoned the project, and the Home did not independently pursue placing out even its relatively few full orphans.[42]

The idea of keeping children with their mothers was not completely new for the board, which in a handful of cases subsidized a surviving mother in lieu of admitting a child into the Home. These cases were rare, however, and at the time resulted seemingly by happenstance, not from a routinely available choice or process. The board did not publicize these actions or preserve a tally of the children or mothers served in this way.[43] Not until the mid-1920s did the board begin to more frequently consider, even if it did not often find, ways to prevent admission by keeping children with their mother.[44] Widowed fathers, who admitted approximately half of the Home's children, presented further complications. Reflecting societal norms that deemed men less capable as caregivers, single fathers were not only excluded from most publicly funded "Mothers' Pensions" but frequently succumbed to pressure from relatives and their communities to relinquish their children.[45] Moreover, neither New Orleans nor the state provided any guidance or role models for child placing in New Orleans or around the state where, as one social work commentator described, conservatism and pride "attached to institutions and methods that are not perfect." Nearly a decade passed before organized child placing slowly took root in the region.[46]

Despite their outcry against the evils of childcare institutions and their professed desire to keep families intact, Leucht's and Heymann's resistance to stipends and outplacing hardened as Eastern European immigration increased. Although Eastern European Jews had been seeking refuge in America from poverty and persecution at the hands of Czarist Russia since the 1880s, the great migration intensified with pogroms of the early 1900s. By 1924, more than two million Eastern European Jews immigrated to America, some of whom made their way to New Orleans. Unlike big cities of the North and even other southern cities like Atlanta, New Orleans was not inundated by these immigrants, who likely were deterred by the city's ongoing epidemics and inadequate drainage. Nevertheless, as with other established Jewish communities in America, acculturated "uptown" Jews in New Orleans responded with a mixture of compassion and condescension. To prevent newcomers' Old World customs and Orthodox religious observances from spurring antisemitism and nativism, they needed to be aided and Americanized as quickly as possible.[47]

The influx of Eastern European Jewish immigrants similarly played out in the Home's population.[48] From 1880 to 1900, while the percentage of all foreign-born wards dropped by nearly half and the percentage of all wards born to immigrant parents remained nearly constant (88 percent to 91 percent), the percentage of Home children born to immigrants from Russia and other Eastern European countries jumped from 20 percent to 51 percent. This trend continued over the next several decades. By 1930, the percentage of foreign-born wards again dropped by half, but the percentage of Home children born to Eastern European immigrants rose to 67 percent.[49]

Some Jewish orphanage managers disparaged the conditions in which these immigrants raised their children. In 1898, as more children of Eastern European descent entered Cleveland's Jewish orphanage, that superintendent lamented that his charges had come from "dirty and shiftless homes," marked by "aimless poverty" and "soulless superstition."[50] Similarly, in 1904, Michel

Heymann underscored the need to separate children from "poor parents living in the congested Ghettos of the large cities . . . especially when the parents are incompetent, ignorant, and sometimes vicious."[51] As late as 1925, reflecting the same disdain, the Home's president explained that one mother was incapable of raising children because she was "a typical Russian immigrant, filthy, hardly capable of expressing herself in the most common English words."[52] Not surprisingly, neither the Home nor its Cleveland counterpart took serious steps to support or keep needy immigrant families intact and instead focused almost exclusively on Americanizing the children within their institutions.

Other Jewish orphanages, in contrast, were open to new systems of dependent childcare. After all, American Jews might never be able to build enough orphanages to keep pace with increasing immigration or, if the population growth reversed, would be saddled with empty structures. By 1905, B'nai B'rith's abandoned proposal for a National Home Bureau spurred the first large-scale effort for Jewish child-placement in New York City. The joint program overseen by the Hebrew Sheltering Guardian Society orphan asylum also involved the Brooklyn Orphan Asylum, United Hebrew Charities, the Hebrew Infant Asylum, and the Hebrew Orphan Asylum. Within five months, the program, which featured a rigorous screening process and follow-up visits, approved 70 of 160 prospective foster homes.[53] In Atlanta, where the Russian Jewish immigrant population rose fivefold between 1890 and 1900, Superintendent Ralph Sonn at that city's Hebrew Orphans' Home was sufficiently drawn to the goal of keeping families intact that he proposed that his board take preliminary steps by asking surviving mothers whether they would retain their children if subsidized and, if so, the amount required.[54]

The creation of Newman School fueled pride in the Home's institutional care, further diverting attention from subsidizing surviving parents or placing out children. In 1907, after proclaiming that the school would save Home children from relying on "the peddler's cart or the counter" to earn a living, B'nai B'rith District 7 president Mike Mohr readily dismissed criticism of institutional childcare and "whatever may be said by those advocating new methods in the rearing of orphans."[55] Even Lee Frankel, just three years before he decried institutional childcare at the Home's jubilee, while addressing the National Conference of Jewish Charities, explained that Jewish asylums had not yet systematically attempted to place out their children because they "have never been institutions, but homes, and most worthily have Jewish family ideals been fostered and perpetuated by them."[56] Even if overly generous, Frankel's statement reveals that improving the quality of care inside Jewish orphanages took priority over finding noninstitutional alternatives.

Just before Newman School opened, while addressing the 1904 national Jewish charities conference, Heymann described "The Ideal Orphan Asylum." In its physical arrangement, Heymann's ideal bore little resemblance to the Home. He favored the "cottage plan," an institutional living arrangement recently devised to approximate private homes, in which no more than twenty-five children, under the guidance of "conscientious women," would live in one of several cottages situated on a large plot of suburban land.[57] His vision of ideal orphan education, on the other hand, mirrored the Home's new reality: manual training in the fullest sense, from kindergarten throughout the child's life in the institution.[58] In the discussion that followed, Leucht refined Heymann's thesis. "Believe me, ladies and gentlemen, there is no Ideal Orphan Asylum" because asylums tend to "destroy the individuality of the child." But the Home, Leucht asserted, had found a way to develop the individuality of its children by building a manual training school.[59] For both Leucht and Heymann, the new school offered a means to make the Home the best institution it could be, which only served to perpetuate the orphanage in lieu of noninstitutional alternatives. Max Senior, president of Cincinnati's United Jewish Charities, offered an insightful rebuttal to the claimed impossibility of finding families in which to place children. "If we didn't have the institution, we would have absolutely no trouble finding the homes."[60]

THE SCHOOL'S SUCCESS AND EXPANSION

By all accounts, the Isidore Newman Manual Training School was a success. Often referred to as "Manual," the letter "M" soon adorned school sweaters and athletic jerseys. As news spread about the state's first manual training school, more parents in the community sought to enroll their children in this well-equipped coed institution with its cutting-edge curriculum. By fall 1906, Newman's enrollment reached 250 and, for the first time, non-Home children outnumbered Home children, 137 to 113.[61] For the remainder of the Home's existence, outside children increasingly outnumbered their orphanage classmates. Buoyed by the success of its first school year, the board voted to add a high school one grade at a time, starting in fall 1905. Leucht secured the commitment of Tulane University president Edwin B. Craighead, who had already enrolled his children, to admit the school's future high school graduates to Tulane and Newcomb College without examination. The board was also motivated by the prospect, as Leucht urged, that the high school would attract "pupils of all classes, who are eager to learn, and whose ambition will stimulate our wards to emulation."[62] Moreover, at a time when school attendance was not yet compulsory and nearly one-third of the state's ten- to fifteen-year-olds were employed, each additional year that the Home's wards attended school gave them an educational advantage they might not otherwise enjoy.[63]

"The school has prospered as few expected it would," remarked Leucht in May 1906 after the addition of ninth and tenth grades. "Children of the best families in the city crowd its limited space, and our wards are thrown together with a selected body of children from the outside."[64] By attracting more pay students, however, enrollment quickly exceeded the school's physical capacity. To address the new problem, the board decided to expand the school's classroom space. Isidore Newman, who supported the plan, donated $25,000, leaving the institution to raise the remaining $10,000.[65] When the annex opened in the fall of 1907, Newman School offered the city's first complete program through high school.[66] The expansion also accommodated the kindergarten, which relocated from the Home. That year, the 23 kindergarten children from the Home joined 10 peers from the community, with whom they would play and learn for years to come. President Kahn predicted that "by next year" the increased revenue from additional paying students would make the school self-sustaining, enabling the Home to "grant our orphans even a high school education, if desired, manual training and all kindred branches, without any expense to our Home."[67]

Despite Kahn's optimism, neither he, Leucht, nor Isidore Newman lived to see the school generate sufficient revenue to cover expenses. Although the board never questioned the merits or efficiency of the school, it acknowledged the "heavy drain" and "burden" the school's maintenance imposed upon the Home's finances—as much as $14,870 in costs over receipts in 1930.[68] The board responded by increasing tuition for pay pupils and by expanding the buildings to accommodate more of them.[69] In 1936, for the first time, the Home did not incur a deficit from the school's maintenance.[70]

ASSURING THE SCHOOL MEETS THE HOME CHILDREN'S NEEDS

Although every Home child attended Newman in the lower grades, not every Home child continued through high school graduation. Many were reclaimed by a surviving parent or relative before reaching or finishing high school, and not every Home child was considered equipped for the high school's rigors. Beginning in 1909, on an undefined, case-by-case basis, some academically proficient children were permitted to finish their Newman education after discharge to a local relative.[71] From 1911, when Louis Fuerstenberg became the first Home student to graduate from Newman, to 1947, the school year during which the Home closed, a total of 1,306 seniors graduated from Newman's high school, of which only 97 (7 percent) came from the Home. In any single year, the largest number of Home kids to graduate from Newman occurred in 1939 when the 37 seniors included 9 Home kids.[72] Although the Home kids were a small fraction of Newman graduates, they represented a significant portion of Home peers in their age group. In 1920, for example, the 8 Home kids who graduated from Newman represented more than half of the 15 Home kids who were age sixteen or older.[73]

In May 1905, Newman's faculty identified five "strong pupils" from the Home as candidates for the anticipated high school.[74] Only one of those students, Morris Burka, returned the following year, the others having been reclaimed by relatives. Principal Addicott hailed Burka's academic prowess, claiming the young man illustrated that "some of the very best pupils in the school are from the Home and, on the other hand, some of the worst."[75]

Although Addicott observed that the most common behavioral issues among Home pupils were "dishonesty, impudence, and stubbornness," neither he nor the Home considered, much less sought ways to address, root causes. Despite the manual training approach of nurturing each student's individual abilities, there is no indication that the school or Home made allowances for seriously noncompliant or misbehaving students, regardless of the reason. Then again, even though special education programs were federally mandated in 1975, only recently have educators recognized that childhood trauma and adverse experience can cause and exacerbate disabilities in learning and behavior.[76] Heymann applied what today might be described as a "tough love" approach, explaining to professional colleagues how he had rescued one "very bad boy" from the board's directive to send him to the city's House of Refuge for juvenile delinquents. After Heymann took him to visit the notorious asylum, the boy vowed to improve his behavior.[77]

By definition, every Home child had experienced the death of a parent, or was admitted because one or both parents had been deemed incapable of rearing their children. For example, in 1906 Newman's faculty recommended the dismissal of fourteen-year-old Home student Sarah H., whose father had died from consumption before her tenth birthday. Addicott added, without detailing her behavioral deficiencies, that Sarah's "influence among the younger girls in the Home must be very questionable." Likewise, Addicott condemned fifteen-year-old Dan B.'s behavior and its possible influence on other Home boys. Children "of this character" and age, Addicott wrote, "must certainly exercise a very undesirable influence on younger minds."[78] Addicott did not mention, if he knew, that Dan was one of four motherless brothers admitted to the Home eight years earlier. In both cases, Addicott's concerns and the Home's problems were short-lived. Within a year, the board discharged Sarah to her remarried mother, and Dan to an individual whose relationship to the boy was unrecorded.[79]

While death or dire straits surrounded all Home children, some faced and remarkably managed to overcome extreme circumstances. Harry, Tillie, and Hirsch were the youngest of eight children of Russian immigrants, Abraham and Jennie Goldstein, who made their home in Natchez, Mississippi. The three youngest Goldsteins were admitted to the Home in 1906 after Abraham was condemned to life imprisonment for Jennie's murder.[80] On appeal, after the defense successfully argued that Abraham had not intended to kill Jennie, the court overturned the murder conviction and replaced it with manslaughter. Mississippi's governor later pardoned Abraham, conditioned on his permanent exile from the state.[81] These legal distinctions, however, could not change the fact that the children had witnessed the death of their mother at the hands of their father. Despite the tragedy, the children garnered no unfavorable mention during their time at Newman School, and in the Home each was elected to a position of leadership.[82] After their discharges at ages seventeen and fifteen to an older, married sister, Tillie and Hirsch moved to Corpus Christi, Texas, where she became a homemaker, and he ran an oil-field supply company and was active in his Temple.[83] Hirsch considered "the highlights" of his life the years he spent in the Home.[84] After high school, with funds from the Home, Harry attended pharmacy school, graduating with top grades. Following Navy service in the First World War, Harry returned to New Orleans, where he worked as a clothing wholesaler, married, and raised a family.[85]

THE HOME CHILDREN IN THEIR NEW SCHOOL

Amid scant firsthand accounts of the school's early years are indications that the children appreciated the educational opportunities they received. Because she thought it would interest readers, seventeen-year-old Fannie Cohen wrote in a 1908 letter published in *Young Israel*, a national Jewish children's magazine, that her manual training school was "not only for regular class work" but "also for extra work" such as "cooking, sewing, gymnastics and a few others."[86] The same year, fifteen-year-old Pearl Metzner provided a more expansive view of her school in the address she delivered at the Home's anniversary. "There we are met by our little friends from all parts and conditions of the city, with whom together we, in friendly combat, strive and struggle for recognition, and in which we sometimes succeed; and if we do not, we feel that we are equals before the law. We know that we have had every opportunity to reach out for the highest within our grasp."[87] Pearl's remarks and her school earned a write-up in the newspaper. "The Home is to be congratulated if little Miss Pearl is a sample of the splendid physical health of its wards, not to say of the manual training received by them."[88]

Further evidencing opportunities equally afforded to Home children and their paying classmates, the school's 1908 Founder's Day Program featured tributes to Isidore Newman that Pearl and two pay pupils delivered.[89] The next year, Home student Yolande Weiss, a motherless Hungarian immigrant, shared the 1909 Founder's Day spotlight with pay pupil Frederick D. Parham, a physician's son. Yolande discussed "Our Opportunity for Industrial Training," which for the girls still consisted of domestic skills, while Frederick spoke about "Our Opportunity for College Preparation."[90] The apparent assignment of topics according to gender recalled one of the original forces driving Leucht's push for a training school—the perceived "over-education" of Home girls in academics and their lack of preparedness to become homemakers. This force was strongly endorsed early in the school's history. One year earlier, Principal Addicott extolled the school's model kitchen and dining rooms for "giving our girls an opportunity to become good housewives and good housekeepers, preparing them to develop one day into real, reliable helpmates, for which woman, in my opinion, has been principally created."[91] Adding incentive to become reliable helpmates, since 1900, Home girls who married received $150 from the Simon Gumbel Dowry Fund.[92] These views reflected the sensibilities of New Orleans's prominent women, who were then calling for "schools of domestic science" to address the "servant problem," which one proponent described as, "How can the housekeeper train her servants if she herself be incapable and ignorant of the art?"[93] While Frederick Parham went on to graduate from Tulane University and become an architect, Yolande Weiss used her Newman education to exceed the housebound life expected of her. After her 1912 discharge to an older sister, Yolande moved to Phoenix, Arizona, where she worked as a public health nurse and made news for averaging thirteen visits per day on behalf of the county's antituberculosis society.[94]

Little is known of the experiences of the community children who received scholarships, which in any case turned out to be short-term. Without explanation, Leucht reported at the close of the 1906 school year, "Under the rules adopted, there are no more scholarships, and those now existing will cease as the pupils holding them leave the school."[95] Although Isidore Newman had earlier publicly described the school's objective as also educating "the poor of other denominations," he neither restricted his gift in this manner nor objected to ending the scholarships.[96] Consequently, when those scholarship students graduated or left, Home children received their Newman education exclusively with children whose parents could afford to pay tuition.[97]

Throughout the following decades, Home children encountered the lifestyles of classmates from the city's wealthiest families. In 1913, third-grader Sam Pulitzer met classmate Isidore "Dede" Newman, grandson of the school's namesake, who arrived at school with his brother, Leon "Red," in a chauffeur-driven limousine. Just seeing the big car pull up and the two small boys get out, said Pulitzer, "was a wondrous event," prompting kids to line up along the fence. Pulitzer believed his friendship with Dede was the envy of many Home boys. "I shudder to think what they might have done if they had known about the sandwiches Dede brought for me from his house."[98]

As with Sam and Dede, the lives of other Home kids intertwined with their city peers. On occasion, Newman students visited the orphanage for cultural events or to socialize with friends; some were even envious of a place offering round-the-clock playmates with whom to play hide-and-seek or make hot chocolate on the radiator.[99] In 1922, Newman high school students, including two Home girls, presented an operetta on the Home's third floor.[100] When issues arose from socioeconomic differences, the Home and the school attempted to address them. In 1920, for example, to buffer the disparity in clothing budgets, the board requested that the school enforce a policy of simplicity of dress at graduation.[101] In 1923, after two Home girls attended a classmate's lavish outing, the honorary matrons helped the girls host a party to reciprocate.[102] Adopting the attitude of the schools' founders, one alumna viewed mixing Newman and Home kids as beneficial for both groups. Home kids got to know wealthy people and see "the better side of things," while the interaction prompted wealthy kids to dispel any negative preconceptions of Home kids and see "another side" of life.[103]

Alumni accounts of their reactions to, and relationships with, their Newman classmates, much like their time in the Home, are highly individualized and varied. Helen Lubow Sizeler and Bessie Mashinka Rothstein are among alumni who recounted being invited to classmates' homes and parties and making "good friends with a lot of them."[104] Joe Samuels dined "many a time" at the home of Newman classmate and lifelong friend David Schwartz, son of Home president Ralph Schwarz. Jimmy Whitehead dated popular Newman schoolmate Catherine Cahn Kahn, and Rose Sherman Meadow married a fellow Newman alumnus.[105] Janet Loeb Pfeifer, who was in the Home from 1930 to 1935, said of her "wonderful" high school years at Newman, "We were never looked down on."[106] Ellis Hart, too, recalled the Home kids "were not treated differently."[107]

At the same time, Albert Fox described feeling "inferior" at Newman and "not wanting it known that I was a Home kid."[108] Hannah Golden Limerick, who was in the Home from 1935 to 1942, said that Newman kids "didn't interact with us" and that "we were pretty much segregated."[109] During his time in school, Pat Samuels, too, thought that his Newman classmates "looked upon us as not equal," although he later considered them among his dearest friends, prompting him to travel regularly from Houston to New Orleans for many years to gather for lunch with former schoolmates.[110] Louis Peters summarized the irony of the excellent education he received in the company of his prosperous Newman classmates. "Only two classes of society could afford the cost of tuition. The children of the affluent and the children of the Home."[111]

Whatever difficulties some experienced in adjusting to wealthy classmates, Home children garnered an impressive record of achievement at Newman School. For years, despite their small numbers, Home kids distinguished themselves in academics, as athletic champions and team captains, and played leading roles in theatrical and musical performances, in school governance, and as commencement speakers.[112] Between 1935 and 1943 alone, at least eight of seventeen Home kids who graduated from Newman won prizes or scholastic honors.[113] In 1944, Morris Skalka, who was also commencement speaker, likely set a Newman record by winning six graduation awards and honors, including the boys' athletic prize for his prowess in football, basketball, and track, the prize for school spirit and endeavor, the best examination on the U.S. Constitution, and induction into the National Honor Society.[114] According to Newman schoolmate Catherine Cahn Kahn, students like Skalka were known as "typical Home kid overachievers."[115] Many went on to become lawyers, social workers, psychologists, teachers, and other professionals.[116] "I'm not atypical," said Home alumnus and 1947 Newman graduate James Whitehead, who became associate professor and head law librarian at William and Mary Law School. "I'm just one of the ordinary kids from the Home given the best education and support from the Jewish community."[117]

ADDICOTT'S RESIGNATION AND HEYMANN'S RETIREMENT

After nearly four years in the role, Principal Addicott submitted his resignation, effective May 1909.[118] Despite Isidore Newman's entreaties to reconsider, Addicott returned to California for the remainder of his teaching career.[119] Fortunately, the board thought highly of former assistant principal Clarence C. Henson, a Columbia University–trained educator whom Addicott hired at the school's founding, and quickly promoted him to principal.[120] With only two years' interruption to superintend the Rapides Parish schools, Henson remained in the position until 1947.[121]

Also in 1909, the board began to look for Heymann's successor. Despite his current good health and fitness, he was seventy-one years old (at a time when average male life expectancy was fifty) and had recovered from a serious health scare two years earlier. He had offered to retire, but Home leaders urged him to stay on as long as he was able.[122] Heymann had reached the pinnacle of his career. In addition to Home superintendent, he had served as president of both the city's Prison and Asylum Commission and the Charity Organization Society of New Orleans, and as vice president of the State Board of Charities and Commissions, which he helped create to coordinate charitable and public institutions. Between 1893 and 1905, three successive Louisiana governors appointed him as a delegate to four international conferences on charities and prisons, where he spoke on a range of issues affecting the care and treatment of dependent children and juvenile offenders.[123] Among his greatest and earliest passions was the field of kindergartens, reflected by his lengthy service on the local Board of Free Kindergartens, one of which was named in his honor.[124]

Apart from gratitude regularly expressed to him by Home wards and alumni in formal speeches, over the last year of Heymann's tenure several Home children wrote about him in letters published in *Young Israel*. After describing her school, Fannie Cohen wrote, "Mr. Heymann is our rabbi and we all certainly love him."[125] Eva Levenberg and Pauline Yarutzky described the secret "charity and good deeds" club they were inspired to form after listening to one of his Sabbath sermons.[126] In their letters, Yolande Weiss and Leon Clausner were as pleased with the top grades they earned in Heymann's Hebrew class as the popular books he awarded them as prizes: *The Five Little Peppers* for Yolande and *Uncle Tom's Cabin* for Leon.[127] Beyond his influence as rabbi and Hebrew instructor, Heymann paid attention to the indelicate minutiae that enhanced the Home children's lives, such as their preference for a particular brand of "Prickly Heat and Baby Powder," an antidote for New Orleans's hot and sticky climate.[128]

In September 1908, while in Chicago for a conference, Heymann suffered a cerebral hemorrhage that partially paralyzed him. Reverend Leucht quickly traveled to the hospital bedside of his ailing, unconscious friend. Within two weeks, Heymann had sufficiently improved to return to New Orleans, but his physician cautioned him to limit his work.[129] By mid-November, Heymann resigned. He and Valentine moved out of the Home to a residence a few blocks away.[130]

On April 28, 2009, just four months after the Home had been placed in his successor's hands, Heymann died with his family and Reverend Leucht by his side. At his funeral in his Valence Street home, Leucht delivered the eulogy. Reportedly interrupted by the "sobs and tears" of the Home's ladies and children, Leucht spoke of Heymann's quarter-century of work for organizations that distributed mercy, charity, and benevolence. Reflecting the breadth of his contributions, Heymann's honorary pallbearers included not only Home leaders and school principal Clarence Henson, but also gentile civic and philanthropic leaders representing the city and state. The active pallbearers were all alumni of the Home from Heymann's tenure, including Max Frishman, who had delivered the 1896 anniversary oration.[131]

Tributes to Heymann's life appeared around the country, attesting to his leadership in national discussions and organizational networks. *Charities* magazine described Heymann as "one of the best known workers in the field of modern care of orphans," and "one of the best loved figures in the New Orleans world of social service."[132] The American Prison Association published a glowing eulogy written by Rev. William J. Batt, president of the national correctional chaplains' association.[133] Heymann likely would have been most pleased by the obituary in Houston's *Jewish Herald* newspaper that was written by the paper's founder and proprietor, Edgar Goldberg, who spent the last four of his seven years in the Home under Heymann's "loving care." Now age thirty-three, eighteen years since his discharge, Goldberg remained deeply grateful to the Home and Heymann for setting his future on sound footing. He described the Home as "that dearly beloved institution over in New Orleans" and, until his death in 1937, regularly reported on the Home and encouraged his readers to support it financially.[134]

Among the former superintendent's highest tributes was an invitation from President Theodore Roosevelt to attend the White House Conference on Dependent Children in January 1909, a gathering that would alter the course of American dependent childcare. In his letter, foretelling the conference's landmark consensus, Roosevelt expressed his personal belief "that the best way in which to care for dependent children is in the family home." He noted that in some states orphans were no longer housed in asylums, but instead were placed, often by religious associations, in private homes as boarders, with payment from private or public treasuries, or as adoptees.[135] No representative from the Home took Heymann's place among the two hundred childcare leaders who attended from across the country.

Heymann's headstone in the Jewish cemetery was carved with his most important title, "Sup't Jewish Orphans' Home."[136] He had overseen the orphanage's move to its new building on St. Charles Avenue and nurtured its kindergarten, while restoring the Home's reputation after the scandal inflicted by his predecessor. In all, Heymann touched the lives of more than five hundred children admitted during his tenure and strove to improve their experiences in the Home.[137]

Beyond his accomplishments and the children's individual experiences, questions remain whether Heymann could have used his passion, expertise, and considerable authority in other ways to enhance dependent childcare. He had recognized the importance of contacting alumni to determine how each was faring, but the extent to which he (and they) succeeded was neither publicly reported nor otherwise preserved. Following the Home's wards might have led to improvements in the Home and school, while offering support for recently discharged alumni.[138] Moreover, in the face of mounting criticism of institutional childcare from other parts of the country, which Heymann acknowledged if not embraced, he did not encourage the board to pursue alternatives. Instead, whether prompted by the local prevailing attachment to institutional care or disdain for recent immigrant parents, Heymann and the board flatly insisted—without trying—that placing children in private homes would be futile or unwise. Above all, Heymann's sudden death punctuated the end of his lengthy, productive, and generally beloved tenure, and the beginning of another era for the Home.

REV. JAMES K. GUTHEIM

JOSEPH SIMON

JOSEPH MAGNER

JOSEPH H. MARKS

MEYER M. SIMPSON

GEORGE JONAS

When demands for relief from recent yellow fever epidemics overwhelmed New Orleans's existing Hebrew benevolent societies, Joseph Simon, Rev. James K. Gutheim, and Joseph Magner convened a "Mass Meeting of the Israelites" of the city in November 1854. By March 1855, the Association for the Relief of Jewish Widows and Orphans was formed, with Joseph H. Marks and George Jonas among the founding members who elected Meyer M. Simpson as president. He served until 1865, when George Jonas succeeded him. All photos courtesy of JCRS.

"The Jewish Home," by George François Mugnier, ca. 1880. Originally located at Jackson and Chippewa streets, the Home opened its doors on February 1, 1856, to twelve Jewish orphans and half orphans and one widow. To accommodate the growing population, the Home's board later bought the adjacent property and erected an addition before moving in 1887 to St. Charles Avenue. Courtesy of the Collections of the Louisiana State Museum, 09813.514.1.

MRS. H. NEWMAN   MRS. L. KLOPMAN   MRS. M. LEMANN

MRS. A. HABER   MRS. J. W. MOSES   MRS. H. ABRAHAM

MRS. M. GODCHAUX   MRS. J. WEIS

In addition to significant cash and in-kind contributions by female members of sewing circles and synagogues throughout the mid-South, an estimated one hundred women served as honorary matrons who, among other duties, visited the children on assigned days. The women shown here served as directress of honorary matrons, beginning with Miriam Jung Haber, who held the position for more than a decade, followed by Caroline Beer Klopman, Rosine Kahn Godchaux, Carrie Mayer Weis, Alice Goldsmith Abraham, Carrie Abraham Lemann, Henrietta Weilman Newman, and Irma Moses Moses. Diamond Jubilee Program Book, 1930, courtesy of JCRS.

The Home's constitution mandated that the children attend synagogue on "Sabbaths and Festivals," a duty fulfilled by men the board hired to teach Hebrew and biblical history. Among them was Rabbi Emanuel M. Rosenfelder, whom the board hired in 1875. When Rosenfelder resigned a year later to serve Temple B'nai Israel in Natchez, Mississippi, he received the board's twofold approval; they also blessed his marriage to Sarah Adler, a sixteen-year-old ward whose parents had died of yellow fever, thus ensuring her an "honorable settlement in life." Both photos courtesy of Susan Katz Miller.

Built in 1887 on St. Charles Avenue, the Home was declared a "magnificent monument to Hebrew benevolence." Designed by architect Thomas Sully, the Home, seen here in 1940, comprised four buildings around a central courtyard, ringed by wide galleries. The girls' dormitory, on the right, ran parallel to today's Jefferson Avenue, while the boys' dormitory ran parallel to Leontine Street. The large structure easily accommodated its changing population, which reached a peak of 173 children only briefly in 1915. Courtesy of JCRS.

The Home's synagogue, 1905. The new Home featured a synagogue in which the children attended worship services on Sabbaths, holy days, and festivals, following Reform traditions. Courtesy of JCRS.

Superintendent Michel Heymann, seated at left, leads a religious class in the Home, ca. 1890. The Hebrew words "Shalom Aleichem," meaning "Peace be upon you," appear on the blackboard; above them two English phrases impart the success ethic the Home sought to instill in its wards: "Man is the architect of his own fortune," and "Knowledge is power." Courtesy of JCRS.

Dormitory, ca. 1890. In keeping with current standards for institutional childcare, the children's sleeping quarters in the new Home were praised for ventilation and light, as well as cleanliness and efficiency. The Home did not prioritize individuality and privacy until the mid-1920s. Courtesy of the Collections of the Louisiana State Museum, T0400.1990.06.11.

Dining room, ca. 1890 and 1940. Regimentation and efficiency were also paramount in institutional dining in the Home's early years. By 1905, chairs replaced long wooden benches, and tablecloths appeared for Sabbaths and holidays. By the mid-1920s, to emulate family dining, the children ate with siblings in groups of six to eight at small tables, each set with distinctive dishware. Top photo, courtesy of the Collections of the Louisiana State Museum, T0400.1990.06.10; bottom photo, courtesy of JCRS.

Kindergarten, ca. 1890. Launched in 1883, the Home's "garden of children" employed the principles of German educator Friedrich Froebel, who advocated the "mothering" of young pupils ages three to six with songs, games, and dances. The floor's divided and concentric circles, shown above, were painted in primary colors to stimulate the senses and encourage movement. The kindergarten remained in the Home until 1907, when it was transferred to the Isidore Newman Manual Training School. Courtesy of the Collections of the Louisiana State Museum. T0400.1990.06.05.

In 1904, with funding from banker and philanthropist Isidore Newman, the Home opened the Isidore Newman Manual Training School, seen here in 1905. The school's cutting-edge curriculum taught manual skills, such as home economics and woodworking, to enhance academic learning. From its founding, the coed, nonsectarian school, which admitted children from the community whose parents paid tuition, quickly became and remains one of the city's finest college preparatory schools. Courtesy of JCRS.

Long before the Home band was organized in 1902, the board provided individual music, voice, and dancing instruction to interested children. Shown in 1903 with bandmaster Professor Johann Wunsch, *back row,* Home Band members included Henry Hirsch, *second from left;* Julius Stabinski, *seventh from left;* Harry Caplan, *seventh from right;* Harry's brother Mike Caplan, *fourth from right;* and Marcus Korn, *second from right.* By the early 1920s, Home girls formed a guitar-and-mandolin club and joined the Home band. Courtesy of JCRS.

In 1890, Abraham Yarutzky, founding president of the Home's alumni association, called upon peers to repay their "inestimable obligation" for the "kindness and tender care" they had received in their youth. Alumni shown here, ca. 1909, include Judith Korn (dark dress) and Esther Korn (white blouse) seated *at far right;* their sister Rose Korn, standing, *second from right;* and Leslie Greenwald, standing, *top row, third from left.* Hannah Frishman, alumni president from 1902 to 1909, is seated *at the middle of the table.* Courtesy of JCRS and Leslie H. Greenwald.

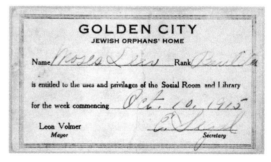

GOLDEN CITY
JEWISH ORPHANS' HOME

Name _____ Rank _____

is entitled to the uses and privileges of the Social Room and Library

for the week commencing _____

Leon Volmer
Mayor

Secretary

Lauded when introduced by Superintendent Chester Teller in 1909, the Golden City was the Home's system of self-governance. The children were divided into "families" run by elected Big Brothers and Big Sisters, some of whom are shown here with "Mayor" Teller. Good citizenship and behavior earned weekly privilege cards (*below right*), which entitled the bearer to outings or use of the social room. Each Fourth of July, the outstanding boy and girl who earned the greatest number of cards received a gold medal (*below left*). Top photo courtesy of JCRS; Max Mendelsohn's Golden City Medallion, 1916, courtesy of Joan Mendelsohn Mehlman; Moses Lew's Golden City Privilege Card, 1915, courtesy of JCRS.

As shown here in 1916 with Superintendent Leon Volmer, Home children celebrated the fall festival of Sukkot by eating meals in the Sukkah they built and decorated. Volmer, an ordained rabbi, proudly described the children's observance of Jewish holidays and Sabbaths, when "the boys pronounce the B'rochoch [blessings] before and after reading the Torah, and the girls read the Hapthtorah and all of the children recite the Hebrew responses and the Kaddish." Courtesy of JCRS.

Nursery children with caregivers, ca. 1920. Given the high risk of illness and death, the Home was among few Jewish orphanages that admitted very young children. In the early 1920s, Nurse Cecile Holleman (*standing at left*) divided her time between the infirmary and the nursery, where Black women served as the youngsters' primary caregivers as was the custom among middle- and upper-class families in New Orleans. Courtesy of JCRS.

Summer camp at Bay St. Louis, ca. 1922. Beginning in 1918, Home children spent several weeks each summer at the Jewish Charitable and Educational Federation's Gulf Coast camp in Bay St. Louis, Mississippi. As advocated by Superintendent Leon Volmer, summer camp got the children out of their daily routine and into nature with fresh air and open water. Swimming in the Gulf, fishing from a rowboat or pier, hiking in the woods, and the fifty-mile train ride aboard the Louisville & Nashville Railroad were summer camp highlights. Both photos courtesy of JCRS.

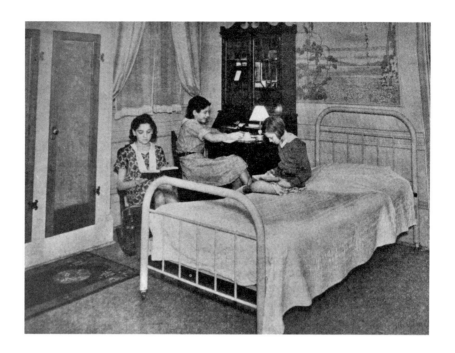

In 1926, as part of his plan to "deinstitutionalize" the Home, Superintendent L. Edward Lashman began to dramatically transform the children's long and sparse dormitories into small, personalized bedrooms (*above*) and study rooms (*facing page*), a reform that was completed three years later by his successor, Harry L. Ginsburg. Both photos date from 1932. Both photos courtesy of JCRS.

In 1926, to integrate the children into the community, Superintendent Lashman closed the Home synagogue and sent the children to the city's three Reform congregations for religious education and worship. In 1925, the last children confirmed in the Home's synagogue (although not necessarily in the order pictured here) were Helen Lubow, Rachel Tannenbaum, Beulah Blondheim, Rosalie Gordon, Rachel Crystal, Etta Miller, Minnie Berebes, Florence Heilbron, Sidney Breen, Morris Offricht, and Louis Turansky. Courtesy of JCRS.

Reflecting the community's generous attention to Home children and the popularity of motion pictures, in the spring of 1926 silent-film stars Lois Wilson, Eileen Percy, and Leatrice Joy (*hatted, left to right*) visited the Home and posed with dozens of children for a photo. Courtesy of JCRS.

Superintendent Harry L. ("Uncle Harry") Ginsburg, who championed the Home's "homelike" ethos, frequently appeared in photographs and articles bearing captions such as "Home Sweet Home" and "The Institution That Is Not an Institution." Here, in 1930, Ginsburg reads to a group of Home children, including Lee (or his twin Sam) Hartman (*standing at left of Ginsburg*), while Helen Eldrich and Milton Fruchtgarten are seated *at right of Ginsburg*. Courtesy of JCRS.

Although the constitution originally slated the event during the festival of "Hannuckah," the Home actually celebrated its anniversary on or near January 8, in honor of General Andrew Jackson's victory in the Battle of New Orleans. For years, orations by rabbis and thought leaders highlighted the day but were later outshone by children's performances. Among the children who participated in the 1932 presentation of Claude Debussy's ballet *Box of Toys*, were: *standing, from left,* Albert Fox (a duck), Alice Naibert, Van Hart, Florette Gordon, and Donald Gordon (another duck); *seated,* Freda Hyde and Helen Garb. From "Will Appear in Home Celebration," *Item-Tribune,* January 3, 1932. With permission of Capital City Press/ Georges Media Group, Baton Rouge.

In January 1960, more than two hundred alumni, spouses, former staff, and friends convened for a gala reunion celebration. The four alumni pictured here are, *from left,* Judge Louis Yarrut, president of the alumni association and the Home's board; Joe Samuels, publisher of the *Houston Jewish Herald Voice* and master of ceremonies; Barbara Winn Grishman, age twenty-three, the youngest alumnus present; and Louis Fuerst, age sixty-six, oldest alumnus present. From "Jewish Children's Home Alumni Will Gather," *Times-Picayune,* January 24, 1960. With permission of Capital City Press/Georges Media Group, Baton Rouge.

chapter seven

CHESTER TELLER'S
GOLDEN CITY
1909–1911

On New Year's Day 1909, Chester Jacob Teller entered the lives of the Home children. At twenty-five, he was handsome and approachable, dynamic and opinionated, with a broad, easy smile and a round, boyish face.[1] Like a nova star, Teller briefly illuminated the Home's sky, serving as superintendent for less than three years. Resulting from what President Gabe Kahn described only as a "conflict of views" over the "plans and methods" of the Home's Manual Training School, Teller resigned before 1911 ended.[2] As the new superintendent, however, he brought enduring changes.

Teller's arrival at the Home coincided with the First White House Conference on the Care of Dependent Children in January 1909—the event that illness prevented Michel Heymann from attending. The conference concluded with a highly publicized consensus among the nation's foremost advocates in dependent childcare: "Home life is the highest and finest product of civilization. Children should not be deprived of it, except for urgent and compelling reasons."[3] Despite this belief, institutional care of dependent children did not immediately cease. Notwithstanding general agreement *in principle* with the consensus, the White House conference prompted few if any institutional managers to close their doors or even drastically reduce enrollments. To the contrary, in most states orphan asylums continued to care for more children than were aided by either mothers' pensions or foster care until the next decade.[4] In the world of Jewish dependent childcare, between 1910 and 1930, when the Pauline Stern Wolff Home opened in Houston, twenty-one Jewish orphanages opened in twelve different states, almost doubling the already existing twenty-eight American Jewish orphanages.[5]

Even at the White House Conference, attendees recognized that prospective foster homes needed to be carefully investigated by competent people and intelligently inspected after children were placed. "Unless and until such homes are found," the conference also decreed, "the use of institutions is necessary."[6] To avoid fruitless controversy among its participants, the chairman of the social workers section at the 1910 National Conference of Jewish Charities, while continuing to explore the feasibility of alternatives to institutional care, took a pragmatic approach: "The majority of Jewish children requiring public care will, for a long time, be cared for in institutions, and that it is, therefore, our duty to maintain our institutions at the high plane of efficiency which they have hitherto occupied, and to adapt to their various needs all progressive improvements in institutional management."[7] While the White House Conference spurred other institutions to pursue ways to keep or place dependent children with their own or other families, the Home continued to devote its energies to improving the institutional lives of its children, a task for which Chester Teller promised exciting new methods.

To marry and start a new job in a new city thirteen hundred miles away within a month would overwhelm most people.[8] Teller, however, embraced the adventure, buoyed by a life of successes. In many ways, he embodied the prevailing American Reform Jewish ideals of education, financial security, social acceptance, and community service—all while maintaining allegiance to the religion. Lacking any obvious Hebrew equivalent, even his given name, Chester—whether a nod to then sitting U.S. president Chester A. Arthur or the Pennsylvania county in which the family resided—suggests his American-born parents intended for him to partake in all that America offered. This is likely just as Teller's grandfather, Rafael, had hoped when he emigrated from Bavaria in 1842 to flee antisemitic restrictions. Thanks to the family's tobacco-trading business, Chester enjoyed a comfortable childhood that included travel to his ancestral German village.[9] Demonstrating a penchant for public speaking, Teller was a winning debater and commencement orator at Philadelphia's Central High School. As one of few, if any other, Jewish students at Haverford College, Teller graduated in 1905 with a Phi Beta Kappa key and honors in political science and philosophy. He won academic prizes and a fellowship that propelled his master's degree at Haverford, followed by a summer studying philosophy and pedagogy at Germany's University of Jena.[10]

Teller embarked on a career in social work, an interest he explored in his college thesis, "The Social Settlement in Theory and Practice," and in a debate where he argued that American Jewish immigration, to address congested ghettos and ensuing xenophobia, should be redirected from large cities to lesser-populated areas.[11] Teller's interests reflected American Jewish philanthropic responses of the day, such as settlement houses that offered community services and the diversion efforts of the Galveston movement, to assist Jews fleeing Eastern European pogroms and to forestall immigration restrictions.[12] He soon headed to New York City to direct boys' clubs for the Educational Alliance, which provided academic and cultural programs for immigrant Jews and other urban poor. After a year, he accepted a similar position overseeing boys' clubs with New York's Hebrew Sheltering Guardian Society orphan asylum (HSGS), where he soon won promotion to assistant superintendent.[13] Having discovered "how little a $5 bill" or "one or two laws" will do to relieve a family's distress, Teller instead sought to achieve social reform through education, which he viewed as the "truest kind of social work." He had decided to devote his efforts to those "who need them most, namely, the homeless children."[14]

Dwarfing the Home, HSGS then housed nearly 1,000 children, ages five to fourteen, and oversaw an additional 260 children placed in homes as part of the program it initiated four years earlier when B'nai B'rith abandoned its proposed national placement bureau.[15] Teller had been hired by HSGS superintendent Ludwig Bernstein, a charismatic educator who introduced sweeping reforms to give his charges more freedom and social interaction. In addition to creating opportunities for "healthy and unrestrained play," Bernstein abolished the "monitoring" system, still used at the Home, in which asylum staff chose older children to help enforce order among their peers, often in a rigid and militaristic manner.[16] Like other institutional reformers across the country, Bernstein had been inspired by the George Junior Republic, an experimental institution founded in 1895 for delinquent and abandoned children by social welfare visionary William R. George in Freeville, New York. As America was moving to protect children from the adult world by passing child labor and compulsory education laws, the junior republic movement emerged to encourage youngsters to play adult roles as lawmakers and managers within the institutions that sheltered them.[17]

As the name suggests, George Junior Republic was structured like a city-state in which children acted as citizens and legislators.[18] Following that model, Bernstein oversaw self-governing boys' and girls' republics that mimicked New

York City's government. With rights and responsibilities spelled out in an elaborate constitution, HSGS's republics—led by peer-elected borough presidents and city councilmen—helped govern the institution and ran a savings bank, cooperative store, and library. Michael Sharlitt, who grew up in HSGS during Bernstein's tenure and later superintended CJOA, extolled his alma mater's self-governing system: "The Republics were a dramatic development, not altogether understood and possibly not appreciated at first by the children themselves, and their establishment was doubtless one of the earliest, if not the earliest, move to recognize the elementary citizenship of children in the sense of partnership in the family. For dependent children, it was a kind of enfranchisement."[19]

As Bernstein's assistant, Teller experienced firsthand the value of giving children—especially dependent children who needed to fend for themselves earlier than most youngsters—a vehicle for self-expression and some control over their lives. Although Teller was highly regarded at HSGS and had developed a strong bond with Bernstein, he was drawn to the leadership opportunity presented by Michel Heymann's retirement. The Home, a small and respected asylum, with its acclaimed manual training school, was perfectly suited for an ambitious and idealistic social worker like Teller. In turn, the board saw in Teller the energy, passion, and an exciting new method to enhance their institution. Despite any opportunity the new superintendent also presented for the Home to adopt HSGS's methods for placing out children, neither Teller nor the board would seize it.

Before starting his new job, however, Teller attended to personal affairs. While still in New York, he married Eva Magnes. Then twenty-seven, Eva had returned to New York after graduating from the University of California at Berkeley a few years earlier. She was a good match for Teller, having grown up in a family committed to education and activism, including her brother Judah Magnes, an influential educator and social activist who served as associate rabbi at New York's Temple Emanu-El.[20] Unlike the wives of prior superintendents, Eva did not serve as matron or other official role in the Home. Instead, in addition to caring for the two children she would soon bear, she was at liberty to engage in community activities.[21]

Once in New Orleans, Teller lost no time infusing the Home with his childcare ideas. While pledging to continue Heymann's "far-sighted" pursuit of the "sacred cause" of "upbuilding" human character, he disdained any childcare institution—whether huge congregate barracks or the small cottages that were becoming a popular replacement—where walls remained blank and children were cautioned to tread lightly, so that order and cleanliness prevailed at the expense of their young souls. Underrating a child's capacity to understand and to suffer, in Teller's view, led to disregard for the child's loyalty to his toys and trinkets, which held a "whole bundle of fancies, dreams, emotions" essential for development.[22] Believing that any policy or action must be done "for" the children, he scoffed at sister institutions who orchestrated their children to "march the streets in long orphan processions," forsaking "energetic action and self-expression." Teller even convinced the board to briefly depart from the anniversary custom of requiring the children's attendance throughout the orations and reports. It was only to the adults' advantage, he argued, to have the children sit in rows and "delight us with their inimitable charm . . . while we grown-ups rehearse the record of our benefactions toward them."[23]

Drawing directly from HSGS, Teller introduced "the Golden City," a system of self-government and clubs. Teller believed this comprehensive program would prepare Home children to become independent adults and useful citizens by giving them what he considered meaningful control over their affairs. Unlike HSGS's bureaucratic-sounding "Republics," however, "Golden City" evoked aspiration and idealism, a place of possibilities. Seeking to create a community, he retained HSGS's miniature government while introducing as its basic component a feature otherwise absent in an orphanage—the family.[24] The Golden City consisted of a Brotherhood and a Sisterhood, which were further divided into these "families," each comprising seven to eight Dwellers and Builders, a sufficiently small number so that each child could fulfill an individual, age-appropriate role. Every child started out as a Dweller, without voting rights, who by age and demonstrated ability to contribute to the household became eligible to move into the voting class of Builders. Each family elected its leader, a "Big Brother" or "Big Sister," who convened weekly meetings to discuss concerns and assign tasks. These family heads were expected to lead by example, modeling manners at mealtime or taking younger members by hand to school.[25] Yet Teller conceded that the Golden City's family groups could never replace a child's real family and that even the best-run asylum could never replace a real home.[26]

Big Brothers and Big Sisters, in turn, were governed by a president and other top officers they elected for a term of six months. In their separate and regular meetings, these young leaders handled the weightiest questions, presented committee reports, and enacted new laws. With the superintendent serving as "Mayor," Teller and his small staff acted as an advisory board of commissioners with certain executive and judicial powers. By combining the family structure with a degree of self-government, said Teller, the children learned the "virtues of cooperation and the spirit of tolerance."[27] According to Teller, the wards took their new roles seriously. "How real it all is to the youthful legislators!" he remarked about his Golden citizens, "Surely there is nothing playful about this, and yet it savors as little of work."[28]

Just as progressive American parenting experts were popularizing the concept of giving spending money to children to teach decision making, Teller introduced allowances to the Home, allocating nearly $400 a year to provide each child a sum commensurate with merit.[29] He created cooperative stores, where the children could use their allowances to buy pencils, stationery, and other small notions. Under the management of peer storekeepers, the children used the shop's profits to benefit the entire community: gifts, decorations for the Home, defraying the costs of making costumes for their Chanukah play, or buying traditional *shalach manos* treats for the festival of Purim. Supervised by peer garden officers, the girls sold flowers and the boys marketed vegetables, all grown on the Home's grounds. The families used the proceeds to buy presents for members' birthdays, self-esteem-boosting celebrations that received little attention before Teller's arrival.[30]

The Golden City also featured a system of discipline that relied on rewards and punishments. To boys and girls who had demonstrated good citizenship in their behavior, appearance, and completion of chores over the prior week, the family awarded Golden City cards. These brightly colored paper cards afforded privileges, such as use of the social room or library. Whoever earned the greatest number of cards over each year was eligible to win a coveted Golden City medal, an engraved gold medallion. Sam Koltun, the medal's ever-proud recipient in 1911, years later made it into a locket for his wife.[31] The award ceremonies and installation of new officers took place on July 4, fusing the children's patriotism with their loyalty to the Golden City.[32] Providing the metaphorical "stick" to the privilege cards and awards' "carrots," the Brotherhood and Sisterhood officers adjudicated alleged infractions of the rules of conduct and meted out punishments. Brotherhood and Sisterhood presidents served as judges while other top officers served as prosecutors to present charges and as clerks to record the proceedings.[33]

From the children's perspective, none of whom had experienced any superintendent other than Michel Heymann, Teller was a whirlwind of youthful energy and activity. He sought to instill that energy in his charges. He embodied the spirit of the nation's playground movement, which had started at the end of the nineteenth century as child labor was losing favor. Providing designated outdoor spaces for physical activity and games, urged playground advocates, improved children's health and social development while it kept them out of trouble.[34] Although the children enjoyed Newman School's state-of-the-art gymnasium during their structured physical education classes, the Home was not equally equipped. Teller transformed the Home's center courtyard into a miniature park with a gazebo and garden, offering spaces for the youngest children to play with dolls and toys. Although Teller removed the long wire fence that divided the courtyard, boys and girls above nursery age continued to play separately, or at separate times, albeit now on a new playground, equipped with seesaws, swings, sand piles, swinging ropes, and ladders.[35] "What we aim here to achieve," said Teller, "is an environment that breathes the spirit of play." To guide and encourage the children's participation in team sports or simple foot races, Teller hired an assistant who served as the Home's first "Director of Play."[36]

Teller also incorporated the children's religious education into the Golden City. Unlike Heymann, Teller thought the quality of Hebrew religious education was measured by how and not which books were used. Instead of the *cheder* or traditional style of teaching elementary Judaism and Hebrew, which he criticized for treating Hebrew as an end rather than a means, Teller sought to tap into the children's natural sense of wonder and humor. He let the children imagine themselves living with Abraham in Canaan, or going down into Egypt to meet the dreamer, Joseph. He viewed the Sabbath and festival holidays as ripe with similar opportunities for imitation and expression.[37] No alumni recollections or outside sources exist, however, to confirm or refute Teller's accounts of his progressive methods of religious education.

To supplement the medical care the children had been receiving, Teller introduced two new clinics in the Home, intended to treat daily scrapes and discomforts before they turned into serious medical problems. In the dental clinic, open twice a week, a visiting dentist regularly examined every child's teeth and treated them as needed. In the medical clinic, each day as many as thirty youngsters appeared, presenting everything from routine chapped lips and splinters to those with more serious ailments of the eyes, ears, or throat.[38] To oversee these efforts, Teller hired the Home's first trained nurse, who called upon a greatly expanded team of consulting physicians as needed.[39]

The Golden City bureaucracy, too, encompassed health. Peer clinic officers' duties included "to take a general interest in the health of all members of the City, and to advise them, particularly the younger ones, when to visit the clinic."[40]

In Teller's Golden City, the elected offices, stores, cards, laws, profits, and good health were all means of building character and moral development. For Teller, the Golden City remedied the "dead hulk of institutionalism" because it constituted "a protest against the all-too-common self-complacency in our child institutions which would have us leave well enough alone."[41]

President Kahn lauded Teller's introduction of "new features in the life and discipline of the Home," which he saw as promoting "the physical betterment and happiness of our children."[42] The board showcased these new features in photographs that appeared for the first time in the Home's annual reports. Snapshots of Gizella Weiss presiding over a meeting of attentive Big Sisters, children tending the cooperative store, and a portrait of "Our Family," consisting of Teller posing on the Home's front steps with more than one hundred neatly dressed and mostly grinning children illustrated the essence of the Golden City and its positive impact on the institution.[43] Impressed by one of Teller's monthly reports, the board voted to distribute one thousand copies to members and patrons.[44] Praise for Teller's Golden City also extended beyond the board. In 1911, *Jewish Charities,* the official bulletin of the National Conference of Jewish Charities, praised the Home's Golden City for making "a distinct contribution to the problem of self-government in orphan asylums," and noted Teller's "particular intelligence" in crafting its judicial department.[45] Philadelphia's *Jewish Exponent* lauded Teller's plan as an "experiment based on an intelligent understanding of conditions as they now exist—experiments which are necessary in the development of public institutions."[46] Teller and his supporters were either unaware of or unswayed by the approach taken by the superintendent of Atlanta's Jewish orphanage, who declared his "unswerving aim" to avoid "Junior republics [and] all attempts at so-called self-government" because they did not resemble normal family life.[47]

The children seemed to approve of and be inspired by Teller and his Golden City. In September 1909, sixteen-year-old Ruth Mayer conceded that, when Teller first introduced the Golden City to the Home's children, "we were not quite prepared to submit to the new rules and regulations that you introduced; we were so accustomed to the old ways." Ruth, a Big Sister, entered the Home in 1893 with her older sister, Beatrice, from Jackson, Louisiana, following the death of their widowed mother. "Now that you have lived among us for a while," continued Ruth just eight months after Teller's arrival, "we can appreciate that your high character, integrity and zeal have not only won the love and confidence of the children of the Jewish Orphans' Home, but also those who were fortunate enough to be brought into immediate contact with you."[48] Later the same year, the Home kids embraced another idea they learned from Teller: the "Boston 1915" visionary movement in which civic reformers dreamed up their future ideal city. They launched "Golden City 1910" to make the Home a child's paradise. They pledged to seek friendship and fairness with one another and by January 1910 planted a grove of sycamore trees in their new playground to benefit future generations.[49]

By all accounts Teller and his wife endeared themselves to the Home's children. "He was very kind and really liked the children," recalled alumna Ruby Simon, who entered the Home in 1910 at age seven. She was touched that, after the birth of his daughter, Teller brought the week-old infant downstairs for the children to see.[50] Alumnus Sam Koltun spoke of the new superintendent's "rapport" with the children, fondly recalling the Tellers taking a group of children for a boat ride and picnic.[51] When Chester and Eva returned from summer vacation in 1910, a group of older Home girls presented them with a play that centered on "girl college life," suggesting that Eva's academic attainments did not go unnoticed. The play was the brainchild of sisterhood president Gizella Weiss who enlisted nine other girls to create music, scenery, and costumes. After the show, which earned the Tellers' applause and appreciative words, the girls served lemonade and cake, which they also had made.[52] Two years later Gizella became the first Home girl to graduate from Newman School and also its first to go to college. She attended Newcomb, where she earned a bachelor's degree.[53]

Drawing on his experience directing HSGS's clubs, Teller supported the Home band and Boy Scout Troop, both of which Heymann had previously introduced. In the summer of 1911, the renamed Golden City Troop organized a camp in the Home's backyard, sleeping in tents as if they were in the woods. The Home band, every member of which also happened to be a scout, led a parade around the backyard, followed by troop members carrying banners and torches.[54] Likely nothing, however, topped the Golden City Troop's experience of leading an honor guard of five hundred city scouts to escort Theodore Roosevelt upon his arrival in New Orleans. Along the route from the train station, down St. Charles Avenue, and past City Hall, crowds applauded each time the band stopped to play. When the procession reached the Grunewald Hotel, the Home band entered the lobby and played several more tunes, reportedly bringing "down the house," before being taken to meet the former president. "I'm mighty glad to see you," Roosevelt told the boys after they played a song for him. "Just the kind of a band the Boy Scouts ought to have." From there, Roosevelt went to the French Opera House, allowing the boys to sit on the edge of the stage while he spoke, paying special compliment—with no mention of his earlier White House Conference—to the "Boy Scout Band from the Jewish Orphans' Home."[55]

THE DEMISE OF ISIDORE NEWMAN AND
THE SHIFT FROM MANUAL TRAINING

During Teller's tenure, two events deeply affected the Home and its school. In November 1909, at age seventy-two, Isidore Newman died. Considered one of the greatest financiers of the South, Newman was best remembered as a philanthropist of unparalleled generosity. This was especially true in regard to the Home and his namesake school, where he coupled his financial contributions with his stewardship of both the Home's endowment as a trustee and the school as a life member of the education committee. The *Daily Picayune* expressed the sentiment of all who had known him and countless others who felt a personal loss in his death: "He was a great and good man."[56]

By the time Newman died, the trend in education that shaped his namesake school had shifted. Once viewed as an ideal method of instruction, manual training had now fallen out of favor. The abstract exercises it employed in shopwork drew criticism; the National Education Association concluded that manual training lacked industrial value.[57] As Principal Clarence Henson explained at the Home's January 1910 anniversary celebration, the school's original manual training courses had proven too limited to provide either complete literary or industrial education. "The policy of the Isidore Newman Manual Training School is not merely to teach boys and girls how to make beautiful and useful articles of wood and iron, and copper and brass, but to industrialize the entire process of instruction in school life. Our work is a deliberate and conscious effort to connect school with industry. . . . Manual training is good as far as it goes, but it does not go far enough. Industrial training is broader and more comprehensive."[58]

For these reasons, the kindergarten and elementary school continued to provide manual arts (such as carpentry and metal work) for boys and household arts (cooking and sewing) for girls, in addition to the conventional studies of spelling, reading, writing, arithmetic, history, and geography. In the high school, however, Henson introduced two tracks of study: a literary track for pupils who intended to go to college and an industrial track for those who did not. This change also reflected the school's recent success in preparing its students for college: six of the nine members of Newman's first graduating class of June 1909 had gone on to college.[59] With board approval, Henson, a practical man, adjusted the school's curriculum to meet the needs of its students, an increasing percentage of whom were college-bound pay pupils from outside the Home.[60]

Newman's college preparatory track yielded dramatic results. It became increasingly successful in preparing academically proficient students from the Home and community for college. The year before Gizella Weiss graduated and went to Newcomb, Louis Fuerstenberg became the first Home boy to graduate from Newman in 1911 and went on to Tulane University, where he studied dentistry. In 1913, no fewer than sixteen of Newman's twenty-seven seniors (59 percent) went on to college, which was a larger proportion than the 35 percent of the nation's college-bound high school graduates.[61] Louis Yarutzky, one of four Home students who graduated that year, joined nine of his Newman classmates at Tulane University where he entered the law school.[62] A decade later, as the proportion of American high school graduates who continued to college dropped to 32 percent (reflecting graduates' increasing demand for jobs instead of higher education), thirty-six of Newman's fifty graduating seniors (72 percent) headed to college, which now also included schools outside the region, such as Wellesley, the University of Chicago, and Massachusetts Institute of Technology. Of five Home seniors who graduated that year, Louis Stein and Reva Levine respectively headed to Tulane University and Newcomb College.[63]

Despite the fact that one of the original reasons for founding the school was to provide its girls with domestic skills for the "practical side of life" instead of "paying too much attention to school advancement," some Home girls especially benefited from Newman's college-preparatory education. Of the Home's ninety-seven Newman graduates from 1911 to 1947, fifty were girls, which generally reflected the national experience of women predominating among high school graduates because men were more likely to enter the full-time workforce.[64] A few Home girls, like a growing number of their middle-class counterparts at Newman and elsewhere, used their high school diplomas to attain postsecondary education, which was still largely reserved for a relatively small number of men. In 1922, Louise Fielschmidt followed the earlier path to college laid by Gizella Weiss and Reva Levine. After graduating from Newman with an academic average of 90 percent or above in all subjects, Louise likewise excelled at Newcomb, where she was elected vice president of the student body and captain of her class basketball team, while earning extra money as dormitory counselor and assistant librarian.[65] In 1925, future legal trailblazer Bessie Margolin also headed to Newcomb where, after two years, she became the first Home girl to attend law school, graduating from Tulane with honors, before obtaining her legal doctorate at Yale.[66] Other Home girls who pursued higher education after completing Newman include Anna Crystal, who studied art at Newcomb in 1926, 1928 Newcomb graduate Ronia Levine, and Helen Gold Haymon and Lucille Pierce Gilberstadt, both of whom, after graduating from Louisiana State University in 1939 and 1942, respectively, obtained master's degrees in social work at Tulane.[67]

The Henry Newman Educational Fund, established in 1907 by the late Home president's bequest, helped finance higher education and professional training for some of these and dozens of other Home students. Among them, the fund helped Alfred Meyer to attend medical school in 1910, enabled Harry Goldstein to attend pharmacy school in 1913, and three years later helped Louis Fuerstenberg pay for dental school and equipment.[68] Such financial assistance, however, did not always pave the way to college. Sam Koltun declined the scholarship Tulane awarded him for graduating first in Newman's class of 1913 because he "had to go to work and support" himself. Instead, he took a job as a stock boy at Leon Fellman's Department Store, while taking night classes at Soule Business College.[69]

Over the same period that Newman expanded its college preparatory track, demand increased for industrial and commercial training for Home wards who, by aptitude or interest, were not destined for college.[70] In 1915, board president Joseph Kohn described a "perplexing question" which he attributed to the "ever-changing conditions of society, immigration, and life in general." As he explained, not all Home children "are mentally equipped or physically qualified to derive full benefit from the excellent education. Some of them for various reasons cannot rise above 5th or 6th grades though they be of an age to enter upon life's serious duties."[71] To meet the needs of some of these students, Newman added new classes in shorthand, typing, and domestic sciences.[72]

For those Home students who struggled to meet the rigors of Newman's commercial or industrial curricula, or who expressed an alternative interest, the board turned to a growing number of public commercial and industrial schools that had not existed when it founded Newman School. Since then, Louisiana's school officials had sought to catch up to "the most progressive states in the country" by offering training in commerce, industry, and domestic science.[73] The choices for Home girls included Frances T. Nicholls Industrial School, which opened in 1913 initially to provide training in apparel manufacturing, and Joseph Kohn High School of Commerce (named in honor of the Home's president), where students learned accounting and other business skills. In addition to the National Farm School, beginning in 1916, the board sent Home boys to Samuel J. Peters Commercial High School for business training. By 1922, Home boys also made their way to Delgado Central Trades School, whose initial courses in metalworking and woodworking later encompassed a wide range of vocational skills.

To assign the appropriate educational track, at least once each year the Home's education committee reviewed the scholastic record of each Home child age thirteen and older, while also considering the child's expressed interests. In consultation with Principal Henson and faculty, the committee determined whether each child should pursue literary studies for college preparation or vocational training at Newman or elsewhere.[74] While there is no extant record of the criteria applied or the consistency of decisions, the committee's summary recommendations suggest a highly individualized approach. In 1916, the board approved recommendations that academically strong students Leroy Swartzkopf and Ida Goldberg continue in Newman's literary courses while Fannie Black and Herbert Morris were selected for courses in stenography and telegraphy, respectively.[75] In 1923, as Jack Margolin began Newman's academic courses, the board placed Hyman Stein in Newman's "business course including printing and shop" with a view toward a "trade career" and Jeanette Tannenbaum in a "special course including English and Physiology: objective, a trained nurse."[76] In 1924, sixteen-year-old Sarah Lampert, whose best subjects at Newman had been cooking and sewing, became one of three Home graduates of Nicholls School. With her certificate in millinery studies, Sarah promptly landed a job with Marks Isaacs Company Department Store and used part of her earnings to pay the five-dollar dues for the Home's alumni association.[77]

TELLER RESIGNS

On January 1, 1911, precisely two years after he arrived, to the board's "surprise and chagrin," Teller submitted his resignation.[78] In his annual report that year, President Kahn disclosed only that the reason Teller gave for his "unlooked for" resignation was "a conflict of views" over the school's "plans and methods." One possible clue lies in an undated, handwritten note, which was loosely inserted in the minute book following the entries for the meeting at which the board discussed Teller's resignation: "Resolved that this Board of Directors wish to go on record as to the non-sectarian character of the Isidore Newman Manual Training School, which is to be maintained in full accordance with the aims and purposes of its founder, whose honored name it bears. By non-sectarianism it is meant that no religious instruction shall be introduced into the school, and there shall be nothing in the curriculum, policy or management of the school to conflict with the intent of this resolution."[79] That Principal Henson also offered his resignation during this time (although the board took no action and he stayed at Newman until 1947) could further point to a conflict between the Home and the school. Kahn, "with a heavy heart," also related without additional explanation that, during the board's discussions, "personal animosities" arose which "clouded the issue" and forced the board to accept Teller's resignation.[80] No doubt deepening Kahn's disappointment, only one year earlier he had praised Teller and Henson for achieving "a complete harmony" between the Home and its school: "What is taught in one, is practiced in the other."[81] Even though the coincidence of the board's resolution and the two men's resignations suggests that the difference of opinion between Teller and Henson involved some aspect of religion, the records simply fail to enlighten due to the board's intriguing decision to expunge from the minutes all reports prepared by the committee to consider Teller's resignation.[82]

Teller's impending departure did not sour his relationship with the board, as he delivered the address at the Home's anniversary a week after submitting his resignation. Given the fact that the Home continued to labor under a deficit, to which the additional expenses for Teller's Golden City and the school's net costs greatly contributed, the board's decision to showcase the superintendent reflected its faith in his ability to generate donations and its respect for him. Rising to the occasion, Teller enthusiastically described the Golden City, earning praise from the local press.[83]

Teller stayed on as superintendent for four months after proposing his resignation and offered to remain for as long as the board desired. Amid this upheaval, President Gabe Kahn died. Leading a delegation of Home children, Teller attended the funeral at Temple Sinai, which reportedly was "packed to the doors" by Jews and gentiles in homage to Kahn's philanthropic works for the entire community. In tribute to Kahn's thirty years of service to the Home, including seventeen years as president, its flag was lowered and the front door was draped in mourning.[84] Joseph Kohn, second vice president since 1908, won unanimous election as president, a position he held until his death in 1921.[85]

The next month, Brooklyn Hebrew Orphan Asylum elected Teller as its new superintendent. Recognizing its efforts to convince him to stay were in vain, the Home's board accepted his resignation.[86] By early August, it hired Rabbi Leon Volmer, requesting that he come to New Orleans as soon as possible to work alongside Teller before he departed.[87]

Teller finished his tenure at the Home with a flourish. Marking his last official duties, he led Rosh Hashanah services in the Home's synagogue, attracting nearly one hundred outside worshippers, his largest attendance yet. Teller selected two children to assist in the service. Reflecting an uncommonly egalitarian approach to worship even by progressive Reform Jewish practices of the time, fourteen-year-old Gussie Burka led prayers and fifteen-year-old Joe Cohn sounded the *shofar,* the ceremonial ram's horn.[88]

After the High Holy Days, Teller and his family boarded a train and left New Orleans.[89] On New Year's Day in 1912, he started his new job at Brooklyn's Jewish orphanage, a large institution caring for 570 boys and girls.[90] A few months later, however, Teller suddenly resigned, permanently leaving the world of institutional childcare, but not Jewish youth or their education.[91] In 1917, after holding a series of positions in New York in which he continued to broaden his managerial skills and communal leadership, he became the first executive director of the National Jewish Welfare Board, which had been created to support Jewish soldiers during World War I and to train rabbis as military chaplains.[92] Along the way, drawing on his time with the Home's scouts and his work establishing New Orleans's first citywide summer boy scout camp, Teller became a pioneer in the nascent field of Jewish summer camping.[93] After partnering with his former HSGS boss Ludwig Bernstein to purchase lakefront parcels in Belgrade, Maine, Teller spent the rest of his career directing Camps Arden, Arcadia, and Winslow for middle-class Jewish girls and boys, demonstrating his undiminished passion promoting children's development through structured play.[94] Teller died in 1962 at age seventy-eight.[95]

Although the far-reaching changes Teller introduced suggest that his predecessor had not kept pace with changing practices in dependent childcare, his Golden City was by no means the only or even the most obvious means to impart self-sufficiency or otherwise improve the Home's daily life. One approach might have been to eliminate the ringing of bells, a practice that Teller failed to alter. So too, if the prior "monitorial system" of empowering older peers to supervise younger ones had proved rigid and militaristic, perhaps the problem stemmed from imposing too much responsibility on older children in lieu of hiring additional adult supervisors. Moreover, Teller did not address the fundamental issue of institutional care, instead perpetuating what Rabbi Leucht had years earlier lambasted as still being "cages" despite their "golden wires." Although Teller drew heavily from the HSGS's self-governing "Republics," he had not similarly brought to the Home any of the New York asylum's considerable experience in placing wards in families outside the institution.

Instead, the Home's board gave to its new superintendent—Teller, a twenty-five-year-old with less than three years of actual childcare experience—unbridled authority to implement a sweeping change in the form of self-government. And yet, based on the existing alumni accounts of that era, Teller's Golden City brightened and enhanced the children's lives, likely owing to the force of his enthusiasm. As HSGS's Bernstein and other experts in the field of institutional self-government cautioned at the time, this approach to child development demanded skillful and judicious adult guidance "exercised along the lines of friendly control without dictation."[96] The future of the Home's Golden City, and the well-being of its young Dwellers and Builders, now rested in the hands of a new mayor, Leon Volmer.

chapter eight

RABBI LEON VOLMER
1911–1925

Leon Volmer's fourteen-year tenure as superintendent spanned the First World War, including the exuberant patriotism and heightened antisemitism it engendered, and the successful fight for women's suffrage. Just as they shaped the nation and New Orleans, these historic events also colored the lives of the Home's children. Likened at the time to a "fine type of Jewish boarding school," the Home offered its wards an increasing array of opportunities and activities to overcome negative stereotypes and develop their capacities not only as Jews and workers, but also as middle-class citizens in a democratic society.[1]

Leon Volmer was born in 1877 in Little Rock, Arkansas, where his father, Louis, a Bavarian immigrant and Confederate veteran, owned a dry goods store. A long-serving alderman, president of Little Rock's Congregation B'nai Israel, and founding treasurer of local B'nai B'rith Lodge 158, Louis instilled in his son an appreciation for civic and religious engagement. After graduating from high school, Leon attended Hebrew Union College in Cincinnati, where he earned his undergraduate degree and ordination as a Reform rabbi. In his first and only pulpit, Volmer served a decade as rabbi of Charleston, West Virginia's Congregation Bene Israel. Beyond his clear and measured sermons and the sanctity he bestowed on congregants' life-cycle events, Volmer won over the community through public service, leading the state's Anti-Tuberculosis League and fundraising for Associated Charities. Tall, large framed, and athletic, the town's rabbi also captured favorable attention by coaching the high school's new football team, leading the Mountain Lions to a winning first season.[2] In 1905, he married native-born Tresa Kaufman who, three years later, gave birth to their only child, Louise.[3] Although seemingly making Charleston his home, in 1911 Volmer accepted the superintendent's post at the Home. "There are few men," lamented the *Charleston Gazette*'s editor about Volmer's departure, "who have endeared themselves to the people of the town with the splendid qualities of brain and energy and soul that have become known to Charleston people as his."[4]

Volmer left no record of what prompted his career change, but a Home employee later offered a motive while retelling his exasperated exchange with the cleric-turned-superintendent: "You could have been a great rabbi but didn't like the congregation telling you what to do. You like to tell others."[5] Any misgivings Volmer harbored about being overseen by yet another group of volunteer leaders were eased by the Home's solid reputation. His Little Rock hometown had entrusted nine needy children to the Home over the years. Moreover, in addition to his father's B'nai B'rith leadership, Volmer had strong links to New Orleans through two HUC roommates: Rabbis Moise Bergman, who had served Congregation Gates of Prayer since 1904, and Judah Magnes, Chester Teller's brother-in-law.[6]

Running the Home presented a dramatic increase and shift in responsibilities for Volmer, whose Charleston congregation comprised fewer than fifty members.[7] Moreover, Volmer's experience with children was limited to teaching his congregants' offspring, coaching the local high school football team, and raising his daughter, who was then only three years old. The first ordained rabbi to serve as Home superintendent, Volmer was also the first superintendent to raise his own child in the Home from toddler to high school graduate. A devoted father, Volmer appeared in a family photo pushing a baby carriage, wearing a tall, dapper bowler and a wide smile.[8] In the Home, Volmer sometimes demonstrated paternal tendencies, referring to "my boys" when praising the lads in his charge.[9] A photo depicted Volmer coaxing a circle of hand-holding Home toddlers to look at the camera. On the back, he wrote, "Our babies."[10] For many Home children, however, Volmer presented himself differently.

THE GOLDEN CITY LIVES ON

From the start, Volmer embraced the Golden City. He had little incentive to do otherwise. Before student governments became common in high schools and colleges, the novelty of the Golden City continued to win favor with the board and in the local press. Moreover, to supplement what he lacked in institutional childcare expertise, Volmer need only look to the thirty-six-page Golden City handbook which detailed the ideals and operations of the children's self-governing community.[11] Only four months after he arrived, Volmer publicly praised the "freedom, initiative, and spontaneity" that flowed from this "modern, scientific plan of child-rearing."[12] Within a few years at the Home, Volmer articulated his views on the essential purpose of a modern orphan home. "If the orphanage has any reason for existing," said Volmer in 1916 and again in 1918, "that reason must be to take the unfortunate child and provide a home for him, the atmosphere, the moral and spiritual life, the education and the activities of which will make the child a Social Force in the Social Construction of Society."[13] As an educational and character-building tool, the Golden City provided another form of "learning by doing."[14] If aware of criticism about self-government from professional peers, such as that voiced by the superintendent of Atlanta's Jewish orphanage, Volmer never mentioned it.[15]

Despite the idealistic moniker and lofty goals, alumni accounts about Volmer's tenure reveal that neither he nor his Golden City did much to eliminate regimentation and harsh discipline. Alumna Helen Gold Haymon recalled that during Volmer's tenure, which coincided with the first six of her fifteen years in the Home, the loud clanging of a bell continued to announce activities and the lengthy list of punishable offenses included tardiness to meals or school, "sassing" staff, not changing into "yard clothes" from "school clothes," or failing to obtain permission to do things. Whether meted out by staff, or by Big Brothers and Big Sisters, breaking rules most often led to extra chores or lost privileges such as Saturday night silent movies and weekend outings.[16] Another common punishment for minor infractions was being sent to sit on one's locker in the basement for varying lengths of time, causing several alumni many years later to remember their locker number, which was also sewn into their clothes for identification.[17]

Sam Pulitzer, who lived in the Home from 1914 to 1918, recalled a typical morning in Volmer's Golden City:

> With us lined up at the foot of our beds, the superintendent, with his starched white shirt and shiny black shoes, would pass in review. We would all stand tall and straight, trying not to move, trying not to attract attention, for if his eyes rested on you for longer than a second, you knew something was wrong. . . . I

will never forget his name—Mr. Volmer—or his face. He would get real close and just scruff the tops of your shoes with his, an indication that they were not clean enough. If your hair needed cutting, he announced it to everyone, telling them you had bangs like a little girl, and better report to the barber before the day was out. Actually, he was a very kind man, but a firm disciplinarian, and every boy knew that he had better toe the line.[18]

Even a decade later, Volmer had failed to mellow. Louis Peters, who entered the Home near the end of Volmer's tenure, recalled avoiding the superintendent after receiving a "caustic tongue lashing" for running inside the building.[19] Mildred Gordon Tobias, who also was admitted to the Home near the end of Volmer's tenure, stated that although she "loved the Home" and, as a compliant child, did not personally encounter difficulties, "Volmer was very hard on the boys."[20] Other alumni of the time recalled physical discipline. Of fifteen alumni interviewed in 1983 who lived in the Home during Volmer's tenure, six recounted paddling or spanking, including five who said Volmer administered the penalty.[21] Of the five, Hirsch Goldstein recalled that, when his brother was caught sneaking off premises without permission, "Rabbi Volmer put Harry's head between his legs and gave him a belt whipping."[22]

Another perspective of Volmer's Golden City comes from William F. Rosenblum, whom Volmer hired in September 1913 as boys' supervisor. A twenty-one-year-old graduate of New York's City College, Rosenblum had just completed a year in a similar position at Cleveland's Council Educational Alliance, which offered classes to East European immigrants. Many years later, Rosenblum, after serving more than three decades as rabbi of New York City's Temple Israel while publicly advocating for social justice, described his years at the Home as "three of the most exciting, difficult and happy of my career, years that molded me into the minister that I was to become."[23] His introduction to New Orleans, however, had raised doubts about his job choice. After Rosenblum slid into a rear seat on the St. Charles Avenue streetcar en route from the train station to the Home, the conductor bellowed at him, "Don't you know betta than to sit there? These seats are for n——s!" Only then did a shaken Rosenblum see the sign, "for colored only," which local law required conductors to use to racially separate patrons. Order resumed when another rider, noting luggage, jumped to Rosenblum's defense, "Cain't you see he's from the Nawth. He don't know no betta."[24]

Within the Home, Rosenblum found a nurturing environment, describing "the love that we showered upon our children, a real parental love that was mixed with all of the gamut of punishment and spoil that strict fathers and harassed mothers would exercise in the typical American home."[25] From Rosenblum's perspective, the Golden City's system of self-governance "for the most part worked wonderfully" and helped older children develop a sense of responsibility and care. Goldie Berger Knobler and Morris Rosenberg concurred, years later proudly recalling being elected to watch over younger peers.[26] Rosenblum conceded that some Big Brothers and Sisters became "minor overlords," sentencing young rule-breakers to extended stints of "locker-sitting" or physical force.[27] Alumnus Sam Pulitzer described some of these overlords in his account of the "Seven Soap Scrubbers," a group of Big Brothers who enforced order by dragging youngsters to the showers, roughing them up, and rubbing a bar of soap over their teeth.[28] To rein in one abusive Big Brother, Rosenblum described how, during inspection, he slapped the boy in the face and told him, "I don't like the way you handle your family. I thought I'd do to you what you've been doing to little M. He's only six." Still satisfied with his actions, years later Rosenblum wrote that the boy became a much better Big Brother and a "solid if stolid citizen of the town to which he returned."[29]

At the time, as reflected by Rosenblum's anecdote, physical forms of discipline were not uncommon. Despite prohibition by the city school board since 1852, Louisiana law continues today to grant each local school jurisdiction discretion to use corporal punishment.[30] Although physical discipline earned increasing disfavor, and was eliminated at the Atlanta Jewish orphanage by 1914, other Jewish orphanage managers, too, continued to use these measures occasionally as a last resort.[31] Neither the Home's board nor Volmer's professional colleagues ever indicated that the Home's methods of discipline, if known, were inappropriate. To the contrary, throughout his tenure the board rewarded Volmer with praise, bonuses, and salary raises.[32] In 1921, after touring the Home, thirty delegates of the Tri-State Conference of Social Workers reportedly came away "very well pleased" from Volmer's lecture on "Discipline in the Home."[33] In 1923, following an inspection during Volmer's tenure, E. R. Johnston, director of the Vineland School for the Feebleminded and an institutional authority, declared the Home "one of the most successful institutions of its kind in America."[34]

Although one alumna summed up her six years under Volmer by saying,

"Life wasn't fun," far more Home alumni (like their peers in other Jewish orphanages) rationalized that these harsh measures were inflicted only upon "naughty" children or those who had done something to "deserve it."[35] Despite characterizing him as "very stern" and "known to spank the children," Bessie Weinberg Smith, for example, described her childhood in the Home, including six years with Volmer, as "wonderful and rewarding."[36] Even Hirsch Goldstein, whose brother Harry received a whipping at the superintendent's hands, considered his twelve years in the Home "the highlights" of his life, all of which were during Volmer's tenure. Other children managed to thrive under the regimentation by avoiding harsh discipline or compartmentalizing negative experiences, aided by increasing opportunities, activities, and friendships. Perhaps this explains the seemingly contradictory descriptions among the children, including by Bessie Margolin, who summed up her twelve years in the Home during Volmer's tenure by expressing gratitude for being pushed to excel and saying, "I always felt loved."[37]

OPPORTUNITIES AND ACTIVITIES

Amid regimentation, Volmer promoted "productive" self-expression by surrounding the children with an increasing array of opportunities and activities. At a time when women clamored for political rights and social freedoms enjoyed by men, Volmer dramatically enlarged the girls' offerings, likely also inspired by his daughter's interests and her close friendship with Home girls her age.[38]

Volmer expanded occasions to enjoy music and play instruments, a novel experience for some wards. Sam Pulitzer quickly learned to play the piccolo, something he had never before seen, in time to march with the Home band in the 1916 Mardi Gras parade, calling it "the most thrilling event" of his young life.[39] The next year, Volmer hired Henry Wehrman, a Paris-trained violinist and composer, to teach stringed instruments to girls aged ten and older.[40] By the next anniversary celebration, the girls' new Mandolin and Guitar Club followed the boys' brass band in a concert for an estimated seven hundred guests, and the two groups later formed a coed ensemble.[41] "The Victrola in one room, the radio in another, and the pianola is still in another room," wrote Esther Cantor in 1925, "the whole atmosphere around here is music."[42]

Volmer also enhanced athletics. By 1915, he supplemented the ongoing twice-weekly classes in games and calisthenics with additional instruction in sports for the boys and folk dancing for the girls.[43] By 1922, tennis joined the Home pastimes for boys and girls, thanks to a local organization's donation of a court and net.[44] Before entering the Home, growing up poor on his family's Texas farm, Ralph Beerman rarely played sports. "But when I got to the Home, we had every conceivable thing you needed for athletics," Ralph remembered with delight. "Not only that, we had a place to play—a big, open yard. Boy, I was in my glory."[45]

As a former football coach, team sports particularly captured Volmer's interest, albeit not always to the children's advantage. As William Rosenblum related, "to stimulate competitive interest and spirit," he and the superintendent headed opposing teams in all three sports. To Rosenblum, Volmer was a "massive man" and a poor sport who argued over calls and played roughly, forgetting that the players were "mere boys." To teach his boss a lesson, during a football game, Rosenblum enlisted little Bennie Samuels to "pull a play." After teammates arranged a block, Samuels grabbed Volmer by the ankles, pulling with all his strength. As Volmer landed "with a thud," recounted Rosenblum, a large swatch of hair flew off, revealing a bald pate to onlookers' shock. After he rose to his feet, realizing the blame lay higher up than with Bennie, Volmer growled, "You're through, Rosenblum."[46] In Rosenblum's telling, after admitting that he orchestrated the stunt to curb the superintendent's bad sportsmanship, a contrite Volmer withdrew the threatened termination to the children's relief.[47]

Although Rosenblum implied that Volmer repented, the children continued to joke about their superintendent's "win-at-any-cost" temperament. One boy sarcastically predicted that Volmer might one day play "without 'crabbing' at the umpire"[48] After losing to Volmer at the Home's regular Sunday game, several alumni playfully threatened to return with "a ball that will not feel like a ton of bricks" and "our own imported umpires."[49] Whether through hard knocks on the field or humor, Home children had to learn to deal with different personalities and leadership styles from one superintendent or supervisor to another.

To encourage socialization and individual interests, Volmer welcomed a proliferation of clubs, about which he encouraged the children to write in the Home's newsletter, the *Golden City Messenger*, along with their poems, short stories, and jokes. The Literary Club hosted high-profile speakers such as Mayor Martin Behrman and Governor Luther Hall, who discussed citizenship and government.[50] The Drama Club performed monthly plays while the Self Helpers delved into subjects "helpful in the mental and moral development of the adolescent girl."[51] In honor of the Jewish U.S. Supreme Court justice, a group of Home boys organized the Brandeis Club, which in 1923 discussed current topics that increased the children's understanding of the challenges in the world around them, including the modern Ku Klux Klan, antisemitism, and "What the American Jew Stands For."[52] As Volmer declared, "[N]othing tends to teach a child the true principles of self-reliance and self-expression more than membership in a club."[53]

While the Golden City Boy Scout Troop continued to flourish, Volmer again turned his attention to the girls. In 1921, a year after the founding of Louisiana's first Girl Scout troop, Volmer opened the experience to Home girls under the leadership of girls' supervisor Bessie Hirschfield, who brought eleven years' experience from Cleveland's Jewish orphanage.[54] After hearing the girls describe their "Daily Good Turns," Volmer happily reported to the board that scouting enhanced the girls' morale and character, making the expenses for uniforms and carfare seem "small and worth it."[55]

Starting with fourteen-year-old Elsmere Hoffstadt's adoption of a stray rabbit in 1919, the Home's Animal Pet Association quickly encompassed pigeons, white rats, dogs, a goat, and a cow, teaching the joys and responsibilities of caring for animals.[56] To further justify the expense, Volmer explained that the animals provided an effective disciplinary tool as even the "hardest to reach child" responded to the sting of losing the privilege of caring for pets even briefly.[57] The program—which the press claimed was "the first and only animal pet association in any such institution in the United States"—soon turned to pedigreed chickens.[58] By April 1923, the chickens had produced more than one thousand eggs, enabling the boys to sell enough to finance the program and incubate the rest. While many of the thirty-three hundred chickens supplied the Home's anniversary banquets, Kronenberg brothers Archie and Isidore captured national attention for their prize-winning Single Comb White Leghorn Cockerels.[59] Consistent with the national trend to promote agriculture through youth organizations such as 4-H Clubs, the Home's pet hobby had transformed into an industry that contributed to the institution's upkeep. At the same time, following in Michel Heymann's footsteps, Volmer hoped these agricultural skills would counter stereotypes to offset the growing antisemitism of the era. Beyond increasingly restrictive immigration laws, industrialist Henry Ford published weekly rants about a worldwide Jewish conspiracy, while even closer to home the major New Orleans newspapers ran ads offering Mardi Gras celebrants their choice of "Jew Masks," with or without a beard.[60]

Volmer dramatically increased the children's opportunities outside the Home, part of his plan to expand their worldview. Generous individuals and organizations donated a steady stream of tickets and invitations for excursions, from picnics and automobile rides to trips to museums and Mississippi River boat rides complete with refreshments.[61] For the boys, "Nothing, absolutely nothing, excited us more than the occasional appearance of Mr. Heineman [sic]," recalled Sam Pulitzer, referring to Alexander Julius ("A. J.") Heinemann, part owner of the city's professional baseball team. Besides driving the boys to play at Pelican Ballpark, Heinemann frequently donated tickets to the games.[62]

Home kids also were encouraged to attend the symphony and other performances, as Ralph Beerman put it, "to be indoctrinated in the culture."[63] In 1921, Home children heard Metropolitan Opera star Mabel Garrison on her world tour and the next year were treated to a concert by renowned "March King" John Philip Sousa.[64] The culture of the time also included blackface minstrelsy, a racially oppressive genre that enjoyed nationwide popularity from the mid-nineteenth century well into the next.[65] Not only were the children frequently treated by donors to attend minstrel performances at local theatres, but they also often performed their own shows.[66] Despite Rosenblum's asserted intolerance of racism, he directed the boys' minstrel performance in 1917, proudly posing for a photograph with his young black-faced cast members in front of an enormous American flag.[67]

Recognizing that this now condemned form of entertainment has a complex history in America's Jewish community, one scholar posits that some Jews—such as Al Jolson in the 1927 talkie *The Jazz Singer*—donned blackface not to disparage but in kinship with the Black experience, a position bolstered by Jolson's support for Black entertainers.[68] In a 1954 article, Judge Louis Yarrut, who spent thirteen years in the Home and graduated from Newman in 1913, suggested such empathy existed among Home children. Recalling that the Home was neighbored by "New Orleans University for Negroes" and the Protestant Orphan Boys' Home, Yarrut wrote, "It was not unusual for us boys to play ball one afternoon with our colored neighbors and the next with the Protestant boys. Never did I hear any vile epithet against race or religion. We were innocent children unsullied with prejudice, having a good time."[69] Perhaps the children were more open-minded than the Home's managers. The only contemporaneously documented communication between the Home and New Orleans University was the Home's 1915 complaint that unpleasant discharges from the university's smokestack had "dirtied our dormitories with smoke and soot."[70] In contrast, in June 1916, when a fire broke out at the Orphan Boys' Home, Volmer welcomed its thirty boys—all white—to take refuge in the Home.[71]

Movies, too, provided regular entertainment for Home children. M. H. Jacobs reserved two dozen seats for Home children each week at his Prytania Theater, as did Mr. Waldorf at his Magazine Street cinema.[72] For years, in partnership with the *New Orleans Item,* the Strand Theater opened its doors for "Orphans' Day," evidencing the city's fascination with real and fictional orphans. In 1919, Home kids joined counterparts from asylums across town to watch America's sweetheart, Mary Pickford, in her much-celebrated comedy-drama *Daddy Long Legs* about an orphan who lives happily ever after with her mystery benefactor.[73] Sufficiently impressed with the power of movies to broaden the children's "mental horizon," Volmer purchased equipment to project movies on a screen in the third floor's Anniversary Hall, where at least once each week the children viewed popular, full-length films ranging from D. W. Griffith's *Child of the Ghetto* to slapstick comedies.[74]

Amid the popularity of motion pictures coupled with wider access to technology, Volmer harnessed the power of movies in another way. In 1920, as chief fundraiser, a role which the board had earlier added to his job, Volmer made a "propaganda" movie of the "true workings of the Home."[75] A professional cameraman filmed the children at morning inspection, walking to school, playing, studying, eating dinner, and tucked in their beds. *A Day in the Jewish Orphans' Home* premiered in New Orleans before Volmer took it on tour with a portable projector, starting in Birmingham, Alabama. Volmer declared the project a success, reporting that the film generated nearly $5,000 in contributions while spreading "the friendly feeling for our institution."[76] Although they thought little about whether movies built character or raised money, many alumni remembered the thrill of the spring of 1926, when silent-film stars Lois Wilson, Eileen Percy, and Leatrice Joy visited the Home and posed with dozens of children for a photo.[77]

THE GOLDEN CITY TAKES ON THE GREAT WAR

The First World War touched all Americans, including Home kids. After an initial financial panic in 1914—when disruption in worldwide commodity markets plunged crop prices—Louisiana enjoyed a wartime economic boom. Farm prices skyrocketed as Britain and France turned to America for war matériel and, after entering the conflict in 1917, the federal government invested heavily in the expansion or creation of military installations and maritime infrastructure, including three new shipyards and a massive warehousing terminal in New Orleans. Louisianians had money in their pockets and used it to support the war effort through fundraising, while aiding the selective service registration of more than seventy thousand men.[78]

Volmer used the Golden City's clubs to foster patriotism and help the children deal with the war's challenges. After the girls' Progress Club learned about the Red Cross, they made bandages and knitted sweaters for soldiers.[79] Like their peers across the nation, Home boys and girls joined the United War Work Victory Campaign by doing odd jobs to earn money to "keep our fighters happy," which also helped the Home face a wartime shortage of custodians.[80] The Golden City Boy Scout Troop earned merit badges by selling war savings stamps and Liberty Bonds and marched in a special bond-drive parade.[81] "We really didn't understand how the bonds helped the fighting," conceded Sam Pulitzer, "but we were full of excitement at the prospect of another parade, especially when we were told that the President was proud of us."[82]

The war had another, less celebrated, consequence for the city and the Home. Venereal disease outbreaks among the troops swiftly reversed decades of apathy toward sexually transmitted infections. To protect the health and virtue of its troops, the federal government prohibited prostitution within five miles of any military base and, amid the city's prominent Navy presence, local officials reluctantly closed Storyville, New Orleans's legal red-light district.[83] To protect boys and girls, sex education in public schools began to win acceptance from a growing number of officials and educators.[84] Volmer took note. Admittedly lacking training to teach this "once-tabooed subject," as he described it, Volmer researched "the proper method of presenting the subject to his boys and having the right person to present it to his girls." For the older boys, he also implemented cold showers before bed, the commonly accepted deterrent to masturbation, which he referred to as "the malpractice indulged in by children reaching puberty." Nurse Anna Levine, known to the children as "Veenie" and whom Volmer deemed efficient and sympathetic, held sessions with the girls. She discussed the reproductive process with the ten- to fourteen-year-olds, while reserving for their elder peers subjective issues such as relationships and sexual impulses. Aided by Assistant Superintendent Harry Ginsburg following his Navy service, Volmer addressed "the boys' problem."[85] For many children in the Home as elsewhere, learning about the facts of life came as a shock. "You mean everybody does it?" asked an incredulous eight-year-old Abe Plotkin. "Even the president of the United States?"[86]

When President Woodrow Wilson proclaimed May 11, 1918, a national day of prayer, Volmer kept the children home from school and conducted a prayer service for them.[87] The next month, the Home dedicated a flag bearing thirty-six stars to honor Home alumni who were serving in the military. Volmer pointed to the flag as evidence of Jews' patriotism, and the Home's contributions to it. "Jews were among the first to rally to the support of the nation when war was declared," said Volmer, "disproving forever the old belief that Jews detest the hardships and dangers of war."[88] Volmer's assertion was not unprovoked; across the country, the war had stirred up old prejudices and prompted new stereotypes of Jews as alleged cowards guilty of disloyalty.[89] Just one year earlier, shortly after the United States declared war against Germany, Professor Henry Gill, director of New Orleans's Public Library, delivered remarks at a public event for the city's Jewish Library Association. Instead of delivering his expected address on library work, Gill shocked the largely Jewish crowd by condemning Jews as unpatriotic. Dr. Mendel Silber, senior rabbi at Congregation Gates of Prayer and an honorary Home board member, had been expected to speak about Hebrew literature; instead, he coolly rebutted Gill's claims by reviewing the services and sacrifices of Jews in the country's wars.[90]

For Home kids, three alumni epitomized Jewish patriotism in the face of danger. Joseph Wolf, who came to the Home in 1911 from Texas, left at age fifteen to enlist, which according to one account made him "perhaps the youngest non-commissioned officer in the American army on the firing line." When he turned eighteen, he triumphantly wrote his aunt, "Now they can't send me back. It's for Old Glory that we're fighting and none are too young to uphold its honor." For his service as a stretcher bearer with the renowned "Lost Battalion," Wolf returned from France bearing the prestigious Croix de Guerre, and later delighted Home children by returning for Sabbath services and a visit.[91]

Two other alumni sacrificed their lives for their country and were later represented on the Home's flag by two gold stars. Max Block, who lived in the Home with his sister, Fanny, from 1904 to 1914, served in the Army's Washington Artillery "Rainbow Division." He was killed in France's Argonne Forest two days before the war ended. Just before learning of his death, Fanny received a letter from her brother. "We are in mud and water up to our necks," wrote Max, referring to the incessant rain. "But that's all right, Sis. I know there is still some sunshine left in the world, and it's in the dear old U.S.A." Volmer recalled the young man who had left the Home just five years earlier as "one of the model inmates of the institution, with truth, honesty and loyalty as his ideals."[92] Alumnus Leon Clausner received fatal wounds while serving in the 161st machine-gun company at Soissons, France. Before his death, he wrote his widowed mother, "I don't ever want you to worry about me for I am one happy boy that I can be over here doing my bit."[93] In a public tribute to their two fallen alumni, the Home's children planted trees in Audubon Park.[94]

RELIGIOUS LIFE

Like most other Jewish orphanages of the time, the Home adhered to Reform Jewish practices, consistent with the cultural and religious attitudes of its board members and benefactors. These affluent New Orleanians largely dis-associated themselves from what they considered archaic rituals of Orthodox Judaism, which lacked relevance in modern society and were associated with poor and unassimilated Jewish immigrants.[95] Along with years of separation from family and regulated visiting privileges, replacing Orthodox with Reform traditions further drove a wedge between some Home children and their immigrant parents. After acquiring the means, East European Jewish immigrants in larger cities, such as New York, Cleveland, and Chicago, established separate Orthodox orphanages, something not feasible in New Orleans given the relatively small Jewish population.[96]

During Volmer's tenure, as before, Home records continued to remain silent of any mention of observing *kashrut*, the Jewish dietary laws. Any effect previously given the Home's bylaw that required the Home's "culinary department" to adhere to "strictly Jewish principles and practice" had ended by the turn of the century. In 1902, for example, the Home acknowledged donations of not only "200 pounds of matzos," but also "3 buckets of shrimps" and "2 hams," along with "Easter eggs for the babies."[97] Traditional Jewish foods were so unusual in the Home that Helen Gold Haymon remembered having a secret "mid-night feast" when one girl, after visiting her mother, returned with "home cooked, Kosher goodies" including gefilte fish.[98] The Home's elimination of its *kashrut* requirement, even if only on paper, would have stirred no objection from B'nai B'rith District 7, the orphanage's funding partner, whose 1886 banquet featured oysters and crabs (violating the prohibitions against eating shellfish) and ice cream and cheeses following courses of beef and roast chicken (violating the prohibition against mixing milk and meat).[99] In the first two decades of the twentieth century, B'nai B'rith's *Jewish Ledger,* which related news of interest to New Orleans's Jewish community, ran advertisements for oysters and crabs alongside those for kosher delicatessens and *mohels,* who perform religious circumcisions.[100]

Although parents and Orthodox rabbis left no record of requesting religious accommodations for any of the children, the board apparently recognized the need to engage the spiritual leaders of the entire Jewish community. In 1920 Home president Joseph Kohn extended honorary directorships, previously held only by New Orleans's Reform rabbis, to rabbis of the local Orthodox congregations.[101] For the most part, the Orthodox clergy quietly attended board meetings, although in 1940, Rabbi Uri Miller of Orthodox Congregation Beth Israel taught a Judaism course in the Home organized by Reform Touro Synagogue's Rabbi Emil Leipziger.[102]

Unlike their secular education, the children's religious studies and observances remained an insular experience confined within the Home and its synagogue.[103] Reflecting the availability of music lessons and the Home's adherence to Reform practices, selected children played the organ during the Home's Sabbath services that Volmer led on Friday evening and Saturday morning.[104] Helen Gold Haymon pleasantly recalled the Home's Yom Kippur eve custom: the children sought and granted forgiveness to resolve lingering squabbles with peers.[105] Morris Rosenberg recalled the Passover seders that Volmer conducted in the dining room, describing them only as "lengthy."[106] Volmer also looked for new ways to brighten the children's weekly religious classes. To engage the children with vivid scenes from Jewish history and Bible stories, Volmer employed a balopticon, the overhead projector's forerunner, and a stereopticon, which displayed three-dimensional views.[107]

Volmer emphasized confirmation, a rite of passage associated with the Reform movement that links attainment of a basic religious schooling (usually at tenth grade) with *Shevuot,* the holiday that commemorates the Jewish people's receipt of the Torah at Mount Sinai. For Reform Jews, confirmation for boys and girls replaced the traditional bar mitzvah reserved for only boys. Each year in the Home's synagogue, after conducting the service from the Union Prayer Book, giving short talks about the Ten Commandments or the holiday, and receiving certificates, the confirmands were feted at a party, which in 1925 featured music supplied by Eugene Aschaffenburg's orchestra.[108] For the occasion, the honorary matrons outfitted the girls with frilly white dresses and the boys with dark suits, and distributed gifts, such as a bracelet or purse for each girl and a pocketknife or belt buckle for each boy.[109] In this way, the Home children's religious coming-of-age ceremony paralleled the pageantry of their peers' confirmation experiences in New Orleans's Reform Jewish community, including their Jewish classmates from Newman School.[110]

SUMMER CAMP

From his quest to expand the children's experiences outside the Home emerged one of Volmer's most profound contributions. In 1918, the Jewish Charitable and Educational Foundation (JCEF) began offering overnight summer-camp experiences for needy members of New Orleans's Jewish community, including Home children. After successfully testing the venture at a rented property, JCEF purchased a waterfront estate at Bay St. Louis, Mississippi.[111] At Volmer's urging, the board began sending the children to the JCEF camp every summer, creating a universally beloved feature of Home life.

An American cultural phenomenon, organized camping originated in the last two decades of the nineteenth century. Progressive educators, physicians, and clergy pioneered this movement with their beliefs that "fresh air" and going "back-to-nature" offered underprivileged children relief from the negative consequences of urbanization and industrialization, such as crowded and unsanitary living conditions, exploitative labor, and even organized crime. American Jewish social reformers, seeking to assimilate and improve conditions for young Jewish immigrants, were among the earliest and most enthusiastic supporters of the movement. As the National Conference of Jewish Charities noted in 1904, summer camping offered "an affordable antidote to urban congestion and the anomie of the slums." By the time the Home children first dipped their toes in the Gulf of Mexico, organized outdoor living was recognized as much for its educational value ("learning by doing") as for its social benefits (teaching self-reliance and cooperation), concepts that closely aligned with the children's experiences at Newman School and in the Golden City.[112]

Finding it "difficult to refrain from using superlatives," Volmer reported in 1919 that the children's close contact with nature during their week at camp gave them "almost a spiritual experience." From the moment they boarded the train, the children were free from all routine activities and regulations. Swimming in the Gulf, fishing from a rowboat or pier, singing, reading in the pavilion, walks to town, and hikes through the woods—all at their choosing—

gave the children a fresh outlook, while aiding their physical, mental, and moral development.[113] By the second year, the Home children began spending two weeks in Bay St. Louis before going back to school; by the mid-1930s the children's time at camp increased to six weeks. For at least a month in advance, the girls happily sewed bathing suits and cover-ups while the boys broke in their baseball gloves.[114]

Neither Volmer's nor the children's enthusiasm for summer camp ever flagged. Upon returning from Bay St. Louis in 1925, Volmer reported that the experience added "incalculable value" to the children's lives, "in a way that is not afforded them by the environment of institutional life."[115] Years later, Ralph Beerman concurred: "We played ball, swam from the pier, fished from a boat. . . . You can't live a better life!"[116] Even after they were discharged, alums Isidore Busch visited the camp to spend time in his favorite spot and Helen Gold Haymon returned to work as a camp counselor.[117] "The joys of out-of-doors life can never be erased from memory," Helen wrote years later, noting it was the only time most of the children ever left New Orleans.[118] Even Hilda Crystal White, who considered "every breathing moment" in the Home "a battle," adored its summer camp. "Here, with a taste—a small taste of freedom," wrote Hilda, "my spirit was always quieted."[119] Years later, after establishing herself as an author, Hilda chose Bay St. Louis as the setting for one of her novels.[120]

INCREASING THE STAFF

Throughout Volmer's tenure, he relied on a male assistant, a position first held by William Rosenblum and then Harry Ginsburg, who arrived in 1917 with strong recommendations from his nearly five years' experience at CJOA. Except for his Navy service during World War I, Ginsburg spent the rest of his life in the Home. Volmer had far less success in hiring, or at least retaining, a girls' supervisor who met his criteria: "a middle-aged Jewish woman of refinement and culture.[121] Over his fourteen years, no fewer than nine such women filled the slot, but left after a time ranging from a few months to four years, to pursue higher education, marriage, or a better job.[122] The turnover apparently was not due to Volmer's failure to advocate for salary increases as staff often received incremental raises.[123] A more likely cause was the demanding nature of the job, which entailed living in the Home and, except for rare vacations, being on duty around-the-clock.

Within the Home, the children interacted with a relatively large number of adults, but the full-time professional childcare staff remained sparse. In 1920 for example, with a population of 130 children, the Home's full-time childcare staff consisted of Volmer, an assistant superintendent (sometimes referred to as boys' supervisor), a girls' supervisor, dietitian, registered nurse, and five nursery caregivers. Thirteen volunteer honorary matrons took turns visiting the children, including to provide car rides, entertainment, and birthday treats. The children also received attention, upon admission and thereafter as needed, from a team of the city's finest medical professionals, consisting of ten consulting physicians (including a psychiatrist), two visiting dentists, and one orthodontist, all of whom donated their services.[124]

For the first decade of Volmer's tenure, even his time with the children was limited. Unlike its treatment of his predecessors, the board had expanded Volmer's duties to include fundraising. The significance of the role was heightened by the Home's decision in 1913 to join the city's newly organized JCEF, following the national trend of "federating" or uniting Jewish charitable organizations in a community to avoid competing for the same dollars.[125] JCEF guaranteed the Home, in exchange for not separately soliciting funds from New Orleanians, a portion of funds the federation generated on behalf of all constituent institutions. To supplement its federation and B'nai B'rith income, the Home turned to other donors outside the city to bridge the budgetary gap—an effort that kept Volmer traveling throughout the region. In 1922, six years after Volmer first recommended that "the proper person" be hired for the consuming task, the board hired L. Edward Lashman, CJOA's former superintendent, as the Home's first full-time field director to raise money as well as enlist communities to look after recently discharged wards.[126]

Alumni who entered the Home as babies most frequently recalled the time they spent with the nursery workers, all Black women. The Home's employment of Black women as nurses for its youngest children and infants followed the longstanding practice in many middle- and upper-class families in New Orleans. In the early 1920s, for example, five Black women cared for the Home's twenty nursery children.[127] One of those children, Helen Gold Haymon, who entered the Home at age two following her mother's death in the 1918 flu epidemic, years later said of the woman she knew as "Mammie," "She was the only mother I've ever known."[128] Hilda Crystal White, too, cherished the Black woman who cared for her, describing her on the back of a photo as "Edna, my nurse and substitute mother in the Jewish Children's Home."[129]

Although they had no official childcare duties, several full-time housekeepers and custodians—all Black men and women—developed strong bonds with the children. Ralph Beerman was one of many alumni who fondly recalled Lottie Hopkins, the Home's longtime cook, and believed the feeling was mutual. Upon returning from World War II military service, Ralph and his brother Morris walked into the Home's kitchen to see Hopkins. "She cried as if we were her children, that we had come back from the war standing up."[130] Joe Bihari, in the Home from 1931 to 1943, and whose career as a record producer was honored in the Blues Hall of Fame, attributed his love of music to the "hours and hours" he spent listening to the radio after chores with Matthew Causey, a Black maintenance worker who lived with his family on the premises.[131] While segregationist laws and societal norms precluded public interactions between the races—from public transit and education to recreation—close relationships between Black staff and white children flourished in the Home's private spaces.[132]

Some alumni openly addressed the role of race in their lives, even if they did not directly attribute it to their time in the Home. Jake Turansky, five years after his 1929 graduation from the National Farm School and discharge from the Home, organized a meeting in New Orleans to protest the racially motivated death-penalty sentences of nine young Black men in Scottsboro, Alabama, all of whom received posthumous pardons and exonerations in 2013.[133] Hugo Fielschmidt, a Home resident from 1910 to 1925, made a point of welcoming Black patients and employed a Black dental assistant, to the apparent consternation of the majority-white Dallas community in which he practiced dentistry.[134] Similarly, Sam Hartman who lived in the Home from 1928 to 1934, later spent his medical career in Beaumont, Texas, where he employed a Black nurse and treated Black and white patients. Sam insisted on greeting all patients respectfully by their last name, at a time when that simple courtesy was rare, and refused to racially segregate his waiting rooms despite complaints from white patients.[135] Ben Shanker, who lived in the Home from 1929 to 1941, took great pride in his World War II service as a gunnery officer aboard a submarine chaser that was selected for a landmark mission to prove the effectiveness of Black commanders in the Navy.[136] "Just thinking about how many doors that had already been opened in my life," said Shanker about the way he approached the assignment, "how would I have room in my constitution and makeup that I would have any opinions to be against people of any kind?"[137] Although the Home's employment of Black staff in nursery and custodial positions perpetuated racial norms, these men and women contributed greatly to the children's care and well-being.

Volmer recognized the need to increase and improve the adult attention each Home child received. Around this time, when confounding institutional census data identified all "paid employees" without distinguishing part-time gardeners from full-time teachers or nurses, Jewish orphanages on average had one "paid employee" for every six to eight children, generally comparing favorably to asylums run by other religious groups. Using the same data, the Home had one paid employee for every fifteen children, although its ratio of actual childcare workers to children approximated one to twenty.[138] In its first published guidelines for childcare institutions in 1927, the U.S. Children's Bureau recommended one full-time childcare worker for every twelve children.[139] Likely driven as much by his awareness of child-staff ratios that came to his attention through his leadership in national childcare associations as by his first-hand observations in the Home, in 1923 Volmer introduced an economical plan to secure additional childcare staff on a part-time basis. He recruited talented young, single, men and women who were studying medicine, law, or social work at Tulane and Newcomb and who sought to reduce their living expenses. In exchange for room and board, Volmer required these students, in the evenings and on weekends, to help the children with homework, keep them out of trouble, and simply lend a sympathetic ear.[140]

Among Volmer's earliest student counselors were Arthur J. Rosenberg, a Tulane student who had earlier worked at Brooklyn's and Philadelphia's Jewish orphanages, and Philip Feingold, a former teacher from New York and current Tulane medical student who was described as a "man of culture and refinement."[141] Volmer later also extended these positions to deserving college-bound wards, such as Hugo Fielschmidt in the summer of 1924 before he entered dental school.[142] Volmer's successors continued his innovative program throughout the rest of the Home's history, exposing the children to dozens of talented and ambitious college and graduate students, all white and mostly but not all Jewish.

WOMEN'S WORK

In the final years before the passage of the Nineteenth Amendment, the board faced a demand for women's participation in the Home's governance. Although women had funded and helped run the Home since its founding, during Volmer's tenure and Joseph Kohn's presidency women finally assumed positions as voting members of the association and leaders of its governing body. In January 1914, twelve women representing the local chapter of the National Council of Jewish Women attended the board's meeting. Leading the group were Nannie Haas Pokorny, a community leader and suffragist who was reportedly one of the city's earliest licensed drivers; Minnie Wexler, the Home's only unmarried honorary matron; and Ida Weis Friend, founding president of New Orleans's chapter of Hadassah. Citing the large number of girls in the Home (70 of 171 children), and the fact that CJOA's board already included female directors, these formidable women asserted that the time had come for the Home to do the same. The board quickly acceded.[143] These southern Jewish women, under the local banner of a national Jewish women's organization, had followed their Cleveland sisters' path to claim their places on the Home's fifty-nine-year-old board to make policy to care for needy children. In so doing they provide further evidence that Jewish women in the South largely replicated the organizational behaviors of their Jewish counterparts elsewhere.[144]

Within three months, the Home board admitted sixty women as association members, paving the way for Pokorny and Wexler to win seats on the board.[145] Beyond crucial committee work, the two women invested themselves in the children's lives. Pokorny oversaw Gizella Weiss's transition from the Home to Newcomb College, and Wexler looked after Irma Maretzky and Lena Tobias as they pursued careers in stenography while living in a nearby boarding house.[146] Recognizing their diligence, President Kohn appointed his female directors as delegates to the National Conference of Jewish Social Service, which they attended with Superintendent Volmer in 1917 and 1920.[147]

Community women also assumed another voluntary role at the Home during this period. During the first half of Volmer's tenure, Home leaders sought ways of providing "aftercare" to assist wards' transition to independence after discharge, a common concern among Jewish orphanages. In 1915, to address this "serious problem," the board launched a Big Brothers and Big Sisters program. Notwithstanding the name's confusing similarity to the children's leadership positions in the Golden City, the program enlisted adult volunteers from the city's Jewish community to personally "aid, encourage and protect" former residents as they learned to negotiate the "uncertainty, trials and temptations" in the world outside the Home. "Let him visit you, or if possible, visit him," urged President Kohn. "Let him know in a kindly way that you are his friend, his older and wiser brother, his counsellor and advisor."[148] Despite repeated calls for volunteers of both genders, few men agreed to become Big Brothers, and that portion of the effort soon languished. The call for adult Big Sisters, on the other hand, quickly struck a sympathetic chord with a wide swath of prosperous Jewish women in the community, drawing volunteers from within and outside the ranks of the stalwart honorary matrons.[149]

For the rest of the Home's existence, long after the demise of the Golden City, adult Big Sisters played a vital role in the children's lives. Perhaps most important were the strong personal relationships that the children individually developed with their Big Sisters, who often introduced their charges to the world of New Orleans's financial and social elite. Home alumni appreciated their Big Sisters for many things, including the chance to visit their homes and learn about "the finer things in life." Bessie Margolin, for example, developed a close relationship with her Big Sister, Hanna Bloom Stern, who had a long history of service to the Home and community. Stern's husband was Home trustee Maurice Stern, a German-born Jew who made his fortune as president of the cotton brokerage firm Lehman, Stern & Company.[150] During the five years Hanna Stern served as Bessie's matron, her son Edgar married Edith Rosenwald, the daughter of Sears, Roebuck & Company magnate Julius Rosenwald, further cementing Hanna's place among New Orleans's Jewish elite.[151] As a Big Sister, Stern exposed Bessie to her family and their lifestyle, including their St. Charles Avenue mansion, and helped Bessie secure housing and other services while transitioning from the Home to Newcomb College.[152]

Certain Big Sisters, like Stern, quickly earned reputations as "favorites" with the children for being especially generous with their time, attention, and affection. Helen Gold Haymon appreciated that Big Sister Anna Baum Naman remembered her birthday, invited her and her sister for dinner, and showed that she cared.[153] Not all Big Sisters lived up to the children's expectations. "I had one, but she was sort of not good," recalled Freda Hyde Lowenthal without offering specifics. "Some of the kids had wonderful ones, like Mrs. Feibelman," Freda said, referring to Mary Ann Fellman Feibelman, wife of Rabbi Julian Feibelman, a social activist who served Reform Congregation Temple Sinai from 1936 until his retirement in 1967.[154] Goldie Schonbach was another "lucky" Home girl who secured her first job in 1923 with the help of another popular Big Sister, Irma Moses Moses, who nurtured relationships with her assigned children that lasted long after their discharge.[155] Dorothy Rosenbaum, who lived in the Home from 1921 to 1929, treasured the China dishes Moses gave her as a wedding present, and later brought her son for visits at Moses's fine Joseph Street home.[156] In a 1929 letter to his father, twelve-year-old Louis Albert raved about his Big Sister, Mrs. B. Isaacs, who had just taken him out to lunch and a show: "She's a peach."[157]

PURSUING "NORMALCY"

Criticism of institutional childcare heightened in the first decades of the twentieth century as a growing cadre of social welfare professionals joined the call for raising dependent children in private homes. Sensitive to this, Volmer implemented the earliest changes to make the Home "cozier and more home-like" in appearance and function. In 1916, starting with the large, impersonal dining room, he directed the boys, using woodworking equipment at Newman School, to saw the long dining tables in half to provide each Golden City family a separate table.[158] In 1921, following the death of Joseph Kohn, the new president, Dr. Jacob Warren Newman, joined Volmer's efforts. Tablecloths and napkins were used daily (instead of only on holidays and other special occasions), despite the increased cost and labor. Newman also donated a complete silverware set and secured new curtains and shades.[159] A year later, when siblings dining together had become a regular practice, Volmer sought to further enhance the "home" feeling by replacing the rectangular "half-tables" with round ones, each furnished with a uniquely patterned set of dishes, and enlivening the room with greenery and framed pictures.[160]

Volmer also took steps to personalize each child's birthday. Through much of his time, each Home birthday celebrant received a small gift and a special meal served on the closest Friday evening. Volmer, who delighted in marking his daughter Louise's birthday with gifts and affectionate telegrams, eventually recognized the shortcoming of trying to celebrate one or more children while everyone else in the dining room ate their regular meal.[161] To resemble a private family's celebration, he directed that each child's birthday be feted at a little gathering with siblings or special friends in one of the parlors on the closest Saturday afternoon with cake, ice cream, and a gift. Despite the added time and expense, Volmer wanted each child to "always remember how happily he celebrated his birthday while in the Home."[162]

A bachelor and son of former Home president Henry Newman and Isidore Newman's nephew, President Jacob W. Newman encouraged these and other changes. He was wealthy and generous to the Home, donating $5,000 in 1925 in honor of his fiftieth birthday.[163] A practicing obstetrician who donated his medical services to poor women and children, Newman also immersed himself in Home activities. In 1921, for example, he secured a larger dwelling for Mrs. Milner, a favored nearby boardinghouse owner, so she could better serve the Home's nonresident wards (older children who no longer lived in the Home but remained under its supervision) and recent alumni.[164] Newman also supported Volmer's requests, such as moving the showers from the basement to adjoin the dormitories (so children no longer negotiated two flights of stairs before and after showering), chilling the water fountains, and adding a private bathroom for older girls.[165]

In June 1923, with 120 children in the Home, Volmer, citing the practice followed by at least two other orphanages and current standards in childcare, convinced a reluctant board to allow older children to spend weekends or vacations with parents or relatives.[166] When Volmer arrived, visitors to the Home were permitted only one Sunday afternoon each month. In 1918, the board granted Volmer's requests to expand visiting opportunities, increasing to afternoons on two Sundays each month in 1918, and by 1925, every Sunday afternoon. Subject to Volmer's approval, visiting parents and relatives could now take children off premises for a meal or movie.[167] For those who lived in or near the city, frequently spending Sunday afternoons with their children enabled them to preserve family bonds. Like Abraham Beerman in West, Texas, this was not the case for the parents of most Home children who lived in distant venues across the B'nai B'rith region and lacked the resources to travel. Widowers Sam Crystal in Chattanooga, Tennessee, and Joseph Tannenbaum, who had moved to New York after admitting his children from Galveston, went to great effort to visit during their children's stays in the Home. To capture these rare family meetings, the Crystals in 1925 and Tannenbaums in 1919 posed near the fountain on the Home's front lawn for cherished photos that descendants have preserved to this day.[168] Some parents who moved to New Orleans to be closer to their children also faced difficulties. In 1917, after finding that eight of eleven parents who moved to the city had become dependent since their arrival, Julius Goldman, director of JCEF, whose Central Relief Bureau provided aid to needy members of the Jewish community, urged the Home to discourage such relocations. Instead, the board required out-of-state lodges to agree to support any Home child's parent who became dependent after moving to the city.[169]

The heightened interest in "normalcy" of living conditions during the Newman and Volmer years coincided with the institution's official name change, including on the building's facade, from "Jewish Orphans' Home" to "Jewish Children's Home." More than semantics, the new name resulted from a 1924 amendment to the Home's constitution, which officially expanded eligible beneficiaries from "Jewish orphans and half-orphans" to a broader population: "Jewish children, who are without adequate means of support, or who are without proper care or supervision."[170] The amendment eliminated the stigma that might attach to youth who lived in a self-styled "orphanage" and obviated the board's longstanding yet inconsistent practice of stretching the words "orphans and half-orphans" to encompass dependent children with a living parent. In 1922, for example, of a total 123 children, 20 were full orphans, 82 were half orphans, while the remaining 21 were dependent children with two living parents.[171]

The Home's decreasing number of full orphans in relation to half orphans and children of two living indigent parents conformed to population trends in America's Jewish and non-Jewish childcare institutions. Not all other orphanages, however, yet saw the corresponding need to eliminate the word "orphan" from their name. CJOA, for example, changed its name in 1919 for the next decade to the Cleveland Jewish Orphan Home, symbolizing its transformation into a more humane place for children to live, if not the parental status of most of its charges.[172]

KEEPING THE HOME AT THE VANGUARD OF CHILDCARE

Throughout his tenure, like his predecessors, Volmer actively participated in local and national conferences, within and beyond the Jewish community, where he networked with institutional managers and other child welfare advocates, coinciding with the evolution of social work as an academic and professional endeavor. Even the organizations' names reflected this change: the National Conference of Charities and Correction and the National Conference of Jewish Charities, which Heymann and Teller had attended, became the National Conference of Social Welfare and the National Conference of Jewish Social Service in 1917 and 1919, respectively.[173] Volmer attained prominence and ultimately leadership roles in these organizations, delivering the invocation, presenting a paper on the effectiveness of self-governance, and presiding over recurring debates (which he described in 1922 as an ongoing "battle royal") on the merits of orphanages versus home placement. In these discussions, Volmer agreed with the goal of keeping children with their mothers when "moral and mental conditions permit," and acknowledged the increasing viability of placing children in private homes but only when a "home of high standards" could be secured. Despite his increased awareness of noninstitutional alternatives and their touted advantages, Volmer's biggest takeaways from the conferences he attended, as he regularly reported to the board, were both to affirm the essential role of a well-run institution in dependent childcare, and to stay abreast of the latest methods for maintaining institutional excellence in all facets of youth development.[174]

Dr. Newman, too, rose to leadership in child welfare associations, serving as vice president of Louisiana's Society for the Prevention of Cruelty to Children (the forerunner to the Children's Welfare Bureau) and president of the Social Workers Conference of New Orleans, while also placing the Home at the vanguard of children's health. Reflecting its eagerness for the latest medical advances, the Home embraced an opportunity to protect its wards from scarlet fever, which prior to the advent of antibiotics in the 1940s remained a leading cause of child mortality, including for five Home children in 1881. In November 1924, renowned husband-and-wife physicians, Drs. George and Gladys Dick, while in town to promote their recent discovery of a scarlet fever cure and vaccine, made news by injecting their serum into the forearms of fifty Home children, and then vaccinated those on whom a tell-tale red dot appeared.[175] The same year, as medical experts sought to promote diphtheria immunization, the press also lauded the Home as a pioneering role model for administering the Schick skin test to all 140 children, followed by antitoxin injections to those children displaying a lack of immunity. By the end of the year, all but 5 Home children were declared immune.[176] Even the Home's system of medical records influenced practices among local peer institutions; following a 1926 round table conference, managers of childcare institutions across the city chose the health record in use at the Home as their model.[177]

Beyond the health care it provided, the Jewish institution and its leaders received high praise. Father Peter M. H. Wynhoven, director of Catholic Charities and a pioneering social justice advocate, honored the Home by delivering the 1927 anniversary address. Noting the Hebrew word *tzedakah* means not only charity but also justice, Wynhoven declared "the Jew among the most desirable of citizens." He lauded the Home as "a model of service to the community."[178] The prominence Volmer, Dr. Newman, and other Home leaders garnered for the institution stemmed largely from centralized activities they implemented and controlled within the building, such as self-governance and health care, and the education the Home provided only two blocks away at Newman School. In resisting home placements, perhaps they simply could not envision a way to achieve similar control or efficiency in caring for 140 children placed in private Homes across the city or the region.

THE END OF VOLMER'S TENURE

Volmer's fourteen years as superintendent suddenly ended on January 1, 1926. The board had asked Volmer to withdraw his resignation, but he declined to do so. He considered himself privileged to have guided "the destiny of the Home and of the children in it" throughout his tenure, creating bonds with the board, staff, and children "which are not lightly severed." With "deepest regret" Volmer explained only that he had received an unexpected business opportunity.[179] Although unmentioned, the timing was good; his daughter Louise had graduated from Newman one year earlier and was now well into her sophomore year at Newcomb College, where she lived on campus.[180] The superintendent revealed humility and self-awareness achieved from hindsight, referring to his "insufficiency in training for the specific work of institutional child guidance at the outset of my career here, and perhaps temperamental lack."[181]

After his resignation, Leon and Tresa Volmer moved to Canton, Ohio, where Tresa's sister lived. There Volmer worked in the insurance business while remaining active in B'nai B'rith and other Jewish organizations. He delivered lectures on Judaism and child development, and helped organize the religious school at the McKinley Avenue Temple, where he occasionally led services.[182] After an extended illness, Leon Volmer died in September 1933 at age fifty-six; he was buried in Charleston, West Virginia, where he had started his career as a rabbi.[183]

Having admittedly embarked on his career at the Home insufficiently trained for "institutional child guidance," Leon Volmer embraced Chester Teller's Golden City model of self-government. Against the backdrop of America's quest to make the world safe for democracy, the Golden City offered the children an object lesson in representative government as well as a framework for contributing to the war effort. Despite ongoing praise from the board and the public for this innovative system of institutional childcare, subsequent accounts from alumni and staff revealed the problem of relying upon youth to govern themselves and younger peers without adequate supervision by adults trained and suited to work with children. Notwithstanding his shortcomings as a disciplinarian, Volmer enhanced the children's lives by expanding activities and programs especially for the girls within and outside the Home that emulated the experiences of middle-class community peers. By launching the Home's student-counselor program, Volmer also economically increased the children's individual exposure to bright and attentive role models. The extent would soon be revealed, however, to which Volmer and the board had overlooked growing trends to "deinstitutionalize" the Home, including by pursuing alternative forms of childcare.

chapter nine

ED LASHMAN STEERS
THE HOME IN A NEW DIRECTION
1926–1929

Having served as the Home's field director since 1922 and superintendent of Cleveland's Jewish orphanage before that, Edward Lashman presented a strong choice to succeed Leon Volmer. A disarmingly slender man of medium height with a trim mustache, in his four years as field director he had shepherded a bold campaign to regain the Home's financial footing while raising its profile throughout the B'nai B'rith region.[1] As an emerging class of professional social workers and evolving childcare standards challenged the authority of institutional lay leaders, Lashman undertook an equally bold campaign as superintendent to make the Home as homelike as possible for its children.

Louis Edward Lashman (who went by Ed) was born 1890, in Riga, Latvia. He came to America as a toddler with his parents, Samuel and Lottie. They lived for more than a decade in Philadelphia before moving to Camden, New Jersey, where Samuel owned a dry goods store.[2] By 1915, after graduating from Columbia University's Teachers College, where he studied social science and psychology, Lashman was drawn to the field of child welfare. After a year directing municipal youth centers and playgrounds in Raleigh, North Carolina, Lashman headed to Chicago to run B'nai B'rith's Big Brother activities, pairing Jewish men with boys in need of attention.[3] His duties there quickly expanded, and by 1918 he also served as executive secretary of the Anti-Defamation League, which B'nai B'rith founded five years earlier "to stop the defamation of the Jewish people and to secure justice and fair treatment to all." In this role, Lashman advocated for social justice, including by protesting antisemitic movies and cartoons.[4]

While in Chicago, Lashman married Edith Deutsch. Born in Cincinnati, Ohio, in 1892 to Austrian parents—her father was a history professor at Hebrew Union College and her mother a homemaker—Edith attended public schools before earning degrees at the University of Cincinnati and Simmons College in Boston. After briefly teaching, she attended Boston's Prince School of Department Store Education, where she learned the fundamentals of retail sales and service, experience she later used to solicit donations and supervise volunteers. While Ed fulfilled his military service during World War I, Edith filled his job at the Anti-Defamation League, honing her advocacy for Jewish and social causes.[5]

A tall woman with an authoritative voice, Edith Deutsch Lashman spoke her mind. At the ADL, she made news when she complained directly to the secretary of the Navy about a form that omitted "Jewish" from the listed religions and obtained his agreement not to use the data to undercount Jewish servicemen.[6] She made news in Cleveland, too, for asking to be excused from lengthy jury deliberations, citing hardship: at night, talkative female jurors kept her awake while sequestered in a hotel and, during the day, patronizing male jurors refused to argue the case with her.[7]

In January 1920, having resumed work at B'nai B'rith after his military service, Ed Lashman became superintendent of what had become known as the Cleveland Jewish Orphan Home (CJOH).[8] He continued his predecessor's work to transform the facility into a more humane place for its five hundred children. With a "ruthless kind of energy," Lashman "shook up the very foundations" of CJOH, wrote an alumnus, "making life richer and freer." He closed the upper grades at the institution's school and sent those children to public school, abolished uniforms, hired a dietitian, and recruited volunteers to run new clubs and organizations. For the first time, he permitted outings for the children and allowed more frequent visits by family. The Lashmans cultivated relationships with Cleveland's prosperous Jewish community. With increased donations, he installed windows in dark corners, purchased a dishwashing machine, and piped dependably warm water into washrooms for the children and staff. To better prepare the children for discharge, he added after-school courses in auto mechanics, typing, and shorthand.[9]

Lashman also introduced self-governance into CJOH. That Lashman's "Sunshine City" closely resembled the Home's "Golden City," with the same rankings of "Dwellers" and "Builders," was no coincidence. Early in his CJOH tenure, while attending a social work conference in New Orleans, Lashman visited the Home on a tour arranged by Volmer.[10] Lashman's favorable impressions of the Home not only led him to introduce similar practices in Cleveland's orphanage, but later drew him back to New Orleans.

As Lashman purged CJOH's grimness and ruggedness, however, his relationship with its board deteriorated. Regarding himself as the expert charged with improving the institution as he saw fit, he responded abrasively to interference, thereby alienating board members. In 1921, after the board rejected his request to discontinue the traditional "First Picnic" anniversary celebration, Lashman resigned, just eighteen months after he arrived. In a farewell statement, Lashman bitterly cautioned the board to spell out his successor's duties so he "may not come here under any false pretenses and may understand whether his position is analogous to that of a factory employee, as intimated by certain members of the Board, or whether he is a professional social worker with the responsibility, dignity, and authority which this position should carry with it."[11] He illustrated the friction between the professionalization of social work and childcare institutions dominated by lay boards.

Lashman briefly returned to Chicago, where he learned that the Home was looking to hire a field director.[12] Not only did Lashman's CJOH experience qualify him for the job, but the new position entailed only a portion of his former responsibilities and for a well-regarded institution with far fewer children. Volmer's steady fourteen-year tenure and Lashman's favorable impressions of the Home allayed any misgivings Lashman held about once again subordinating himself to a lay board. Furthermore, the Home's superintendent would not second-guess him because the field director reported to the board, reflecting the importance it attached to the new position.

By the time Volmer resigned, Lashman felt deep commitment to the Home. For four years, Lashman had traveled the region, appealing for the Home's children while inculcating in donors a practice of annual contributions.[13] New Orleans had become home for the Lashmans as well. Edith's brothers had moved to New Orleans years before Ed and Edith, quickly making names for themselves. Hermann B. Deutsch, a political reporter for the *Times-Picayune*, was becoming one of the city's most renowned writers, and Eberhard P. Deutsch, who married a wealthy New Orleans socialite, established what became a prominent law firm bearing his name.[14] Ed and Edith arrived in 1922 with their three-year-old daughter, Hermine. In 1924, Edith gave birth to a son, L. Edward Jr., although sadly just two months later, Hermine died.[15] Lashman expressed gratefulness to the Home's board, as he wrote after their daughter's death, whose "sympathetic understanding on the occasion of our tragic loss helped much to give Mrs. Lashman and me the courage and will to 'carry on.'"[16]

Edith withstood the tragedy by staying active in community affairs, assuming leadership roles as chair of the Young Women's Hebrew Association and president of the parent teacher association of Newman School, which her son, L. Edward Jr., or "Sonny," attended. Edith often used her full name, Edith Deutsch Lashman, an uncommon practice at the time, which connected her to the prestige her brothers had already earned in their careers and among the city's social circles. Adding intellect, grace, and the favorable reputation she had acquired in supporting her husband's work, Edith easily navigated New Orleans's Jewish and gentile community as a goodwill ambassador and fundraiser for the Home.[17] Assuming more visibility in the community than previous Home superintendents' wives, Edith represented the changing role of women in a male-dominated society and provided a new model for Home girls.

Two important resources guided Ed Lashman in his new role as superintendent. He turned first to Harry Ginsburg, who had a decade of experience as the Home's assistant superintendent. "His intimate acquaintance with the details of the institution's workings," wrote Lashman in support of raising Ginsburg's salary, "and his rare ability as a supervisor of boys and girls relieved me of considerable detail and helped much to lighten the burden in the change of administration."[18] Equally important, the Child Welfare League of America ("League"), a newly formed national organization created to set childcare standards, had just completed a comprehensive study of New Orleans's thirty-four child welfare institutions and agencies, including the city's twelve orphanages that together housed thirty-five hundred children. The report's forty-two pages devoted to the Home represented the institution's first independent critical evaluation by childcare experts. Delivered just two weeks after Lashman assumed the superintendency, the report revealed operational shortcomings and provided a roadmap for steering the institution in a new direction.[19]

Overall, the League's report reflected the dramatic shift in priorities for dependent childcare taking place since the turn of the century. In prior years, the Home and other institutions received praise for physical layouts and processes that prioritized orderliness, cleanliness, and efficiency, such as large, spartan dormitories, peer behavioral management in the form of self-government, and the efficiencies obtained from bulk purchasing of clothing and other items. By 1926, with the focus on meeting the individual child's needs, those same features and systems drew condemnation as outmoded and antithetical to proper dependent childcare. While the Home had gilded its institutional cage with expanded programs and improved facilities, to borrow Rabbi Leucht's metaphor from the end of the last century, it had resisted calls to keep or place children in private homes.

Simultaneously, while 205,000 children lived in institutions or received care from agencies across the United States, the field of childcare, nationally and locally, grew dramatically. The League emerged from the recommendations of the landmark 1909 White House Conference. In addition to the priority placed on preserving family life, the conference called for standards that could emerge only from cooperation and regulation among interested institutions and agencies.[20] A second White House Conference in 1919 intensified the scrutiny on institutional childcare. Held in what President Woodrow Wilson declared the Year of the Child, the 1919 conference led to national recognition of children's fundamental rights (including a normal home life, education, recreation, and vocational preparation) and fundamental principles of institutional administration.[21]

The conference also shifted public perception, contributing to wide attacks on orphan asylums throughout the ensuing years. "Abolish the Orphan Asylum," announced child welfare leader Sophie Irene Loeb's 1925 essay that ran in newspapers across the country, calling on Americans to support mothers' subsidies and home placements instead of institutions.[22] In New Orleans, as well, newspaper headlines the same year announced "Great Campaign Begun to Abolish Orphan Asylums," "A Home for Every Child," and "Abolition of Asylums Is Sought by Women's Organization."[23] The president of the featured women's organization, the Louisiana Federation of Women's Clubs, was none other than volunteer activist Ida Weis Friend, who a decade earlier had won seats for women on the Home's board and in 1917 served as a director.[24]

Despite these public and prominent rejections of institutional childcare, just as with the initial White House Conference of 1909, the nation's orphanages remained open. Instead of closing, many institutional managers, as one commentator described, "subjected themselves to vigorous heart searching and a great effort . . . to place institutional service on a sound basis and to determine where the lines between the different kinds of care for different individuals or groups should be drawn."[25] Throughout the first decades of the twentieth century, as Volmer had observed, the vigorous debate around childcare continued as academics and seasoned practitioners challenged and defended old and new childcare and social welfare policies and practices. However, these conferences and debates began to coalesce into a body of professional ideals and standards.[26]

In New Orleans, this led to the creation of the Central Council of Social Agencies, organized in 1921 to provide uniform standards and practices that would, in turn, promote greater cooperation among its member agencies. The Central Council, of which Volmer and Lashman were members, and its fundraising arm the Community Chest of New Orleans, had commissioned the League's survey, which Dr. Jacob W. Newman fully endorsed in his dual roles as president of the Home and of the Louisiana Society for the Prevention of Cruelty to Children, soon renamed the Child Welfare Bureau. After the League conducted its observations over several weeks in October 1925, the city eagerly awaited its findings. The Community Chest planned to use the report to set its annual fundraising goals while the Home and other surveyed institutions looked forward to the expert guidance.[27] Most urgently, the League's report would help determine the future of the Waifs' Home, a municipal asylum, now rocked by shameful news that its superintendent, while intoxicated, had seriously beaten a boy on Christmas Day. Further reflecting the community's high regard for the Home and its leaders, Dr. Newman later headed efforts to select personnel for the Waifs' Home's new nonpolitical board.[28]

League founder and lead investigator, Dr. Christian Carl Carstens, advocated a nuanced, child-centered approach to dependent childcare. While asserting the primacy of keeping children in their own homes whenever possible, Carstens never pitted private foster homes against institutions. "His concern was always focused upon the quality of service, and not upon the type of organization," wrote Carsten's colleague Emma Octavia Lundberg, the first social services director of the U.S. Children's Bureau.[29] Foster care of any kind would be greatly reduced, urged Carstens, if community resources were used to prevent the removal of children from their own homes. At the same time, he viewed the League's surveys not as mere jobs to be done and reports to be written but rather each one "was a crusade for a square deal for children."[30]

Carsten's approach characterized the League's report on the Home, which he coauthored with his staff member Mary Irene Atkinson, who later succeeded Lundberg at the U.S. Children's Bureau. Based on a full day of observation and scrutiny of records, the report covered all aspects of the institution, including governance, staffing levels and qualifications, the building, children's medical care and diet, the children's daily lives and education, and overall social policies. The report applauded many aspects of the Home's operations while raising serious questions about others. The League commended the children's "natural and spontaneous" interactions with visitors and administrators, which it attributed to the many social opportunities, cultural advantages, and community contacts the Home provided. It also lauded the Home's superior medical services, educational and vocational advantages, and "splendid physical care," all of which the League attributed to the board's commitment to giving Home wards "a wholesome environment."[31]

In keeping with Carsten's child-centered views, the League urged the Home to overhaul its approach to admitting and retaining children. The Home should "exhaust all resources" before "depriving a child of the environment which is still considered the most desirable for rearing the young of the human race, namely the family home." For children whose dependency arose from purely economic factors, the League advocated the use of family casework, state mothers' pensions, and granting of mothers' aid by private agencies to prevent and decrease institutional admissions.[32] It called on the Home to adopt "a more flexible social program" to offer alternatives to institutional care whenever appropriate. To do so, the League recommended the Home hire a "person trained in the technique of social casework and having broad experience in the field of children's work" who would report to the superintendent and be responsible for intake, discharge, and aftercare.[33] Just as the Home had commendably relied upon scientific principles and trained experts in providing medical care, wrote the League, the Home should not in its social decisions rely "upon the kindly interest, sympathy and good intentions of lay men; upon employees responsible first of all for other duties; upon social agencies outside of New Orleans which in many instances were newly organized and inadequately staffed; and upon the New Orleans Jewish Welfare Bureau whose case methods, as revealed by recent studies, are not entirely consistent with accepted standards of procedure."[34]

The League expressed concern that communities across the B'nai B'rith region found it easier to send children to the Home rather than support them locally. In one of its most poignant observations about the vast majority of children admitted to the Home from outside the New Orleans area (then 120 of 137), the League wrote, "It seems a travesty on human kindness for a child who has been deprived of one parent by death to be deprived of the other solely for economic reasons and to be removed hundreds of miles from his original environment in order to receive aid."[35] For this reason, the League cautioned, the Home should not assume that all children B'nai B'rith proposed for admission needed institutional care.

For the League, the work a series of superintendents and board presidents had done to make the Home feel more like a home failed to suffice. Their biggest concern about the building was the "unfortunate" barracks-style dormitories. With children housed in such large groups, rather than in smaller bedrooms, stressed the League, approximating family life was an "impossibility."[36] Believing that creating individual rooms would be unfeasible, the League instead suggested that if and when the board considered constructing a new facility, it should erect small cottages to care for groups of no more than twelve children as a family unit.[37] This "cottage plan," which Michel Heymann had years earlier touted in his "ideal orphan asylum," had become a popular alternative to traditional institutions, including among Jewish orphanages. In 1912, New York's Hebrew Sheltering Guardian Society had moved from the city to a two-hundred-acre campus in Pleasantville; in 1921 Baltimore's Hebrew Orphan Asylum moved from its large building on the city's westside into a new cottage facility in "the country" (before closing five years later); and in 1929 CJOH moved from that city's declining Woodland Avenue neighborhood to a thirty-acre suburban campus while adopting the agreeably modern name "Bellefaire."[38]

The League also did not mince words in decrying the Golden City's shortcomings. It disapproved of the Golden City's methods of self-governance and discipline, noting that giving "checks" and "privilege cards" for unsatisfactory and good behavior, respectively, created expectations of reward for doing what was right. In the League's view, the entire scheme promoted tattling and imposed excessive responsibility on older children. The League also viewed the cooperative store as an artifice that prevented the children from patronizing neighborhood shops as they would do as part of a private family. To teach economy and life experience, the report recommended giving the children, especially older girls, greater control in selecting and buying their clothing.[39] On other points, the League recommended the Home hire an additional supervisor for the seventy girls in the Home and a trained caregiver, in lieu of the current babysitters, to attend to the nursery children.

After acknowledging Newman School's "exceptional educational advantages," the League posed a series of questions for the board. Was association with a "selected group of outside children" as desirable for the Home children's social and emotional development as association "with an unselected group such as is found in the public schools"? Did the Home children develop "a definite class consciousness" from attending Newman School? Was the large financial investment warranted by the results achieved? Deeming itself unqualified to address these questions, the League urged the board to secure an expert to conduct the necessary study. The Home's board had never before faced such concerns about its school. Less than two years earlier, the *Golden City Messenger* boasted that the school afforded Home children "unusual advantages" while teaching that "wealth is no evidence of worth," which instead must be measured by "honorable achievement and personal decency."[40]

The League's report inspired Lashman, who knew from his time at CJOH how to implement swift and dramatic reforms. He was prepared to do nothing less for the Home's children. Unlike his CJOH experience, the Home's board fully endorsed Lashman's reforms, which President Newman proudly described as a plan "to approximate the normal family home and duplicate the conditions as nearly as possible."[41] Lashman first turned his attention to the younger children, who as young as age six previously had been turned over from the nursery to the care of a fourteen- or fifteen-year-old Big Sister. Instead, Lashman retained children in the nursery under direct adult supervision until they were nine years of age.[42] He also recruited a volunteer to direct a preschool class for children ages two to five and hired a nursery supervisor. At the time, nursery schools—professionally supervised environments for young children that promoted social and emotional development while enhancing motor skills and sensory discrimination—were rare and catered almost exclusively to children of affluent parents.[43] When the honorary matrons, whose roles were undermined by the League's report, objected to the proposed preschool as "a luxury only children of wealthy parents enjoy," Lashman nevertheless convinced the board to proceed with the novel concept.[44]

Neither Lashman nor the board, however, addressed the League's concern that Home children might develop a "definite class consciousness" by attending Newman School. Instead, the board acknowledged that the city's public commercial high schools and trade schools were now better equipped for vocational training than Newman. Over the past two decades, Newman had become a general high school geared toward college preparation, where one or two teachers taught all specialized studies, rather than the manual training program envisioned by its founders. For this reason and with the expectation of reduced expenses, the board voted to discontinue Newman's commercial and industrial departments.[45] By 1930, Lashman reported that 20 of 142 Home children attended Delgado Trade School (14), Samuel J. Peters Commercial School for Boys (3), and Joseph Kohn Commercial School for Girls (3). In place of vocational training and consistent with national educational trends, Newman School introduced a new and enlarged "arts and crafts department" to give "greater opportunity for creative work, the standard of achievement to be measured by artistic excellence," and not vocational preparation.[46] In view of the curricular changes, the board recognized that the name "Isidore Newman Manual Training School" conveyed an outdated and inaccurate impression of the school.[47] In June 1931, when Home pupil Ida Rose Beerman won the prize for the school magazine's best editorial, she graduated not from "Manual," but from the newly named Isidore Newman School.[48]

Experiences recounted by Ida's brother, Ralph, tend to confirm not only the wisdom of the Home's decision to rely on specialized public schools to meet the vocational needs of some children, but also—contrary to the League's concerns—the value of exposure to socioeconomic differences. In 1926, Ralph "jumped at the chance" to leave Newman's rigorous academics to attend Delgado, where he learned metal work and drafting that qualified him for machine shop jobs after he left the Home. By attending both schools, Beerman met "two different worlds of people," by which he meant Newman's "rich kids" and Delgado's "working poorer class of people" who offered a "touch of the real world." Looking back years later from his position as president of a national industrial business, Ralph appreciated what both schools offered. "I don't believe I could have gotten that exposure to life anywhere else."[49]

Lashman focused on an overriding goal to avoid Home children being "stamped as institutional children." To this end, he also began dismantling the Golden City's insular activities. "The best way to fit children in institutions for life outside," he argued, "is to make them a real part of society."[50] He abandoned the cooperative store, as the League recommended, and increased the children's allowances to enable them to purchase candy, stationery, and small notions at nearby stores. Despite their popularity, he abolished the Home's Boy and Girl Scout groups, and distributed the children to local troops.[51]

Attending local synagogues furnished another means for Home children to become part of the wider Jewish community. With the endorsement of local rabbis, the board assented to Lashman's request to close the Home synagogue, which he saw as an outdated relic. Beginning with Rosh Hashanah and Yom Kippur in September 1926, the children were distributed among the city's three Reform synagogues—Temple Sinai, Touro Synagogue, and Congregation Gates of Prayer—all within walking distance or a brief streetcar ride. Impressed by their new congregations—or perhaps the company of their Jewish community peers—several Home children requested permission also to attend services at these synagogues on Friday nights and Saturday mornings.[52] Lacking Volmer's rabbinic training, Lashman felt added incentive to enroll the children in the religious schools and confirmation classes conducted by the synagogues they attended for services.[53]

Although the board decided to invite local parents and relatives to take their children to services at their synagogue, which would have enabled children to worship at the city's Orthodox congregations, no record remains of any such notice or requests.[54] Before Sam Levitan was admitted to the Home at age three in 1927 following the death of his mother, his family worshipped at Orthodox Congregation Anshe Sfard. Throughout his nine years in the Home, Sam attended Sunday school and services at Reform Temple Sinai. Whether Sam's father was apprised of the alternative or chose not to seek an accommodation is unknown. Years later, the board commented, "In all our years of experience, we have had no such [religious] insistence from any parent or guardian."[55] After discharge, Sam's remarried father sent him to Communal Hebrew School, where he studied to become a bar mitzvah, a traditional ritual not then observed in Reform congregations or in the Home.[56] Considering the dependence of parents and guardians on the Home for childcare, which would tend to chill requests for accommodations, Sam likely was not the only Home child who forwent the Orthodox upbringing he would have received with his family.

Lashman continued to oversee the children's celebrations of religious traditions as would be conducted in a private Jewish home, including Friday evening *kiddush,* with the lighting of candles and blessings over wine and *challah.* Home children celebrated other traditional Jewish holidays and festivals typically commemorated in private households, such as Passover seder, eating Hamantaschen on Purim, and taking meals in an elaborately decorated *sukkah.*[57] They celebrated Chanukah by kindling the festival lights and receiving small gifts, as would be done in a private Jewish home but, at Lashman's direction, with a view to offset the ubiquity of Christmas. In December 1926, after the children presented a play about the Maccabees, the heroes of Chanukah, the superintendent treated his charges to a dance party.[58]

Further exceeding the League's recommendations, Lashman ended practices that dehumanized or failed to individualize the children. To identify laundry, the housekeeping staff began sewing into the children's clothing fabric tags rubber-stamped with their names instead of the previously assigned numbers. On Friday nights, Lashman, his wife, and other staff members, began sitting with the children for dinner and *kiddush* service, rotating among the tables weekly, to model table manners and increase personal contact.[59] He began declining and discouraging wholesale invitations for all the children from well-meaning donors, such as riverboat cruises, trolley rides, and "Orphans' Day" at the movies, in favor of outings and opportunities offered individually or to small groups of interested children. Previously welcomed and publicly applauded, these large group activities had fallen into disfavor with child welfare professionals for the institutional stigma they carried.[60]

By the end of 1928, as part of his "de-institutionalizing plan" to address one of the League's biggest concerns, Lashman began breaking up the large, "prison-like" dormitories into small bedrooms, each accommodating one to three children, resulting in one of the most dramatic changes in Home life.[61] "Privacy," marveled Rabbi David Lefkowitz after touring the Home, contrasting his childhood in New York's Hebrew Orphan Asylum with the small bedrooms Lashman created, was something "we never knew—a little like a home."[62] For some Home children, having a private room, or even one they shared with only one or two other children, offered a new and treasured experience. Seventeen-year-old Beulah Blondheim, newly discharged from the Home in 1929 after living there for fifteen years, cried over leaving behind not only her friends and her comfortable routine, but also her "private little room." "I'm telling you," recounted Beulah years later, "I wanted to go back."[63]

Although Lashman followed the League's recommendation and abolished the "check" system by which Big Brothers and Sisters tallied demerits for their young charges, he retained other aspects of the Golden City, such as the weekly family meetings during which the children proposed ways to improve their daily life.[64] He valued these sessions as a means of promoting independence and a "homelike" environment. "We don't do a thing for the children that they can themselves do," he told national childcare professionals at a 1928 conference in a discussion on character building.[65] However, eliminating some aspects of the Golden City to which the children had grown accustomed provoked temporary repercussions. As Ginsburg later recounted, a few older children, having adjusted to the Golden City's scant adult supervision, expressed a sense of injustice from being deprived of their authority and resented that their actions were now being too closely watched. "No longer could older children use younger children as 'flunkies' and intimidate them," Ginsburg wrote for the first time in 1934 about the "child government." "No longer could older children abuse younger children on the pretense that they 'were trying to make them behave.'" Suggesting that a higher degree of neglect if not abuse may have existed in the Golden City than had been previously revealed, Ginsburg now saw self-government as "a cruel misnomer" for letting children rule each other.[66] If either Lashman or Ginsburg harbored these concerns before the League issued its report, they left no such record. To the contrary, the League attributed the children's "sustained interest" in the self-government program to Ginsburg, whose enthusiasm "vitalized" the whole plan.[67]

Despite Lashman's remarkable achievements to modernize and deinstitutionalize the Home during his time as superintendent, neither he nor the board took steps to offer a "flexible program" to care for children in a noninstitutional environment wherever possible, or to employ a trained social caseworker to implement those services, as the League had recommended. Nor is there any record of serious consideration to do so. Although neither Lashman nor the board explained their inaction, as early as 1921 child welfare advocates elsewhere recognized the challenges of foster family placements, including finding suitable families, children who needed re-placements, separation of siblings, and oversight.[68] Whether from the weight of the Home's established and publicly applauded practices, the absence of adverse fiscal or regulatory consequences, or the lack of local norms and structures to aid parents in keeping their children or to support foster care, the League's recommendations apparently could not overcome the Home's institutional inertia.

On May 4, 1929, following what was described as a "protracted illness," Ed Lashman suddenly died. Three of the Home's oldest boys and two alumni served as pallbearers at his funeral.[69] The board's memorial tribute, prepared by rabbis of the three Reform congregations that embraced the Home's children, lamented the loss of "an executive of great force" who was "scholarly in his approach to his chosen work, kindly in his dealings with children, indefatigable in his efforts both for the spiritual good of the child and the material wealth of the Institution."[70] According to alumnus Louis Peters, whose daily chores included emptying the superintendent's wastebasket, Lashman was an "intelligent, soft-spoken, kindly person" who was "dearly loved by the children."[71] Before he died, Lashman made known that, typical of Jews who eschew floral offerings for funerals, he preferred any memorial contributions be put toward the Home children's enjoyment. "It was more than a gesture, that last request," wrote the editor of the *Times-Picayune*. "Mr. Lashman was a man to whom the care of orphaned or neglected children was more than a job and more than a career. It was his life. . . . It was his idea, therefore, that the Home should be what its name implies, rather than an institution which would bend each child to fit its requirements." For years to come, the Lashman Fund ensured each child received a fitting Chanukah gift.[72]

During just three years as superintendent, Lashman led the Home's lay board to embrace many, although not all, of the Child Welfare League's recommendations, which reflected evolving standards of childcare. We are left to imagine what additional changes Lashman would have instituted had his career not been cut short. Beyond other accomplishments, Lashman engendered the support of his staff, who, in the board's words, "caught the fever of Edward Lashman's zeal, fervor of belief in the sacred cause."[73] Among the most zealous of Lashman's staff and supporters were Harry Ginsburg and Edith Deutsch Lashman.

chapter ten

"UNCLE HARRY" GINSBURG TAKES CHARGE 1929–1940

Ed Lashman's interrupted quest to make the Home more "homelike" quickly found its champion in Harry Ginsburg, whose tenure spanned the Great Depression and World War II. By his former boss's death in 1929, Ginsburg already had worked in Jewish orphanages for fifteen of his forty-one years, including a decade at the Home as boys' supervisor and then assistant superintendent, capably substituting for Volmer and Lashman during their absences. If appointing the Home's first unmarried superintendent raised concerns, neither the board nor its bachelor president wasted any time on them—although within a year after his promotion, Ginsburg added a familial female presence by hiring his widowed sister, Sonya, to work and live in the Home as a supervisor.[1] Three weeks after Lashman's death, without soliciting applications, Dr. Jacob W. Newman announced the board's unanimous decision to put the popular Ginsburg in charge.[2] Home children reportedly hailed their new superintendent, whom many of them had known for years, with "loud cheers."[3] For the rest of the Home's existence, and his life, "Uncle Harry" personified the institution.

The board also recognized that Ed Lashman's widow, Edith, possessed the skills and ambition to carry out her late husband's fundraising work as field director, a position that had remained unfilled during his tenure.[4] And yet, the capable woman had a tender, sensitive side that almost kept her from accepting the post. It would be too difficult emotionally, she had first thought, to see the same children's faces in the same rooms where she had lived for more than three years with her late husband, and so she originally planned to move to California, where her sister was launching a career as a public health nurse. Edith Lashman, however, quickly reassessed the situation. Not only did assuming her husband's job of raising money from seven states fill her hours; she also felt emotionally attached to the children, whom she had unofficially "mothered" while living in the Home during her husband's time as superintendent, advising the girls about what sort of hat to buy, or finding six little boys turning somersaults in the beds during their "rest hour." "My capacity as 'mother,'" she explained soon after taking the position, "has made my life so full of small, homely interests that I don't have time for loneliness."[5] Moreover, after Ginsburg volunteered to occupy other quarters in the Home, the board permitted Lashman to retain her three-bedroom apartment with her young son, who continued gratis at Newman School. Amid expanding boundaries for women, the position also promised a career that included travel and public speaking for a cherished cause.[6]

Despite the all-too-common resistance to ambitious career women, Lashman found a supportive colleague in Harry Ginsburg, who had long endorsed women's rights. "The world is not going to the dogs," he wrote in support of suffrage in 1912, "because the mothers of men feel able to take an active interest in the affairs of their community and their country."[7] Moreover, the board's decision to place Lashman in charge of fundraising left Ginsburg more time to focus on the children and running the Home. As superintendent, "Uncle Harry" Ginsburg embraced the transformative work launched by his predecessor and made it his mission for the next seventeen years to replicate private family life as closely as possible for the Home's children.

Harry Lincoln Ginsburg was born on August 13, 1886, in Petrograd, Russia, and spent his childhood in Denver, Colorado.[8] Unlike most other Jewish orphanage superintendents by this time, Ginsburg never finished college or received a degree. Instead, he obtained a broad education in a variety of academic settings: he studied American literature, history, and French at New York City's rigorous Townsend Harris Hall School; Latin, German, and physics at Central Institute in Cleveland, Ohio; and spent a summer studying art in London. After arriving in New Orleans in 1917, Ginsburg twice enrolled part-time at Tulane University, once before and once after his World War I Navy service. On both occasions, however, due to the demands of his job at the Home, Ginsburg withdrew without receiving grades or credits.[9] After that, other than two summer courses at New York's School of Social Work, Ginsburg set aside any dreams of higher education and made rearing the Home's children his life's work.[10]

In his first exposure to childcare, Ginsburg volunteered at New York's Hebrew Sheltering Guardian Society and was there when it adopted the system of self-government that Chester Teller later brought to the Home as the Golden City.[11] Drawn to the field by this experience, twenty-five-year-old Ginsburg started his professional life in childcare as a boys' supervisor at Cleveland's Jewish orphanage.[12] After five years, he left Cleveland to answer Superintendent Volmer's ad for a similar position in the Home.[13]

Ginsburg enjoyed working with children and, by all accounts, it came to him naturally. He was recalled in his early years at CJOA as one of the better-liked boys' supervisors. Short and stocky but a speedy runner, Ginsburg enjoyed being on the playground year-round, where he deftly organized the kids into teams. Yet Ginsburg brooked no nonsense and was remembered by one former resident for physically disciplining an unruly CJOA boy by what was described as "mopping" him around the playroom. "Anyway, the kids liked him," added the alumnus, recalling how Ginsburg introduced a Victrola into the dormitory, recounted stories of his travels, and read *Huck Finn* to the boys in the evening.[14]

Home children, too, liked their "Uncle Harry." According to visitors, the children showed him casual affection, neither stiffening to attention nor showing embarrassment in his presence. Hearing him approach, for example, a boy glanced up from his book and said "'Lo, Uncle Harry," before returning to his reading.[15] A reporter visiting in 1940 remarked that the children would no sooner "call him Mr. Ginsburg than forego an ice cream dessert."[16] Another visitor noted that, as Ginsburg walked through the building, children greeted him pleasantly with demonstrations ranging from a wave to a "hug accomplished with nine-year-old enthusiasm."[17] He was described as "father, advisor, confession-receiver, friend, as well a genial but shrewd student of human character and child character in particular."[18] He was frequently photographed encircled by eager, smiling Home boys and girls—sometimes with one or two of the smallest perched on his lap—with whom he is reading, playing checkers, or simply paying close attention. Although many were staged for the cameras, these recurring images captured Ginsburg's prominence in the life of the Home and its children.[19]

Ginsburg's large personality also inspired a wide range of emotions and recollections from Home alumni. He loved music and played the flute, recalled Beulah Blondheim Harvith, who spent fifteen years in the Home.[20] Ralph Beerman recalled Ginsburg as "quite an orator" from whom he "learned an immense amount about life, people, and many other things."[21] Sonia Packman

Washofsky, placed in the Home at age eleven by her widowed father, "loved Uncle Harry," who in her words, was a "tough man . . . you had to respect." Returning after a leisurely summer visit with an aunt, Sonia complained to Ginsburg about resuming her chores, which then consisted largely of keeping one's room straight and other odd jobs as needed, just as would be expected of children in any private home. "You're part of the team," Ginsburg quietly but firmly replied to Sonia's sassy resistance, which she found far more effective in winning her cooperation than any punishment.[22] Albert Fox, remembered Ginsburg's response to a boy who objected to "wasting all of this time" painting and fixing up the girls' rooms. "If these young ladies never have a chance to have anything good," Fox recalled Ginsburg gently explaining, "they'll never appreciate good things in their lives."[23] Helen Gold Haymon took comfort in Ginsburg's presence. "I can yet hear," the alumna reminisced, "in the still of the night, the rhythmic beat of Uncle Harry's walking stick as he strolled on the sidewalk below our dormitory, checking to be sure all was well with his 'kiddies,' as he called us."[24]

By far, most alumni who spoke about Ginsburg offered only praise for the man who took time with them, as he had at CJOA, to play ball, tell stories about his Navy days, or read aloud from *The Count of Monte Cristo*.[25] A few alumni, however, who otherwise spoke positively of their time in the Home, harbored criticism of the superintendent. Joe Samuels, among the Home's most dedicated alumni, convened reunions and listed his name in the Houston phone book as "Samuels, Joe ExHK," so other "Ex-Home Kids" could stay in touch. And yet privately, Joe, who had become the publisher of Houston's *Jewish Herald Voice*, expressed strong dislike for the superintendent. Admitted to the Home at age thirteen in 1929 after the board waived its twelve-year age limit to keep him with his younger siblings, Joe claimed to family members that "Ginsburg was always on his case," such as by routinely "confiscating" newspapers and other items Joe purchased with his own money, and once, falsely accusing the shy boy of "touching girls." Joe also claimed that Ginsburg intercepted letters that he wrote to his younger brother Pat, who remained in the Home after Joe's discharge in 1934.[26] Freda Hyde Lowenthal, who lived in the Home from 1925 to 1938, considered Ginsburg's social work methods "very advanced" for his time, perhaps even "far-fetched," citing his practice of allowing the female supervisors to bathe the youngest boys and girls together until "the minute we got bosoms and something else." In the same published interview, Lowenthal lodged a more troubling claim without specifics, that "one of the girls," who was "probably" no more than eighteen, "became his girl-friend."[27] For other alumni, even Ginsburg's evening ritual prompted suspicion. Unlike Helen Gold Haymon's reassuring recollection, Alvin "Pat" Samuels, Joe's younger brother, and Lilyan Golden Milner separately criticized Ginsburg's practice of "patrolling" the halls of the girls' dormitory either during shower time or after lights out.[28] However, beyond these vague accounts, no further record or evidence exists of Ginsburg behaving inappropriately with female wards. Hannah Golden Limerick, too, who continued to live in the Home for two years after her sister Lilyan's discharge, remembered the sound of Ginsburg's cane striking the floor as he walked through the girls' dormitory every night, a routine she less cynically had attributed to making sure no boys had snuck over.[29]

THE HOME DURING GINSBURG'S TENURE

By 1930, and throughout the rest of its years, the Home consistently received praise in the press as "the institution that is not an institution," a "home-like Home," and a "real home for its youthful inhabitants."[30] With funds raised by Edith Lashman and the board's support, Ginsburg worked hard to create this reality inside the Home and keep it prominently in the public eye. By 1932, he completed the renovation of the children's sleeping accommodations Ed Lashman had started, transforming all four dormitories into small, individual rooms for one to four children, outfitted with modest beds, desks, and dressers ordinarily found in private homes, providing space for clothing, photographs, trinkets, toys, and some privacy. This "homelike" ethos permeated the entire facility. Visitors noted "graciously appointed common rooms and wide game rooms."[31] The "bright, cheerful bedrooms, with gay wallpaper," captured one reporter's attention, while another likened the "cozy" atmosphere, in which children read, built a model plane, or laughed, to the "residence of one of your neighbors," albeit larger.[32] While social work experts continued to do so, neither the press nor the general public ever again questioned whether the Home should be doing more to keep children with their own or place them with a foster family.

Albert Fox welcomed the changes Ginsburg introduced. In 1925, when Albert was three, their father, Samuel, admitted him and his siblings to the Home. Samuel moved his family to New Orleans in the hope that the change from Cincinnati's climate would ease Albert's mother's depression following the death of two children from measles. In New Orleans, Samuel opened a tailor shop on Rampart Street, while his wife, whose condition deteriorated, entered the state mental hospital. Seeing the tailor struggle to raise his four children alone, a customer—Dr. Jacob W. Newman—suggested that Samuel admit his children to the Home. Albert's sister, Sylvia, was among the first girls to move into the newly remodeled bedrooms, which they decorated to their taste with framed pictures on the walls and favorite books and mementos on shelves.[33] With the expectation that they exercise good judgment and care, Sylvia, Albert, and the rest of the Home children, when not studying or doing chores, were free to enjoy the social rooms and common spaces, equipped with pianos, radios, magazines, and games. Except perhaps for the large colorful Bible-story murals that a visiting artist painted in the main entrance hallway, the first-floor chandeliers, rugs, clocks, and upholstered furniture created the aesthetic of a large and attractive private home.[34]

Beyond physical alterations, Ginsburg continued to modify the Home's programs with the goal of making life "normal" and helping the children learn to conform their behavior to engage in society beyond the Home's brick walls. Unlike Golden City days, when tardiness, unkempt appearance, or rudeness resulted in the loss of privileges, Ginsburg used no such tactics. It was absurd, he explained, to enact a "penal code" for children and wait for them to transgress. He now saw the "artificial behavior system" the Home previously enforced as an attempt to save staff time at the expense of individual attention and measured discipline. In Ginsburg's experience, children liked to evade rules and escape through technicalities. Instead, by teaching children to exercise judgment and "what they know are our wishes," Ginsburg reported that he no longer heard the excuses, "it wasn't announced" or "I didn't know what you meant." Believing that most children's "sins" resulted from thoughtlessness, he advocated a gentle approach, letting them see the consequences of their actions. Staff interventions with children on a case-by-case basis became learning opportunities they later discussed at regular meetings. In more complicated adolescent problems, Ginsburg acknowledged without offering specifics, "we sometimes have to be more subtle and surround the offense with unpleasant circumstances and consequences."[35] Calling Ginsburg a "master in child psychology," alumnus Louis Peters recalled occasional visits to his office during which, with a "touch of a smile" and a "calm voice," the superintendent invited him to "intelligently and logically see if we can find the 'psychological reason' for your actions."[36]

The shrilly clanging bells that once summoned children to activities from morning to night, and which threatened demerits if ignored, were now silenced. The children were taught to pay attention to the clocks placed throughout the Home. If the hall clock says that it "is a half hour before dinner," one happy resident wrote in March 1930 about the change, an older child now encouraged younger peers, "'Come on kiddies, it's time to take your bath. You don't want to come late for dinner and displease Uncle Harry, do you?'"[37]

The changes Ginsburg instituted also impacted the children's personal choices, such as attire. During Ginsburg's tenure, the children wore clothes they selected, within budgetary limits, to mingle easily with their wealthy and middle-class peers at Newman School and the Reform synagogues without being viewed as objects of charity. This comported with the federal Children's Bureau recommendation, first articulated in 1927, that the standard of dress for institutional children should "be as high as that for the average child with whom he associates in the community."[38] Some girls sewed their own clothes with the help of the Home's seamstress, Eola, and older boys and girls, depending on their maturity, went or were taken by supervisors downtown to purchase clothing. Holding donated clothing to the same standards, the Home inspected, washed, and ironed each item before distributing to the children. Bessie Mashinka Rothstein recalled that she and her twin sister, Pearl, when young, picked out different color outfits.[39] Even the boys, recalled Albert Fox, who nevertheless considered his wardrobe inferior to his Newman classmates, had sufficient clothing in number and style to accommodate rough-and-tumble play in the yard, appear presentably at school, and dress up for synagogue and Sunday school.[40] As he and Rothstein explained, Home kids were expected to change out of their school clothes when they played in the yard and to change back into school clothes each evening for dinner.[41]

To foster ties to the community, any clubs, teams, or other organized social groups within the Home that Lashman had not disbanded were eliminated. Instead, Ginsburg and his staff encouraged the children to join outside organizations, to mingle in the community they would soon enter. "Why center their life here," asked Ginsburg, "when the goal is to develop the children's social instincts to prepare them to be at ease in their future lives."[42] Children who formerly played in the Home band, for example, now found their places among bands organized at Newman, other schools, or the Rotary Club. Athletic Home kids played on their school's teams while the alumni association supplemented the institution's playground and recreational facilities for tennis, football, baseball, and basketball by donating a wading pool.[43] In place of the Home's social and cultural clubs, Home high-schoolers joined sororities such as "LT" (as girls' club "Lucky Thirteen" was publicly known) and fraternities such as Tau Beta Phi, which was nonsectarian, and Sigma Alpha Rho, whose members were Jewish students from Newman and other local high schools.[44]

With the same view of emulating life in a private family, Ginsburg also enlarged the children's freedom and privileges. After dinner, they could gather in sitting rooms near their bedrooms or in the downstairs library and drawing room. Alumnus Ralph Beerman described an overall "jovial" atmosphere that filled the Home throughout Ginsburg's tenure, in which boys and girls "kidded around with each other" and learned to dance while playing records on the Victrola.[45] The older girls received dates at the Home, whom Ginsburg required be Jewish, while all children were encouraged to invite over friends, including to Friday night dinner, just as other children did.[46] As part of Ginsburg's minimal approach to rules and regulations, mealtime became flexible. When older children expected to be late for dinner, due to a ball game or other activity, they called to request that their dinner be kept warm.[47]

Despite the freedom to come and go through the front door, alumnus Harry Kovner recalled taking further liberties. At night, he and his teen pals snuck out—and back in—the rear door into the boys' dormitory which Bill Parker, resident carpenter and treasured friend to many Home children, unlocked for them.[48] Sam Brody, too, who lived in the Home from 1936 to 1946, similarly tested the boundaries of Ginsburg's free rein. Viewing a 1942 photo that captured him, at age thirteen, and three Home buddies seated atop a tractor, the retired chemist and multiple patent holder explained, "We had freedom of movement and we just went down Jefferson Avenue to the levee and that's where this picture was taken." Other photos depicted Brody and friends perched on the building's rooftop.[49] Although children in private families then generally had more unstructured, unsupervised time than today, these undetected adventures suggest either the shortcomings of Ginsburg's reliance on good judgment alone to guide the behavior of adolescents in his care, or that they behaved much like other adolescents regardless of the institutional setting.[50]

After the demise of the Home's Animal Pet Association, Ginsburg ensured that the backyard continued to retain plenty of space for children's pets.[51] Illustrative of the Home's encouragement of individual interests, Emanuel Ginsburg was permitted to claim a small square in the yard, where he raised five chickens and tended his "farm," which he started with one stalk of corn, a dozen sunflowers, and radishes.[52] Earl Foreman years later proudly recalled his pets in the Home, a privilege he was denied at the Catholic orphanage in Memphis in which his widowed mother first briefly placed him. In addition to a dog that he found and named "Brother," Earl's pets in the Home included guinea pigs, rabbits, and chickens. He later boasted about the business skills he honed by selling small animals to schoolmates. "If their mother wouldn't let them keep it, there were no refunds, but I would take the animal back."[53]

Ginsburg went further than his predecessors in personalizing birthdays, making sure each of the children celebrated on the actual date of their birth. Sonia Packman Washofsky enjoyed Ginsburg's practice of inviting each celebrant, along with a special friend of their choosing, whether from school or the Home, to his apartment to enjoy cake, ice cream, and Coca-Cola, a special treat.[54] Adele Karp Cahn, a Home resident from 1923 to 1935, years later cheerfully recalled that Ginsburg wrote poems for each child's birthday, including one he composed for her.[55]

Early in his tenure, Ginsburg substituted adult supervision in place of self-governance and increased the direct care staff.[56] He divided the children by age into three departments, consisting of a combined Nursery and Junior Department for children eleven and younger, and Boys' and Girls' departments for older children, with each department run by a head supervisor. Within the Nursery and Junior Department, two assistant supervisors each worked with no more than twelve nursery children up to age seven, and four additional part-time employees worked with junior children, ages eight to eleven. He further divided the Boys' and Girls' departments by age into two groups, with about twenty-five children in each. One supervisor and four part-time workers oversaw each group.[57]

In July 1929, Ginsburg hired Jack Margolin as boys' supervisor. Jack, who had grown up in the Home for fifteen years, had graduated from Newman and was attending Tulane's School of Commerce, with aid from the Home's Henry Newman Educational Fund.[58] Before Jack left New Orleans in fall 1932 to attend Dartmouth College, where he obtained his master's degree in business administration, he left a positive imprint on his charges. Looking back decades later, alumnus Sam Hartman acknowledged Margolin as "a friend and a counselor" who successfully encouraged Sam to become a physician.[59]

When Ginsburg hired Margolin, he also hired twenty-two-year-old Anna Berenson as girls' supervisor. Utilizing her experience from prior teaching positions, the talented young woman also taught the children music and oversaw their Hebrew homework, enabling Ginsburg to economize on staff.[60] By fall, Berenson enrolled in Tulane's School of Social Work, which she attended in the evenings. Her time in the Home laid the foundation for her further education and lifelong career in social work, including a doctorate from Columbia University, coauthorship of a monograph for the Ford Foundation that helped shape the federal Head Start program, and her years teaching at Columbia, New York University, and Rutgers.[61]

Beyond attracting salaried professionals, Ginsburg greatly expanded Volmer's initiative of hiring student counselors in exchange for room and board. Over his tenure, Ginsburg introduced the children to nearly three dozen bright college and graduate students, many studying medicine and social work, with up to sixteen in residence at a time. They were instructed to oversee homework but give only such assistance as needed, to approximate an attentive parent's care and support.[62] Eunice Howsmon, a Newcomb student from Mobile, Alabama, worked evenings in the Home's nursery for four years before receiving her social work degree in 1934. Each day, Howsmon and her cohorts attended their nearby college classes before returning to care for their charges. When the children were tucked in for the night, counselors began their own studies.[63] Freda Hyde Lowenthal enjoyed getting to know the "wonderful counselors" who often stayed for several years, while James Whitehead appreciated their "great informal influence."[64]

Student counselor Hippolyte Peter ("H.P.") Marks Jr., a talented Jewish medical student who later became a pediatrician, served as a role model for young Albert Fox. In his room, located on the same floor as Albert, Marks maintained an extensive personal library and a love for classical music, both of which he shared with the children. Joe Stamm, another inspiring student counselor attending medical school, showed Fox how to use a microscope by viewing snail eggs they scraped from the aquarium. Counselors like Marks and Stamm, said Fox, showed him the value of a college education. "I believe that I am what I am today," said Fox, who later graduated from LSU's Engineering School before running his own building and remodeling company, "because of these young students who acted as mentors and big brothers."[65] Several Home alumni returned to work as student counselors, including Sam Hartman while he attended LSU medical school.[66] Another Home alumnus and LSU medical student who served as student counselor, Woodrow "Woody" Polewada shared his love of photography with Home kids.[67] In the summer of 1942, when medical students were asked to study year-round to graduate sooner to begin military service, Albert Fox, who had just completed ROTC training and awaited orders to report to the Army Reserve Officers' Corps, filled Woody's slot as camp counselor for the summer.[68]

Counselors, too, appreciated the program. Without the Home's room and board from 1939 to 1942, Gertrude Balkan, from Drew, Mississippi, could not have afforded to complete her studies at Newcomb. On a typical evening, Balkan joined five or six Home children at dinner, where she engaged them in conversation as she modeled table manners, before overseeing homework or keeping them company while they listened to records or the radio.[69] According to Samuel K. Cohn, who held the position from 1938 to 1941 while he attended Tulane Medical School, working as a Home counselor became a coveted job among Jewish medical students who were looking to cut expenses. While in the Home, Cohn enjoyed a private bedroom and three "very good" meals. In his later surgical practice, Cohn used his counselor experience to win the trust of pediatric patients, including by not wearing the traditional—but often frightening—white coat.[70]

THE CHANGING WORLD OF DEPENDENT CHILDCARE

Despite the homelike features, during Ginsburg's first few years, the Home had made little if any progress in determining the extent to which its children might benefit from noninstitutional alternatives, or in securing an experienced social caseworker to make that determination, as the Child Welfare League had urged in 1925. Like his predecessors, Harry Ginsburg instead focused his attention on improving the Home. In 1930, upon returning from the National Conference on Social Work, Ginsburg still considered the shifting perspectives on childcare as fads, not serious solutions. He commended the board for declining to rush to adopt any of the "latest modern methods" as they would have been forced repeatedly to change course with each new panacea. Whether called institution, cottage plan, or placing out, urged Ginsburg, these names obscured the actual level of care the children received. He spoke of shocking conditions he had seen in one of New York's large congregate institutions, where children were herded, fed in large groups, infrequently bathed, and lacked proper medical care. But he had been equally shocked to see a "cottage plan" where small groups of children received no meaningful personal attention from "cottage mothers" who delegated supervision to older children. Ginsburg conceded that "in some cases" placing children in private foster homes would be preferable to institutional care "if proper homes could be found." However, he criticized the Atlanta Jewish orphanage, which had recently transitioned to a general policy of foster family care and parental support, for placing children in families at such a distance that their "professional visitor sees them only once a year," and for frequently relocating children from home to home.[71]

In contrast, in defending the Home's "homelike" version of institutional care, Ginsburg reassured the board that its program of individualized care avoided the disadvantages of group rearing: "No other home in the country has eliminated all rules and behavior systems, treating each child as though he were the only one in the family." He encouraged the board to continue making the Home "an ideal place for rearing children," using "no methods which should not be used by a good parent."[72] He continued to resist foster care, decrying it in 1932 as a method which had "not yet justified universal approval" and placed a child "in a home where he is not really a family member.[73] His views comported with the prevailing negative attitude toward foster care throughout New Orleans, as reflected in a 1932 news article, "Foster Home Plan Not Preferred Here." In a survey of sixteen cities, the U.S. Children's Bureau found that eleven cared for more children in institutions than foster care, with the percentage of institutionalized children ranging from 53 percent in Buffalo to 95 percent in New Orleans.[74] Moreover, of the total 233 children that the local children's bureau had placed in foster care as of 1933, there is no indication that any of them were Jewish.[75] Louis Peters, who lived in the Home at the time, recalled that Ginsburg, ever philosophical, anticipated the situation would eventually change. "He preached that one day, when society became more enlightened, children would be raised in foster homes, supervised by professionals, rather than large institutions."[76] But for Ginsburg, that day had not yet arrived.

THE GREAT DEPRESSION

As Ginsburg noted with pride in his January 1933 report to the board, "We are passing through possibly the greatest economic difficulties we have experienced in a century, and yet have not forgotten the purposes for which our Home is maintained."[77] The entire country continued to reel from the stock market's cataclysmic plunge in October 1929. Although New Orleans's press and politicians claimed the city fared better during the early days of the Depression than other parts of the South, it was those other parts upon which the Home also depended for financial support, and which sent their needy children.[78] Edith Lashman, while traveling for fundraising, saw and heard the tragedies firsthand. In 1933, she reported that it was difficult for New Orleanians who had not experienced even one bank failure to visualize conditions in Corinth, Mississippi, where not one bank remained open, or in Alabama, where rural schools had closed in twenty-five counties, or in Texas, where fundraising campaigns were underway to feed and clothe children.[79] These conditions, and their lingering aftermath, prompted the admission of additional children and lengthened their stay amid declining donations.

Oklahoma, too, was hit hard by the Depression, sending Hannah Golden, age seven, and her eleven-year-old sister, Lilyan, to the Home from Tulsa. Across that state, three out of every eight urban residents were jobless, while farm income fell by 64 percent.[80] In 1931, after the girls' father, William, lost his upholstery business and their grandparents lost the family farm, their mother died. Before the local B'nai B'rith recommended the girls' admission in 1935, William tried desperately to find work. When not being shuttled between relatives, the girls were on the street, sometimes stealing empty milk bottles to buy a ticket to spend the day in the movie theater.[81] Also from Tulsa came Joe, Rose, and Maxine Bihari, the youngest of eight children, who were admitted by their mother in 1931 a year after their father died.[82]

Despite early efforts to downplay the Depression's impact on New Orleans, the grim reality soon set in. Happenings on Wall Street did not stay there. In January 1930, A. J. Heinemann, New Orleans's Baseball and Amusement Company owner who had long provided recreation and tickets for Home kids, fatally shot himself in the grandstand of his beloved ball park. Although friends attributed Heinemann's death to ill health, others pointed to his $300,000 loss in the stock market crash.[83] The public debate over whether he was the city's first suicide victim of the Depression revealed the overall financial anxiety. By December of that year, unemployed and financially desperate New Orleanians sold oranges the city provided at low cost, mimicking New York's apple-selling campaign.[84] As tax revenues declined, the budgets of the city and school board were slashed. The community's charitable organizations had to cope with increased pressures for services in the face of diminishing finances. The Community Chest, the nonsectarian pooled funding mechanism upon which the Home depended to cover a significant portion of its operating expenses, fell $80,000 short of its citywide goal for 1930; its revenues continued to plunge downward over the next three years, collecting $175,000 less than needed for

1933.[85] In early 1934, in response to a deficit created by the Community Chest's funding cut and the Home's decreased donations from outside the city, the board directed Ginsburg to find additional costs to cut.[86]

As a result, the Bihari and Golden children lived in the Home while it eliminated all unnecessary purchases, postponed physical improvements, and even charged alumni and guests to attend the Home's popular Passover seder. Beyond reducing the salaries of most employees, the Home also discharged half the domestic staff. Instead, the children took on greater responsibility for cleaning their rooms, painting walls and windows, washing dishes and floors, and mending and cleaning clothes.[87] Sam Freedman, who had been admitted to the Home in 1928, recalled that the meals under what he called the Home's "austerity program" remained wholesome but featured more red beans and less meat and chicken.[88] Considering the hard times everywhere else, Joe Bihari recounted that he and his sisters were so "well taken care of" in the Home, "where we had everything, . . . we didn't know what it was to be in a Depression."[89] Ginsburg's cost-cutting proposals, however, addressed far more than the Home's finances. Because decreasing the Home's population offered one way to reduce operating costs, he used the opportunity to educate the board about his evolving approach to admission and discharge policies. Girls' supervisor Anna Berenson had inspired her boss's new thinking.

In June 1933, just six months before the board requested Ginsburg's proposed budget cuts, Berenson earned her master's degree in social work from Tulane University. Enhanced by her insider's view, her thesis explored the extent to which a congregate childcare institution like the Home could approximate family life and satisfy the individual needs of the children under its care. "Even the most fervent advocates of child-placing in families . . . do not demand that all institutional care of even normal children cease, nor do they ask that all normal children shall at once be placed in private families," wrote Berenson.[90] But even if appropriately placed in an institution, she added, the Home should "steadily and systematically" prepare each child to return to a family home, preferably their own rehabilitated home.[91] Noting that the Home "does not place its children in private family homes," Berenson echoed the Child Welfare League's report eight years earlier in suggesting the institution undertake a "more flexible social program" using professional social casework methods to determine which of the children might benefit from living in a private family home. She noted that the board had made a good first step in 1928 by authorizing children to summer with friends and relatives.[92]

Berenson also revisited the League's questions about Newman School but went even further. Just as the board had determined that the specialized public high schools now offered superior commercial and trade facilities, Berenson queried whether the public grammar and general high schools were of "sufficiently high order" to render the Home's school "unnecessary." Moreover, noting that private schools, by attracting children from a higher social and financial level than public schools, generally have "the tendency to foster snobbery and class prejudice," she also questioned whether Home children faced an "added problem" or, instead, whether Newman offered features that "more than make up for the possible undesirable aspects of this situation." For these reasons, Berenson renewed the League's call for "a special study of the whole school problem."[93]

In Berenson's words, "The Jewish Children's Home attempts to give the child a home which will be to him a haven of security, a place where he is wanted, loved and protected from those experiences which adults alone should be called upon to face." However, Berenson asserted, determining the extent of the Home's success required a comprehensive, qualitative evaluation of the results achieved, possibly through a case study of both the children in the Home and those discharged over at least the last decade.[94] Ginsburg took Berenson's recommendation to heart and assigned her to conduct a "case review" and "analysis" of each current child's records. As Ginsburg explained to the board, the goal was to better understand each child's background and environment to develop his or her character and behavior more effectively, while probing possibilities of returning the child to a surviving parent or a family relation. The case review approach reaped prompt results. As an active if not voting member of the admission and discharge committee, based on the review, Ginsburg began urging "the rejection of children for whom any decent family care can be provided, and also the discharge of children wherever a similar situation arises." He credited this approach for the five admissions and twenty-four discharges over calendar year 1933, which reduced the population from 136 to 117 children.[95]

The board's request for budget cuts prompted Ginsburg to advance other bold proposals, especially considering his earlier general opposition to foster care. He noted that the need for individual adult attention for six Home children who were under age eight prevented him from further cutting staff. Recommending that the Home depart from its historic practice and cease admitting children this young, Ginsburg wrote, "It is much more desirable to have such children remain in a private home environment," which he suggested might be a foster home overseen and supported by their own community.[96] For the Home's oldest children, although he believed the Home was meeting the needs of children over eight who benefited from group life, including by "re-educating damaged personalities" in ways that foster homes could not, Ginsburg cited the "damage" done to children who remain in the Home beyond the "childhood period." Because keeping children too long reinforces some parents' belief that the Home assumed full and permanent responsibility, he urged the board to return children before they become self-supporting so that the parent has a chance to renew a normal relationship. For this reason, he recommended that the board discharge children at an age "as close to sixteen as possible."[97]

In making these recommendations to set age parameters, which might require foster-care placements, Ginsburg characterized his role in a new light. Referring to himself as a "technician, prepared by years of study and practice," he explained that his responsibility for adjusting childcare methods to the children's needs compelled him to "make recommendations to a lay board for which the members are not entirely prepared." Ginsburg had correctly foreseen that the board remained unprepared to accept his proposals; it rejected as "unwise" the adoption of age limits for admission and discharge. In so doing, the board evaded even a limited test of foster care and perpetuated the Home's unusual practice of admitting children as young as two years.[98]

Perhaps Ginsburg's boldest proposal, likely also spurred by Berenson's thesis, was for the Home to "decide whether we need the Newman School for the education of our children." Inasmuch as the school no longer offered vocational training, he argued for the first time that the reasons that drove the school's creation no longer existed. He believed that the public primary, grammar, and high schools would satisfy the children's educational needs while also enabling Home children to form lasting friendships with peers of their own economic status. "Their contact with a special group at the Newman School has a tendency to give false economic and social notions," wrote Ginsburg. "I see no good argument in favor of the private school as against the public school for our children, regardless of expense."[99] The total savings Ginsburg estimated from eliminating Newman School from the Home's operations, exclusive of proceeds from selling the property, was $14,000, which included the current school deficit of nearly \$4,000.[100] This too was a recommendation the board was not prepared to receive, and the subject lay dormant for another eight years.

By the end of 1935, the Home's population had dropped to eighty children, ranging in age from three to eighteen. Ginsburg attributed the nearly 20 percent decrease in population over the prior year, the net result of eight admissions and twenty-five discharges, to "better social work" and increased government aid under the New Deal, which made communities "less hasty" in asking to admit a child, coupled with the Home's efforts to keep children with, and promptly return them to, family or relatives.[101] While noting that some communities in the B'nai B'rith region placed out some children while sending others to the Home, Ginsburg continued to reject "a complete foster home plan." The Home served a genuine need by working with "problem children" in ways that foster homes could not, he argued, and thereby remained unique among institutions by providing its children with "genuine adult care" and not mere supervision.[102]

"Problem children" attracted attention across the country. In the 1930s, as the nation's orphanages witnessed a marked decline in the total number of children requiring placement outside their families for financial reasons, they also witnessed a corresponding increase in the proportion of "difficult or problem children" needing placement, whether due to emotional or behavioral difficulties or intellectual differences. Consequently, as reflected by Carl Carstens's 1932 lecture, "Use of Institutional Placement or Foster Care or Both," foster homes could not provide a single solution for all children needing placement.[103] "Problem children" required special programs. Although the number and identity of Home children Ginsburg considered a "problem" are unknown, he generally characterized them, "Most children are problems," and later qualified his remark: "Some of our children come from undesirable surroundings and have already formed habits which are destructive" and which "require not merely correction but practically re-education." Provided such children did not suffer from "feeblemindedness" (as measured by intelligence tests the Home regularly began administering in 1927) combined with "arrested development" that prevented getting along with peers, Ginsburg viewed the Home as "the right place for them, even though we find greater difficulty in preparing them to earn a livelihood than in the case of other children."[104] Guided by a psychiatrist and psychologist who joined the Home's medical consultants in 1927, the Home sought to address the needs of these children through tutoring and "special" academic courses, coordinating supervisory approaches among staff. To address mental health issues, the Home transferred a small number of children to New Jersey's Vineland Training School or later to Cleveland's Bellefaire, the former CJOA.[105]

ANNIVERSARY CELEBRATIONS

Ginsburg's attempts to reform the children's participation in the Home's anniversary celebrations also faced resistance from the board. Although Chester Teller had relieved the children of attending the lengthy speeches, these annual events continued to feature elaborate children's performances to the delight of the attending public. In 1932, for example, some eighty Home children in handmade costumes performed ballet and pantomime in a production of Debussy's *La Boîte à Joujoux* ("Box of Toys"), followed the next year with nearly as many young actors staging a six-scene rendition of *Alice in Wonderland*.[106]

Beginning in February 1934, Ginsburg called on the board to discontinue the children's public performances. He could not justify devoting as much as "one-third" of the children's school year to produce an extravagant play and noted that "progressive agencies" had ceased using children to elicit public support, being neither effective nor desirable publicity. Moreover, eliminating the performances could save the Home as much as $200 per year, at a time when he was asked to cut all unnecessary expenses.[107] The board, however, countered that the children's performances provided "important contact with the community" and that discontinuing them did not serve the best interest of the Home or its children. Even when the honorary matrons unanimously endorsed Ginsburg's request, the board saw no reason the event could not proceed in a way to avoid unduly disrupting the children's activities.[108]

Several years passed before the board lived up to its stated intention of avoiding undue disruption for the children. Until then, in 1939, for example, with a reported seven hundred people in attendance at Gates of Prayer's Leopold Weil Center and a Home population of seventy children, the eighty-fourth anniversary celebration opened with a discussion, "Should FDR Be Elected for a Third Term?" among Home high-schoolers Ralph Ginsberg, Lilyan Golden, Raymond Howell, and Bennie Shanker. The panel discussion preceded a three-act production of *Rebecca of Sunnybrook Farm*, accompanied by a four-piece ensemble led by Arthur Zack, conductor of New Orleans's Philharmonic Symphony Orchestra.[109] Finally, in 1943, the board cut the children's anniversary performances, instead confining the day's celebration to a public open house and reception.[110] Despite the merits of Ginsburg's pleas to avoid exploiting the children, the change more likely stemmed from the small size of the remaining population, which by then was about thirty-six children—too few to mount the full-scale productions that had earlier drawn large crowds.

Unaware of Ginsburg's concerns about exploitation and unbothered by the time spent practicing, Hannah Golden Limerick, who enjoyed dancing and acting at the Home and school, loved participating in the anniversary performances. Although she did not remember her older sister's stance on FDR's third term, Hannah happily recalled the Home's 1939 production of *Rebecca of Sunnybrook Farm,* in which she played "bad kid" Minnie Smellie, while her best friend Nellie Skalka was cast as Clarabell Simpson. The anniversary event left Hannah with only happy memories, including an audience member's compliment that she was "a born actress."[111] What Hannah and other children disliked about anniversary celebrations was opening the Home to visitors for public tours, which caused her embarrassment from being put "on display" where she lived.[112] Neither Ginsburg nor the board considered this aspect of the scaled-back event.

STRUGGLES WITH B'NAI B'RITH

In 1938, two controversies emerged between B'nai B'rith and the Home, the first over money and the second over the adequacy of the children's religious education. The financial dispute proved easier to resolve. When the two organizations first affiliated in 1875, B'nai B'rith agreed to pay the Home annually a sum based per capita on its membership, in exchange for a specified number of seats on the Home's board and admission of eligible children referred by its lodges. The arrangement worked until 1914 when B'nai B'rith, apparently enjoying increased membership, sought to decrease its payment. The two organizations agreed that B'nai B'rith would instead pay a flat sum of $20,000 per year, an amount the Home characterized as a contractual obligation. In the 1930s, B'nai B'rith, then also supporting the Jewish Home for Aged in Memphis, Tennessee, unilaterally decreased its payments, a likely consequence of the Depression. In 1937, the Home alleged underpayments for several prior years totaling $50,000, which the fraternal organization denied. In 1938, after heated exchanges, the parties resolved the dispute. B'nai B'rith's seats on the Home's board decreased to nine, the Home waived its claim to the $50,000, and B'nai B'rith agreed to pay the Home an annual sum equal to the amount it paid to the Memphis Home for the Aged, never to be less than $10,000 nor more than $20,000.[113]

Meanwhile, B'nai B'rith grew dissatisfied with what it considered the Home's insufficient Hebrew and religious education.[114] For more than a decade, as part of the Home's concerted efforts to increase outside contacts, the children received religious instruction from New Orleans's three Reform synagogues, alongside community peers. Among the three synagogues, two conducted compulsory coed Hebrew classes for thirty minutes weekly, and the third held a compulsory Hebrew class only for the boys of the Confirmation class.[115] In 1936, B'nai B'rith called for the Home to introduce additional instruction in Jewish subjects and Hebrew language. Attempting to address those concerns, Rabbi Emil Leipziger, chair of the Home's Jewish education committee, with the assent of the rabbis who held honorary board seats and represented three Reform and two Orthodox congregations, began conducting "religious cultural" sessions for Home children, exploring selected religious themes and Jewish historical figures for forty-five minutes weekly. B'nai B'rith's insistence on further "intramural" religious and Hebrew instruction, Leipziger stressed, conflicted with the Home's efforts to eliminate institutional activities not characteristic of private home life.[116]

At the end of 1939, with B'nai B'rith still unsatisfied, Leipziger's committee surveyed Jewish orphanages across the country about the nature and extent of their religious education. Thirty institutions responded, including those classified as Reform, Conservative, and Orthodox. Out of what Leipziger described as a "hodge-podge of methods," one fact emerged: none of the responding orphanages had decentralized their activities as fully as the Home.[117] Citing decentralization as "one of the main influences which has given our Home our rank among child-care institutions of our country," Leipziger reported, the committee "looks upon any departure from that policy as a backward step . . . even [for] such a laudable desire as a more intensive Hebrew education." If additional Hebrew instruction is desired, urged Leipziger, the Home should ask the three Reform congregations to provide it.[118]

B'nai B'rith disagreed, soon blaming the Home's insufficient Jewish atmosphere and training for "several" recent Home alumni marriages outside the faith. Even if the intermarriage rate was no greater than that of New Orleans's Jewish community, the fraternal organization insisted it had "the right to expect a higher standard" of Jewishness in the Home than might exist in a private family. "What is necessary is something of a Jewish atmosphere on the highest level" as reflected by training the children in "the tradition, history, literature and Hebrew language of the Jewish people."[119]

As much as the Home's leadership objected to B'nai B'rith's proposal for additional, insular religious education, the idea was anathema to Home children. Some, like athlete Pat Samuels, resented the time religious education already took from his sports activities at Newman. "Every Wednesday we had to take a course in Jewish history and that interfered with football and basketball practice. That we didn't like but we had no choice."[120] Bessie Mashinka Rothstein, who attended Temple Sinai after beginning her religious education in the Home, admitted, "None of us liked taking Hebrew."[121] Harry Kovner, who attended Gates of Prayer, went to Sunday school through confirmation. As for Hebrew lessons, he replied, "It didn't sink in. I couldn't learn it."[122] Their gripes reflected those of most Jewish kids raised in families.

Amid increasing calls from professionals for alternatives to institutional care, superintendents Ed Lashman and Harry Ginsburg focused on improving Home life by removing all vestiges of insular activity. In a city cited for its resistance to foster care, the Home received consistent applause from the public and no urgent call to close its doors. The dire financial conditions of the Depression, coupled with the help of a novice social worker, provided strong motivation for Ginsburg and the board to prevent admissions and promote discharges for a greater number of children. Keeping the institution open for the reduced population now commanded their full attention.

chapter eleven

FINAL YEARS
1940–1946

A DECLINING POPULATION PRESENTS
NEW CHALLENGES

The Home on St. Charles Avenue, once considered a magnificent monument to Hebrew benevolence, embodied the founders' dream to offer parentless Jewish children permanence in a world filled with misfortune and uncertainty. By 1940, however, national forces converged to reduce demand for institutional childcare, including in the Home. The cost of maintaining the cavernous, aging structure threatened the Home's ability to serve the children entrusted to its care, whose diminishing number now totaled sixty-five. Over the next six years, as the country endured World War II and the institution's presidency was shouldered by a succession of four prominent leaders, the board determined the Home's fate.[1]

With declining birth rates often attributed to urbanization and industrialization, the nation's percentage of children ages five to seventeen dropped from 35 percent in 1870 to 20 percent in 1947. At the same time, fewer of these children were becoming dependent due to the death of a parent; medical advances and improved working and living conditions had sharply decreased the death rate of parent-age adults.[2] Yellow fever, the deadly scourge that drove the Home's creation, finally attributed to mosquitoes in 1901, inflicted its last bout in Louisiana and the United States in 1905.[3]

Even when a child lost a parent, the surviving spouse now faced an increased chance of guarding her or his children against dependency. In addition to increases in average worker income, the national government had assumed greater responsibility for families. Most notably, starting in 1935, federal Aid to Dependent Children, made possible through the New Deal's Social Security program, provided essential funding to invigorate existing state and local mothers' pensions programs. Old Age and Survivors Benefits and general relief, along with the increase of retirement systems and pensions, also bolstered families. At the same time, service and relief programs run by private charitable agencies, especially in Jewish communities, employed counseling and funding to rehabilitate family situations that might otherwise lead to dependent children. According to the U.S. Children's Bureau, between 1933 and 1943, children in care of all institutions and agencies decreased by 24 percent, with an even greater decline in the Jewish childcare population. For Jews and non-Jews alike, amid growing acceptance of foster home placements, the greatest decline was in the number of children being cared for in institutions.[4] Although New Orleans was much slower than the rest of the country to join the foster home movement, the city's population of children in institutions had decreased between 1930 and 1940 from approximately 1,450 to 1,100 children (24 percent).[5]

These trends did not bypass the Home. Its population shrank from 151 children in 1929, when Ginsburg became superintendent, to 85 in 1936 when Ralph J. Schwarz was elected president, to 65 in 1940, and continued to decline thereafter.[6] With Ginsburg's heightened attention to identifying desirable family circumstances, coupled with increased community efforts to keep children with parents and relatives, the Home's discharges outpaced a decreasing number of admissions.[7] The smaller population, in turn, made it easier to create the homelike environment for which the Home received consistent public praise. With fewer children, more space opened for each of them to enjoy a greater amount of privacy, while still leaving room to house professional staff and unpaid student counselors. Additional staff, in turn, translated into greater individualized attention per child.

With its dwindling population, the Home struggled with high fixed costs resulting from maintaining its large, half-century-old structure. Inflation was already accelerating by the time the bombing of Pearl Harbor drew America into World War II, reflected by a nearly 10 percent rise in the Bureau of Labor Statistic's Consumer Price Index during 1941. Over the first five months of 1942, the index rose at almost a 13 percent annual rate, with food prices leading the way.[8] Refusing to lower its standard of care, albeit for fewer children, the Home faced dramatic increases in its per capita costs.[9] The Home's annual spending per child increased from $901.50 in 1938 to $959.95 in 1941. Compared to nine other American Jewish children's institutions, the Home's 1938 expenditure of $2.47 per child per day was the highest, followed most closely by $2.15 spent by New York's Hebrew Sheltering Guardian Society, down to Philadelphia's $1.25.[10] In clothing alone, in 1940, the Home spent $57.40 per child per year, a higher outlay than most institutions.[11]

Meanwhile, despite Edith Lashman's vigorous regional fundraising efforts, the Home's revenues lagged behind expenses. Even before Congress declared war in December 1941, contributors tightened their purse strings or diverted their philanthropy to lessen the plight of Jewish children and adults overseas. B'nai B'rith, too, shifted its priorities.[12] As District 7 president Julius Livingston announced in November 1941, after the organization purchased a $10,000 national defense bond, "The day is passed when the major part of B'nai B'rith activities is philanthropy."[13] The fraternal order redirected its focus from supporting Jewish charitable institutions to enlarging its anti-defamation work and supporting the war effort, such as by providing Red Cross vehicles and establishing recreational facilities at military bases.[14] Through its Hillel movement, which by 1943 operated on nearly 150 American college campuses, B'nai B'rith enlarged its broad religious, cultural, and educational programs for students to reintegrate veterans and to combat college antisemitism.[15]

The war also spurred the Home to expand its authority to care for Jewish children who were refugees from Nazi Germany, if necessary. At the same time, nearly fifteen years after the Child Welfare League first recommended the Home provide alternatives to institutional care, the board empowered itself via charter amendment to help children in their own homes or the homes of their relatives, place children in foster homes or in special care institutions, and conduct supportive welfare work with their parents and relatives.[16] But the board was never called upon to aid refugee children. Nor did the board rush to implement foster care; it did not take its first serious step toward offering this service until 1944, when it hired an experienced social worker.[17]

New Orleans prospered during World War II, including from the employment Higgins Industries and other shipbuilding plants provided, and welcomed servicemen en route to the combat zone or stationed locally.[18] Within the Jewish community, volunteers from the local chapter of the National Council of Jewish Women (NCJW) smoothed the path for refugees, meeting every ship that docked.[19] Although no call ever came to house refugee children, the Home did open its doors to adults from war-torn Europe. In spring 1940, about one dozen women, all refugees of Hitler's regime, gathered each morning in one of the Home's spacious parlors. There the women sewed clothing and made handicrafts, while practicing their English, in an NCJW-sponsored program.[20] The same year, Harry Ginsburg took in Claude Jacoby, who had fled Dusseldorf, Germany, leaving behind parents who later died in the Holocaust. The twenty-two-year-old photographer appeared at the Home looking for work. Because the Home previously offered no-cost room and board only to college students who worked as counselors, Jacoby considered himself "very lucky" when Ginsburg offered him a position teaching photography to Home children. Jacoby remained in the Home until August 1941, just two months before being inducted into the U.S. Army.[21]

Nazi oppression of Jews in Germany and Italy brought governess Inge Friedlander to the United States, whom Ginsburg hired in 1940 as girls' supervisor. Despite Friedlander's fluency in five languages, her English was not yet perfect, but she quickly learned the girls' expressions. The Home's progressive childcare pleased her, including giving children their own rooms with freedom to decorate and responsibility to maintain. After working at the Home each day, she took evening classes at Tulane's School of Social Work, which accepted her practical experience to satisfy the field placement requirements. In addition to supervising other staff, she enjoyed working with the children. She took younger girls shopping at downtown department stores and accompanied those who attended Temple Sinai, making sure they wore hats and gloves.[22]

World War II touched the Home in other ways as well. Alumni serving in the military, especially those abroad, retained important ties to the institution, their peers, and Harry Ginsburg. Hyman Stein, who left the Home in 1926 after graduating from Delgado Trades School, brought to the military skills he honed in the Home's band. "I got a special assignment," he wrote to Ginsburg in 1943, "so I guess I'll be in Uncle Sam's band," which he emphatically deemed "a *damn good cause.*"[23] Stein had kept in touch with Home alumnus Hugo Fielschmidt, the Houston dentist, who was also in the Army. While serving as a combat medic, Hugo was captured by the Germans in 1944 while attempting to rescue three hundred wounded servicemen from the caves at Anzio, Italy, a feat for which he was awarded the Bronze Star and a Presidential Unit Citation.[24] Home alumnae twins, Bessie and Pearl Mashinka, who lived in the Home from 1920 to 1934 before graduating from Joseph Kohn Commercial High School for Girls, enlisted in the Women's Army Auxiliary Corps in Houston, making headlines as "the twins who joined the army." When other

WACs accepted the chance to leave the service at the end of the war in Europe, Bessie and Pearl opted to join the regular Army and served eight months in Berlin. After finding Ed Lashman Jr., Edith's son, who was recuperating from a military service injury, they passed along the news to his grateful mother.[25] David Ladner, from Port Arthur, Texas, entered the Home in 1928 at age nine and lived there until 1937. In the early morning of June 6, 1944, Technician Fourth Grade Ladner stood atop a tank-landing ship watching the invasion of Utah Beach in Normandy, France, where he later transported wounded soldiers to the hospital ship. Two weeks later, from "somewhere in France," Ladner wrote to Ginsburg, enclosing a donation: "Many times during my tour in the service I have thought of pleasant years spent in the Home."[26] To honor all Home alumni who served during World War II, including six who gave their lives, the children of Temple Sinai's Religious School presented the Home with a bronze plaque engraved with their names.[27]

World War II also prompted the Home to venture into day care, a form of early childcare that gained national prominence by women's wide-scale entry into the workforce.[28] Jennie Silverman Ogden, a Latvian immigrant and divorced mother of twin girls, Jennie and Sara, espoused two primary goals: secure a job for herself and a good education for her daughters. For herself, she joined the U.S. Army Nurse Corps to serve her adoptive country. For her daughters, she turned to the Home, which accepted the seven-year-old girls on a part-time basis. After attending Newman School each weekday, the girls remained in the Home's care until their mother retrieved them after dinner. This part-time arrangement continued until June 1943, when Mrs. Ogden, now a second lieutenant stationed outside the city, admitted her girls full-time. Consistent with the Home's policy to strengthen bonds between children and financially capable parents, Lieutenant Ogden contributed a monthly sum to help defray the girls' costs.[29]

The weighty problems about the Home's future were of little concern to Jennie and Sara, who enjoyed "simple and basic pleasures" while tasked with "simple and basic responsibilities." When they were not tending to their clothes or fulfilling rotating tasks such as stuffing envelopes in the office or helping in the dining room, they played with other children at the goldfish pond in the Home's courtyard, roller-skated, or spent time in the private room they shared. Both girls loved attending Newman School, and prided themselves, after reaching the age of ten, with taking the streetcar "all by ourselves" for shopping trips to Canal Street or the dentist's office.[30] And, like Home children before them, the girls relished the weeks they spent at summer camp in Bay St. Louis, with twice-a-day swims in the bay, fishing trips, picnics, and bonfires.[31]

TAKING STOCK AND LOOKING AHEAD

In 1941, to evaluate operations and plan for the future, the board invited the Child Welfare League, the same entity that studied the Home in 1925, to again conduct a survey. This time the League partnered with the Council of Jewish Federations and Welfare Funds, a research organization which had been founded in 1932 by Jewish federations in fifteen cities.[32] B'nai B'rith, on its initiative, separately evaluated the institution. As it shifted priorities away from charitable institutions, B'nai B'rith sought to contain costs and ensure its annual contribution to the Home, now $13,000, was being well spent.

By the time the board received both reports, long-serving board member Leon C. Simon had been elected president. Simon, a civic-minded businessman and Federal Reserve Bank board chair, had earlier won the Times-Picayune Loving Cup for founding the city's Association of Commerce.[33] Before year's end, President Simon convened a special meeting to determine the board's next steps, with William P. Bloom, B'nai B'rith District 7's new president, in attendance. The board focused on the League's findings and recommendations, which included but exceeded the areas studied by B'nai B'rith and in far greater depth.[34]

Among other favorable findings, including those regarding health care and nutrition, the League again bestowed high praise on the Home's success in its children's socialization, especially as a congregate childcare institution. It generally described the children as friendly, at ease, and polite, while showing "a measure of inner restraint which comes from good emotional growth." It also noted that most Home children demonstrated "a high cultural level" and "poise which will permit them to fit into almost any group."[35]

The board also expressed pleasure with the League's assessment of Harry Ginsburg as "suited by personality, training and experience to care for children." While acknowledging that Ginsburg lacked formal social work training, the League found, "Members of the staff have continuously looked to him for leadership. He maintains excellent rapport with both children and staff. The children know him as 'Uncle Harry' and the name is well deserved." It lauded the freedom he gave the children to move freely in the community to go to movies, attend Hebrew school, visit friends, and shop, and the individualization he oversaw in clothing, birthdays, allowances, and problem resolution.[36]

B'nai B'rith, in stark contrast to the League, condemned the superintendent as "decidedly backward" in his childcare views and found his "personality and social outlook [was] not conducive" to achieving the Home's objectives "both from the Jewish as well as general social point of view." According to B'nai B'rith, "A person with warmer Jewish feelings as well as a more gregarious social relationship and a more civic attitude . . . could better develop the personality of the children."[37] B'nai B'rith's observations may have stemmed not only from its lingering complaints about the Home's lack of "Jewishness," but also from Ginsburg's reportedly antagonistic behavior during the survey team's site visit. According to B'nai B'rith's survey chair, Ginsburg dismissed methods taught by Tulane's School of Social Work, provided only an approximate number when asked for the Home's population, minimized the need for records by remarking that "a father doesn't need records," and discussed a young boy's troubled family history in the boy's presence.[38] Ginsburg's reportedly cavalier behavior toward B'nai B'rith's inspectors, combined with his later unfounded claims that they lacked childcare experience, may suggest an insecurity stemming from his lack of social work credentials or some other resentment he harbored toward them. For board members, however, the League's findings greatly outweighed those of B'nai B'rith and vindicated their superintendent.[39]

The League's report repeated much of what had been in the 1925 assessment. However, this time the board adopted some of the recommendations that it or its superintendent had previously resisted. Most notably, the board finally accepted the League's advice to hire a social caseworker, properly qualified by training and experience. Although novice social worker Anna Berenson's limited casework during her time as supervisor was the closest the Home had come to filling this position, she had left in 1936 to pursue her promising career. In accepting the League's recommendation this time, the board acknowledged "the growth of case work in child caring and the possible extension of our work to supervision of children in their own homes or placing them in foster homes." Given the shortage of workers caused by the war, however, the board committed to making earnest effort to secure a caseworker only "if available at reasonable compensation."[40] To finally address the League's renewed recommendation that the Home expand its work to encompass foster home care and family rehabilitation, the board offered to seek out assistance in these aspects of childcare with New Orleans's Jewish Charitable and Educational Federation (JCEF), whose direct involvement in the lives of Home children thus far, in addition to providing direct aid to needy families, largely consisted of vetting local applications for admission and overseeing children discharged locally.[41] The board also agreed to make use of social service agencies during admission and discharges to and from communities outside New Orleans, in lieu of relying on B'nai B'rith's lay lodge members, no matter how well-meaning or plaintive the petitions.[42] The Home's board agreed to rely on its superintendent, and the caseworker when hired, for gathering relevant social work data and advice, but declined to relinquish ultimate authority over admission and discharge decisions, as the League had recommended, reflecting the lay leaders' ongoing reluctance to yield to professional childcare staff.[43]

Although it disputed the League's finding that the Home's fundraising appeals too heavily emphasized the religious imperative of *tzedakah*, the board reluctantly abolished the Field Department. The League had concluded that the revenue the department generated from appeals to individuals did not justify its expense, especially in light of the Home's need to access funds from federations and other organized sources.[44] In recognition of Edith Lashman's dedicated service and prize-winning fundraising appeals, the board nonetheless retained her on a part-time basis as financial secretary.[45]

Once again, the Newman School "problem" captured the attention of both the League and B'nai B'rith, albeit in different ways. The League recommended the Home should "more carefully" study its children with a view to transferring to other schools those who could not benefit from Newman's rigorous program. It observed that fifteen Home children who had been transferred from Newman to commercial, trade, and other public school programs appeared on the whole "to be doing fairly well."[46]

Rather than Newman's academic appropriateness, B'nai B'rith raised concerns over "the false sense of values" and "difficulties" the Home children might develop from socioeconomic disparities with their Newman classmates. The fraternal organization recommended the Home should send as many children as possible to the city's public schools "so as to enter more adequately into the scheme of things with which children from average economic and social backgrounds who likewise attend the public schools, concern themselves."[47] As it had when the same issues had been raised by the League in 1925, by Anna Berenson in 1933, and by Harry Ginsburg in 1934, the board again sidestepped the issue. Instead, it expressed complete confidence in the education most Home children received at Newman School.[48]

Rather than a difficult situation, the board saw Home children's exposure to "the best families in the city" as an "intangible advantage" of attending Newman School. Although not mentioned by the board, being exposed to wealthy Newman classmates was much like the children's exposure to the often-rarified lifestyles of New Orleans Jewish community through the Home's Big Sister program, in operation for nearly three decades. These personal relationships with prominent Jewish women and their families imbued the children with social capital that enabled them to navigate and aspire to join middle- and upper-class society. The most common description of the program by alumni was that Big Sisters had taught them "to appreciate the finer things in life."[49] At school, however, one practice commonly cited by alumni sharpened the socioeconomic disparity without advantage. Every rainy day, so its children would not need to walk back midday as they usually did, the Home sent paper-bag lunches to the school. Home alumni described how they cringed when the school's public address system broadcast the predictable announcement: "Attention Home children: your lunches are in the office." "Everybody felt that was kind of wrong," recalled Harry Kovner about the indignity of being differentiated needlessly from non-Home classmates.[50] Putting aside the regrettable rainy day announcement, the benefits the board discovered from educating Home children at Newman School (and from pairing them with Big Sisters and ambitious student counselors) portended what leading economic researchers are only today fully comprehending: meaningful connections across socioeconomic class lines promote long-term upward economic mobility and help disadvantaged youth to succeed.[51]

Apart from all other issues raised in the League's and B'nai B'rith's 1942 reports, for the board the issue of the building still loomed large. If the population continued to decline, the structure simply was too large to justify its continued use and expense, yet the board believed it "would be folly" to sell the building to obtain smaller quarters that would require additional expenditures. Also, the board reasoned, for the duration of the war, selling the building for a reasonable price and securing adequate quarters elsewhere were highly unlikely. The Home might yet be called upon to care for war refugees.[52] It pledged to remain vigilant to changing conditions and trends, declaring in December 1942, "We shall be the first to recognize that the Institution should no longer be maintained. That time, in our opinion, has not yet arrived."[53] Nor was there any public call to close the Home, as reflected by the favorable press surrounding the next month's celebration of the Home's eighty-eighth anniversary.[54]

THE HOME'S NEW SOCIAL CASEWORKER

In early 1944, with thirty-one children remaining, the board hired Nathaniel W. Bronstein, the institution's first trained social worker since Anna Berenson's departure nine years earlier. Born in Russia and raised in Toronto, Bronstein graduated from University of Toronto's School of Social Work and received further postgraduate education at Harvard, Simmons School of Social Work, New York School of Social Work, and the Psychoanalytical Institute in New York. Bronstein, thirty-eight, came to the Home with experience in institutional work, family casework, child guidance, and community organization. Reporting to Harry Ginsburg, Bronstein was entrusted with ensuring that the Home admitted only those children for whom care was needed outside of their family.[55] Coupled with the cooperative agreement the board had reached with JCEF, the social worker's hiring finally provided the Home the resources needed to determine whether to admit a child to the Home *or* place and oversee her or him in a foster family, whichever served the child's best interests.[56]

Although two more years passed before the Home actually placed a child into foster care, the continued success of efforts to resist avoidable admissions and promptly encourage discharges, coupled with increased government funding and community support for families, further reduced the Home's population. With fewer children in residence, the Home's financing became increasingly unsustainable. By September 1945, during the presidency of Leon Heymann, the population dipped to twenty-five children and annual per capita operating expenses rose to $1,821, nearly double what they had been in 1941. Although operating costs had been reduced to "to the irreducible minimum" consistent with the Home's appropriately high standards, the committee entrusted to advise the board delivered its bottom line: "The maintenance of the present facilities at such an exorbitant cost should not be continued for a population of only twenty-five, nor a population under 75."[57] That the committee's spokesperson was board member Louis Yarrut, a distinguished lawyer and second-generation alumni association president whose sister and niece also had been raised in the Home, underscored the gravity of the situation.

In early 1946, newly elected president Justin V. Wolff charged another special committee "to consider all aspects of the Home's work and operation." By April, the committee debated either "drawing up a drastic plan of reorganization" or merging with the Pauline Stern Wolff Home, the small Jewish orphanage in Houston that had opened in 1930.[58] In June, despite his outreach through speaking engagements and notices in synagogue newsletters, Bronstein had not yet located any suitable foster home candidates but was optimistic "that some results will be forthcoming in the Fall."[59]

THE DEATH OF HARRY GINSBURG

On June 25, 1946, Harry Ginsburg died of a heart attack. Rabbis Julian Feibelman of Temple Sinai and Nathaniel Share of Congregation Gates of Prayer conducted funeral services in the Home.[60] Some children, like Sonia Packman Washofsky, were out of town, spending summer vacation with relatives, as was encouraged. Years later, given Ginsburg's prominence in her life, Washofsky was surprised she could not recall what she thought or felt at the time about his death. All she remembered was that her widowed father, who had moved from Arkansas to New Orleans to be near her, paid his respect by attending the funeral.[61] Bettye Sawilowsky Eisner, like most other Home kids at the Bay St. Louis summer camp, returned by car or train for the funeral. The inquisitive thirteen-year-old felt particularly close to "Uncle Harry," having become his grandniece Selwyn's favorite playmate during her frequent visits. For Eisner, admitted six years earlier by her widowed mother, Ginsburg's death was like "losing a second father."[62]

In Ginsburg's memory, the board issued a tribute: "The fruits of his labors are visible in the lives of the hundreds of children whom he guided toward responsible and well-adjusted adulthood. Inspired by a progressive philosophy of childcare, he converted the institution into a true Home which duplicated nearly as possible the atmosphere of normal family life. Thus he brought into our program an emphasis upon the psychic care of children equal to the emphasis upon their physical welfare."[63] The *Item* similarly praised the self-educated superintendent who many times had been depicted with the Home's children in heartwarming photographs on its pages: "He brought to his task not only the competence and industry to which he had schooled himself, but a warm personal affection for his charges, which they returned in rich measure. If he disregarded the cliches of social service formulas, he espoused the humanities more earnestly."[64] The headstone atop Ginsburg's grave at Hebrew Rest Cemetery read simply: "Our beloved Uncle Harry."[65]

Beyond all else, Ginsburg's death removed any remaining doubt among the board that the time to close the Home had arrived. When it convened in early September after its usual summer recess, the board unanimously agreed that the Home would no longer house children. Instead, the organization would find new life as a regional, nonresidential children's service. The board appointed Edith Lashman as acting superintendent, while Nathaniel Bronstein continued to evaluate the most appropriate placement for the remaining thirty-one children.[66] For the first time in its history, the Home would offer a flexible program of childcare services in which institutional care—provided elsewhere—was chosen only for those children who, following professional diagnosis, were deemed in need of specialized care not possible in their own or a foster home. Keeping children with their families, promptly returning those once removed, and finding foster home care for others became the Home's paramount responsibilities.

In September 1946, the board began placing the remaining children, ranging in age from three to sixteen years, in accordance with Bronstein's recommendations. The board discharged thirteen children to parents or relatives, under the oversight of JCEF. After Bronstein determined that twelve other children had emotional or behavioral needs that exceeded the care a private foster home could offer, the Home transferred them to Bellefaire, the former CJOA, which now offered therapeutic services in a residential group setting.[67] To ensure the children arrived safely at their out-of-state destinations, supervisor Inge Friedlander Elsas served as travel companion. "I wanted to see all my children safe," recalled newlywed Elsas, who thought of them as family. The children had attended her wedding, which was held in the Home a few weeks before Harry Ginsburg died.[68]

To address the needs of six children for whom foster home care was determined most appropriate, Bronstein placed an advertisement in the local newspapers:

WANTED: GOOD FOSTER HOMES

We are in need of a number of good Jewish foster homes for several normal children, formerly of the Jewish Children's Home. These children are not for adoption. They need understanding foster parents who can provide affectionate care and a healthy environment which is not otherwise available to them. We will pay reasonable monthly board to good Jewish homes with stable income, adequate living quarters and a genuine liking for children. Clothes, medical care and allowance for children will be provided.[69]

By November 1, 1946, all six children had been placed in foster homes vetted by Bronstein.

Meanwhile, the board turned its attention to the school and the building. Finding no impediment in the wishes Isidore Newman expressed when he made his momentous gift, the board separately incorporated Isidore Newman School and transferred the assets and property to the new corporation. The historic alliance between the Home and its prestigious private school was memorialized in the terms of the school's new charter, which required that any qualified child under the Home's care, now or in the future, be admitted for "such equitable contribution as the Home's board shall determine."[70] In 1947, the board leased the Home building to the Jewish Community Center for a year before transferring ownership.

Although the board closed the Home as a residential facility in 1946, the organization did not disband. To the contrary, after the last child had been evaluated and placed, the ninety-one-year-old organization embarked on a new era of regional services for Jewish families and children in need. No longer shouldering the weighty responsibilities of the building and school that had long embodied its fundamental mission and crowning achievements, the Jewish Children's Home now followed the trend of most other American orphanages, which were transforming their operations to either provide non-residential services or serve residential populations with special needs.[71] As board president Justin Wolff put it, "We are actively supervising the field work in this area. Under modern views, where placing a child in a group home is the exception and not the rule, this is an important activity."[72]

The Home played a crucial (if at times imperfect) role in caring for children whose families were struck with disaster—furnishing food, clothing, shelter, medical care, and education—at a time when public aid was unavailable or insufficient. Given that the vast majority of its children were returned to a parent or relative, the Home provided a vital service in meeting both short- and long-term family needs. For children who remained only a few months or even a few years, the Home, by enabling a parent to regain stability and reclaim them, supported the family's long-term survival. Children who spent most or all of their youths in the Home received a safe and stable environment. The Home's willingness to admit large sibling groups further promoted family unity, whereas today an estimated 70 percent of siblings are separated in foster care placements.[73]

Through the years, the Home's leaders demonstrated in many ways their dedication to improving the care and securing the future of their charges by their relatively early adoption of innovations in child development such as kindergarten, Sloyd training, manual training, self-governance, clubs, summer camp, and student counselors who served as role models and mentors, all coupled with the latest advances in medical care. They also demonstrated dedication to their mission by inviting critique from leading childcare experts, to which they responded by making significant reforms, including creating a homelike physical environment and integrating the children into neighborhood religious and social activities.

What made the Home diverge from counterparts in other cities such as New York, Atlanta, and Philadelphia which more readily embraced noninstitutional childcare? Historian Gary Polster posed a similar question about Cleveland's Jewish orphanage where, before converting in 1940 to a residential facility for emotionally troubled youth, he described leaders who "stubbornly held fast to the principle of institutionalizing dependent ghetto children" and "never seriously considered" foster family care. As Polster posited, "Perhaps their reluctance to do so was an indication of Jewish nervousness about their place in America, especially at a time when Fascism was beginning to emerge both here and abroad. Perhaps they thought that anti-Semitism would lessen somewhat if they kept under cover and made over some of those who appeared conspicuously Jewish—those who might cause them more trouble if they were permitted to roam free on the city streets."[74] Polster's singular theory, however, even if it partially describes the situation in New Orleans, fails to explain why foster care was more readily embraced by Jewish communities elsewhere, which presumably were equally fearful of antisemitism.

The Home's resistance to foster care must also account for its leaders' conformity to the norms of the surrounding community, which long adhered to institutional childcare. Like their lay counterparts who led New Orleans's non-Jewish childcare institutions, Home board members—experts in business, medicine, and law—were slow to abandon local tradition in favor of foster care, a system that to this day demands ongoing strategic and evidence-based reforms among a complex network of stakeholders.[75] Even after the city's non-Jewish childcare agencies embarked on foster care placements, the Home continued to decry the lack of suitable Jewish foster homes, reflecting one Jewish orphanage manager's earlier observation, "If we didn't have the institution, we would have absolutely no trouble finding the homes."[76] This was particularly true in New Orleans where the Home epitomized the Jewish community's integration into the city's life and landscape. For its leaders, closing the Home threatened that achievement. Apart from the city's Jewish cemeteries, the Home on St. Charles Avenue was New Orleans's oldest, continuously operating institutional structure built by and for its Jewish citizens.[77] Prominently positioned in uptown New Orleans, near the prestigious Isidore Newman School it founded and operated, the Home was a bold and tangible measure of Jewish philanthropy and the respect accorded by the surrounding community. From its founding to its resisted closure, the Home's physical structure and location embodied its leaders' visions of their rightful place within New Orleans and society.

Separating the organization's identity from the prominent building in which it formerly sheltered children took even longer than closing the doors. It continued to be known as the "Jewish Children's Home" until 1956, when the board changed the name to "Jewish Children's Home *Service*," to convey its increasing array of nonresidential functions: foster care, placement in specialized facilities, consultation, and scholarships to college and Jewish summer camps. "Home" was not removed from the name until 1972 when the agency, which had added research and community education to its programming, became the "Jewish Children's *Regional* Service" to properly acknowledge the wide geographical area it had been serving and to this day continues to serve. Moreover, until moving to a high-rise building in Metairie in 2000, JCRS maintained its offices within the JCC, marking 113 years in the same location. Even today, having been re-embedded during the JCC's 1964 reconstruction, the Home's 1887 marble cornerstone remains visible to St. Charles Avenue passersby, honoring the founders' vision of creating a Jewish institution "as enduring as time."

Each year on the High Holy Days, Jews reaffirm the quintessential duality of human existence. According to Reform interpretation, although we are limited in controlling life's fate, we have the power through *t'shuvah* (repentance or returning to the rightful path), prayer, and *tzedakah* (righteous giving) to lessen the "harshness of the decree." Despite our frailties and inevitable short-comings, through humility and introspection we can transform ourselves and, in turn, improve our communities and the world.[78] These spiritual concepts add meaning to the history of the Home, whose 1855 constitution declared the founders' hope in Hebrew and English, "With God We Shall Do Valiantly." Spanning 168 years and counting, this Jewish institution has demonstrated an enduring capacity to lessen the "harshness of the decree" for the least fortunate members of its community through reassessment, growth, and change.

EPILOGUE

In January 1960, 105 years after the Home's founding, and fourteen years since it closed, more than two hundred alumni, spouses, and supporters gathered for a reunion. Although stalwart alumnus Joe Samuels had earlier organized reunions for "Ex-Home Kids" in and around Houston, this was the first official Home reunion organized by the alumni association since 1930. The Home they knew remained standing, but the large building was now owned and occupied by the Jewish Community Center (JCC). Deteriorated beyond repair, the ornamental towers and the third floor that once held grand anniversary celebrations and movie screenings had years earlier been removed.[1] Among other changes, a large swimming pool now filled the courtyard where the Home children had roller skated, fed goldfish in a small pond, and swung from the jungle gym.[2] These alterations, however, did not dim the memories or enthusiasm of the Home's former residents.

The attendees spanned a wide segment of the Home's history. At age sixty-six, Louis Fuerst was the oldest alumnus present. Formerly known as Fuerstenberg, in 1911 he became the first Home student to graduate from Newman School, and before his discharge in 1914 experienced life in the Home under superintendents Heymann, Teller, and Volmer. Twenty-three-year-old Barbara Winn Grishman, who lived in the Home for its last two years, now married and living in New Orleans, was the youngest attendee.[3] Reunion committee chair Jean Segal Avegno, who lived in the Home from 1905 to 1916 and later returned to work as Harry Ginsburg's secretary, carefully orchestrated all event details and communications with Joe Samuel's help.

But it was Judge Louis Yarrut who represented the greatest breadth and depth of the Home's history. Though one year younger, Yarrut had been admitted to the Home in 1896, six years before Fuerst arrived. Yarrut's connections to the Home traced back even earlier. His father, Abraham Yarutzky, after having lived in the Home from 1877 to 1881 when it was still on Jackson Avenue, presided over the alumni association at its founding in 1890. The father had called upon its members to repay "their inestimable obligation" to the Home for equipping them "to go out into the great world as architects of our own fortunes." When Abraham Yarutzky's wife died six years later, he placed his son and daughter in the Home, knowing from his own experience they would be well cared for. Yarutzky's son, who grew up to be Louis Yarrut and married Home alumna Eva Levenberg, repaid his obligation to the Home by becoming president of the alumni association and the first alumnus president of the Home's board. In 1945, as chair of the board's special committee to assess viability, he delivered the somber news that the Home would soon need to close. At the reunion's grand banquet, Judge Yarrut, newly elected to Louisiana's Fourth Circuit Court of Appeal after a dozen years on the bench of the Orleans Parish Civil District Court, delivered the evening's keynote address.[4]

Despite his memories of marching to meals and to school at the sound of bells that typified the regimentation of his youth, he spoke fondly of his time in the Home and what he knew of his peers' experiences.

> When we consider the wonderful home we had: the finest shelter; the finest clothing; the finest meals; the finest medical attention; and educated in one of the finest schools, the Newman School, we know we had no reason to envy the poor little rich boy who had everything but love and companionship. Just think, with 150 children in the Home, at the drop of a hat we could organize a baseball game, an indoor baseball game, a basketball game, or any of the many games that children would engage in those days. And just think how easy it was to get a group to study together, exchange ideas and assist one another.[5]

Former staff members, too, returned for the special event. Boys' supervisor Rapp Lawes, nurse Anna Levine "Veenie" Kamin, and girls' supervisor Louise Simone were there, along with dietitian Elizabeth Josephson Kaiser, whom the children called "Miss Joe." Also attending was Bill Parker, the Home's maintenance supervisor and cherished friend to many Home children, who continued to maintain the building for the JCC. That evening, according to Jean Segal Avegno, Parker "was still looking after everybody." Former financial secretary Edith Lashman, who was then serving on the board of the Home's successor agency, attended as well.[6] The event's printed program included a photograph of superintendent Harry Ginsburg, wearing a smile and his trademark bowtie, surrounded by a dozen Home children, the smallest on his lap. The caption read, "Uncle Harry, please tell us a story!" As alumna author Hilda Crystal White, described the photo, "It is Uncle Harry as I remember him best."[7]

At this and other reunions, the Ex-Home kids who attended joyfully shared recollections and delighted in each other's successes in professional and personal life. By far the most common sentiment expressed was gratitude for the care and opportunities that the Home had provided when their own families could not. Even alumni who complained about their childhood found it difficult to envision an alternative. Most Home alumni, who considered themselves fortunate for the care they received, could not miss what they had not known.

Although Yarutzky and Yarrut are the only parent-and-child alumni duo who held elected offices for the Home, its history abounds with multigenerational alumni connections, revealing both the precariousness of family stability for southern Jews and the potential for children to overcome adversity with social and educational opportunities. Indeed, Judge Yarrut's sister, Pauline, and his niece, Tillie Slobotsky, also were raised in the Home, marking three generations of Home alumni in one family.[8]

Alumni brothers Ellis, Van E., and Carol Hart, who repaid their gratitude in funding and service, also traced their family legacy back to the Home's earliest days. Their grandfather, Isaac Tobias Hart, was a successful auctioneer who delivered the Home's 1863 anniversary oration, imploring the crowd to remember their "sacred and holy duty" to provide for the Home's widows and orphans.[9] Isaac's sisters, Frances and Julia, were among the Home's earliest teachers, from 1857 through 1869. Seventy years later, following the sudden death of Isaac's son H. Van Hart, the Home admitted H. Van's three youngest boys. Van E., a businessman, served a term on the board in the 1960s that overlapped his brother Carol, an attorney, whose six years of board service preceded his 1969 election to president, a position he held for four years. They predeceased their older brother, Ellis, who at age ninety-nine proudly attended the 2016 gala celebration of the Jewish Children's Regional Service, as the Home's successor agency is known today.[10]

While the Home remained open, alumnus Harry Caplan (whose brother Mike led the Home band at the fiftieth anniversary in 1905) began his many years of service as board secretary, following earlier alumni directors Nathan Goldstein and Max Tobias. After the Home closed, the board welcomed alumni Helen Gold Haymon, brothers Bernard Shanker and Benjamin Shanker, Sam

Levitan, Jennie Ogden Schneider, Adele Karp Cahn, Hyman "Herc" Levine, Joe Samuels, Ralph Beerman, and Janet Loeb Pfeifer. Representing the affection former staff held for the Home, Dr. Samuel K. Cohn, a student counselor while he attended medical school, later served on the JCRS board.[11]

Alumni children and grandchildren who have served as JCRS president include Marc Beerman, son of alumnus Ralph Beerman, and Bruce Miller, grandson of alumna Esther Korn Groff. JCRS board member Louis Yarrut Fishman carried on the tradition of service to Jewish children set by his alumni grandfather and great-grandfather, Louis Yarrut and Abraham Yarutzky. Children of alumni who have served as directors include Clara Jean Berry, daughter of alumnus Jack Pulitzer; Judge Max N. Tobias Jr., son of alumni spouses Max Tobias and Mildred Gordon Tobias; Morris Burka Jr., son of alumni association president Morris Burka Sr.; and Jim Pfeifer, son of alumna Janet Loeb Pfeifer.[12]

Reflecting the ongoing esteem in which the community holds the organization, the board roster also reveals a legacy of service passed down within families from prior generations of non-alumni board leaders, such as David Schwarz, son of Ralph Schwarz, and Neil Kohlman, great-nephew of Solis Seiferth, each of whom served as president of the Home or JCRS. Former JCRS president Leon Rittenberg III is the great-grandson of Home board member Robert Polack.[13] The late Sara Berenson Stone, the grand dame of New Orleans's Jewish community who chaired JCRS's education scholarship committee for many decades, proudly acknowledged the important contributions made to the Home by her cousin Anna Berenson Mayer, who served as girls' supervisor from 1929 to 1936, during and after her studies at Tulane's School of Social Work.[14]

In addition to personal service, countless alumni and their families supported the Home and have supported JCRS with generous financial contributions. For Ben Shanker, establishing a permanent fund in the early 1970s to help students defray their college expenses was one of his "greatest pleasures." Like many other Home alumni, he modestly considered his gift "a small, small payback" for how much, years earlier, he and his siblings had received.[15]

Today's Jewish Children's Regional Service serves at-risk, dependent, and financially challenged Jewish children and families across Louisiana, Texas, Oklahoma, Mississippi, Alabama, Arkansas, and Tennessee.[16] As the nation's only regional child service agency for an exclusively Jewish clientele, JCRS provides case management for children with special needs, scholarships for college and Jewish summer camps, disaster relief, and outreach programs to build Jewish identity. Nearly 40 percent of JCRS clients come from single-parent homes, and many are being raised by someone other than their biological parents, such as grandparents, other relatives, or foster home care. In 2022, JCRS served over eighteen hundred Jewish children across the seven-state region.[17]

Isidore Newman School remains one of the finest college preparatory schools in New Orleans, as well as the city's only accredited, coeducational, nondenominational independent day school. In 1967, albeit seven years after local public schools began to comply with court-ordered desegregation, Newman became the city's first private, non-parochial school to admit Black students.[18] With a current enrollment of 1,055, early childhood through twelfth grade, Newman provides 23 percent of its students more than $3 million in financial aid.[19] Preserving the historic relationship between the Home and the school, JCRS holds a seat on Newman's board of governors.[20] Yielding an impressive alumni roster, including best-selling authors Walter Isaacson and Michael Lewis and sibling football phenoms Eli and Peyton Manning, the school's motto remains unchanged: *Discimus Agere Agendo*—We learn to do by doing.

NOTES

AJA	American Jewish Archives
AJA-BB	American Jewish Archives, B'nai B'rith Collection, No. 180
AMM	Home Annual Meeting Minutes
AR	Home Annual Report
BMM	Home Board Meeting Minutes
DD	*Daily Delta* (New Orleans)
DP	*Daily Picayune* (New Orleans)
GCM	*Golden City Messenger*
HB	Home "Biography" registry books
ICCC	*Proceedings of the International Congress of Charities and Correction*
INSA	Isidore Newman School Archives
ISJL	Institute of Southern Jewish Life
JCRS	Jewish Children's Regional Service
NCCC	*Proceedings of the National Conference of Charities and Correction*
NCJC	*Proceedings of the National Conference of Jewish Charities*
NOI	*New Orleans Item*
NOPL	New Orleans Public Library
NOS	*New Orleans States*
NOT	*New Orleans Times*
NYT	*New York Times*
RGD-LA	R. G. Dun & Co. Reports, Louisiana vols.
TD	*Times Democrat* (New Orleans)
T-P	*Times-Picayune* (New Orleans)
TSC	Tulane University Library Special Collections
TSC-JCH	Tulane University Library Special Collections, Jewish Children's Home Records, no. 180

INTRODUCTION

1. U.S. Census Bureau, *Benevolent Institutions, 1904*, 16 (table 4), 56–126 (listing 1241, "Orphanages, Children's Homes, and Nurseries").

2. Friedman, *These Are Our Children*, 12, 204n4; Tobias, *The Hebrew Orphan Society of Charleston*, 10–11 (housed orphans in repurposed building only for a "brief period just before the Civil War"); Bernard, *The Children You Gave Us*, 8 (New York's Hebrew Benevolent Society, est. 1822, opened the Hebrew Orphan Asylum in 1860 in a repurposed building).

3. The prevailing style among university presses at this time is to capitalize "Black" and lowercase "white." That is the style adopted in this text. For a different and (to this author) compelling view on this point of style, see Kristen Mack, "Capitalizing Black and White: Grammatical Justice and Equity," MacArthur Foundation, August 26, 2020, www.macfound.org.

4. Cleveland's Jewish Orphan Asylum (CJOA), which B'nai B'rith's District 2 opened in 1868, served children primarily from Ohio, Indiana, Kentucky, Missouri, Kansas, and Colorado. Similarly, B'nai B'rith's District 5 opened the Atlanta Hebrew Orphan Asylum in 1889 to serve children primarily from Georgia, Maryland, the District of Columbia, Virginia, and the Carolinas. Wilhelm, *Independent Orders of B'nai B'rith*, 63, 138, 141, 143.

5. Friedman, *These Are Our Children*, 67, 197n105; Bernard, *The Children You Gave Us*, 118.

6. Bureau of Jewish Social Research, "Statistics of Jews," 291.

7. In addition to portions of *Fair Labor Lawyer* that describe Bessie Margolin's time in the Home, 1913–25, scholarly works about the Home, in whole or significant part, are Caroline Light's book *That Pride of Race and Character*, Wendy Besmann's article "The 'Typical Home Kid Overachievers,'" Mark Bauman's article "Variations on the Mortara Case" (reprinted in his 2019 book, *A New Vision of Southern Jewish History*), and master's theses by Anna Berenson, 1933, and Olive Andrus, 1938. Arthur Bielfeld, 1962 (AJA SC-8877), and Solomon T. Greenberg, 1964 (AJA SC-8869), while students at Hebrew Union College, wrote brief but notable History term papers about the Home. Founder Joseph Magner's *Story of the Jewish Orphans' Home* provides an important institutional chronology through 1905 while Anne Konigsmark's *Isidore Newman School*, a highly informative book which the school published in 2004 to commemorate its centenary, advises (iv) that it "is not meant to be a comprehensive historic document but rather the story of a wonderful school."

8. Harvey Wolff and Calvin Wolff interview (Moritz); Stone, "Edgar Goldberg"; "Two Orphanage-Reared Men Hold Reunion After 63 Years," *New Orleans States-Item*, January 13, 1966 (Butler); Jeanne Samuels interview.

9. *The Sphinx*, July 1906, 50, February 1907, 138; "David Swift, Merrimaker Magician," *Minneapolis Star*, November 21, 1955; Stifft interview.

10. "Funeral Held for Ex-Mayor," *Enterprise-Journal* (McComb, MS), January 5, 1981.

11. "Samuel Pulitzer, 84, A Maker of Neckwear," NYT, October 21, 1989; "E. S. Pulitzer, Orleans Exec, Is Dead at 65," *New Orleans States-Item*, September 11, 1967; Andrea McElfresh, "New Orleans Clothing Mainstay Perlis," Nola.com, March 21, 2021.

12. Broven, *Record Makers and Breakers*, 39–42, 154–157; "Joe Bihari, Founder of Blues Record Company," *Los Angeles Times*, December 2013.

13. "Silver Tea Will Honor Mrs. Leah Goot," *San Antonio Light,* April 15, 1966; "Mrs. Leah Goot, pioneer Hadassah leader," *Jewish Herald-Voice* (Houston), September 25, 1969.

14. Trestman, *Fair Labor Lawyer.*

15. White, *Wild Decembers,* jacket copy; "False Starts—Autobiography," n.d., Hilda Crystal White Papers, Howard Gottlieb Archival Research Center, Boston University ("White Papers"), box 8, folder 6.

16. BMM 1: January 19, 26, 1862. The Home's 1862 Annual Report states that Mengis (elsewhere spelled "Mengers" and "Menges") was discharged to "Mr. Lucas, Jeweler." The registry, however, states that he was "Expelled." See also "A Life of Bold Projects: Adventurous Ups and Downs of Mr. Menges," *Baltimore Sun,* June 15, 1904; "Morris C. Menges, Horseman, Is Dead," *Brooklyn Daily Eagle,* March 8, 1921; "Morris C. Menges," *New York Tribune,* March 9, 1921; "Well Known Horseman Dies," *Seattle Daily Times,* March 9, 1921; "Three Prominent Railroad Men Dead," *Omaha World Herald,* March 9, 1921.

17. Joe Pichirallo, "The Odyssey of Norman Mayer," *Washington Post,* December 19, 1982; Kassondra O'Hara, "One Man's Radical Plan to Blow Up the Washington Monument," *Medium. com,* December 17, 2020.

18. "Report of the Grand Jury," *TD,* April 17, 1865.

19. Berenson, "A Study of the Jewish Children's Home" ("Berenson thesis"), 96–99.

20. Berenson thesis, 176.

21. AR 1887: 22–23; "The Orphan Home Scandal," *T-P,* February 9, 1886.

22. "The Institution That Is Not an Institution," *Item Tribune,* January 12, 1930.

1. A PERMANENT HOME, 1853–1856

1. "Babette Baer Schwartz," accessed June 19, 2021, www.findagrave.com/memorial/18731896 /babette-schwartz; "Wolff Benjamin Schwartz," accessed June 19, 2021, www.findagrave.com /memorial/135566734/wolff-benjamin-schwartz.

2. Carrigan, *Saffron Scourge,* 71; NOPL, Louisiana Division, "Yellow Fever Deaths in New Orleans, 1817–1905," January 31, 2003, accessed June 19, 2021, nutrias.org/facts/feverdeaths.htm.

3. Heller, *Jubilee Souvenir,* 27; *The Occident* 11, no. 10 (January 1854): 61–63. The *Daily Picayune's* interment reports from July 30 through October 4, 1853, listed ninety-six yellow fever burials in the city's Jewish cemeteries.

4. Carrigan, *Saffron Scourge,* 4.

5. Robinson, *Diary,* 152–53; Humphreys, *Yellow Fever and the South,* 23.

6. *T-P,* August 28, 1853; *DeBow's Review* 15, no. 6 (December 1853): 627.

7. Robinson, *Diary,* 153; Carrigan, *Saffron Scourge,* 67.

8. "The Epidemic," *T-P,* August 21, 1853; "City Intelligence," *T-P,* August 26, 1853; Robinson, *Diary,* 153.

9. "The Plague in the Southwest," *Debow's Review* 15, no. 6 (December 1853): 595–635, 614–15; Robinson, *Diary,* 153; Carrigan, *Saffron Scourge,* 62.

10. Carrigan, *Saffron Scourge,* 8–9.

11. Carrigan, *Saffron Scourge,* 10–11.

12. Kern interview; HB 1: 9–14 (Schwartz family); www.findagrave.com/memorial/135566734/wolff-benjamin-schwartz.

13. Langston, "James K. Gutheim," 70; "Rabbi James Koppel Gutheim," *The Sabbath Visitor* 16, no. 9 (January 1887): 519; Zola, "James Koppel Gutheim"; Shpall, "Rabbi James Koppel Guttheim [*sic*]," 166–67.

14. "Special Notices," *DP*, August 29, 1853.

15. Ashkenazi, *The Business of Jews in Louisiana*, 10.

16. Reinders, *End of An Era*, 7; Wilson, ed., *Queen of the South*, 25.

17. Olmsted, *A Journey in the Seaboard Slave States*, 583; Ford and Stiefel, *The Jews of New Orleans and the Mississippi Delta*, 45.

18. Fussell, "Constructing New Orleans," 847.

19. Carrigan, *Saffron Scourge*, 49.

20. Rogers, "History of the New Orleans Flood Protection System."

21. Wilson, ed., *Queen of the South*, xx, 10–12.

22. Carrigan, *Saffron Scourge*, 49; Ford and Stiefel, *The Jews of New Orleans and the Mississippi Delta*, 39.

23. Korn, *The Early Jews of New Orleans*, 3–4, 8, 29–34.

24. Campanella, "From Landmark to Parking Lot," 12; Magner, *Story*, 5 (New Orleans's Jewish population in 1854 was "2000 souls").

25. Singer, "The 10 Best, Most Classic Jewish Jokes."

26. "Ashkenazi versus Sephardic Jews," Ask the Rabbi, accessed October 13, 2021, www.aish.com/atr/Ashkenazi-versus-Sephardic-Jews.html.

27. Telushkin, *Jewish Literacy*, 214–15.

28. Korn, *The Early Jews of New Orleans*, 248; Lachoff and Kahn, *The Jewish Community of New Orleans*, 7; Ford and Stiefel, *The Jews of New Orleans and the Mississippi Delta*, 37–40.

29. Korn, *The Early Jews of New Orleans*, 239; Malone, "New Orleans Uptown Jewish Immigrants," 244–45; Alexander, "Congregation Gates of Prayer," 12–13.

30. Clement, "Children and Charity," 339, 341.

31. *DP*, August 26, 1853.

32. *DP*, August 26, 1853; November 10, 1854; August 7, 1855.

33. Wisner, "The Howard Association of New Orleans," 41; Hildreth, "Early Red Cross," 49–50; *The Occident* 11, no. 6 (September 1853): 329.

34. Dollinger, *Quest for Inclusion*, 19.

35. "No fewer than 36 times": Rabbi Uri Topolosky, Eulogy for Lillian G. Rodos, January 9, 2012, New Orleans.

36. "City Intelligence," *DP*, March 8, 1846.

37. *DP*, October 16, 1853.

38. Robinson, *Diary*, 280–85.

39. HBA Report for July–December, 1853, rpt. in *The Occident* 11, no. 11 (February 1854): 580–83 (noting only two orphans and one pensioner under HBA care).

40. For the week ending August 22, 1854, the city's yellow fever deaths reached 258. "Mortality," *T-P*, August 22, 1854. The *Daily Picayune*'s interment reports from August 20 through October 29, 1854, attributed 24 Jewish burials to yellow fever.

41. HB 1: 7–8; BMM 1: January 29, 1856.

42. "Three Founders of the Jewish Home Survive," *DP*, December 25, 1904.

43. Magner, *Story,* 6; "Three Founders of the Jewish Home Survive," *DP*, December 25, 1904.

44. Clement, "Children and Charity," 339, 341. In 1854, non-Jewish orphanages in New Orleans included: Asylum for Catholic Orphan Boys, third district; Fourth District Boys' Orphan Asylum; Poydras Female Orphan Asylum (est. 1817 by Protestant women); Catholic Female Orphan Asylum; St. Mary's Orphan Boys Asylum (est. 1835 by Catholics); St. Joseph's German Boys' and Girls' Orphans Asylum; Camp Street Orphan Asylum; Asylum for Relief of Destitute Orphan Boys (est. 1824 by Protestant men); and St. Anna's Asylum for Destitute Females and their Helpless Children on Prytania Street (est. 1853).

45. Tobias, *The Hebrew Orphan Society of Charleston,* 10–11.

46. Rebecca Gratz, "A Foster Home," *The Occident* 8, no. 1 (April 1850): 1; Fleischman, *The History of the Jewish Foster Home,* 11; Ashton, *Rebecca Gratz,* 210–11.

47. Bogen, *The Luckiest Orphans,* 10–12.

48. Korn, *The Early Jews of New Orleans,* 247–48, 255; Hanger, *A Medley of Cultures: Louisiana History at the Cabildo,* chap. 2, 34.

49. "Judah Touro's will," *DP*, January 24, 1854.

50. Notice, *DP*, November 25, 1854; Magner, *Story,* 6.

51. "Meeting of the Israelites," *New Orleans Crescent,* November 27, 1854; "Hebrew Widows and Orphans," *DP*, December 9, 1854; "A Golden Wedding to Gladden Tuesday," *DP*, November 24, 1901; Magner, *Story,* 6–7.

52. Bogen, *The Luckiest Orphans,* 17.

53. "A Jewish Orphans Home," *The Israelite,* December 15, 1854; "The Jewish Widow and Orphan Asylum," *The Israelite,* January 19. 1855.

54. *DP*, December 8, 1954; Magner, *Story,* 7.

55. AMM 1, March 18, 1855.

56. AMM 1, March 18, 1855.

57. Magner, *Story,* 8.

58. "Death of Meyer M. Simpson," *NOS*, August 12, 1977; *History of the Jews of Louisiana,* 33.

59. U.S. Census for New Orleans, 1850 and 1860; "Shirts-shirts-shirts," *DP*, December 5, 1850; "HBA leadership," *DP*, October 5, 1847; "Special Notices—Hebrew Benevolent Association," *DP*, May 29, 1851; "Consecration of a Synagogue," *DP*, March 6, 1851; "Hebrew Congregation," *DP*, October 29, 1852.

60. Friedman, *"Legal, Political, and Religious Legacy,"* 81, 82–83; "The Death of Gov. Henry M. Hyams," *T-P*, June 26, 1875.

61. "Death of Joseph Cohn," *T-P*, May 14, 1882; "Mr. Daniel Goodman," *T-P*, August 31, 1850. Elected as directors were Joseph Simon, Manuel Goldsmith, Lionel L. Levy, Louis Rose, Benjamin Florance, I. H. Marks, Lambert B. Cain, and Ezekiel Salomon.

62. *Constitution of the Association for the Relief of Jewish Widows & Orphans* (New Orleans: Sherman, Wharton & Co., 1855) (*1855 Constitution*), "Preamble," 6–7.

63. BMM 1: March 27, 1855; Magner, *Story,* 10.

64. Founders who were born or earlier lived in Charleston include: Meyer Simpson, Henry Hyams, Benjamin Florance, and David Cohen Labatt. Charleston native Dr. Samuel Harby, who

although not a Home founder, was married to founding Honorary Matron Sarah Levy Harby. Samuel's father, Isaac Harby, and David Cohen Labatt's father, Abraham, were members of Charleston's Hebrew Orphan Society. Tobias, *The Hebrew Orphan Society*, 35, 36; Hagy, *This Happy Land*, 71–73. Founders from Mobile included Benjamin DaSilva, sexton of Mobile's synagogue, and brothers-in-law business partners Abraham Haber and Manuel Goldsmith.

65. Founder David Cohen Labatt, for example, was Henry M. Hyams's nephew. Friedman, "*Legal, Political, and Religious Legacy*," 83. Joseph Simon married Labatt's niece, Rosina ("Matrimony Notice, *T-P*, December 1, 1851). Manuel Goldsmith was married to the sister of Abraham Haber, with whom he sold wholesale dry goods. See Trestman, *Online Supplement*, for additional information about Home founders.

66. Malone, "New Orleans Uptown Jewish Immigrants," 249.

67. Founders affiliated with Gates of Mercy included Isaac Hart, Joseph Simon, Manuel Goldsmith, Joseph Cohn, Lambert Cain, and Leopold Klopman. Gates of Mercy Board minutes, 1853–56, Touro Synagogue Collection, no. 24, TSC. Founders affiliated with Dispersed of Judah included Rev. James K. Gutheim, Henry Hyams, Daniel Goodman, and Benjamin Florance. See Trestman, *Online Supplement*, for additional information about Home founders.

68. Founder David Labatt's father, Abraham, also was a member of the Reformed Society. Elzas, *The Reformed Society of Israelites*, 23–25, 43.

69. Swierenga, *The Forerunners*, 222, 386n36.

70. *1855 Constitution*, Bylaws XIII and XIV. The Kashruth requirement remained in the bylaws until at least 1890, although its enforcement is unclear. The only explicit reference to the Home's observance of Kashruth in the nineteenth century was in an 1865 report by Union inspectors regarding the needs of the city's charitable associations following the Civil War: the Home's customs "prevent them from using beef as killed by the usual method." "The Orphan and the Destitute," *NOT*, November 13, 1865. By the early twentieth century, Home menus noted dairy served with meat, and donations-in-kind included shellfish. In 1880, the board delegated authority over worship to a redesignated religious education committee.

71. Magner, *Story*, 25, 30, 39, 44, 51.

72. "Three Surviving Founders," *DP*, January 8, 1905.

73. The author compiled founders' enslavement data from microfilmed copies of city tax ledgers for 1852 through 1858, NOPL. See Trestman, *Online Supplement*.

74. *DP*, October 18, July 18, and August 6, 1853. "Griffe" referred to a person of mixed European and African or African and Native American ancestry. "Free People of Color in Louisiana: Terminology," LSU Libraries Special Collections, accessed June 22, 2021, lib.lsu.edu/sites/all/files/sc/fpoc/terminology.html.

75. Abraham Haber, 1860 U.S. Census for New Orleans.

76. Greenwald, "Purchased Lives," 15; *Cohen's New Orleans Directory for 1855*, AI. According to tax records, board minutes, and census data, the Home did not enslave Blacks. Instead, throughout the nineteenth century it employed only whites (natives of Louisiana and other southern states, as well as immigrants from Ireland, France, Switzerland, and Germany) as resident cooks, infant nurses, washwomen, carpenters, and gardeners. The Home's earliest recorded Black employee was Alice Cohn, a forty-two-year-old cook from Mississippi, as enumerated in the 1910 census.

77. Korn, "Jews and Negro Slavery in the Old South," 158, 199.

78. Monaco, "Moses E. Levy of Florida," 382; Adler, ed., "David Einhorn," 78–79.

79. Evans, *The Provincials*, 264–65.

80. "Mass Meeting of the Jews," *DD*, November 27, 1854; "Amusements last week," *DP*, March 13, 1853.

81. "Mercantile Inquisition," *New Orleans Weekly Delta*, December 8, 1851; "Mercantile Agencies," *New Orleans Weekly Delta*, December 15, 1851.

82. RGD-LA, 9: 75 (July 1848).

83. RGD-LA 9: 75 (March 1852); "Blackleg": cjewords.blogspot.com/search/label/blackleg.

84. RGD-LA 9: 260 (June 1849).

85. RGD-LA 11: 212 (November 1856).

86. RGD-LA 10: 364 (March 1852; July 1854).

87. "Death of Joseph Cohn," *T-P*, May 14, 1882; RGD-LA 11: 101 (August 1854, June 1855).

88. RGD-LA 9: 143 (May 1860).

89. RGD-LA 12: 22 (January 1861).

90. RGD-LA 10: 529 (January 1855).

91. RGD-LA 10: 363 (March 1852, January 1854).

92. *The Occident* 13, no. 7 (October 1855): 370.

93. *The Occident* 13, no. 7 (October 1855): 370.

94. Richard Campanella, "When Lafayette City Became New Orleans," *T-P*, June 9, 2017.

95. BMM 1: May 8, 1855; Hennick and Charlton, *The Streetcars of New Orleans*, 7, 10.

96. BMM 1: May 1, 1855.

97. BMM 1: August 1, 1855.

98. BMM 1: August 21, 1855.

99. "Local Affairs," *DD*, January 9, 1856; "Muddy streets": Local Affairs, *DD*, January 9, 1856.

100. Bishir, "William A. Freret."

101. Photograph of the Home, ca. 1880, by George François Mugnier, Collections of the Louisiana State Museum, 09813.514.1 (C-115), reproduced on page 126 herein.

102. Tyler, *New Orleans Women*, 55–56; Van Zante, *New Orleans 1867*, 203.

103. Before 1855, Jewish orphanages existed in London; Amsterdam; and Fuerth, Germany. Any involvement in these orphanages by founders from those locales is unknown, and there is no indication that the practices of these orphanages (such as London's and Amsterdam's separate institutions for Sephardi and Ashkenazi children, or Amsterdam's and Germany's single-gender institutions) influenced the Home's founding. Focke, "Jewish Orphanages in Dutch Society"; Conway, "The Origins of the Jewish Orphanage," 57; Barbeck, "History of Jews in Nuremberg and Fuerth."

104. Van Zante, *New Orleans 1867*, 14, 207–8.

105. *Dedication of the Home*, 4.

106. *Dedication of the Home*, 4–5.

107. Ophir, "Where does the blessing of 'shehechiyanu' come from?"

108. *Dedication of the Home*, 6.

109. BMM 1: December 18, 1855.

110. Roumillat, "The Glorious Eighth of January"; Hemard, "New Orleans Nostalgia: Celebrating Victory"; Gerome, "Battle of New Orleans once was national holiday."

111. *Dedication of the Home,* 6.

112. As adopted in 1855, Article IX of the constitution provided, "The Anniversary of this Corporation shall be celebrated during the Feast of Dedication (Hannuckah)." AMM 1: March 18, 1855. In 1858, to comport with practice, the board amended the provision to permit the anniversary to be celebrated *either* "during the Feast of Dedication (Hannuckah) or on the 8th of January" and by 1880 set the celebration "on the 8th of January, or as near that date as practicable." TSC-JCH, box 1, folder 2; AMM 1: March 1880. For the popularity of the January 8 holiday, see Roumillat, "The Glorious Eighth of January," and Gerome, "Battle of New Orleans once was national holiday."

113. BMM 1: November 27, 1864; "What is Asarah B'Tevet," Chabad.org, accessed October 18, 2021, www.chabad.org/library/article_cdo/aid/3170662/jewish/What-Is-Asarah-BTevet-Tevet-10.htm.

114. For accounts of annual celebrations by other Jewish orphanages (identified by newspaper location), see "The Jewish Orphan Asylum Third Anniversary," *Plain Dealer* (Cleveland, OH), July 14, 1871; "Jewish Orphan Asylum—Annual Picnic and Inspection Held Yesterday," *Democrat and Chronicle* (Rochester, NY), July 8, 1886; "Simchath Festival Celebrated at Hebrew Hospital and Orphan Asylum—Anniversary of the Institution," *Baltimore Sun,* October 26, 1891; "The Jewish Foster Home and Orphan Asylum," *Philadelphia Inquirer,* May 20, 1894; "Holiday for the Hebrew Orphans," *San Francisco Call,* September 28, 1896; "Inmates of Jewish Orphans' Home Entertain—Religious Festival and Anniversary of Institution Founding Are Jointly Celebrated," *Chicago Tribune,* December 7, 1896; "Hebrew Orphans' Annual Show," *Atlanta Constitution,* April 13, 1896;

115. Other Home orators who used race language to ascribe a favorable place for Jews in society include attorney Henry L. Lazarus (1882: "extraordinary conduct of the Jewish race"), Julius L. Beer (1884: the Home was "a reminder of the greatness of the race which has given it birth"), and merchant Samuel J. Kuhlman (1885: "does not the charity of our race elicit the admiration of the world"). For discussion of Jewish racial identity in the South, see Rogoff, "Is the Jew White," 201–3, and Light, *That Pride of Race and Character,* 38–40.

116. "Home for Jewish Widows and Orphans," *T-P,* January 11, 1859.

117. AR 1861: 6.

118. See, for example, "Jewish Orphans: Thirty-Eighth Anniversary," *DP,* January 9, 1893 (Charles Levy noted the bravery and loyalty of "many" coreligionists who fought in the battle); "Jewish Children Present Program," *T-P,* January 28, 1928 (children performed tableaux about the Battle of New Orleans). Fannie Barnett Linsky's "America and the Jew," a Thanksgiving pageant the Home children performed at the 1927 anniversary, typifies what historian Jonathan Sarna calls the "cult of synthesis" by which American Jews interwove their "Judaism" with their "Americanism." Sarna, "The Cult of Synthesis in American Jewish Culture," 63–64.

119. Friedman, "Legal, Political, and Religious Legacy," 76–77, 82–83, 85–86; "Anniversary Celebration," *Daily True Delta* (New Orleans), January 9, 1858; "Anniversary of the Jewish Widows and Orphans' Home," *Jewish Messenger* (New York City), January 29, 1858; Ira Rosenwaike, "Eleazar Block," 142–49; "Home for Jewish Widows and Orphans," *T-P,* January 11, 1859.

120. Bauman, *A New Vision of Southern Jewish History,* 306, 354–57; Bauman, *Jewish American Chronology,* 58; Korn, *Early Jews of New Orleans,* 225.

121. Korn, *Early Jews of New Orleans,* 227; Friedman, "Legal, Political, and Religious Legacy," 87.

122. "Jewish Widows and Orphans' Home," *Daily Crescent,* March 3, 1856.

123. AMM 1: October 7, 1855.

2. FIRST YEARS, 1856–1861

1. "Local Intelligence," *Daily Crescent,* February 2, 1856.

2. BMM 1: May 1, 30, and June 26, 1855; AMM 1: October 7, 1855. DePass's life before or after her work in the Home is unknown. As for religion, Bertram Korn identified DePass as a Sephardic name, held by several Jewish men in New Orleans (*Early Jews of New Orleans,* 248, 327).

3. "First Anniversary Ball," *DP,* December 15, 1849 (nine men listed as managers); "First Annual Fancy Dress and Masquerade Ball," *DD,* December 6, 1864 (Mr. I. Wise, secretary); Ladies Hebrew Benevolent Society, *TD,* April 2, 1865 ("Isaac Hart, Hon. Secretary"); "Ladies Hebrew Benevolent Society," *DP,* December 24, 1865 (Mr. S. Marx, chairman).

4. For southern Jewish women's organizations that enlisted or allowed men to conduct activities, see Bauman, *A New Vision of Southern Jewish History,* 79, 392nn13–15.

5. Tyler, *New Orleans Women,* 28–29.

6. Fleischman, *The History of the Jewish Foster Home,* 11–12; Ashton, *Rebecca Gratz,* 210–11.

7. BMM 6: January 4, 1914.

8. Charter, Constitution & Bylaws, 1855 (list of contributors), TSC-JCH box 1, folder 2.

9. *Dedication of the Home,* 19 (list of contributors).

10. BMM 1: May 22, 1866; Miriam Haber, New Orleans Census 1860; Ira Rosenwaike, "Eleazar Block," 142–43, 147.

11. Friedman, *These Are Our Children,* 12–13.

12. Neither the board nor Joseph Magner, the association's 1905 historian, recorded why the children did not initially attend nearby public schools. Magner, *Story,* 103.

13. BMM 1: March 9, 1856.

14. BMM 1: January 25, 1857; Kobrin, "Teaching Profession in the United States."

15. BMM 1: February 22, 1857. Frances's father was New Orleans auctioneer and Home supporter Isaac Tobias Hart, a native of Kingston, Jamaica, who in later years moved to Woodville, Mississippi. He was not related to founder Isaac Hart (no middle initial), a native of London who later moved to Detroit. Both men's names first appear together in the Home's 1862 annual report. See Trestman, *Online Supplement,* for additional information about these men.

16. BMM 1: March 28, 1859; BMM 2: June 6, 1875.

17. BMM 1: April 18, 1956.

18. BMM 1: July 14, 1856.

19. AMM 1: March 7, 1880; Magner, *Story,* 41–43, 62.

20. Jennie Goldstein, a native of Frankfurt, Germany (and of no known relation to either the matron or earlier resident, both named Jeanette Goldstein), had been admitted in 1876 at age sixty-two, and was discharged in 1885 to Touro Infirmary. HB 1: 365.

21. Magner, *Story,* 62; AR 1922: 49.

22. BMM 1: March 8, 1857.

23. BMM 1: February 22, 1857.

24. BMM 1: February 22, 1857.

25. BMM 1: March 8, 1857.

26. BMM 1: December 28, 1856.

27. BMM 1: December 28, 1856.

28. BMM 1: February 1, 8, 1857.

29. Orleans Parish School Board Minutes, July 5, 1852, 46–47, accessed March 24, 2022, louisianadigitallibrary.org/.

30. BMM 1: February 22, 1857.

31. BMM 1: March 8, 1857.

32. AMM 1: March 18, 1857.

33. BMM 1: May 21, 1857.

34. BMM 1: February 15, 1857.

35. BMM 1: June 1, 1857, January 17, 1858.

36. BMM 1: July 2, 1857.

37. BMM 1: September 3, 1857.

38. BMM 1: September 24, October 13, 1857.

39. BMM 1: October 21, 1857.

40. Hacsi, *Second Home*, 5.

41. "Report of the Grand Jury of the Parish of Orleans for the Term ending June 30th, 1858." (Emphasis added.) The author thanks Ronald P. Joullian, University of New Orleans Special Collections, for the report.

42. "Grand Jury Report," *T-P*, October 23, 1856; "Report of the Grand Jury," *T-P*, July 7, 1857; "The Courts," *T-P*, April 6, 1858.

43. BMM 1: July 4, 1858 (board authorized president to respond to the "disparaging paragraph," but did not record any response).

44. Wilson, ed., *Queen of the South*, 174, 176; Carrigan, *Saffron Scourge*, 77.

45. *DP*, October 10; November 16, 23, 1858; Carrigan, *Saffron Scourge*, 77.

46. Carrigan, *Saffron Scourge*, 80.

47. *The Occident* 16, no. 8 (November 1858): 410; *no*. 9 (December 1858): 457.

48. BMM 1: October 3, 24, 1858.

49. "Abstract of Grand Jury Report," *New Orleans Crescent*, July 11, 1859.

50. BMM 1: November 4, 1860.

51. BMM 1: November 18, 1860.

52. The board's liberality in admissions continued. As Superintendent Michel Heymann, who served 1868–70, and again 1887–1909, noted in 1902, "We have made it a rule not to admit any children whose parents are living, and we have made rules to exclude children whose surviving parent later married, but these rules are generally broken. We take all classes of children." *NCJC 1902*, 139.

53. BMM 1: February 7, 1858. The board did not explain the other two rejections between May 1855 and May 1858; in denying the Dyan siblings' admission, the board reported only, "the applicants not coming under the provisions of our constitution." BMM 1: October 13, 1857.

54. Magner, *Story*, 9.

55. BMM 1: May 30, November 29, 1858.

56. AR 1862: 11–13.

57. BMM 1: March 4, 1866 (St. Louis); BMM 1: February 2, 1868 (Memphis).

58. AR 1874: 12–13; 1875: 17–19.

59. Rosenbaum, *Cosmopolitans,* 20; Voorsanger, *Chronicles of Emanu-El,* 26, 40, 43.

60. HB 1: 32. BMM 1: September 4, 1859; July 21, 1861.

61. AMM 1: October 25, 1857; HB 1: 67–69 (Posner), 91–94 (Goldstein).

62. Friedman, *These Are Our Children,* 48; Bogen, *The Luckiest Orphans,* 188.

63. Clement, "Children and Charity," 143; Friedman, *These Are Our Children,* 48, Hacsi, *Second Home,* 118–119.

64. The author compiled age and family size data from the Home's registries and annual reports. See Trestman, *Online Supplement,* for additional information.

65. BMM 1: October 17, 1858; HB 58–66.

66. HB 3: 1393–98 (Tannenbaums); HB 3: 1538–43 (Beermans).

67. BMM 1: November 18, 1866.

68. BMM 2: November 1, 1874.

69. BMM 2: March 4, 1883 (denying application "for the admission of a so-called deserted child"); BMM 3: October 8, 1895 (denying mother's application to admit her children, "her husband having deserted her"); BMM 4: December 27, 1899 (denying application of mother, whose husband was absent, to admit her daughter, "as both father and mother were living").

70. Friedman, "'Send Me My Husband Who Lives in New York City'"; Baker, "The Voice of the Deserted Jewish Woman"; Sperber, "Agunot, 1851–1914."

71. BMM 3: November 3, December 1, 1889.

72. BMM 2: October 5, 1873.

73. BMM 2: June 1, 1882.

74. BMM 3: April 7, May 5, 1889.

75. HB 2: 681–84, 690.

76. Vandal, "Curing the Insane in New Orleans," 181.

77. Korn, *The Early Jews of New Orleans,* 225, 227; Jumonville, "Nameless Graves," 34.

78. BMM 1: January 11, 1857.

79. BMM 1: July 9, 1867 (Nedde and Hannah Ellmann); BMM 4: October 6, 1906 (board admitted the uncircumcised son of a widowed Jewish mother who had married out of the faith but "remained a Jewess").

80. BMM 1: January 30, February 6, 1859.

81. "A Circumcision Story in New Orleans," *American Israelite* (Cincinnati), January 28, 1859; "News Item from New Orleans," *The Occident* 17, no. 1 (March 31, 1859): 6; Berman, "The Trend in Jewish Religious Observance in Mid-Nineteenth Century America," 41. The author thanks Irwin Lachoff for sharing his April 1992 correspondence with David W. Bernard, great-grandson of Jacob Bernard, about the circumcision.

82. Bauman, *A New Vision of Southern Jewish History,* 15.

83. "The Outrage at Bologna: Proceedings at New Orleans," *The Occident* 16, no. 12 (March 1859): 12.

84. BMM: December 26, 1858; AMM 1: March 27, 1859; Bauman, *A New Vision of Southern Jewish History,* 21; Marcus, *United States Jewry,* 302–4.

85. AMM 1: March 27, 1859.

86. Bauman, *A New Vision of Southern Jewish History*, 15.

87. Vigil, *Escandalo Dado Al Mundo en Asunto Mortara*, 37; Frankel, "Notizen," 227–32.

88. Bauman, *A New Vision of Southern Jewish History*, 23.

89. BMM 1: April 23, May 18, 1857.

90. BMM 1: March 29, 1868.

91. *Daily Advocate* (Baton Rouge), March 15, 1856 (comments of A. W. Jourdan).

92. The author compiled state and city appropriations from annual reports and *New Orleans Item* lists of city disbursements to orphanages. In 1905, founder Joseph Magner mistakenly asserted that the Home received state funds only once. Magner, *Story*, 15.

93. Firestone, "Why Jews Don't Proselytize."

94. BMM 1: September 18, 1855; September 5, 1858; November 6, 1859; May 6, 1860; September 9, 1860; March 10, 1861.

95. BMM 1: April 3, 1864.

96. *GCM*, January–February 1933, 2.

97. See Friedman, *These Are Our Children*, 189–90.

98. HB 3: 1593; "One-Armed Player Wins Berth on Manual Eleven," *NOS*, October 5, 1932; "Newman Elects Maurice Garb," *NOI*, January 10, 1934; "Two Schools Hold Final Exercises," *NOS*, June 10, 1936.

99. BMM 1: December 14, 1856; HB 1: 19.

100. HB 1: 18 (Emanuel Goodman), 31 (Moses Barent), 26 (Myra Emanuel), and 23 (Solomon Weil).

101. BMM 1: February 6, 1859 (Sarah and Pauline), May 1, 1859 (Esther).

102. From data available for 1,383 of 1,623 children, which the author obtained from Home registries and annual reports, the board discharged 757 children to a parent and 229 children to a sibling or other relative.

103. Friedman, *These Are Our Children*, 170; Clement, "Children and Charity," 148–51.

104. Robert N. Rosen observed that Jewish immigrant women at the time, drawing on their European experiences, could be found working beside (or presumably following the death of) their husbands as storekeepers, peddlers, grocers, dressmakers, and small boardinghouse operators. Rosen, *Jewish Confederates*, 226.

105. Tyler, *New Orleans Women*, 13; Schafer, *Brothels, Depravity, and Abandoned Women*, 13.

106. AR 1862: 6.

107. Thompson, "Journeys of an Immigrant Violinist," 65–66. As the story has been passed down to Carillion descendants (also spelled Carillon), Benjamin died of yellow fever and his wife Rebecca Levy died when her ship sunk en route to Amsterdam for the reading of her father's will. Email from Rose Gilbert (great-great-granddaughter of Esther Carillion Gilbert), October 13, 2014.

108. BMM 1: December 18, 1859.

109. BMM 1: March 8, 1860.

110. BMM 1: March 19, 1860.

111. BMM 1: May 6, 1860.

112. AR 1900: 21, 27.

113. BMM 1: October 14, 1860.

114. "Herman Gilbert Guggenheim," *TD*, July 28, 1901.

115. BMM 1: September 9, 1860.

116. Bynum, *Unruly Women*, 45; Pelger, "Lives Through the Looking Glass," 15–17.

117. AR 1862: 6.

118. Korn, *Early Jews of New Orleans*, 196–97.

119. BMM 1: May 1, June 19, 1859.

120. Hacsi, *Second Home*, 94; Tyler, *New Orleans Women*, 43–44.

121. BMM 1: April 7, 1861.

122. BMM 1: November 17, 1861.

123. BMM 1: January 5, June 15, 1862.

124. Mintz, *Huck's Raft*, 138–40; Friedman, *These Are Our Children*, 115; Hacsi, *Second Home*, 133–36.

125. Navy enlistment age: www.history.navy.mil/research/library/online-reading-room/title-list-alphabetically/1/living-conditions-in-the-19th-century-us-navy.html; House of Refuge: NOPL, accessed July 6, 2021, nutrias.org/~nopl/inv/neh/nehtx.htm.

126. BMM 1: January 19, 26, 1862; AR 1862: 9.

127. "Morris C. Menges, Horseman, Is Dead," *Brooklyn Daily Eagle*, March 8, 1921; "Morris C. Menges," *New York Tribune*, March 9, 1921; "Well Known Horseman Dies," *Seattle Daily Times*, March 9, 1921; "Three Prominent Railroad Men Dead," *Omaha World Herald*, March 9, 1921.

128. "A Life of Bold Projects," *Baltimore Sun*, June 15, 1904.

129. Friedman, *These Are Our Children*, 64.

130. Pugh, *Juvenile Laws of Louisiana*, 190–91.

131. The author thanks Bobby Dobbins Title (whose husband was previously married to Henry Ber Kaufman's granddaughter) and Jonathan Rose (a possible descendant of Henry) for sharing family records, and Florence Jumonville for providing Touro Infirmary admission records. Although sources differ on Henry's mother's name, all other data align, including the hospital record which assessed her expenses to "J. K. Gutheim."

132. BMM 1: August 2, 1855.

133. BMM 1: February 7, 1858; *Gardner's New Orleans*, 1861, 56.

134. "Family History of Henry Ber & Caroline 'Carrie' Gottlieb Kaufman," unpublished work provided by Bobby Dobbins Title.

135. BMM 1: October 21, 1861.

136. BMM 1: July 2, 1861.

137. Kelley, "Erin's Enterprise," 261–62 (Camp Street Asylum for Girls and St. Mary's Asylum for Boys); Friedman, *These Are Our Children*, 64.

138. AR 1861: 6.

139. AR 1861: 7.

140. See, for example, "Thirteenth Anniversary of the Home for Jewish Widows and Orphans," *DP*, January 7, 1868 ("Bright intelligent young faces. . . . The little girls were dressed in dark purple with dove colored sacks and little straw hats. . . . The boys were dressed in grey cassimere suits, very neat, and showed that their physical as well as intellectual comfort was cared for by the managers of the Home").

141. "Home of the Jewish Widows and Orphans," *Daily True Delta*, January 10, 1864.

142. See, for example, "Local Intelligence," *NOT*, January 11, 1865.

143. AR 1860: 7.

144. "Grand Vocal and Instrumental Concert," *T-P*, May 11, 1858; "The Concert This Evening," *T-P*, May 12, 1858.

145. "Home for Jewish Widows and Orphans, *T-P*, January 11, 1859.

146. "Children's Home of the Protestant Episcopal Church of Louisiana," *DP*, April 20, 1885.

3. CIVIL WAR AND FEDERAL OCCUPATION, 1861–1868

1. Marten, *The Children's Civil War*, 211.

2. Wilson, ed., *Queen of the South*, 244.

3. Roland, "Louisiana and Secession," 389–90, 391, 392.

4. Address of George Williamson, commissioner from Louisiana to the Texas Secession Convention, February 8, 1861, qtd. in E. W. Winkler, ed., *Journal of the Secession Convention of Texas*, 1861, 120–23.

5. "Memorial," *Commercial Bulletin* (New Orleans), June 27, 1857 (listing J. L. Levy & Simpson among those "representing the majority of the Cotton Trade in New Orleans").

6. *Daily Crescent*, January 4, 1861; "The Secession Movement: From Louisiana," *NYT*, November 28, 1860.

7. Johnson, *Life and Letters of Benjamin M. Palmer*, 222.

8. Wilson, *Queen of the South*, 245.

9. Wilson, *Queen of the South*, xix; Rosen, *Jewish Confederates*, 248.

10. Rosen, *Jewish Confederates*, 248.

11. Rosen, *Jewish Confederates*, 248.

12. Rosen, *Jewish Confederates*, 248; Ashkenazi, *Civil War Diary*, 343–45.

13. Rosen, *Jewish Confederates*, 248; Ashkenazi, *Civil War Diary*, 399.

14. Ashkenazi, *Civil War Diary*, 11.

15. Capers, "Confederates and Yankees in Occupied New Orleans," 406; Doyle, "Civilian Life in Occupied New Orleans," 12.

16. Samuel Mayer Isaacs, "Stand by the Flag!" *Jewish Messenger* (New York City), April 26, 1861.

17. "A Dignified Rebuke," *DP*, May 9, 1861.

18. After April 1861, the *Jewish Messenger* (New York City) no longer listed DaSilva as an agent.

19. Rosen, *Jewish Confederates*, xii.

20. AR 1862: 11.

21. Rosen, *Jewish Confederates*, xi, 31.

22. AR 1862: 11–12.

23. Rabbi Bernard Illowy, "Fast Day Sermon: The Wars of the Lord," delivered January 4, 1861, accessed October 15, 2021, www.jewish-history.com/Illoway/sermon.html; Lachoff, "Rabbi Bernard Illowy," 53; Weiner, "A Conflict of Interests," 82, 84.

24. *DP*, October 16, 1861.

25. "A Card," *DP*, March 7, 1862.

26. Mehrlander, *The Germans of Charleston, Richmond and New Orleans*, 140.

27. Doyle, "Civilian Life in Occupied New Orleans," 164.

28. BMM 1: April 27, 1862.

29. BMM 1: July 2, 1862; James Chen, "Confederate Dollar (CSD)," *Investopedia*, May 8, 2021, www.investopedia.com/terms/c/confederate-dollar.asp.

30. BMM 1: February 3, 13, 1861.

31. AMM 1: August 31, 1862; "Grand Jury Report," *New Orleans Crescent*, March 25, 1861.

32. AMM 1: March 24, 1861.

33. BMM 1: May 5, 1861.

34. BMM 1: May 19, 1861.

35. AR 1862: 5, 6.

36. BMM 1: December 28, 1862.

37. BMM 1: August 3, 1862.

38. BMM 1: September 20, 1862.

39. AMM 1: August 31, 1862; BMM 1: September 7, 1862; Doyle, "Civilian Life in Occupied New Orleans," 34.

40. "The Orphan and the Destitute," *NOT*, November 13, 1865.

41. Doyle, "Civilian Life in Occupied New Orleans, 1862–1865," v.

42. Campbell, "'The Unmeaning Twaddle about Order 28,'" 11; Parton, *General Butler in New Orleans*, 327–29; Rosen, *Jewish Confederates*, 252.

43. Parton, *General Butler in New Orleans*, 467–68; Heller, *Jubilee Souvenir*, 134; Kendall, *History of New Orleans*, 283.

44. BMM 1: August 3, 1862.

45. Doyle, "Civilian Life in Occupied New Orleans," 36–37, 49–51.

46. BMM 1: May 3, 1863.

47. BMM 1: October 3, 1864.

48. HB 1: 100, 101.

49. BMM 1: October 19, 1862.

50. BMM 1: January 3, 1864; January 3, March 20, May 7, August 20, 1865.

51. BMM 1: July 17, 1864; HB 1: 13, 14 (Regina and Wolf Schwartz). Lazar also delivered orations at anniversary events. "Home for Jewish Widows and Orphans," *TD*, January 7, 1867; "Celebration of An Israelitish Anniversary," *TD*, January 7, 1868.

52. BMM 1: January 12, 1868.

53. Kern interview; "Babette Baer Schwartz, Memorial," accessed October 19, 2021, www.findagrave.com/memorial/18731896/babette-schwartz.

54. Marten, *The Children's Civil War*, 211; Wilson, "The Irish Angel of New Orleans."

55. Polster, *Inside Looking Out*, 5.

56. Sarna and Mendelsohn, eds., *Jews and the Civil War*, 237; Debbie Nathan, "A Very Jewish Civil War," *Tablet Magazine*, November 15, 2015.

57. HB 1: 99–101, 102–4.

58. HB 1: 105–18. In 1865 and 1866, the board admitted a total of thirty-one children, seven of whom were discharged to their fathers after the war's end, but left no clue about what prompted the admission of the other 24. HB 1: 119–49.

59. Parton, *General Butler in New Orleans*, 473; Doyle, "Civilian Life in Occupied New Orleans," 223.

60. Doyle, "Civilian Life in Occupied New Orleans, 223, 227.

61. BMM 1: March 15, 1863.

62. "Joseph H. Marks Dies at Eighty-Eight," *T-P*, January 31, 1907; *History of the Jews of Louisiana*, 176; "Jewish Home's Golden Jubilee," *DP*, January 9, 1905.

63. AR 1863 and 1864 (published jointly): 34. George Jonas's brother, Abraham Jonas, a friend and political ally of Abraham Lincoln, "grieved" that his two sons, Benjamin Franklin Jonas (the Home's 1856 orator), and George (named for his uncle), joined the "rebel army." Sarna and Shapell, *Lincoln and the Jews*, 172, 174.

64. BMM 1: May 6, 1863.

65. Korn, *American Jewry and the Civil War*, 48–50; Rosen, *Jewish Confederates*, 257.

66. Zola, "James Koppel Gutheim."

67. BMM 1: March 2, 1862 ("Jos. Magner, Secretary, in Camp as soldier"); *History of the Jews of Louisiana*, 175; "Joseph Magner," *DP*, November 22, 1908; "Mr. Joseph Magner," *Jewish Herald* (Houston), December 1908.

68. BMM 1: May 17, 1863.

69. Magner, *Story*, 22.

70. Parton, *General Butler in New Orleans*, 474 (adding, "Before General Butler left the department, 60,000 of its inhabitants had taken the oath").

71. Rosen, *Jewish Confederates*, 249.

72. "Domestic Record," *American Israelite* (Cincinnati), July 3, 1863.

73. BMM 1: September 1862–January 1866 (attendance).

74. Parton, *General Butler in New Orleans*, 474.

75. "Grand Jury Report," *DP*, May 8, 1863.

76. "The City," *DP*, May 13, 1863.

77. Doyle, "Civilian Life in Occupied New Orleans," 83, 86, 91–93.

78. "The Situation," *DP*, April 11, 1865; "Late from the North," *DP*, April 11, 1865.

79. "Report of the Grand Jury," *TD*, April 17, 1865; "Local Intelligence," *NOT*, April 17, 1865.

80. "The Jewish Home and the Grand Jury," *TD*, April 19, 1865.

81. "The Jewish Home and the Grand Jury," *TD*, April 19, 1865.

82. BMM 1: October 3, 1858, May 7, 1865.

83. AR 1866: 15.

84. The closest the board came to seeking a religious accommodation was in 1864, when the public school's examinations conflicted with the festival of Shevuoth. Although the board voted to request a postponement, the school (for unknown reasons) rescheduled the tests before the board made its request. BMM 1: June 5, 1864.

85. BMM 1: July 16, 1865.

86. Lachoff, "Rabbi Bernard Illowy," 60–61.

87. Somers, "War and Play," 4, 28; Chatelain, "The Persistence of the Mardi Gras Spirit in Civil War New Orleans."

88. AR 1866: 14, 16.

89. HB 1: 91–94; BMM 1: June 15, 1862; Tom Bassing, "Greenville's Exemplar of Civic Responsibility," *Delta Democrat Times* (Greenville, MS), December 26, 2014. The author thanks Camille Calman, great-great-granddaughter of Nathan Goldstein, for sharing family history.

90. BMM 1: January 17, 1864.

91. BMM 1: February 7, 1864; AR 1864, 39.

92. AR 1866: 13 ("endeavors to soothe the anguish" of the "widow whose husband has gone to God"); AR 1864: 31 ("the lonely lot of the widow").

93. BMM 1: February 4, 1866.

94. "Services Held Yesterday for Nathan Goldstein," *Delta Democrat-Times* (Greenville, MS), November 23, 1937; "Mississippi Man, Father of Local Woman, Succumbs," *The Times* (Shreveport, LA), November 22, 1937; *Biographical and Historical Memoirs of Mississippi 1*: 804–5; Rowland, *Mississippi* 3: 277–78; Calman interview.

95. AR 1873, 29; 1875, 22.

96. "Orphan Alumni," *DP*, February 13, 1893; AR 1900: 3.

97. "Orphan Alumni," *DP*, February 13, 1893; "Goldstein Remembers Home," *GCM*, June 1927; Calman interview.

98. Stolp-Smith, "New Orleans Massacre (1866)"; Bardes, "The New Orleans Streetcar Protests of 1867." The city's streetcars remained integrated until prohibited by law in 1902.

99. Corrigan, *The Saffron Scourge*, 99.

100. *DP*, September 22, 1867; Corrigan, *The Saffron Scourge*, 99.

101. AR 1869: 15; BMM 1: September 6, 1868.

102. AR 1868: 18.

103. AR 1868: 26–27; gender-segregated public schools: Blokker, *Education in Louisiana*, 20.

104. BMM 1: July 5, August 2, September 6, 1868.

105. BMM 1: July 5, 1868.

106. BMM 1: September 15, 1868. Favorable grand jury reports: *New Orleans Crescent*, March 14, 1868; *New Orleans Republican*, July 15, 1868.

107. Polster, *Inside Looking Out*, 10; Bogen, *The Luckiest Orphans*, 19. As for the only two other Jewish orphanages in operation in 1868, Philadelphia's Jewish orphanage was run by women until the election of a male superintendent in 1879 (Fleischman, *The History of the Jewish Foster Home*, 31–32) and information is unavailable about the early management of the Hebrew Orphan Asylum in Newark, New Jersey.

108. AR 1869: 15.

109. BMM 1: September 20, 1868.

110. BMM 1: February 2, 1868; "Recitation by the Orphans," *TD*, January 7, 1867; "Thirteenth Anniversary of the Home," *DP*, January 6, 1868.

111. Nightingale, *Notes on Nursing*, 42. Ashkenazi, *Civil War Diary*, 324, 403, 438.

112. BMM 1: February 2, 1868; "Severely Burned," *New Orleans Republican*, January 31, 1868; "Serious Accident," *New Orleans Commercial Bulletin*, January 31, 1868.

113. BMM 1: February 2, 18, 1868.

114. Friedman, *These Are Our Children*, 43, 53; Tyler, *New Orleans Women*, 126–27. See Trestman, *Online Supplement*, for additional information about Home children's deaths.

115. O'Neill, "Child Mortality in the United States 1800–2020." Thanks to Dr. Robert Trestman for assisting with child mortality statistics.

116. Tyler, *New Orleans Women,* 128.

117. "Death of Major Isaac Scherck," *DP,* February 3, 1889; *History of the Jews of Louisiana,* 33; "Married," *DC,* February 12, 1866. The author thanks Anne Scherck Morrison, great-granddaughter of Isaac Scherck, for family history and photographs.

118. BMM 1: April 22, 1866; Miriam Haber obituary, *Occident* 24, no. 4 (July 1866): 192.

119. "Klopman v. Klopman," *Daily True Delta,* February 4, 1858.

120. New Orleans's divorce rate in 1870 was 0.1 per 1,000 population. U.S. Dept. of Health, Education, and Welfare, *100 Years of Marriage and Divorce Statistics,* 51. The first divorce in New Orleans between Jewish spouses is believed to date to 1839. Korn, *The Early Jews of New Orleans,* 171.

121. "Legal Notices," *Daily True Delta,* January 21, 1858.

122. Lachoff, "Reform in Mid Nineteenth-Century Jewish New Orleans," 189; Langston, "James K. Gutheim," 73–74.

123. Lachoff, "Reform in Mid Nineteenth-Century Jewish New Orleans," 182, 185–88.

124. Heller, *Jubilee Souvenir,* 51; Touro Synagogue, "One Hundredth Anniversary, 1828–1928," New Orleans, 1928, 13.

125. BMM 1: June 21, 1868.

126. BMM 1: November 1, 1868.

4. A SERIES OF SUPERINTENDENTS, 1868–1886

1. Downs and Sherraden, "The Orphan Asylum in the Nineteenth Century," 274–75.

2. Crenson, *Building the Invisible Orphanage,* 42, 43.

3. "Louisiana at the Prison Congress," *DP,* July 26, 1895; "Biographical Sketches," *American Jewish Year Book,* 70; "Michael [sic] Heymann," *Jewish Herald* (Houston), May 13, 1909; Batt, "Michel Heymann," 147; Mills-Nichol, *Louisiana's Jewish Immigrants,* 152–53.

4. Michel Heymann, U.S. Passport Registration forms, May 2, 1895, April 7, 1900.

5. Mills-Nichol, *Louisiana's Jewish Immigrants,* 153.

6. "Louisiana at the Prison Congress," *DP,* July 26, 1895.

7. Heller, *Jubilee Souvenir,* 40. The Hebrew Educational Society closed in 1881. Langston, "James K. Gutheim," 89.

8. Langston, "James K. Gutheim," 78–79; Stern, *Race and Education in New Orleans,* 41–44.

9. BMM 1: November 1, 1868.

10. Eugenie Heymann Jacobs, Find a Grave, www.findagrave.com/memorial/138814442/ eugenie-jacobs.

11. BMM 1: December 6, 1868.

12. Polster, *Inside Looking Out,* 12.

13. BMM 1: November 1, 1868; Magner, *Story,* 103. Prior to Heymann's arrival, beginning in Gutheim's absence, the children learned Hebrew and religion from Rabbi Emanuel Rosenfelder, a native of Germany who married Home ward Sarah Adler, and later from Moses Aletrino, a native of Amsterdam.

14. BMM 1: January 10, 1869.

15. BMM 1: February 7, 1869.

16. BMM 1: May 12, 1869.

17. BMM 1: November 7, 1869; April 3, 1870. BMM 2: June 14, 1870; August 10, 1870. Heymann's silver loving cup was passed down to Kristin Flanigan, his great-great granddaughter.

18. Leon Heymann, Find a Grave, www.findagrave.com/memorial/139685304/leon-heyman.

19. AR 1870: 3.

20. HB 1: 116 (Fanny Goldstein), 235 (Mayer Block), 246 (Rachel Block).

21. BMM 2: April 10, 1870, June 7, 1870. The name was also spelled Schoenberg.

22. "Jewish Widows and Orphans Home," *DP*, June 16, 1878.

23. "Jewish Widows and Orphans Home," *DP*, January 17, 1870; "Report of the Grand Jury," *DP*, March 24, 1872.

24. AR 1871: 15.

25. AR 1871: 16.

26. Lachoff, "Reform in Mid Nineteenth-Century Jewish New Orleans," 194–96, 197; Heller, *Jubilee Souvenir*, 51–53; Zola, "James Koppel Gutheim"; Shpall, "Rabbi James Koppel Guttheim [*sic*]," 169; Langston, "James K. Gutheim as Southern Reform Rabbi," 74.

27. BMM 2: December 6, 1874.

28. Wilhelm, *Independent Orders of B'nai B'rith*, 62, 63, 68, 141–44.

29. BMM 2: February 28, 1875 (letter from M. Ulman, February 5, 1875).

30. "Jewish Widows and Orphans Home," *DP*, January 18, 1875; "Jewish Widows and Orphans," *NOT*, January 18, 1875; "Jewish Widows and Orphans Home," *New Orleans Bulletin*, January 19, 1875.

31. "Jewish Widows and Orphans Home," *New Orleans Bulletin*, January 19, 1875.

32. AR 1875: 38–39.

33. AR 1875: 6–7.

34. AR 1876: 17.

35. AR 1922: 17.

36. AR 1875: 16–19 (25 of 89 children); AR 1876: 13, 15, 16–18 (35 of 100 children).

37. AR 1916: 55–60; Trestman, *Online Supplement* (Whence Received).

38. Beerman interview, 1998.

39. Garonzik interview.

40. HB 1: 393 (Bernhold); HB 1: 498 (Frishman).

41. "Jewish Widows and Orphans," *DP*, January 7, 1884.

42. 1895: Ida Barnett, New Orleans. 1896: Max Frishman, Natchez, MS; Jack Bernhold, Helena, AR. 1898: Ferdinand Henriques, Woodville, MS. 1899: Alex Moskowitz, Birmingham, AL.

43. HB 1: 304; Winegarten and Schecter, *Deep in the Heart*, 68; "Jews Mark Yom Kippur," *Longview News-Journal* (Longview, TX), September 21, 1988; Wyman, "Jewish Contributions to Marshall, Texas," 8–9; David Weaver, "Hochwald an avid promoter of baseball, education and region," *Marshall News Messenger*, March 7, 1999; "Oldest Alumnus Salutes New Orleans," *Southern Israelite* (Atlanta), January 7, 1955, 6. Thanks to Mark Bauman for providing the last-cited article.

44. AR 1876: 8–9; AMM 1: March 19, 1876.

45. AR 1877: 7.

46. AR 1877: 35.

47. BMM 2: January 3, 1875.

48. AR 1877: 7; "Jewish Widows and Orphans Home," *DP,* June 16, 1878; Friedman, *These Are Our Children,* 111.

49. Hacsi, *Second Home,* 149–50; Friedman, *These Are Our Children,* 43.

50. "Jewish Widows and Orphans Home," *DP,* June 16, 1878; "A Haven and a Rest," *DD,* September 20, 1879.

51. "Jewish Widows and Orphans Home," *DP,* June 16, 1878; "A Haven and a Rest," *DD,* September 20, 1879.

52. BMM 2: July 2, 1878.

53. "Telephone Subscribers, New Orleans Telephonic Exchange December 1879," accessed October 18, 2021, louisianadigitallibrary.org/islandora/object/hnoc-clf%3A4409; "A Selection of Orleans Parish Medical Society Firsts," *125th Anniversary Newsletter of the Orleans Parish Medical Society,* 2003, accessed August 18, 2022, www.opms.org/images/stories/OPMS-History-Profile.pdf.

54. BMM 2: April 15, 1877.

55. BMM 2: July 3, 1877.

56. "Drowned," *New Orleans Bulletin,* August 31, 1875; "The Late Accident on the River," *New Orleans Bulletin,* September 3, 1875.

57. "Jewish Widows and Orphans Home," *DP,* June 16, 1878.

58. BMM 2: September 5, 1875.

59. BMM 2: December 10, 1877; February 10, 1878.

60. BMM 2: March 5, 1878.

61. Carrigan, *The Saffron Scourge,* 112, 115, 121.

62. AR 1879: 7.

63. The Home children who died were Aaron Serwinski and Mina Levi, both two years old, and Sam Unger, an infant who lost his parents to the same disease. HB 1: 364, 414, 415.

64. AR 1879: 7, 11.

65. "Death of Mrs. Mary Schoenberg," *DP,* October 23, 1878.

66. Mary Shoenberg, Find a Grave, www.findagrave.com/memorial/139206633/mary-shoenberg.

67. AR 1879: 11.

68. "Death of Mrs. Mary Schoenberg," *DP,* October 23, 1878.

69. BMM 2: May 7, 1876.

70. "Hebrew Benevolent Association," *DP,* October 26, 1878; AR 1879: 9.

71. "Licensed to Wed," *Chicago Tribune,* February 29, 1880; Lee Schoenberg, 1880 U.S. Census, Chicago; Marriage of Ida Schoenberg to Martin Levy, September 11, 1894, Marriages Index for Cook County, IL; Martin Levy obituary, *Chicago Tribune,* July 6, 1934; Eda [*sic*] Schoenberg obituary, *Chicago Tribune,* January 2, 1947.

72. HB 3: 335.

73. BMM 2: February 16, 1879.

74. Home for Jewish Widows and Orphans, 1880 U.S. Census, New Orleans; Marriage of Nathan J. Bunzel and Regina Cohen, February 14, 1869, Missouri Marriage Records (Ancestry.

com); "Special Notice," *Arkansas Gazette*, December 7, 1871, "The Jewish Sabbath," *TD*, August 4, 1882; Nathan J. Bunzel, Find a Grave, www.findagrave.com/memorial/64672203/nathan-j-bunzel.

75. "A Haven and a Rest," *DD*, September 27, 1879; *American Israelite* (Cincinnati), August 31, 1883. See also "Jewish Widows and Orphans," *DP*, March 27, 1882; and "Our Pet," *American Israelite* (Cincinnati), March 11, 1881.

76. BMM 2: October 9, 1881, January 1, 1882; "More Hoodlumism," *NOI*, March 1, 1881; "Burglars in the Orphan Asylum," *DP*, June 18, 1881.

77. "Jewish Widows and Orphans," *DP*, March 27, 1882.

78. BMM 2: July 15, 1883.

79. "St. Louis, MO," *Jewish Messenger* (New York City), December 3, 1886.

80. "Annual Message," *Jewish Voice* (St. Louis, MO), May 17, 1889; "Aged Israelites," *St. Louis* (MO) *Post-Dispatch*, March 11, 1888.

81. For history of the professionalization of social work, see Roy Lubove, *The Professional Altruist: The Emergence of Social Work as a Career: 1880–1930* (Cambridge, MA: Harvard University Press, 1965), and, within the Jewish community, Stein, "Jewish Social Work in the United States, 1654–1954."

82. "City Notes," *Daily Commercial* (Vicksburg, MS), September 12, 1879.

83. "A Brilliant Jewish Wedding," *TD*, May 30, 1882; "The Jewish Temple," *Woodville Republican*, April 22, 1882; "Lecture on 'Man and Earth,'" *Woodville Republican*, April 7, 1883.

84. *Pointe Coupée Banner* (New Roads, LA), July 15, 1882; "A Good Appointment," *Pointe Coupée Banner* (New Roads, LA), August 25, 1883.

85. "Educational Notice," *St. Louis* (MO) *Globe Democrat*, June 27, 1875; St. Louis, Missouri City Directories for 1877 (teacher) and 1878 (principal of Baden School); 1880 U.S. Census, Woodville, Mississippi (minister); "Educational," *Woodville Republican*, August 19, 1882.

86. "Rosh Hashanah," *DP*, October 3, 1883.

87. "Jewish Widows and Orphans: 29th Anniversary," *DP*, January 7, 1884.

88. BMM 3: February 7, March 7, 1886; AR 1886: 21–23; "An Unpleasant Subject," *Jewish Free Press* (St. Louis, MO), August 13, 1886. The victim was publicly identified in a news article that quoted Jennie Weil's divorce complaint. "A Jewish Divorce Case," *Inter Ocean* (Chicago), April 28, 1887.

89. "An Unpleasant Subject," *Jewish Free Press* (St. Louis MO), August 13, 1886.

90. "An Unchristian Rabbi," *St. Paul Daily Globe*, February 9, 1886; "A Grievous Scandal," *Sacramento* (CA) *Daily Union*, February 9, 1886; "A Missing Rabbi," *Evening Leader* (Grand Rapids, MI), February 9, 1886; "Un Scandale a la Nouvelle-Orleans," *Courrier de États-Unis* (New York City), February 9, 1886; "A Rabbi Seduces An Orphan," *Plain Dealer* (Cleveland, OH), February 10, 1886; "The Charge Against a Rabbi," *Morning Journal and Courier* (New Haven, CT), February 10, 1886; "A Missing Rabbi," *Argus* (Rock Island, IL), February 10, 1886; "A New Orleans Scandal," *Emporia News* (Emporia, KS), February 11, 1886; "A Lecherous Rabbi," *Weekly Bee* (Sacramento, CA), February 12, 1886; *Martin County Democrat* (Shoals, IN), February 12, 1886; *Burlington Independent* (VT), February 12, 1886; *Tammany Farmer* (Covington, LA), February 13, 1886; *Owyhee Avalanche* (Silver City, ID), February 13, 1886; *Weekly Town Talk* (Alexandria, LA), February 13, 1886; "Rabbi Weil a Fugitive," *Rocky Mountain News* (Denver, CO); *Jewish Messenger* (New York City), February 19, 1886.

91. "Shocking Crimes in an Orphans' Home," *St. Louis* (MO) *Globe Democrat*, February 8, 1886; "A Jewish Rabbi's Crimes," *NYT*, February 8, 1886.

92. "A Grievous Scandal," *DP*, February 8, 1886.

93. "The Orphan Home Scandal," *DP*, February 9, 1886.

94. BMM 3: April 23, July 20, 1885.

95. BMM 3: February 7, 1886.

96. "An Unpleasant Subject," *Jewish Free Press* (St. Louis, MO), August 13, 1886.

97. HB 3: 475 (discharged February 12, 1886).

98. AR 1886: 23.

99. BMM 3: March 7, 1886.

100. Zola, "Southern Rabbis," 358, 361.

101. BMM 3: March 7, 1886.

102. BMM 3: April 4, 1886.

103. Light, *That Pride of Race and Character*, 93.

104. AR 1886: 23; "Jew Orphan Home," *DP*, March 22, 1886.

105. "Wandered Back," *DP*, July 28, 1886; Sinclair, "Seduction and the Myth of the Ideal Woman, Law & Inequality," 51–52.

106. Curet, "All Rape Is Not Created Equal," 483–85.

107. Cocca, *Jailbait*, 23, table 1.1; Louisiana Act 115 of 1896 (state's first statutory rape law).

108. BMM 3: May 2, 1886.

109. AR 1886: 22.

110. "Rabbi James K. Gutheim," *Sabbath Visitor* 16, no. 9 (January 1887): 519–21, 519; "James K. Gutheim, The Scholar, Orator and Priest Passes Away," *DP*, June 12, 1886.

111. Heller, *Jubilee Souvenir*, 73; Rosen, *Jewish Confederates*, 363–64.

112. Langston, "James K. Gutheim," 82–83, 86–100.

113. Rosen, *Jewish Confederates*, 363–64; Leo Shpall, "Rabbi James Koppel Guttheim [*sic*]," 169–70; "The Last Rites," *DP*, June 15, 1886.

114. Langston, "James K. Gutheim," 82–83, 98.

115. "James K. Gutheim: The Scholar, Orator and Patriot Passes Away," *DP*, June 12, 1886; Langston, "James K. Gutheim," 98.

116. Langston, "James K. Gutheim," 78, 79, 80; Korn, *American Jewry and the Civil War*, 60.

117. "The Last Rites," *DP*, June 15, 1886; Heller, *Jubilee Souvenir*, 73.

118. Hannah Frishman, "In Memoriam," *Sabbath Visitor* 16, no. 4 (August 1886): 205, 206.

119. "An Unpleasant Subject," *Jewish Free Press* (St. Louis, MO), August 13, 1886.

120. BMM 3: August 3, 1886.

121. "Wandered Back," *DP*, July 28, 1886.

122. BMM 3: July 21, 1886.

123. BMM 3: December 5, 1886.

124. BMM 3: August 3, 1886; "The Jewish Orphan Home: Resignation of the Matron," *DP*, July 30, 1886.

125. *Jennie H. Weil v. Simon L. Weil*, Circuit Court of Cook County, Illinois, case no. 61484–2398, December 23, 1887. After describing her husband's assault on Lena F., Jennie Weil alleged

her husband had committed adultery with three other New Orleans women, but she did not state when or how she learned of those other acts.

126. Simon L. Weil, Find a Grave, www.findagrave.com/memorial/39496952/simon-1.-weil; Simon Weil, 1910 U.S. Census, St. Louis, MO; Simon Weil obituary, *The Monad*, December–January 1918–19, 38.

127. BMM 3: August 3, 1886.

128. BMM 3: August 17, 1886; "Death of Mrs. Hyams," *Dallas Morning News*, August 20, 1896.

129. BMM 3: May 2, 1886, August 3, 1886.

130. BMM 1: March 6, 1870.

131. BMM 2: June 7, 1870.

132. "An Unpleasant Subject," Jewish Free Press (St. Louis, Mo.), August 13, 1886; *American Israelite* (Cincinnati), February 19, 1886.

133. "Hebrew Charity: The Laying of the Cornerstone," *DP*, November 26, 1886.

134. "Rev. Isaac L. Leucht," *DP*, August 7, 1887; "Knife Fails to Save Life of Noted Rabbi," *NOI*, June 5, 1914; Lachoff, "Reform in Mid Nineteenth-Century Jewish New Orleans," 194, 196–97; Lachoff and Kahn, *The Jewish Community of New Orleans*," 36.

135. BMM 1, December 5, 1869; BMM 2: December 22, 1878; BMM 3: April 14, 1885, October 5, 1885.

136. BMM 3: January 3, 1886; AMM 1: March 20, 1887.

137. "The New Jewish Home," *DP*, November 21, 1886; Baumann, *A New Vision of Southern Jewish History*, 233.

138. "Hebrew Charity: The Laying of the Cornerstone," *DP*, November 26, 1886; "The Jewish Home: Laying the Corner-Stone of the New Building," *TD*, November 26, 1886; "Historic Time Capsule, 80 Years Old, Given to New Orleans Agency," *Southern Israelite* (Atlanta), August 28, 1964, 1; "Capsule Found in Cornerstone," *T-P*, August 10, 1964.

139. Classified ad, *DP*, September 23, 1877; *American Israelite* (Cincinnati), August 31, 1877; "Iberia Immigration Society," *The Louisiana Sugar Bowl* (New Iberia, LA), December 9, 1880; "Card of Thanks," *New Iberia Enterprise*, July 7, 1885.

140. BMM 3: December 5, 1886; January 2, February 6, 1887.

141. BMM 3: April 3, 1887.

142. AR 1886: 17.

5. A NEW HOME AND THE DREAM OF
A NEW SCHOOL, 1887–1903

1. "Jewish Orphans' Home Meeting Held," *DP*, April 3, 1905.

2. BMM 3: September 1, 1887; "Jewish Orphans: The Opening of the New Home on St. Charles Avenue," *DP*, September 5, 1887.

3. Mariano, "The 1884 Cotton Expo."

4. Campanella, *Geographies of New Orleans*, 276.

5. "The Jewish Home: First Anniversary in the New Building," *DP*, January 9, 1888.

6. "300 unique New Orleans moments," Nola.com, December 2, 2017, accessed July 6, 2022,

www.nola.com/300/article_09852351–76af-5975-b16b-446167c8eeba.html; "Walking on Neutral Ground: New Orleans' Unique Landscape Feature," accessed July 6, 2022, www.smartcities-dive.com/ex/sustainablecitiescollective/walking-neutral-ground-new-orleans-unique-landscape-feature/186151/.

7. Dominique Hawkins, "City of New Orleans HDLC—St. Charles Avenue Historic District," May 2011, accessed July 7, 2022, www.nola.gov/nola/media/HDLC/Historic%20Districts/St -Charles.pdf.

8. Thomas Sully, "Architectural Drawings for Jewish Orphans' Home, 1886," TSC Southeastern Architectural Archive ("Sully Drawings"); Thomas Sully, Specifications for Jewish Orphans Home, TSC-JCH, box 35, folder 1 ("Sully Specifications"); "Jewish Orphans: The Opening of the New Home," *DP*, September 5, 1887; Otis, "New Orleans Notes."

9. "The New Building of the New Orleans University," *DP*, February 5, 1888.

10. See, for example, "Jewish Orphans: The Opening of the New Home," *DP*, September 1, 1887.

11. "The Children's Fountain at the Jewish Home," *DP*, October 19, 1897; "Mrs. Jas. K. Gutheim Passes Away," *DP*, May 7, 1904.

12. BMM 7: November, December 1915 (Superintendent Reports). By March 1916, the population dropped to 166 and never again exceeded that number. AR 1916: 55.

13. Friedman, *These Are Our Children*, 78–79, 234n19.

14. "Jewish Home," *NOI*, August 24, 1894; Rothman, *The Discovery of the Asylum*, 228–29.

15. "Jewish Home," *NOI*, August 24, 1894; photograph of dining room, ca. 1890s, JCRS.

16. "The New Orleans Home," *Sabbath Visitor*, January 1887, 551; "Jewish Home," *NOI*, August 24, 1894.

17. BMM 3: May 13, 1888; Bernstein interview.

18. "Jewish Home," *DP*, January 7, 1895.

19. "The New Orleans Home," *Sabbath Visitor*, January 1887, 551; "Jewish Orphans," *DP*, September 5, 1887; "Recognition of Mr. Magner's Work," *DP*, October 29, 1898.

20. AR 1899: 34; *Reports of the Boards of Commissioners of McDonogh School Fund*, 33.

21. Stern, *Race and Education in New Orleans*, 42, 44, 267n51.

22. Friedman, *These Are Our Children*, 99–100, 101–2. CJOA, in contrast, did not close its school until 1920, as its superintendent believed that maintaining control over the children was the best way to train productive American citizens.

23. Jones, "A History of Compulsory School Attendance," 73.

24. AR 1891: 82.

25. "The Jewish Home: Annual Meeting," *DP*, March 26, 1883; "An Exhibition of the Kindergarten School," *DP*, May 28, 1882.

26. "Hebrew Relief," *DP*, March 30, 1885 (the board hired Emma Bruff as its first kindergartner teacher and alumna Hannah Levy as Bruff's assistant).

27. Haven, "The Relation of Kindergarten to Manual Training," 443–48; Gutek, *An Historical Introduction to American Education*, 255; MacKenzie, "Free Kindergartens."

28. Mackenzie, "Free Kindergartens."

29. *Report of the Commissioner of Education for 1884–1885*, 103; "The Kindergarten School of Mrs. Seaman," *DP*, May 28, 1882; Bauer, "The Kindergarten Movement in New Orleans," 385.

30. Heymann, "Reminiscences of a Kindergarten Friend," 283.

31. Sully Drawings; "Jewish Orphans," *DP*, September 5, 1887; "Jewish Home," *NOI*, August 26, 1894.

32. "Jewish Home," *NOI*, August 26, 1894; Hanson, "The New Orleans Normal Kindergarten Training School, 389.

33. Heymann, "Reminiscences of a Kindergarten Friend," 282.

34. "Louisiana at the Prison Congress," *DP*, July 26, 1895.

35. Sully Drawings; Sully Specifications; Interior Photo of Synagogue, n.d., JCRS; Interior Photo of Synagogue (ca. 1905) in Magner, *Story*; "Jewish Orphans," *DP*, September 5, 1887; Otis, "*New Orleans Notes*." Although architect Sully's drawings planned the synagogue on the second floor, an exterior photograph of the Home from the 1920s, which shows the children walking past Star of David stained-glass windows, indicates that the synagogue was located on the first floor.

36. "Jewish New Year," *DP*, September 23, 1892; "Jewish New Year Services Are Ended," *NOS*, September 28, 1916; AR 1894: 38; AR 1895: 29–30.

37. AR 1896: 35; Friedman, *These Are Our Children*, 136–38.

38. "Death of Henry Newman," *NOI*, December 26, 1906.

39. BMM 3: January 3, 1886. Leucht's 1886 call for industrial training had been heard outside the boardroom. In January 1887, Isaac Mayer Wise wrote in his national publication, "The Sabbath Visitor," that the rear building of the future Home "will be fitted up for a Manual Training School."

40. "Rev. Isaac L. Leucht," *DP*, August 7, 1887; Louisiana Educational Society, *Constitution and Bylaws*, 9; *Biographical and Historical Memoirs of Louisiana*, 109.

41. Friedman, *These Are Our Children*, 106, 107.

42. AR 1889: 17–18; Tyler, *New Orleans Women*, 129.

43. AR 1889: 17–18.

44. AR 1890: 18.

45. AR 1900: 23–24.

46. AR 1900: 43.

47. Friedman, *These Are Our Children*, 111.

48. AR 1891: 11; Friedman, *These Are Our Children*, 108.

49. BMM 3: September 6, 1891.

50. "Death of Gabriel Bamberger," *Chicago Daily News*, January 10, 1903; "Gabriel Bamberger," *Kindergarten Magazine* 15, no. 6 (February 1903): 393–94; "Gabriel Bamberger," *Indianapolis Journal*, January 25, 1903.

51. Dye, "Woodward and Manual Training," 20; Westerink, "The Manual Training Movement."

52. McEvoy, *The Science of Education*, 211; "Manumental," *Art Education* 1, no. 1 (October 1, 1894): 4; "Manual Training for Children, *DP*, December 18, 1898.

53. BMM 3: November 1, 1891.

54. BMM 3: January 3, 1892.

55. HB 1: 471; BMM 3: September 6, November 1, December 6, 1891.

56. HB 1: 578.

57. HB 1: 578; BMM 3: June 1, 1888, May 4, 1890.

58. "The Jewish Home," *NOI*, February 13, 1893; "Soule's College Commencement," *T-P*, June 29, 1895; "Public School Night Terms End," *DP*, May 29, 1909; "Notary Public," *NOS*, September 2, 1928; Phelps interview.

59. AR 1892: 5.

60. *History of the Jews of Louisiana,* 99; "New Officers of Grand District Lodge No. 7," *The Menorah* 2 (January–June 1887): 335; "Gabe Kahn, The Good Samaritan," *DP,* April 22, 1911.

61. "The Conference of Charities Invites the National Body to Meet Here," *DP,* May 15, 1896.

62. AR 1893: 13–14.

63. AR 1894: 37.

64. See, for example, AR 1895: 11–12; 1896: 35–36; 1897: 37.

65. Friedman, *These Are Our Children,* 182; AR 1891: 11.

66. HB 1: 402; "Orphan Alumni," *DP,* January 5, 1891.

67. HB 1: 495.

68. "The Home's Forty-First Year," *DP,* January 13, 1896; AR 1896: 11–13.

69. Moskowitz: HB 2: 765; AR 1899: 35. Bernhold: HB 1: 392; "The Jewish Home," *DP,* January 10, 1897; "The Forty-Second Home Anniversary," *DP,* January 11, 1897; AR 1897: 10–13. Henriques: HB 2: 718; "Jewish Home's Anniversary Day," *DP,* January 10, 1898. For Henriques's career in admiralty law, see "Law Leader's Funeral Today," *T-P,* July 27, 1966; Martinez, *The Story of the River Front at New Orleans,* 136–38.

70. "The Jewish Home's Anniversary Day," *DP,* January 9, 1899; AR 1899: 12.

71. AR 1899: 35–36.

72. AR 1898: 43; 1899: 18. "The Jewish Home's Anniversary Day," *DP,* January 9, 1899.

73. HB 2: 646. After working in the Home until 1910, Bella moved to Donaldsonville, where she helped raise her ten nieces and nephews. *Donaldsonville Chief,* July 23, 1910; Casso, *Lorenzo,* 127–30.

74. "Jewish Home for Widows and Orphans," *NOI,* August 24, 1894. AR 1895: 31; 1897: 36. "The Jewish Home's Annual Meeting," *DP,* March 22, 1897.

75. Friedman, *These Are Our Children,* 121.

76. AR 1900: 24, 43; undated photograph of the Home's Sloyd workshop, JCRS; Ramey, *Childcare in Black and White,* 169–70 (explanation of "educational Sloyd").

77. Friedman, *These Are Our Children,* 109–10.

78. AR 1898: 44–45.

79. HB 2: 710; "The National Farm School," *Bucks County Gazette* (Bristol, PA), September 6, 1900; "Six Graduated at Farm School," *Philadelphia Times,* June 27, 1902.

80. HB 2: 787; AR 1902, 29; NCCC 1897, 108–10.

81. See Trestman, *Online Supplement,* for the Home's National Farm School graduates.

82. HB 1: 512; BMM 3: June 7, August 4, August 11, 1891 (HUC admitted Bernstein), July 3, 1892 (eye treatment), November 13, 1892 (board voted to "have nothing more to do" with Bernstein).

83. Polster, *Inside Looking Out,* 17, 135; Friedman, *These Are Our Children,* 139–40.

84. AR 1895: 30.

85. Otis, "New Orleans Notes."

86. See Trestman, *Online Supplement,* for information about Home children discharged to apprenticeships and jobs (1888–99).

87. HB 1: 386; Davis interview. The author thanks Dr. David B. Davis II, grandson of alumnus David Davis, for sharing family history and photographs.

88. HB 2: 905; BMM 4: November 5, 1905; 1910 U.S. Census, Assumption Parish, Louisiana; "Personal," *Louisiana Planter and Sugar Manufacturer*, July 31, 1897, 77; *Donaldsonville Chief*, August 14, 1915.

89. 1920 U.S. Census, New Orleans (Alphonse, Rose, and Alan Pincus); "Welcome Home, Holmes Soldier," *T-P*, April 28, 1919; Alphonse Pincus obituary, *T-P*, September 27, 1966.

90. Moritz: Harvey Wolff and Calvin Wolff interview. Sonnenberg: "Police Force Maintains Its Mounties," *T-P*, April 21, 1946. Henriques: Ray Bellande, "The Henriques-Slay House," accessed August 8, 2022, biloxihistoricalsociety.org/biloxi-homes.

91. BMM 3: June 2, August 27, November 3, 1889.

92. AR 1894: 6; "Good Times Will Change All," *DP*, May 20, 1895; Young Men's Business League, *New Orleans of 1894*, 3; Edwards, "The Depression of 1893."

93. AR 1898:18–19, 23, 42; "Jewish Home: Forty-Third Anniversary," *TD*, March 21, 1898.

94. AR 1899: 15; "Children Seriously Ill," *New York Tribune*, August 15, 1898; "His Long Life for Helpless Babies," *New York Journal*, August 30, 1898; "Hebrew Orphan Asylum," *Jewish Messenger* (New York City), August 26, 1898.

95. "Southern Rabbis to Gather Here," *T-P*, January 4, 1900.

96. Handwritten Notes from Sermon, "Home," n.d., Leucht Papers, AJA, MS-596, box 1.

97. "Jewish Home Anniversary Made the Occasion of a Gathering of Rabbis," *DP*, January 8, 1900; AR 1900: 17.

98. "Jewish Orphan Alumni," *DP*, March 12, 1900.

99. BMM 4: April 6, 1902.

100. "The Jewish Home Will Have a Manual Training School," *DP*, April 28, 1902.

101. "The Jewish Home Will Have a Manual Training School," *DP*, April 28, 1902.

102. BMM 4: May 4, 1902 (Educ. Comm. Report, May 3, 1902).

103. BMM 4: May 4, 1902 (Educ. Comm. Report, May 3, 1902); Magner, *Story*, 88.

104. BMM 4: May 4, 1902 (Educ. Comm. Report, May 3, 1902).

105. BMM 4: May 4, 1902; Magner, *Story*, 89.

106. BMM 4: May 4, 1902; "surprised": AR 1903: 23.

107. Konigsmark, *Isidore Newman School*, 14–18; "Picayune Loving Cup Awarded to Isidore Newman," *DP*, February 15, 1903.

108. AR 1890: 27 (trust funds valued at $29,471.00); AR 1909: 48 (same trust funds valued at $117,148.00).

109. BMM 4: May 4, 1902. Newman's reference to "having read" Bamberger's "able and convincing address" is curious because there is no evidence that the educator prepared a written report in connection with his 1902 visit or that his oral remarks were transcribed.

110. BMM 4: May 18, 1902.

111. *Plessy v. Ferguson*, 163 U.S. 537 (1896); Acts of Louisiana, 1890, no. 111; Acts of Louisiana, 1894, no. 98; "Separate Car Bill," *NOI*, June 26, 1902; Reed, "Race Legislation in Louisiana," 383; Acts of Louisiana, 1894, no. 54 (anti-miscegenation); Acts of Louisiana, 1900, no. 70 (prisons); Acts of Louisiana, 1902, no. 92 (mental institutions); Constitution of Louisiana, 1898, article 248 (public schools). The author thanks Walter C. Stern for his insights on this topic.

112. Louisiana Educational Society, *Charter and Bylaws*, article 3.

113. "The Picayune Loving Cup Awarded to Isidore Newman," *DP*, February 15, 1903. Newman did not explain his use of the word "sectional," which then commonly referred to lingering animosity over the Civil War and Reconstruction.

114. "Magnificent Memorial Tablet," *NOI*, March 21, 1905. In 1946, when asked in connection with the Home's closure whether the school's disposition was subject to any restrictions, the board's law committee concluded, "At the time the original gift of money was made by Mr. Isidore Newman, no conditions were attached thereto." BMM: November 12, 1946.

115. "Formal Dedication of Training School," *TD*, January 9, 1905.

116. AR 1907: 38, 39; 1908: 29, 30; 1910: 53.

117. Konigsmark, *Isidore Newman School*, 29.

118. AR 1903: 21, 51.

119. Friedman, *These Are Our Children*, 17–20, 99, 132–33.

6. ISIDORE NEWMAN MANUAL TRAINING SCHOOL, 1904–1909

1. Magner, *Story* (photographs); Konigsmark, *Isidore Newman School*, 13, 32.

2. "The Merry Jingle of the School Bell Sounds," *DP*, October 2, 1903. Nationally, public elementary schools were almost always coeducational, and by 1900, most American public high schools were coeducational as well. "Single-Sex Education," academics.hamilton.edu/government /dparis/govt375/spring97/Gender_Equity/singlesex/ge3.html; "Co-education," Britannica, www .britannica.com/topic/coeducation.

3. BMM 4: October 31, 1904 (Educ. Comm. Report).

4. Stern, *Race and Education in New Orleans*, 76, 78, 81–82.

5. "The Merry Jingle of the School Bell Sounds," *DP*, October 2, 1903.

6. "Public Night School, *DP*, October 25, 1903; "Miss Sophie Wright's Night School," *DP*, October 17, 1903.

7. Konigsmark, *Isidore Newman School*, 13; "Leader Arrives for the Newman Manual School," *DP*, September 19, 1904; "Manual Training School Opening Great Event," *DP*, September 23, 1904; "School Nearly Ready," *TD*, September 25, 1904; "James Edwin Addicott," *Who's Who in California, 1928–1929*, 348.

8. "Newman Manual Training School's Dedication," *DP*, January 9, 1905.

9. Andrus, "Isidore Newman School," 83–84; "Manual Training School," *DP*, September 1, 1904; "Manual Training School Nearly Ready to Open," *DP*, September 11, 1904; "The Isidore Newman [sic]," *TD*, October 4, 1904; "Newman Manual Training," *DP*, October 4, 1904.

10. BMM 4: February 5, March 5, 1905.

11. BMM 7: May 7, 23, 1916.

12. BMM 7: May 7, 1905.

13. Hacsi, *Second Home*, 154.

14. "Damper May Be Thrown on Anniversary Music," *TD*, January 3, 1905; "Musicians' Union," *DP*, January 3, 1905; "Threat to Boycott Charity," *DP*, January 3, 1905.

15. "Marks Golden Jubilee Jewish Orphans' Home," *TD*, January 9, 1905.

16. Hacsi, *Second Home*, 200; Shansky, *Hebrew Orphan Asylum Band*.

17. AR 1903: 26.

18. AR 1905: 45.

19. "The Jewish Home," *TD*, January 9, 1905; "Jubilee Celebration," *DP*, January 9, 1905.

20. Andrus, "Isidore Newman School," 76.

21. "Description and history of the Athenaeum of the Young Men's Hebrew Association in New Orleans," ca. 1930, accessed July 12, 2022, louisianadigitallibrary.org/islandora/object /state-lwp%3A6775.

22. Magner, *Story,* 110.

23. "Manual Training School," *DP*, January 9, 1905; "Formal Dedication of Training School," *TD,* January 9, 1905.

24. District 7's proposal to stop funding CJOA, raised and defeated in 1884 and 1886, finally passed in 1904 by a vote of sixty-two to twenty-four after five hours of heated debate. "B'nai B'rith: An Exciting Session of the District Grand Lodge Convention," *DP*, May 7, 1884; "B'nai B'rith Orphan Asylum Matter Settled Harmoniously," *DP*, May 11, 1886; "A Battle Royale in B'nai B'rith Convention," *San Antonio Express,* April 21, 1904; "B'nai B'rith Grand Lodge," *Vicksburg* (MS) *Herald,* April 21, 1904; "B'nai B'rith," *Philadelphia Jewish Exponent,* April 29, 1904.

25. B'nai B'rith Report of Committee on Institutions, April 8, 1942, TSC-JCH, Box 49, Folder 11.

26. AR 1905: 24–25.

27. AR 1905: 28.

28. Heymann's professional papers included: "Jewish Child-Saving in the United States," *NCCC 1897;* "Youthful Habitual Offenders," *International Prison Commission, 1899;* "Child Saving in New Orleans," *ICCC 1900;* "The Treatment of Needy Families in their Homes," *NCCC 1903;* "The Ideal Orphan Asylum," *NCJC 1904;* "Homes for the Aged and Infirm," *NCJC 1906.*

29. AR 1894: 38.

30. "Sectional Meetings," *NCCC 1894,* 349; Heymann, "Jewish Child-Saving in the United States," *NCCC 1897,* 108.

31. Heymann, "Jewish Child-Saving in the United States," *NCCC 1897,* 108.

32. *NCJC 1902,* 140.

33. *NCJC 1902,* 139.

34. "The New Orleans Conference," *Charities Review* 6, no. 2 (March 1897): 150–51.

35. *NCJC 1902,* 144.

36. Joseph and Rudolph Bernstein interview.

37. Letter from Sam Koltun to Viola Weiss, October 24, 1983, JCRS; Sam Koltun interview.

38. Email from Richard Draper, August 8. 2020 (grandson of alumna Sybil Bianchini Dehougne).

39. Brooks interview.

40. Friedman, *These Are Our Children,* 37–38, 45; Crenson, *Building the Invisible Orphanage,* 113–15.

41. BMM 4: June 7, 1903.

42. "Abandoned": Lee K. Frankel, "Placing Out of Jewish Children," *NCJC 1904,* 205.

43. Between 1905 and 1920, the board considered paying a stipend in lieu of admission in six cases. In three of those cases, after approving or briefly paying stipends to a mother or female

relative, the board later admitted the children. BMM 4: May 7, 1905 (Segal); BMM 4: June 4, November 5, 1905 (Koltun); BMM 6: November 5, 1911 (Pulitzer). In the other three cases the board approved stipends in lieu of admission. BMM 5: June 8, 1908 (not identified); BMM 6: October 10, 1910 (Yarnoff); BMM 6: September 3, October 8, 1911 (Stein).

44. The board's 1925 treatment of four Redman siblings from Houston is illustrative. After citing the "best policy" of keeping children with their mother and noting this could be accomplished in this case by Houston's Jewish federation, the board nonetheless admitted the children the next month. BMM 9: July 31, 1925.

45. Sribnick and Johnsen, "Mothers' Pensions," 29–32; Ginsburg, "Institutional Intake," 134–35.

46. Wyckoff, "Louisiana Notes," 410, 411.

47. Friedman, *These Are Our Children,* 17–18; Malone, *Rabbi Max Heller,* 44–45.

48. Between 1881 to 1924, approximately 2.25 million East European Jews arrived in the United States, the great majority from Czarist Russia, and the remainder from Romania, Austria-Hungary, and other countries. Friedman, *These Are Our Children,* 17.

49. U.S. Census, 1880, 1900, and 1930. In 1910, the census taker simply listed all Home children's parents' birthplace as "unknown"; in 1920, the percentage of children born to parents whose birthplace was listed as Russia was 70 percent. Atlanta's Jewish orphanage experienced a similar change in its population. Light, *That Pride of Race and Character,* 66–67.

50. Polster, *Inside Looking Out,* 74.

51. Heymann, "Ideal Orphan Asylum," *NCJC 1904,* 199.

52. *GCM,* January 1925, 2–3.

53. Trevathan, "Hebrew Orphans' Home of Atlanta," 39–40; "Placing Jewish Children in Orphan Homes," *The Menorah* 39 (October 1905): 217–19.

54. Trevathan, "Hebrew Orphans' Home of Atlanta," 12, 38.

55. "B'nai B'rith in Memphis Meeting," *DP,* April 22, 1907.

56. Lee K. Frankel, "Report of the Committee on Dependent Children," *NCJC 1902,* 121.

57. Heymann, "Ideal Orphan Asylum," *NCJC 1904,* 70.

58. Heymann, "Ideal Orphan Asylum," *NCJC 1904,* 70.

59. *NCJC 1904,* 91.

60. *NCJC 1904,* 130–31.

61. BMM 4: November 4, 1906 (Addicott's report).

62. BMM 4: May 7, 1905 (Education Comm. Report).

63. Jones, "A History of Compulsory School Attendance," 73.

64. BMM 4: May 3, 1906 (Educ. Comm. Report).

65. BMM 4: July 1, 1906.

66. BMM 4: October 7, 1906.

67. AR 1907: 29; BMM 4: February 2, 1908.

68. See, for example, AR 1912: 32; 1913: 28; 1914: 31; 1915: 30; BMM 11: December 9. 1931 (Finance Comm. Report).

69. AR 1919: 8–9.

70. Andrus, "Isidore Newman School," 72–73 (noting, however, if capital investment and endowment interest were considered, the Home paid a higher tuition for its wards than was paid for outside pupils).

71. As two early examples, the board permitted Bella Fuerstenberg (BMM 5: December 5, 1909; HB 2: 970) and Louis Yarutzky (HB 2: 823) to continue at Newman School after their discharges in 1909.

72. Newman Commencement programs, INSA.

73. AR 1920: 14.

74. BMM 4: May 5, 1905.

75. BMM 4: November 4, 1906 (Addicott's report).

76. See, for example, United Federation of Teachers, "Considering Trauma in Special Education Evaluations"; Tuchinda, "The Imperative for Trauma-Responsive Special Education," 769.

77. "The Care of Dependent, Neglected and Wayward Children," *ICCC 1893*, 122.

78. BMM 4: November 4, 1906 (Addicott's report).

79. HB 2: 880 (Dan B.), 992 (Sarah H.); BMM 4: November 4, 1906 (Addicott's report).

80. HB 2: 1088, 1089, 1096; BMM 4: November 4, 1906.

81. BMM 4: November 4, 1906; *Goldstein v. State* (Mississippi Supreme Court Case #12449, 1907) and Certificate of Pardon by Gov. Earl Brewer, April 11, 1913, Mississippi Dept. of Archives and History.

82. AR 1912: 53 (Harry, Golden City Big Brother); AR 1915: 51 (Tillie, Golden City Big Sister); AR 1919: 14 (Hirsch, Treasurer, Golden City Brotherhood).

83. "At Temple Beth El Congregational Dinner," *Corpus Christi Times*, March 7, 1966; "Goldstein Last Rites Monday," *T-P*, February 27, 1972.

84. Letter from Hirsch Goldstein to Viola Weiss, September 6, 1983, JCRS.

85. "Raise Service Flag Above Jewish Home," *T-P*, June 3, 1918 (military service); BMM 6: June 1913 (Supt's Report); BMM 7: May 27, 1915 (Educ. Comm. Report).

86. *Young Israel*, July 31, 1908, 190.

87. "Jewish Orphans' Anniversary Day," *DP*, January 13, 1908.

88. "Miss Metzner's Address," *T-P*, January 19, 1908.

89. "Newman Training School Celebrates Founder's Day," *DP*, February 29, 1908.

90. "Founders' Day at the Newman Training School," *NOI*, March 1, 1909.

91. "Newman Training School Celebrates Founder's Day," *DP*, February 29, 1908.

92. BMM 4: July 5, 1900; AR 1901: 21.

93. "Leading Women Discuss the Servant Problem," *DP*, December 25, 1904.

94. Frederick Duncan Parham, World War I draft registration card, June 5, 1917; Tulane *Jambalaya*, 1918, 119; HB 2:1000 (Yolande Weiss); "Nurses Averaged 13 Calls Each Day," *Arizona Republican*, January 14, 1921; "Clinic Cares for Many in December," *Arizona Republican*, January 11, 1922.

95. BMM 4: May 3, 1906 (Educ. Comm. Report).

96. "Formal Dedication of Training School," *TD*, January 9, 1905.

97. Newman School later awarded scholarships (see Konigsmark, *Isidore Newman School*, 160), but there is no record of the practice resuming before the Home closed.

98. Pulitzer, *Dreams Can Come True*, 114. See also Besmann, "Typical Home Kid Overachievers," 142, 149. Subtitled "Instilling a Success Ethic in the Jewish Children's Home in New Orleans," Besmann's 2005 article, which roughly divides the Home's ninety-one-year history into three eras (featuring survival, producing middle-class American Jews, and finally emulating

family care), cogently argues that the Home's leadership sought to supply its children in each era with the goal of career success and the tools to achieve it, including Newman School in the third era. The author is indebted to Besmann for her scholarship and insights.

99. Helen Gold Haymon, "Memories of Days in J.C.H., 1920–1935," JCRS ("Haymon Memories"), 6, 10; Hornikel interview.

100. "Pupils Give School Treat in Operetta," *T-P,* June 4, 1922.

101. BMM 7: January 4, 1920 (Educ. Comm. Report).

102. BMM 8: June 3, 1923 (Educ. Comm. Report).

103. Simons, *Jewish Times,* 174 (quoting alumna Freda Hyde Lowenthal, 1925–1938).

104. Sizeler interview, 1982; Rothstein interview, 2003. See also Jennie Ogden Schneider, "Remarks to JCRS Panel, 1995," JCRS ("Often after school, Newman classmates would join us to play in team games").

105. Joe Samuels interview, 2003; Whitehead interview; Meadow interview, 2003.

106. Pfeifer interviews.

107. Ellis Hart interview, 2017.

108. Fox interviews, ISJL 2003, 2004.

109. Limerick interview, 2018.

110. Alvin "Pat" Samuels interview, 2018.

111. Louis Peters, "Fortunate Unfortunates—Part I," *Jewish Herald-Voice* (Houston), May 22, 1980.

112. Home students Louis Fuerstenberg (1911), Sam Koltun (1913), and Bessie Margolin (1925), the highest-ranking members of their Newman graduating classes, won scholarships to Tulane and Newcomb. Newman Coach Claude "Monk" Simons Sr., praised Leroy Swartzkopf (1917) as "one of the best Prep School pitchers ever in New Orleans," before the talented Home athlete (and future San Antonio advertising executive) pitched winning seasons for Tulane and then as a semiprofessional. "Swartzkopf Twirls Alamo Bank to Title," n.d., and other undated clippings generously provided by Swartzkopf's daughter, Kay Swartzkopf Smith.

113. In 1935, Van Eaton Hart won Tulane's scholarship for the highest-ranking Newman graduate. He also won awards for French, chemistry, and boys' athletics. In 1936, Helen Gold Haymon and Maurice Garb were graduation speakers. In 1938, Lucille Pierce won the certificate for excellence in sewing. In 1939, Ralph Ginsberg won prizes for chemistry and *Pioneer* business management, and was a graduation speaker. In 1940, Lilyan Golden was senior-class president and graduation speaker. In 1943, Carol Hart won awards for U.S. history and loyalty. In 1941, Benjamin Shanker was a graduation speaker. Commencement Programs, INSA. Thanks to Van Hart for sharing his father's Newman School records.

114. Commencement Program, June 1944, INSA.

115. Besmann, "Typical Home Kid Overachievers," 155.

116. Besmann, "Typical Home Kid Overachievers," 155.

117. Besmann, "Typical Home Kid Overachievers, 121–22.

118. BMM 5: January 5, 20, 1908.

119. "James Edwin Addicott," *Who's Who in California, 1928–1929,* 348.

120. BMM 5: March 5, 1908.

121. Ellen Foley, "Henson, Ending 42 Years in Education," *T-P,* February 2, 1947.

122. BMM 5: April 5, 1908; Life expectancy: u.demog.berkeley.edu/~andrew/1918/figure2 .html.

123. "Michel Heymann Dead," *T-P*, April 29, 1909; "Mr. Heymann Honored," *TD*, June 21, 1905; "Michel Heymann Returns," *DP*, November 5, 1906; "Biographical Sketches," *American Jewish Year Book*, 70.

124. "Fifteenth Annual Meeting of the International Kindergarten Union," *Kindergarten Review* 18, no. 10 (June 1908): 603.

125. *Young Israel*, July 31, 1908, 190.

126. *Young Israel*, August 7, 1908, 204.

127. *Young Israel*, August 14, 1908, 222 (Weiss); September 4, 1908, 268 (Clausner).

128. "Heat," *Montgomery* (AL) *Advertiser*, May 24, 1908.

129. "Rabbi Leucht Returns," *DP*, September 13, 1908.

130. "Supt. M. Heymann Resigns," *Jewish Herald* (Houston), November 19, 1908; "Michel Heymann Honored," *DP*, February 1, 1909.

131. "Michel Heymann Dead," *DP*, April 29, 1909; "Michel Heymann," *DP*, April 30, 1909; "Mr. Heymann Is Claimed by Death," *NOI*, April 28, 1909; "Many Pay Tribute to Memory of Michel Heymann," *NOI*, April 29, 1909; "Michel Heymann's Burial Rare Tribute of Esteem," *DP*, April 30, 1909. Maurice Greenwald, Marcus Korn, David Kraus, David Marcus, Morris Burka, Harry Kaplan, and Sol Stern also served as alumni pallbearers.

132. "Twenty-One Years of Service," *Charities and the Commons* 21 (December 19, 1908): 438.

133. Batt, "Michel Heymann," 146–49.

134. "Mitchael [sic] Heymann," *Jewish Herald* (Houston), May 13, 1909; HB 1: 549. See also Stone, "Edgar Goldberg," 78–79; Stone interview.

135. Letter from President Theodore Roosevelt to Michel Heymann, January 6, 1909, provided by Kristin Flanigan, Heymann's great-granddaughter. See also, "Michel Heymann Invited to White House," *DP*, January 19, 1909.

136. "Michel Heymann," Find a Grave, www.findagrave.com/memorial/139580770/michel -heymann.

137. The Home admitted 24 children during Heymann's first tenure (1868–70), and 481 during his second tenure (1887–1908). HB 1 and 2.

138. In 1902, Heymann estimated that the Home had produced "perhaps 10 percent" successful professionals. As for the rest, he replied, "I do not know. They have to fight a hard battle. So it becomes our duty to make our orphan asylum as perfect as we can." *NCJC 1902*, 140.

7. CHESTER TELLER'S GOLDEN CITY, 1909–1911

1. Chester J. Teller, U.S. passport application, June 19, 1906; AR 1909: 32, 104 (photos).

2. AR 1911: 24; *Jewish Herald* (Houston), March 30, 1911.

3. *Proceedings of the Conference on the Care of Dependent Children, January* (Washington, DC: GPO, 1909) ("*White House Conference 1909*"), 5.

4. Hacsi, *Second Home*, 4.

5. See Trestman, *Online Supplement*, for a list of American Jewish orphanages.

6. *White House Conference 1909*, 10.

7. *NCJC 1910*, 205.

8. "Teller-Magnes," *Philadelphia Jewish Exponent*, November 27, 1908.

9. Hurwitz, "How Lucky We Were," 31–32; "Chester Jacob Teller," *Brooklyn Daily Eagle*, December 29, 1911; U.S. Census 1900, Philadelphia.

10. "A Twentieth Century Club at High School," *Philadelphia Inquirer*, March 28, 1901; "High School Speakers Selected," *Philadelphia Inquirer*, May 14, 1901; "Wins Haverford Alumni Prize," *Philadelphia Inquirer*, May 26, 1905; "Main Line Society on Haverford Campus, *Philadelphia Inquirer*, June 16, 1905; *Biographical Catalog of the Matriculates of Haverford College, 1833–1922* (Philadelphia: Haverford Alumni Association, 1922), 466–67; "Chester J. Teller's Appointment," *Philadelphia Jewish Exponent*, June 28, 1907; Hurwitz, "How Lucky We Were," 32.

11. Haverford College Archives, Graduating Theses, 1905, vol. 2, shelf R80E; "A Discussion of Immigrant Problems," *Philadelphia Jewish Exponent*, February 23, 1906.

12. "Settlement Houses," Jewish Virtual Library, accessed February 14, 2022, www.jewish-virtuallibrary.org/settlement-houses; Bauman, *Jewish American Chronology*, 76–77.

13. "Chester J. Teller's Appointment," *Philadelphia Jewish Exponent*, June 28, 1907.

14. "Chester Teller's Timely Talk," *DP*, April 14, 1909.

15. *Twenty-Ninth and Thirtieth Annual Report of the Hebrew Sheltering Guardian Society of New York, October 1, 1907–September 30, 1909*, 90, 93.

16. Sharlitt, *As I Remember*, 36–37; Hacsi, *Second Home*, 157–58.

17. Light, *States of Childhood*, 1–2, 6–7.

18. "Historical Note," Hebrew Sheltering Guardian Society Records, American Jewish Historical Society, archives.cjh.org//repositories/3/resources; Light, *States of Childhood*, 91–92; "Our Legacy: William R. George," September 27, 2018, boysrepublic.org/our-legacy-william-r-george/.

19. Sharlitt, *As I Remember*, 38.

20. "Weddings: Teller-Magnes," *Philadelphia Jewish Exponent*, November 27, 1908; Finding Aid, Magnes Collection on Judah L. Magnes, 1870–2004, Bancroft Library, University of California, Berkeley, accessed October 22, 2021,

oskicat.berkeley.edu/search/0743436271.

21. Walter Magnes Teller was born in October 1910; sister, Sophia, was born in August 1911.

22. AR 1909: 34.

23. AR 1910: 28–29.

24. "A Golden City," *Jewish Charities*, August 1910, 4–5.

25. "The Golden City of the Jewish Orphans Home," 1911 ("Golden City Handbook"), 25–27, JCRS; "Jewish Women Gather, *TD*, April 14, 1909; AR 1910: 19, 35–36; "Notable Jewish Event," *TD*, January 9, 1911.

26. "Jewish Home Celebrates Another Anniversary Day," *DP*, January 9, 1911; Teller, "Some Child Caring Ideals."

27. Golden City Handbook, 26–27; "Chester Teller's Timely Talk," *DP*, April 14, 1909.

28. Golden City Handbook, 17; "Jewish Home Celebrates Another Anniversary," *DP*, January 9. 1911.

29. "Allowances," *Encyclopedia of Children and Childhood*.

30. Golden City Handbook, 17–18, 30.

31. Koltun interview, 1983.

32. "Golden City's Golden Fourth," *DP*, July 5, 1911; "Celebration by Jewish Orphans," *NOI*, July 5, 1911.

33. Golden City Handbook, 33–34; AR, 1910, 19.

34. Duff, "The Playground Movement"; Hacsi, *Second Home,* 196–201.

35. Golden City Handbook; AR 1909, 1910, 1911.

36. BMM 5: July 1, 1909 (David A. Morgenstern from New York).

37. "Jewish Relief Society Meets," *TD,* April 17, 1911; Golden City Handbook, 19–20; AR 1909: 36.

38. AR 1909: 25–26.

39. AR 1910: 4. Teller hired the Home's first nurse, Amelia Greenwald, a recent graduate of Touro Infirmary's Nursing School, who later pioneered international public health nursing. Mayer, "Amelia Greenwald and Regina Kaplan," 83.

40. Golden City Handbook, 30.

41. Teller, "Some Child-Caring Ideals."

42. AR 1909: 25.

43. AR 1909: 10 photos; AR 1910: 6 photos.

44. BMM 5: September 2, 1909.

45. "A Golden City," *Jewish Charities* 2, no. 1 (August 1911): 4, 5.

46. Teller, "Some Child-Caring Ideals"; editorial, "The Golden City," *Philadelphia Jewish Exponent,* February 10. 1911.

47. Trevathan, "Hebrew Orphans' Home of Atlanta," 26.

48. "Manual Training Summer School Conducted for the Benefit of Jewish Asylum," *T-P,* September 4, 1909.

49. AR 1910: 40; "Anniversary Ceremony at Jewish Orphans' Home, *TD,* January 10, 1910; "Jewish Orphans' Home," *T-P,* January 10, 1910.

50. Simon interview.

51. Koltun interview.

52. "Orphans at Play," *T-P,* September 1, 1910.

53. HB 2: 998; "Newman High Graduates Twenty," *DP,* June 5, 1912.

54. "Clermont Harbor Scout Summer Camp," *DP,* June 7, 1911. "Boy Scouts," *DP,* June 16, 1911.

55. "Col. Roosevelt Spends Five Hours in City," *TD,* March 12, 1911; "Boy Scouts," *DP,* March 11, 1911.

56. "Isidore Newman Dead," *DP,* December 1, 1909; Andrus, "Isidore Newman School," 49–50. See also, "Isidore Newman," *NOI,* December 1, 909; "Isidore Newman Makes Some Public Bequests," *DP,* December 9. 1909.

57. Andrus, "Isidore Newman School," 50.

58. AR 1910: 41–42.

59. AR 1910: 41–45.

60. Of 340 Newman students enrolled for the 1909 school year, 127 came from the Home. Of Newman's 89 high school students, only 14 came from the Home. AR 1910: 48; Konigsmark, *Isidore Newman School,* 41, 44.

61. Goldin, "How America Graduated from High School," table 2.

62. Commencement program, June 5, 1913, INSA. In addition to Yarutzky, the class also included brothers Meyer and Sam Koltun, and Fannie Stafsky. The Koltuns went to work for department store owner Leon Fellman; Stafsky's plans were not recorded.

63. Goldin, "How America Graduated from High School," table 2; commencement program, June 7, 1923, INSA; BMM 8: May 6, 1923.

64. U.S. Dept. of Education, *120 Years of American Education*, 54.

65. HB 2: 1121; BMM 8: February 4, 1923; Gubin interview; Salky interview. Fielschmidt also served as Golden City Sisterhood vice president (AR 1922: 12).

66. Trestman, *Fair Labor Lawyer*, 13, 25.

67. HB 3: 1444; Tulane *Jambalaya*, 1928, 46; Haymon Memories; Gilberstadt interview.

68. BMM 6: September 6, 1910 (Meyer); BMM 6: June 1, 1913 (Goldstein); AR 1916: 62 (Fuerstenberg).

69. Koltun interview.

70. "Newman School to Add to Curriculum," *NOI*, June 1, 1912.

71. AR 1915: 28.

72. AR 1914: 32; AR 1916: 26.

73. "Biennial Report of the State Superintendent of Public Education," *DP*, December 30, 1913.

74. BMM 7: July 4, 1915; Andrus, "Isidore Newman School," 54; Berenson thesis, 140.

75. BMM 7: July 2, 1916.

76. BMM 8: May 6, 1923.

77. *GCM*, June–July, 1924.

78. BMM 6: January 1, 1911; AR 1911: 24.

79. BMM 6: Between entries for February 9 and March 6, 1911.

80. AR 1911, 24; *Jewish Herald* (Houston), March 30, 1911.

81. AR 1910: 21.

82. BMM 6: May 7, 1911.

83. "Jewish Home Celebrates," *DP*, January 9, 1911; "Notable Jewish Event," *TD*, January 9, 1911.

84. "Pay Tribute to Mr. Kahn," *TD*, April 24, 1911.

85. BMM 6: May 7, 1911.

86. BMM 6: June 8, 1911.

87. BMM 6: July 30, August 8, 1911.

88. "Jewish New Year," *DP*, September 24, 1911; HB 2, 887 (Cohn), 981 (Burka).

89. "Mr. Teller Leaves," *T-P*, October 31, 1911.

90. "Chester Jacob Teller, New Superintendent of H.O.A.," *Brooklyn Daily Eagle*, December 29, 1911.

91. "Prof. Geismar Coming Here," *Brooklyn Daily Eagle*, March 28, 1912.

92. Hurwitz, "*How Lucky We Were*," 33; "Jewish Education," *Newark Evening Star*, December 16, 1912.

93. "Clermont Scout Camp Biggest in South," *TD*, June 18, 1911; "Well-known Social Worker Heads Unique School Corporation," *American Israelite* (Cincinnati), August 21, 1913.

94. Hurwitz, "*How Lucky We Were,*" 45–46. In 1924, Teller hired Home alumna Ida Goldberg as a Camp Arden counselor. *GCM,* September 1924.

95. "Chester Jacob Teller, 78, Retired Welfare Worker," *NYT,* May 21, 1962.

96. Light, *States of Childhood,* 118–19.

8. RABBI LEON VOLMER, 1911–1925

1. AR 1917: 32 (address by Harry L. Glucksman, superintendent, Young Men's Hebrew Association).

2. LeMaster, *Corner of the Tapestry,* 120; "Photograph Portrays Scene Typical Half Century Ago," *Arkansas Gazette,* April 12, 1931; "Rabbi Leon Volmer," *Arkansas Democrat,* September 29, 1898; "Honors for Leon Volmer," *Daily Arkansas Gazette,* June 12, 1901; "Prince Fallen: Notable Memorial Sermon by Rabi Leon Volmer," *Arkansas Democrat,* September 27, 1901; "Anti-Tuberculosis League of the State," *Clarksburg* (WV) *Telegram,* December 24, 1908; "Charleston High School's First Football Team," *Charleston Daily Mail,* September 8, 1935.

3. "Weddings," *Arkansas Gazette,* September 17, 1905; Crosby interview.

4. "New Superintendent for New Orleans Orphans Home," *Jewish Herald* (Houston), August 31, 1911; "Rev. Leon Volmer Is Given a Promotion," *Arkansas Gazette,* August 27, 1911.

5. Unpublished memoir, n.d., William Franklin Rosenblum Papers, Center for Jewish History, P-327 ("Rosenblum Papers"), box 1, folder 1.

6. Kotzin, *Judah L. Magnes,* 24.

7. Adler, "West Virginia."

8. Thanks to Liz Crosby for sharing photos and memories of her grandparents, Leon and Tresa Volmer, and her mother, Louise Volmer Sloane.

9. See, for example, BMM 7: April 2, 1916 (Superintendent Report).

10. The photo, provided by Liz Crosby, is displayed at the Museum of the Southern Jewish Experience.

11. Golden City Handbook.

12. AR 1912: 40.

13. AR 1916: 62; Leon Volmer, "Jewish Charity Order Is Proud of Its Record," *Houston Chronicle,* April 18, 1918.

14. Light, *States of Childhood,* 97, 242.

15. Trevathan, "Hebrew Orphans' Home of Atlanta," 26.

16. Haymon Memories, 3, 11.

17. Knobler interview.

18. Pulitzer, *Dreams,* 4–5.

19. Louis Peters, "Fortunate Unfortunates—Part II," *Jewish Herald-Voice* (Houston), May 29, 1980 (Peters, "Fortunate Unfortunates—II").

20. Mildred Gordon Tobias interview.

21. Pilsk interview (saw others "paddled" for misbehavior or rule breaking); Bessie Weinberg Smith interview (Volmer was "very stern" and "known to spank children, especially the boys"); Pailet interview (Volmer spanked "naughty children" with a hair brush); Simon interview (Vol-

mer "kicked" Mildred Moskowitz "very hard on her bottom"); Knobler interview ("Volmer did spank some children"); Goldstein interview (Volmer "belt-whipped" Hirsch's brother).

22. Goldstein interview. As evidenced by his later election as Big Brother, Harry's behavior improved considerably. AR 1912: 53.

23. Rosenblum Papers, box 1, folder 1.

24. Rosenblum Papers, box 1, folder 1.

25. Rosenblum Papers, box 1, folder 1.

26. Knobler interview; Rosenberg interview.

27. Rosenblum Papers, box 1, folder 1.

28. Pulitzer, *Dreams*, 5; Besmann, "Typical Home Kid Over-Achievers," 138. Not all Golden City Big Brothers and Sisters were tyrants. Many if not most lived up to their leadership roles. Big Brothers Max Tobias, "a good-hearted, fair young man," and Isidore Busch, a solo cornetist and star athlete, recalled Pulitzer, used their charm to secure larger portions for their Home family's supper and remained his lifelong friends. Pulitzer, *Dreams*, 132.

29. Rosenblum Papers, box 1, folder 1.

30. La. Rev. Stat. 17: 223 ("Each parish and city school board shall have discretion in the use of corporal punishment"); Will Sentell, "Louisiana Students were physically disciplined nearly 1,000 times in 2019," *The Advocate* (Baton Rouge), April 18, 2021.

31. Friedman, *These Are Our Children*, 82–83; Trevathan, "Hebrew Orphans' Home of Atlanta," 26.

32. See, for example, BMM 7: February 4, 1917 ($500 bonus for Volmer's "devotion to the children").

33. BMM 8: April 2, 1921 (Superintendent Report).

34. *GCM*, February 1925.

35. Haymon interview; Gorden interview (she was a "quiet child and never got into any trouble over rulebreaking"); Yasnyi interview (some "bad children" talked back or sneaked out to a nearby store); Pilsk interview (paddling she saw was "undoubtedly justified"); Friedman, *These Are Our Children*, 83 (similar views by alumni of other Jewish orphanages).

36. Bessie Weinberg Smith interview.

37. Trestman, *Fair Labor Lawyer*, 15.

38. Crosby interview; Pilsk interview (Volmer encouraged Louise's friendships with Home girls).

39. Pulitzer, *Dreams*, 10–11.

40. BMM 7: November 4, 1917.

41. "Jews Celebrate 63rd Anniversary of Orphans' Home," *T-P*, January 14, 1918.

42. "Children's Page," *GCM*, June 1925.

43. BMM 7: August 1, 1915.

44. BMM 8: February 4, 1922.

45. Beerman interview, 2004.

46. Rosenblum Papers, box 1, folder 1.

47. Rosenblum Papers, box 1, folder 1.

48. *GCM*, July, September 1923.

49. *GCM*, June 1925,

50. BMM 6: April 5, 1914 (Superintendent Report).

51. AR 1914: 55–56; BMM 7: June 2, 1918 (Superintendent Report).

52. BMM 8: January 7, 1923; *GCM*, April 1923.

53. AR 1914: 56.

54. "Celebrating 107 Years of Girl Scouting," Girl Scouts Louisiana East, March 2012, www.gsle.org/content/dam/girlscouts-gsle/documents/about-us/GSLE-Council-Timeline.pdf.

55. BMM 9: July 5, 1925 (Superintendent Report).

56. *GCM*, June 1923, 4.

57. BMM 7: August 3, 1919 (Superintendent Report).

58. "Parker Talks Farming to Ambitious Boys in Jewish Orphans' Home, *NOI*, February 23, 1920.

59. BMM 8: April 3, 1923 (Superintendent Report); O. R. Ernst, "Three Thousand Birds at Shreveport, Louisiana State Fair," *Leghorn World*, December 1921; "Orphan Boys and Their Dumb Friends," *T-P*, January 13, 1922; "Orleans Poultry Wins Fair Prizes," *T-P*, November 10, 1921; "Fine Chickens in N.O. Backyards," *NOI*, November 6, 1921; "Pretty Poultry Agent Comes to Organize Youngsters," *NOI*, February 18, 1921.

60. U.S. Immigration Acts of 1921 and 1924; Michael Feldberg, "Henry Ford Invents a Jewish Conspiracy," accessed July 26, 2022, www.myjewishlearning.com/article/henry-ford-invents-a-jewish-conspiracy/; "Jew Masks": advertised by Economical Drug Store, Canal Street, in *T-P*, January 30, 1921, *NOS*, February 6, 1921, and *NOI*, February 6, 1921.

61. "In-Kind Donations" were regularly recorded in the annual reports, *Golden City Messenger*, and superintendent's monthly reports.

62. Pulitzer, *Dreams*, 10.

63. Beerman interview, 2004.

64. BMM 7: December 5, 1920 (Superintendent Report); BMM 8: February 5, 1922 (Superintendent Report).

65. Katya Ermolaeva, "Dinah Put Down Your Horn: Black face Minstrel Shows Don't Belong in Music Class," GEN, October 30, 2019, accessed August 22, 2022, gen.medium.com/dinah-put-down-your-horn-154b8d8db12a.

66. BMM 6: August 2, 1914 (Superintendent Report).

67. Photo provided by Leslie H. Greenwald, grandson of five Home alumni: Leslie Greenwald, alumni association president, who married Lillian Neuberger Dover after the death of his first wife, Judith Korn; and Henry Hirsch who married Bertha Seligman. For additional family history, see www.hankgreenwald.com.

68. Steve Lipman, "Jews and Blackface: A Complicated History," *New York Jewish Week*, February 6, 2019 (quoting historian Jonathan Sarna).

69. Yarrut, "The Reflections of a Jew at a Catholic Retreat," 18–19. The author thanks Jari C. Honora for providing this article.

70. BMM 7: February 7, 1915. In 1935, after New Orleans University left St. Charles Avenue to merge with another Black college (later becoming today's Dillard University), the complex became home to Gilbert Academy, which until it closed in 1949 served as the university's preparatory school. Although a few Home alumni recalled watching from their bedroom windows as Gilbert students practiced sports, none recalled any personal interaction between the young

occupants of the neighboring properties. Brody interview, 2018; Levitan interview, 2018. "There was never any interaction between them and us," emphasized the late jazz musician Ellis Marsalis, who attended Gilbert Academy shortly after the Home closed and the JCC occupied the building. Pervasive segregation laws and mores prevented social contact between white and Black youth. Marsalis interview.

71. BMM 7: June 4, 1916 (Superintendent Report); "Jewish Asylum Offers Shelter to 51 Boys," *NOI*, May 23, 1916.

72. BMM 7: May 2, 1915 (Superintendent Report).

73. "N.O. Orphans Guests at Item Strand Party," *NOI*, June 18, 1919.

74. BMM 7: August 6, 1916 (Superintendent Report), January 1917 (Superintendent Report).

75. BMM 7: December 7, 1919 (Superintendent Report).

76. BMM 7: January 4, 1920 (Superintendent Report), April 5, 1920 (Superintendent Report), May 1, 1920 (Superintendent Report). BMM 8: June 5, 1921 (Superintendent Report); "Jewish Orphan Home to be Shown in Movies," *NOS*, May 1, 1920; "Herzl Lodge Celebration, *Houston Post*, July 13, 1920. Efforts to locate the film have been unsuccessful.

77. See this image on page 145. *GCM*, May 1926; Clairfield interview; Neiman interview; Raden interview; Garonzik interview; White Papers, box 7, folder 13 (copy of photo). Thanks to Joseph Yranski, former senior film and video historian, New York Public Library (email to author, October 19, 2022), for identifying the silent film stars in the photo.

78. Matthew Reonas, "World War I," March 17, 2019, accessed July 21, 2022, 64parishes. org/world-war-i.

79. BMM 7: May 5, 1917 (Superintendent Report).

80. BMM 7: November 3, 1918 (Superintendent Report).

81. BMM 7: July 1, 1917 (Superintendent Report); October 6, 1918 (Superintendent Report).

82. Pulitzer, *Dreams*, 11.

83. Paris Permenter, "Last Days of Storyville," *New Orleans Magazine*, October 2017.

84. Lord, *Condom Nation*, 36–37; Imber, "The First World War," 47, 52.

85. BMM 7: March 2, 1919 (Superintendent Report); BMM 8: April 3, 1923 (Superintendent Report).

86. Plotkin interview.

87. BMM 7: June 2, 1918 (Superintendent Report).

88. "Raise Service Flag Above Jewish Home," *T-P*, June 3, 1918; "Jewish Orphans' Home Raises Service Flag," *NOS*, June 3, 1918; "Service Flag Has Thirty-One Stars," *T-P*, June 2, 1918.

89. United States Holocaust Museum, "Antisemitism in History: World War I," *Holocaust Encyclopedia*, accessed September 8, 2021, encyclopedia.ushmm.org/content/en/article /antisemitism-in-history-world-war-i. In his 1923 anniversary address, alumnus Louis Yarrut cited Wolf's and Block's sacrifices, urging "that intolerance be dispelled." "Jewish Orphan Home Finishes its 68th Year," *NOI*, January 8, 1923.

90. "Jewish Patriotism," *American Jewish Chronicle*, May 11, 1917,

91. HB 2: 1193; "18 Now, Can't Stop Him," *NOI*, September 1, 1918; "Declares He Is Getting All Decorated," *NOI*, December 15, 1918; "Two War Heroes Go from Jewish Orphans Home," *NOI*, January 10, 1919; BMM 7: August 3, 1919 (Superintendent Report).

92. HB 2: 1021; Index Record for Max R. Block, American Battle Monuments Commission; "Orleanian Killed in Last Fighting," *T-P*, January 29, 1919; Likes interview.

93. HB 2: 1011; "Leon Clausner," *Semi-Weekly Spokesman-Review* (Spokane, WA), September 8, 1918; "Leon Clausner Gives His Life Over in France," *Spokane* (WA) *Chronicle*, September 20, 1918; Augustson interview.

94. AR 1920: 10; "Jewish Federation in Annual Session," *T-P*, February 9, 1920.

95. Ferris, *Matzoh Ball Gumbo*, 112.

96. See, Friedman, *These Are Our Children*, 144–45, 169.

97. AR 1902: 130.

98. Haymon interview.

99. Ferris, *Matzoh Ball Gumbo*, 112; "B'nai B'rith: Thirteenth Annual Session," *DP*, May 10, 1886. B'nai B'rith's silk souvenir napkin, imprinted with the menu, is on display at JCRS.

100. See, for example, *Jewish Ledger*, August 7, 1925, 12 (adjacent ads for Orpheum Restaurant's oysters and F. Sherman Kosher Groceries and Delicatessen).

101. Rabbi Moses H. Goldberg of Congregation Chevra Thilim, the first Orthodox rabbi to serve as honorary director, was later joined by Orthodox Rabbis Zodek Rubenstein, H. Raphael Gold, and Uri Miller of Congregation Beth Israel and Maurvin Elefant of Congregation Anshe Sfard. AR 1920: 2; *GCM*, January 1928, November–December 1932; BMM 14: January 16, 1939.

102. "Tell-A-Vision" brochure, 1940, JCRS.

103. AR 1916: 44–45.

104. Knobler interview.

105. Haymon interview.

106. Rosenberg interview.

107. BMM 6: December 6, 1914 (Superintendent Report); BMM 8: 1922 (Superintendent Report).

108. *GCM*, June 1923; *GCM*, June 1925. Eugene Aschaffenburg's five aunts and uncles resided in the Home for six months in 1887.

109. *GCM*, July 1925; Simon interview (received silver thimble).

110. See, for example, "100 Boys, Girls Are Confirmed," *NOI*, June 3, 1922.

111. "Jewish Charity Federation Aids Scores in Year," *NOS*, July 21, 1918; "San Felipe Will Be Summer Home," *NOS*, May 8, 1919.

112. Lorge and Zola, eds., *A Place of Our Own*, 1–6.

113. BMM 7: October 5, 1919 (Superintendent Report).

114. BMM 7: October 2, 1921 (Superintendent Report).

115. BMM 9: September 8, 1925 (Superintendent Report); "Orphans Happy at Coast Camp," *NOS*, August 15, 1926.

116. Beerman interview, 2004.

117. *GCM*, September 1924.

118. Haymon Memories, 7–8.

119. "Autobiography: The 'Outsider,'" n.d., White Papers, box 8, folder 6.

120. "Manuscript—Solange's Boy—A Novel by Hilda White, 2003" (unpublished), White Papers, box 8, folder 5.

121. Classifieds, *Jewish Social Service* 10, no. 7 (January 1920): i.

122. The girls' supervisors Volmer hired included: Sarah Jacobs (December 1915–1917); Ruth Boehm (1917–1918); Irene Tedesche (1918–August 1919); Corinne Nathan (October 1919–January 1920); Bessie Hirschfield (1920–1923); Sarah Radoff (1923); Sara Doris Itzkovitch (December 1923–1927).

123. See, for example, BMM 6: May 21, 1912 (raises for cook and dietitian); BMM 7: September 2, 1919 (Home engineer); BMM 7: December 5, 1920 (dietitian); BMM 6: January 7, 1923 (asst. superintendent and seamstress).

124. AR 1920: 2.

125. Jones, "The Jewish Community in New Orleans," 30, 56–57; Joseph Jacobs, "The Federation Movement in American Jewish Philanthropy," *American Jewish Year Book* 17 (September 9, 1915, to September 27, 1916): 159–98.

126. BMM 7: February 6, 1916 (Superintendent Report); *GCM* April 1, 1923.

127. BMM 8: August 3, 1924 (Superintendent Report).

128. Haymon Memories, 1; Aesha Rasheed, "Former orphanage residents reunite," *T-P,* March 19, 2004.

129. Scrapbook photo, White Papers, box 1, folder 10.

130. Beerman interview, 2004; Aesha Rasheed, "Former Orphanage Residents Reunite," *T-P,* March 19, 2004.

131. Bihari interview, 1995. Alumni also fondly recalled Black maintenance worker Bill Parker as a positive influence. Gerson interview ("all the children loved Bill Parker); Morris Skalka interview (children "revered" Parker); Kovner interview (Parker "used to take care of me, teach me to fix things."

132. Light, *That Pride of Race and Character,* 81–82.

133. "Protest Meeting Today on Scottsboro Cases," *NOI,* November 18, 1934; Douglas Linder, "The Scottsboro Boys Trials: A Chronology," accessed October 14, 2022, famous-trials.com/scottsboroboys/1601-chronology.

134. Fieldsmith interview.

135. HB 3: 1604; Anderson interview.

136. Purdon, *Black Company,* 179–81, 191–201, 245–46; Shanker interview; "Benjamin Shanker," *The Oklahoman,* October 11, 2022.

137. Lindley, *Opening Doors,* 215–221.

138. Hacsi, *Second Home,* 87, 103 (table 3.1). Hacsi used data from U.S. Census Bureau's *Benevolent Institutions, 1910;* the 1920 institutional census did not capture "paid employees." In 1910, the Home employed 7 childcare workers for 125 children; by 1920, at least 10 Home employees cared for 135 children.

139. U.S. Children's Bureau, *Handbook,* 13.

140. BMM 8: October 7, 1923 (Superintendent Report).

141. BMM 8: October 7, 1923 (Superintendent Report); BMM 9: October 6, 1925 (Superintendent Report).

142. BMM 8: July 6, 1924 (Superintendent Report).

143. "Nannie Haas Pokorny," accessed May 23, 2023, findagrave.com/memorial/8035838; Leatham, "Ida Weis Friend"; BMM 6: January 4, 1914.

144. For Southern Jewish women's organizational behavior in the late nineteenth and early twentieth centuries, including regional similarity, see Bauman, *A New Vision of Southern Jewish History*, 78–100.

145. "Jewish Home Puts Women on Board," *DP*, March 30, 1914; BMM 6: April 5, 1914.

146. BMM 7: January 3, 1915; January 7, 1917 (Big Brothers & Sisters Comm. Report).

147. BMM 7: May 6, 1917, April 4, 1920.

148. AR 1915: 28–29; "Jewish Orphans to Be Given Start by Big Brothers," *T-P*, March 29, 1915.

149. BMM 8: May 11, 1924 (Big Brothers & Sisters Comm. Report).

150. Goodkind, "Maurice Stern," 294–95.

151. Klein, *A Passion for Sharing*, 47–48.

152. Trestman, *Fair Labor Lawyer*, 11, 18.

153. Haymon Memories, 5.

154. Simons, *Jewish Times*, 173.

155. BMM 8: June 3, 1923 (Superintendent Report).

156. Portnoy interview.

157. Letter from Louis Albert to his father, December 1, 1929, kindly provided by his daughter, Sharon Albert Brier.

158. BMM 7: April 2, 1916 (Superintendent Report).

159. BMM 8: July 10, 1921 (Superintendent Report).

160. BMM 8: March 5, 1922 (Superintendent Report).

161. Telegram, Leon Volmer to Louise Volmer, January 31, 1915; Crosby interview.

162. BMM 9: June 2, 1925 (Superintendent Report); *GCM*, June 1925.

163. *GCM*, January 1925.

164. "Dr. J. W. Newman Rites Tomorrow," *NOS*, May 2, 1936 (donating medical services); BMM 8: July 10, 1921 (boarding house).

165. BMM 8: August 14, 1921. "Dr. J. W. Newman Honored by Many on his 50th Birthday," *NOI*, January 23, 1925; "Dr. J. W. Newman Rites Tomorrow," *NOS*, May 2, 1936; "New Orleans Resident Leaves $300,000 Estate," *The Times* (Shreveport, LA), May 28, 1936.

166. BMB 8: June 3, 1923.

167. BMB 7, June 2, 1918.

168. Crystal family: Singer interview; photo of Sam Crystal with Hilda, Ann, Rachel, and Ida, White Papers, box 6, folder 14. Tannenbaum family: Raden interview; Neiman interview; photo of siblings with their father, Joseph, courtesy of Irene Raden and Harriet Beth Neiman.

169. BMM 7: October 30, 1917.

170. BMM 8: January 27, 1924.

171. AR 1923: 13; *GCM*, July 1923.

172. Friedman, *These Are Our Children*, 168; Polster, *Inside Looking Out*, 176.

173. Hansan, "National Conference of Charities and Correction"; "JPro: History," accessed December 5, 2022, *www.jpro.org/history*.

174. See Volmer's reports to the board following his annual attendance at professional conferences, including BMM 7: July 1, 1917 ("provided suitable homes were available"), May 2, 1920, and BMM 8: July 2, 1922 ("battle royal"), August 3, 1924, and July 20, 1925.

175. "Serum Combats Scarlet Fever," *NOS*, November 28, 1924; "Science Scores Another Victory in War on Ills," *T-P*, November 28, 1924.

176. "Says Recreation Is Big Problem," *NOS*, March 21, 1924; BMM 8: December 1924 (Superintendent Report).

177. "Orphans' Health Records Are Aim," *NOS*, October 20, 1926.

178. "Father Wynhoven Lauds Patriotic Charity of Jews," *T-P*, January 10, 1927; "Jewish Children's Home Celebrates," *NOS*, January 10, 1927; *GCM*, January 1927.

179. BMM 9: December 1, 1925. But see *GCM*, February 1926 (reporting that Volmer resigned due to "serious illness" in his family).

180. "Dr. Lashman Is New Home Head," *NOS*, January 7, 1926; "Dr. L. E. Lashman to Direct Home," *T-P*, January 7, 1926.

181. BMM 9: December 1, 1925.

182. "School at Temple to Open Saturday," *Repository* (Canton, OH), September 3, 1930; "Jewish University Group Will Hear Book Review," *Repository* (Canton, OH), February 21, 1931; "Temple Service Friday," *Repository* (Canton, OH), July 2, 1932.

183. "Leon Volmer Dies After Long Illness," *Repository* (Canton, OH), September 11, 1933; "Leon Volmer, Former Home Head Is Dead," *NOI*, September 11, 1933.

9. ED LASHMAN STEERS THE HOME IN A
NEW DIRECTION, 1926–1929

1. "Dr. Lashman's New Home: Succeeds Leon Volmer," *NOS*, January 7, 1926.

2. "Louis Edward Lashman," *American Biography* (American Historical Society, 1931) ("Lashman Biography"), 294–96. Samuel and Lottie Lashman, 1900 U.S. Census, Philadelphia; 1910 U.S. Census, Camden, NJ.

3. "L. Edward Lashman Heads Cleveland Orphans Home," *Chicago Sentinel*, December 12, 1919, 15; "Dr. Lashman Is New Home Head," *NOS*, January 7, 1926; *Meredith College Quarterly Bulletin*, March 1916, 15; "Edward Lashman," *The Sentinel* (Chicago), November 24, 1916, 8.

4. *American Israelite* (Cincinnati), May 2, 1918; "Tactics of Anti-Defamation League," *Exporters' Review* 24 (May 1918).

5. "Edith Ruth Deutsch," *Walnut Hills High School Year Book* (Cincinnati, OH, 1909), 15; "Daughter of Dr. Gotthard Deutsch Marries L. Edward Lashman," *Chicago Sentinel*, May 31, 1918, 15; "Notice," *Reform Advocate*, November 9, 1918, 322; "New Orleans," *American Israelite* (Cincinnati), June 14, 1929, 3.

6. Daisy Weinberg, "She's Mother to Children at The Home," *NOI*, January 10, 1930. "Correspondence Between the IOBB ADL and the Navy," *American Jewish World*, November 22, 1918, 5.

7. "Edith Deutsch Lashman," *American Israelite* (Cincinnati), June 14, 1929; "Woman Juror Asks Release," *NOI*, January 23, 1921.

8. "Come to New Orleans," *Jewish Charities Magazine*, May 1920, 204.

9. Polster, *Inside Looking Out*, 178.

10. Polster, *Inside Looking Out*, 178–79; National Conference of Social Work, *Conference Bulletin* 24, no. 1 (August 1920).

11. Polster, *Inside looking Out*, 182.

12. Lashman Biography, 295.

13. Lashman Biography, 296.

14. "Hermann Deutsch Dies in NY at 81," *T-P*, June 26, 1970; "Eberhard P. Deutsch," *NYT*, January 18, 1980; Daisy Weinberg, "Famous Names in Her Album," *NOI*, February 10, 1930.

15. *American Israelite* (Cincinnati), September 4, 1924.

16. BMM 9: January 11, 1925 (Field Director's Report).

17. "New Orleans," *American Israelite* (Cincinnati), June 14, 1929.

18. BMM 9: February 3, 1926 (Superintendent Report). There is no record that Ginsburg sought the post, although one alumnus understood that the board wanted to hire a married superintendent. Peters, "Fortunate Unfortunates—II."

19. Child Welfare League of America, "Report on Jewish Children's Home, New Orleans, Louisiana" (Report No. 16): Submitted to the Committee on Child Care of the Council of Social Services, 1925, TSC-JCH, box 49, folder 13 ("CWL 1925"); "Child Welfare Survey Planned," *T-P*, October 26, 1925.

20. "History," Child Welfare League of America, accessed September 20, 2021, www.cwla. org/our-work/cwla-standards-of-excellence/history/; "Child Welfare League of America," Social Welfare History Project, accessed September 20, 2021, socialwelfare.library.vcu.edu/programs /child-welfarechild-labor/child-welfare-league-of-america/.

21. U.S. Dept. of Health, Education, and Welfare, *The Story of the White House Conferences on Children and Youth*.

22. *Richmond Times-Dispatch*, February 4, 1925; *Daily Illinois State Journal*, February 11, 1925; *Syracuse Herald*, February 4, 1925.

23. "Great Campaign Begun to Abolish Orphan Asylums," *T-P*, August 2, 1925; "Mother's Care of Child Costs Less Than Institution's," *T-P*, February 22, 1925; "Abolition of Asylums Is Sought by Women's Organization," *NOI*, May 31, 1925.

24. "New President, Pension Fight Clubdom Topics," *T-P*, November 8, 1925; AR 1917: 2.

25. "Book Review, *The Work of Child-Placing Agencies; Handbook for the Use of Boards of Directors, Superintendents, and Staffs of Institutions for Dependent Children*," *Social Service Review* 1, no. 2 (June 1927): 349–51, 351.

26. The U.S. Children's Bureau's 1927 release of two publications, each featuring a different method of dependent childcare, evidenced the continuing acceptability of both options amid emerging professional ideals and standards: *The Work of Child Placing Agencies* and *Handbook for the Use of Boards of Directors, Superintendents, and Staffs of Institutions for Dependent Children*.

27. The Community Chest of New Orleans, the forerunner to the United Way for the Greater New Orleans Area, was first proposed in January 1924, after similar nonsectarian pooled funding mechanisms for social services had previously been adopted in Atlanta, Baltimore, Cincinnati, and other cities. Rabbi Emil Leipziger, a Community Chest organizer, and fellow Home board members Alfred Danziger and Sylvan Newberger were elected to leadership positions in the secular organization. By November the CJEF and its affiliated organizations (the Home, Touro Infirmary, Jewish Welfare Fund, the Young Men's and Young Women's Hebrew Association, and the Ladies' Aid and Sewing Society) joined the Community Chest as charter members. "The Community Chest," *NOS*, April 22, 1924; "Name Seven More to Direct Community Chest Work," *NOS*, July 25, 1924; "Chest Drive to Be Aided by Hebrews," *NOI*, November 26, 1924.

28. "Child Welfare Survey Planned," *T-P*, October 26, 1925; "Rigaud Enters Not Guilty Plea in Waif Attack," *State-Times Advocate*, January 27, 1926; "Reforms for Waifs' Home Near—Newman," *NOI*, March 3, 1926.

29. Lundberg, *Unto the Least of These*, 252.

30. "C. C. Carstens: Interpreter of the Needs of Dependent Children (1865–1939)," accessed September 20, 2021, socialwelfare.library.vcu.edu/programs/child-welfarechild-labor/c-c-carstens-interpreter-of-the-needs-of-dependent-children/.

31. CWL 1925, 20, 39–40.

32. CWL 1925, 37.

33. CWL 1925, 40.

34. CWL 1925, 39.

35. CWL 1925, 38.

36. CWL 1925, 14–15.

37. CWL 1925, 15.

38. "New Home of Jewish Children's Republic Is Dedicated to Its High Use," *New York Tribune*, October 20, 1912; Zmora, *Orphanages Reconsidered*, 186–88; Polster, *Inside Looking Out*, 196; Sharlitt, *As I Remember*, 196.

39. CWL 1925, 22, 23.

40. CWL 1925, 24–25; *GCM*, July 1923, 1.

41. "Jewish Charity Workers Urged to Help Chest," *T-P*, January 17, 1927.

42. Berenson thesis, 96.

43. Cahan, *Past Caring*, 23.

44. BMM 9: June 18, 1926 (May 31, 1926 letter from Cora L. Goldsmith).

45. Berenson thesis, 140–41; Andrus, "Isidore Newman School," 53.

46. "Isidore Newman Manual Training School," *NOI*, August 3, 1930.

47. BMM 9: June 1927 (INMTS Comm. Report); BMM 9: October 4, 1927 (Superintendent Report).

48. "42 Get Diplomas in Exercise at Newman School," *T-P*, June 12, 1931.

49. Beerman interview, 2004.

50. "Care of Children in Asylums is Studied," *T-P*, November 24, 1926.

51. BMM 9: October 5, 1926 (Superintendent Report).

52. BMM 9: October 5, 1926 (Superintendent Report).

53. Lashman briefly employed a teacher from New Orleans's non-congregational Communal Hebrew School before enrolling the children in the Reform synagogues' religious schools. BMM 9: October 5, 1926.

54. BMM 9: May 4, 1926 (Superintendent Report); October 5, 1926 (House Comm. Report). "Children Attend Outside Services," *GCM*, October 1926.

55. "Report of Special Committee of Jewish Children's Home to Board of Directors Concerning the Child Welfare League Survey," December 3, 1942 ("Home Special Committee Report 1942"), AJA-BB, box 4, folder 3.

56. Levitan interview, 1983. The author located only two references to "Bar Mitzvah" in the Home's records, both unexplained: the donation of a "suit of clothing for a 'Bar Mitzvah'" in the 1872 Annual Report (36); the caption ("Bar Mitzvah") of a photograph in the 1916 Annual

Report depicting a boy holding a *torah* while another stands at the *bima* (pulpit) in the Home's synagogue (25).

57. See, for example, text and photos in *GCM*, October 1926 ("the Children's Sukkah"), April 1927 (Passover seder), March 1928 (Hamantaschen at Purim).

58. BMM 9: December 7, 1926 (Superintendent Report).

59. BMM 9: January 4, 1927 (Superintendent Report).

60. BMM 9: May 4, 1926 (Superintendent Report). See also Haymon Memories, 5.

61. BMM 10: January 10, 1928.

62. Rabbi David Lefkowitz, "Eulogy to L. Edward Lashman," *Proceedings of Fifty-Sixth Annual Convention, District Grand Lodge No. 7, B'nai B'rith, Mobile, AL, May 5–7, 1929*, 166–67, AJA-BB, box 10.

63. Harvith interview.

64. BMM 9: January 4, 1927 (Superintendent Report).

65. "Central Council Social Agencies Hold Conference," *T-P*, January 26, 1928.

66. BMM 12: April 10, 1934 (Survey Comm. Report, February 22, 1934); Berenson thesis, 96–97.

67. CWL 1925, 23.

68. Zmora, *Orphanages Reconsidered*, 186.

69. "Children Attend Edward Lashman Funeral Service," *T-P*, May 6, 1929.

70. BMM 10: June 4, 1929.

71. Peters, "Fortunate Unfortunates—II."

72. "L. E. Lashman, Friend of Jewish Children, Dies," *T-P*, May 5, 1929; "Child Happiness Fund Is Started," *T-P*, May 12, 1929; "A New Orleans Philanthropist," *Shreveport* (LA) *Journal*, May 8, 1929; "Edward Lashman," *Hattiesburg* (MS) *American*, May 7, 1929.

73. *GCM*, May 1929, 3.

10. "UNCLE HARRY" GINSBURG TAKES CHARGE, 1929–1940

1. According to one alumnus, Ginsburg threatened to quit if not chosen as superintendent because he was single, arguing that "he was married to the Home, his family were the kids." Peters, "Fortunate Unfortunates—II."

2. BMM 10: May 23, 1929 (Report of Special Comm.), Herman Seiferth, "Hearts Hail New Heads at the Old Home," *GCM*, June 1929, 2.

3. "Ginsberg [sic] Chosen Head of Jewish Children's Home," *T-P*, May 26, 1929.

4. "New Orleans," *American Israelite* (Cincinnati), June 14, 1929.

5. Daisy Weinberg, "Arranges Jubilee Fete: She's Mother to Children at the Home," *NOI*, January 10, 1930.

6. BMM 10: May 23, 1929.

7. "The Old-Fashioned Mother," *Plain Dealer* (Cleveland, OH), June 23, 1912, 4.

8. Although Lashman's and Ginsburg's East European backgrounds reflected the ancestry of most children under their charge, no record exists that the coincidence influenced the board's hiring decisions. Nor is there any indication that the two men's backgrounds affected their relationship with the board, whose leadership remained largely of Central European origin,

despite the social and religious divisions over country of origin that otherwise permeated New Orleans's Jewish community. For an account of the city's intra-ethnic divergence from the perspective of two women, including Home psychologist Ruth Dreyfous, see Malone, "As Told to Memoirs: Ruth and Rosalie."

9. Ginsburg's draft registration cards, June 5, 1917, and April 1, 1942; BMM 7: January 7, 1917 (Superintendent Report); "Jewish Children's Home to Observe 82nd Milestone," *T-P*, January 3, 1937; "Jewish Children's Home Celebrates 85th Anniversary," *NOI*, December 31, 1939; "Harry Ginsburg Dies at Age of 59," *T-P*, June 26, 1946. Special thanks to Ann E. Smith Case, Tulane University archivist, for providing Ginsburg's student file.

10. HLG to Ralph J. Schwarz, April 22, 1942, TSC-JCH, box 44, folder 10.

11. Berenson thesis, 17n11.

12. Polster, *Inside Looking Out,* 128, 183.

13. Polster, *Inside Looking Out,* 170.

14. Polster, *Inside Looking Out,* 128–29; Ginsburg draft registration cards.

15. Edmund Lebreton, "Jewish Home Fete," *NOI*, January 7, 1934.

16. Fred Michalove, "Jewish Children's Home Celebrates 85th Anniversary," *NOI*, December 31, 1939.

17. Edmund Lebreton, "Jewish Home Fete," *NOI*, January 7, 1934.

18. Harnett T. Kane, "Jewish Children's Home Is Unique Institution, *NOI*, January 24, 1937.

19. Newspaper photos of Ginsburg surrounded by children include: "Where Youngsters of Seven States Receive Care," *T-P*, December 15, 1929; "Three of Staff and Youngsters at Jewish Institution," *T-P*, January 9, 1933; "Jewish Children's Home Celebrates 79th Anniversary," *NOI*, January 7, 1934; "'Uncle Harry' Ginsburg Entertains Some of His Happy Young Charges," *NOI*, January 24, 1937; "It's Really 'Home Sweet Home' for Jewish Children," *NOI*, January 9, 1938; "Pets and Books Play Major Role at Jewish Home," *T-P*, December 31, 1939; "Celebrates 86th Anniversary of Home, *NOS*, January 6, 1941; "Jewish Children's Home Conducts Open House," *T-P*, January 8, 1945.

20. Harvith interview.

21. Beerman interview, 2004.

22. Washofsky interview.

23. Fox interview, 2004.

24. Haymon Memories,

25. "Autobiography: The 'Outsider,'" White Papers, box 8, folder 6. "Only praise": for example, Ellis Hart interviews; Pfeifer interviews; Levitan interviews; Lillian Smith interviews; Eisner interview.

26. Jeanne Samuels interview.

27. Simons, *Jewish Times,* 172–73. According to his widow, Joe privately claimed that Ginsburg had been "very much involved" with a young woman who lived in the Home, although it remains unclear whether the alleged relationship began before or after the young woman's discharge, and if after, how many years had passed. Jeanne Samuels interview. As with Lowenthal's remark about Ginsburg's "girlfriend," neither first-person account(s) nor contemporaneous documentation exists to determine what if anything transpired (and with whom) despite the gravity of the accusations.

28. Alvin "Pat" Samuels interview, 2018; Milner interview.

29. Limerick interview.

30. In addition to photographs previously cited, titles of numerous other articles and photo captions reflect the Home's favorable reputation, including: "Family Life Is Preserved in Unusual Institution," *T-P*, January 12, 1930 (with photo, "The Institution That Is Not An Institution"; "Children Given Real Care, Education," *NOS*, December 21, 1930; Katherine Daly, "Jewish Orphans Live as Children of Private Home: Institutionalism Ends and Individuality Enjoys Full Sway," *T-P*, January 3, 1932 (with photo, "Home Become Series of Happy Family Groups"); "Children's Home Praised by Club," *T-P*, June 20, 1935; Harnett T. Kane, "Jewish Children's Home Is Unique Institution," *NOI*, January 24, 1937; Katherine Daly, "New Orleans Institution Is Ranked High throughout the Nation as a Model of its Kind," *NOI*, January 9, 1938; "No Regimentation, Children Grow Up in Informal Home Like Atmosphere," *Sunday Item-Tribune*, January 9, 1938; Glendy Culligan, "Jewish Children's Home Holds Open House on 84th Birthday," *NOI*, January 8, 1939 (with photo, "Unique Among Institutions"); Fred Michalove, "Understanding of Childhood to Make Place a Normal Home Is Philosophy Behind Red Brick Walls on Avenue, *NOI*, December 31, 1939; "Child Home to Observe 88th Year," January 19, 1943 ("children's lives as nearly like normal family life as is possible").

31. Edmund LeBreton, "Jewish Home Fete," *NOI*, January 7, 1934; "Home for Jewish Children Marks 80th Milestone," *T-P*, January 6, 1935.

32. Glendy Culligan, "Jewish Children's Home Holds Open House on 84th Birthday," *NOI*, January 8, 1939; Michalove, "Jewish Children's Home Celebrates 85th Anniversary," *NOI*, December 31, 1939.

33. Fox interview, 2004.

34. Berenson thesis, 27–31; "Jewish Children's Home Celebrates Diamond Anniversary," *Item-Tribune*, January 12, 1930; photos, *GCM*, 1932; Eisner interview (murals).

35. BMM 10: September 30, 1929 (Superintendent Report); Edmund LeBreton, "Jewish Home Fete," *NOI*, January 7, 1934.

36. Peters, "Fortunate Unfortunates—II."

37. *GCM*, March 1930, 6.

38. *GCM*, September 1928; Berenson thesis, 163.

39. Rothstein interview.

40. Fox interview, 2004; Besmann, "Typical Home Kid Overachievers," 149.

41. Rothstein interview; Fox interview, 2004.

42. Lebreton, "Jewish Home Fete," *NOI*, January 7, 1934.

43. *GCM*, January 1930, 7; Berenson thesis, 26.

44. Washofsky interview; Buckman interview.

45. Beerman interview, 2004.

46. Pfeifer interview, 1999; Bessie Smith interview (no interfaith dating); Lillian Smith interview (inviting friends to dinner); Berenson thesis, 99, 102; Daly, "Jewish Children's Home," *NOI*, January 9, 1938.

47. Brody interview; Berenson thesis, 102–3; Quentin Ault, "Collegians 'Brother' Boys," *T-P*, April 28, 1946.

48. Kovner interview, 2018.

49. Brody interview, 2018.

50. Jeffrey R. Young, "How Childhood Has Changed (and How That Impacts Education)," July 11, 2017, accessed March 4, 2022, www.edsurge.com/news/2017-07-11-how-childhood-has -changed-and-how-that-impacts-education.

51. "Jewish Home Fete Is Ready," *NOI*, January 3, 1932.

52. "Boy Runs Thriving Farm," *NOI*, May 15, 1935; Gayner interview.

53. Foreman interview.

54. Washofsky interview.

55. Cahn interview, 2016.

56. Berenson thesis, 98; BMM 12: February 22, 1934.

57. Berenson thesis, 98.

58. BMM 10: October 1, 1929 (Superintendent Report).

59. Sam F. Hartman to Bessie Margolin, February 25, 1986, Margolin Papers, TSC-JCH, box 1, folder 33.

60. BMM 10: July 2, 1929 (Superintendent Report, July 1, 1929).

61. "Anna B. Mayer, 91, Social Policy Planner," *NYT*, November 5, 2000; Mayer with Kahn, *Day Care as a Social Instrument*.

62. BMM 12: January 9, 1933 (Superintendent Report); Berenson thesis, 147; Quentin Ault, "Collegians 'Brother' Boys," *T-P*, April 28, 1946.

63. "Jewish Home Fete Is Ready," *NOI*, January 3, 1932; "Three of Staff and Youngsters at Jewish Institution," *T-P*, January 9, 1933; "Students Work at Orphanage for Schooling," *NOI*, October 16, 1932.

64. Simons, *Jewish Times*, 174; Whitehead interview.

65. Fox interview, 2003, ISJL.

66. Hartman interview.

67. Brody interview, 2018.

68. Fox interview, 2004.

69. Balkan interview, 2004.

70. Cohn interview, 2004. For additional information about the Home's student counsel-ors, see Trestman, *Most Fortunate Unfortunates Newsletter* 11 (April 2021) and Trestman, *Online Supplement*.

71. BMM 11: August 5, 1930 (Superintendent Report).

72. BMM 11: August 5, 1930 (Superintendent Report).

73. *GCM*, July–August 1932, 2.

74. "Foster Home Plan Not Preferred Here," *T-P*, November 4, 1932.

75. "Foster Mothers Make Sacrifices to Care for Tots," *T-P*, May 21, 1933.

76. Peters, "Fortunate Unfortunates—II."

77. BMM 12: January 10, 1933 (Superintendent Report).

78. Heleniak, "Local Reaction," 290–91, 306.

79. BMM 12: January 10, 1933 (Field Director Report)

80. William H. Mullins, "Great Depression," *Encyclopedia of Oklahoma History and Culture*, accessed August 10, 2022, www.okhistory.org/publications/enc/entry.php?entry=GR014.

81. Limerick interview; Milner interview.

82. HB 3: 1643–45; Bihari interview, 1995. Thanks to John Broven for sharing this and other Bihari interviews.

83. Heleniak, "Local Reaction," 292–93. See also Higgenbotham, "A. J. Heinemann."

84. Heleniak, "Local Reaction," 296.

85. Heleniak, "Local Reaction," 303–4.

86. BMM 12: January 9, 1934 (Superintendent Report).

87. BMM 12: March 14, 1933 (Superintendent Report), April 11, 1933 (Superintendent Report); BMM 13: January 15, 1935 (Superintendent Report).

88. Sam Freedman interview.

89. Bihari interview, 2000.

90. Berenson thesis, 166.

91. Berenson thesis, 167.

92. Berenson thesis, 170–71.

93. Berenson thesis, 175–76.

94. Berenson thesis, 178.

95. BMM 12: January 9, 1934 (Superintendent Report).

96. BMM 13: January 15, 1935 (Superintendent Report).

97. BMM 12: February 22, 1934 (Survey Comm. Report). See also BMM 13: January 15, 1935 (Superintendent Report).

98. BMM 13: April 4, 1935 (Admin. Comm. Report). The minimum age for admission at CJOA was five years. In 1923, the latest year for which comprehensive data is available, thirty-three of forty-one reporting Jewish childcare institutions imposed a minimum age of three or older. Apart from three small Jewish institutions dedicated for infants, the Home was one of only five Jewish institutions that admitted children younger than three. U.S. Census Bureau, *Children Under Institutional Care, 1923*, table 22, 48–139.

99. BMM 12: February 22, 1934 (Survey Comm. Report).

100. BMM 12: February 22, 1934 (Supplement to Survey Comm. Report).

101. For changes precipitated by the Community Chest and New Deal programs on Atlanta's Jewish social services agencies, see Bauman, *A New Vision of Southern Jewish History*, 59–77.

102. BMM 13: December 10, 1935 (Superintendent Report).

103. "Child Welfare Conference Set," *NOS*, October 16, 1932; "Childcare, Yesterday and Today," address by Alan S. Geimar, president of Bellefaire, Cleveland, OH, at Jewish Children's Home Banquet, New Orleans, January 8, 1955, TSC-JCH, box 50, folder 3.

104. *GCM*, January–February 1933, 2.

105. *GCM*, October 1927. In April 1927, Dr. Charles Holbrook, a psychiatrist, and Ruth Dreyfous, a Newman and Newcomb graduate who earned her master's degree from Columbia in Child Development, joined the Home's medical consultants. Dreyfous, who later helped establish Newman's admissions testing procedures, administered IQ tests to all Home children. *GCM*, April, August 1927; Malone, "As Told to Memoirs: Ruth and Rosalie," 127.

106. "Jewish Home Fete is Ready," *NOI*, January 3, 1932; "Children's Home Has Anniversary," *T-P*, January 9, 1933.

107. BMM 12: February 22, 1934 (Survey Comm. Report).

108. BMM 13: January 15, 1935; April 4, 1935 (Admin. Comm. Report). See also BMM 14: December 14, 1937 (Anniv. Comm. Reports, November 18 and 23, 1937).

109. BMM 14: January 10, 1939.

110. "Child Home to Observe 88th Year," *T-P,* January 10, 1943.

111. Limerick interview.

112. Limerick interview; Brody interview, 2018.

113. BMM 14: September 14, 1938 (Memorandum of Agreement Between B'nai B'rith and Jewish Children's Home).

114. BMM 14: June 4, 1937 (B'nai B'rith resolutions regarding Hebrew Education, May 19, 1937, and its relationship with the Home, May 10, 1937).

115. BMM 14: December 12, 1939 (Jewish Educ. Comm. Report).

116. BMM 14: June 4, 1937.

117. BMM 14: December 12, 1939 (Jewish Educ. Comm. Report).

118. BMM 14: December 12, 1939 (Jewish Educ. Comm. Report).

119. B'nai B'rith Report of Committee on Institutions, April 8, 1942, TSC-JCH, box 49, folder 11, ("B'nai B'rith Report 1942"), 12.

120. Alvin "Pat" Samuels interview, 2018.

121. Rothstein interview. In an ironic twist, Rothstein worked in the religious school office of Houston's Congregation Emanu El for forty years. "Bessie Rothstein's Death Mourned," undated news clipping, generously provided by Rothstein's daughter, Debbie Rothstein Wizig.

122. Kovner interview, 2018.

11. FINAL YEARS, 1940–1946

1. Ralph Schwarz, an attorney, who was elected board president following the death of Dr. Jacob W. Newman in 1937, was succeeded in 1942 by businessman Leon C. Simon. In 1944, Leon Heymann, president of Krauss Dept. Stores, assumed the board's presidency, followed by attorney Justin V. Wolff in 1946, who held the position until his death in 1951.

2. U.S. Department of Education, *120 Years of American Education,* 6; Aaron O'Neill, *"Life Expectancy in the United States, 1860–2020," accessed December 6, 2020, www.statista.com/statistics /263724/life-expectancy-in-the-united-states/.*

3. Carrigan, *Saffron Scourge,* 167; Staples, "Yellow Fever," 960.

4. Hacsi, *Second Home,* 42–51; B'nai B'rith, "Report of Committee on Institutional Trends," 1946, 7, TSC-JCH, box 48; Meryl Baer, "History of American Income," accessed December 8, 2022, bizfluent.com/info-8346144-jobs-work-during-19th-century.html.

5. Henry L. Zucker, "A Study of Case Work Services for Children and Families in the City of New Orleans and Orleans Parish, Louisiana," June 1, 1946, 55, AJA-BB, box 4.

6. BMM 10: May 7, 1929 (Superintendent Report); BMM 13: June 10, 1936 (Superintendent Report).

7. "Report of Survey of the Jewish Children's Home, New Orleans, La., made under arrangements with Child Welfare League of America, Inc., and Council of Jewish Federations and Welfare Funds Inc., June 1942" ("CWL 1942"), 134.

8. U.S. Bureau of Labor Statistics, "One hundred years of price change," 11.

9. Zucker, "A Study of Case Work Services," 55, AJA-BB, box 4.

10. CWL 1942, 168.

11. CWL 1942, 171.

12. "Holds Anti-Semitism Makes Masses Forget Their Troubles," *NOI*, February 14, 1939; "Anti-Semitism in U.S. Feared," *NOI*, November 15, 1941.

13. CWL 1942, 9; "Sam Wahl First Vice President B'nai B'rith," *Jackson (TN) Sun*, November 25, 1941; "Buys $10,000 Defense Bond," *NOI*, May 26, 1941.

14. "B'nai B'rith Is Electing New Officers," *NOI*, May 5, 1943; "Facilities of B'nai B'rith for Armed Forces Total 335," *T-P*, May 5, 1943.

15. Harry Kaplan, "The B'nai B'rith Hillel Foundations—Retrospect and Prospect," *Jewish Forum*, October 1944; "Bloom Elected B'nai B'rith Head," *Selma* (AL) *Times Journal*, April 29, 1942.

16. Home Charter, March 1940 (as amended).

17. "Report on Jewish Children's Home Made by Henry E. Spitzberg to B'nai B'rith Southeastern Regional Conference in Atlanta, GA., on December 9, 1944," AJA-BB, box 4 ("Spitzberg Report"), 2.

18. Ambrose, "New Orleans in the Second World War."

19. Barbara Kaplinsky, "Looking Back and Leading Forward: Celebrating 125 Years of NCJW in New Orleans," *Southern Jewish Life*, March 28, 2022.

20. "Crafts Are Outlet for Refugees," *NOI*, May 26, 1940.

21. Jessica Jacoby, director, *Roads* (film), 2015; Claude Jacoby's journal entries for April 21, 1940; January 1, November 11, 1941, generously shared by his daughter, Jessica Jacoby.

22. Elsas interview; "Welfare Worker Met Mussolini and Hitler," *NOS*, October 8, 1941; "Inge Elsas, teacher and community volunteer," *Crescent City Jewish News*, July 8, 2017.

23. Hyman Stein to Ginsburg, August 29, 1943 (emphasis in original), JCRS.

24. Capt. Hugo Fielschmidt, typescript, February 22, 1944; undated news clippings: "Falls into Nazi Hands" and "Combat Medica Are Called Great Builders of Morale." These items were generously provided by Fielschmidt's son, Dr. Wayne Fieldsmith.

25. Rothstein interview; "Bessie Rothstein's Death Mourned," news clipping provided by Debbie Rothstein Wizig

26. David Ladner to Ginsburg, July 21, 1944, JCRS. Ladner's journal entries and military records were provided by stepchildren David Mazie and Lisa Mazie, supplemented with information from daughter Susan Ladner Saparow.

27. Today the Home's World War II service plaque hangs in JCRS's office.

28. Lundberg, *Unto the Least of the These*, 289.

29. Jennie Ogden Schneider, "Bringing Back the Orphanages," March 19, 1995, JCRS; Jennie Ogden Schneider interview, 2004.

30. Schneider, "Bringing Back the Orphanages."

31. Schneider, "Bringing Back the Orphanages."

32. CWL 1942.

33. "A. of C. Founder Will Be Honored," *T-P*, September 23, 1946. Simon, a bachelor, was the nephew of an earlier board president, Joseph Kohn.

34. B'nai B'rith Report 1942. The League's comprehensive 198-page report (in contrast to B'nai B'rith's 21 pages) contained sixteen tables of data and cited prevailing childcare standards from authoritative sources in support of its recommendations.

35. Home Special Committee Report 1942, 15–16.

36. CWL 1942, 91.

37. B'nai B'rith Report 1942, 7–8.

38. Proceedings of Sixty-Seventh Annual Convention, B'nai B'rith District Grand Lodge No. 7, Birmingham, AL, April 26–28, 1942, AJA-BB, box 11, folder 6, 139–140.

39. HLG to Schwarz, April 22, 1942, TSC-JCH, box 49, folder 10.

40. Home Special Committee Report 1942, 17.

41. Home Special Committee Report 1942, 17–18. In 1948, JCEF created the Jewish Family Services of Greater New Orleans (JFS), as it is known today, to provide social services to Jewish individuals and families. In 1982, JFS began to serve people of all faiths and today serves the entire community (jfsneworleans.org/history-mission/).

42. Home Special Committee Report 1942, 9.

43. Home Special Committee Report 1942, 14.

44. Home Special Committee Report 1942, 2, 16–17.

45. "Photograph Award List Is Announced," *T-P*, May 16, 1941; untitled, *Southern Israelite* (Atlanta), April 1, 1934 (national award for institutional advertising). Lashman's creative brochures included illustrations by cartoonist John Chase, including "The Jewish Children's Home Tells Its Story," April 1931 (TSC-JCH, vol. 25) and "Tell-A-Vision," 1940 (JCRS).

46. CWL 1942, 64–65, 114–19.

47. B'nai B'rith Report 1942, 13–14.

48. BMM 12: February 22, 1934 (cost containment report); Home Special Committee Report 1942, 14. Notwithstanding Newman School's excellence for college preparation, several Home students who chose to transfer to public high schools later went on to college. In 1943, for example, the Home transferred Harry Cohen from Newman to Alcee Fortier High School in response to his "earnest plea," which his family believes may have been motivated by his desire to play on the public school's baseball team instead of at Newman. Letter from HLG to Ralph Schwarz, February 9, 1943; Blume interview; Cohen interview. After high school, with a BA and law degree from Tulane and a JSD from Yale, Professor Cohen taught at the University of Alabama's law school for thirty-seven years. "Professor Harry Cohen," *Alabama Lawyer* 69, no. 1 (January 2008).

49. For example, Sizeler interview, Haymon interview, Knobler interview, Alvin "Pat" Samuels interviews, Neiman interview.

50. Kovner interview, 2018. Other alumni who criticized the practice include Pat Samuels, Lilyan Golden Milner, Hannah Golden Limerick, and Carol Hart.

51. Reeves and Fall, "Seven Key Takeaways from Chetty's New Research on Friendship and Economic Mobility" (discussing Raj Chetty's 2002 studies on economic mobility and connectedness, "Social Capital I" and "Social Capital II").

52. Home Special Committee Report 1942, 16.

53. Home Special Committee Report 1942, 18.

54. Herman Chatelain, "Just Kids, 50 of Them Are Excited as Home's Anniversary Approaches," *NOI*, January 7, 1943.

55. Spitzberg Report, 2.

56. Spitzberg Report, 3.

57. "Report of the Special Committee to Study Present Costs of Operation of the Home and to Make Recommendations for the Future," September 29, 1945, TSC-JCH, box 1, folder 26.

58. BMM: April 9, 1946.

59. BMM: June 11, 1946.

60. "Harry Ginsburg Dies at Age of 59," *T-P*, June 26, 1946.

61. Washofsky interview.

62. Eisner interview.

63. BMM: September 11, 1946.

64. "Harry Ginsberg [*sic*]," *NOI*, June 27, 1946.

65. Harry L. Ginsburg, Find a Grave, accessed August 20, 2022, www.findagrave.com/memorial/139206572/harry-1-ginsburg.

66. BMM: September 11, 1946.

67. BMM: November 12, 1946 (Bronstein Report).

68. Elsas interview.

69. "Wanted Good Foster Home," *T-P*, September 29, October 21, 1946.

70. Isidore Newman School Charter, November 22, 1946.

71. The board hired Sanford Weiss, a social worker from Cleveland's Bellefaire, as the agency's first executive director; he worked in tandem with his social worker wife, Viola Wolfson Weiss, who ran the agency from her husband's death in 1979 until her retirement in 1988. Ned Goldberg next served as executive director until 2021, when Mark Rubin assumed the post.

72. BMM: February 9, 1947 (Annual Meeting, President's Remarks).

73. Casey Family Programs, "Strategy Brief: Strong Families," August 2020, 2, accessed August 22, 2022, caseyfamilypro-wpengine.netdna-ssl.com/media/20.07-QFF-SF-Sibling-placements.pdf.

74. Polster, *Inside Looking Out*, 197.

75. For more than two decades, the Annie E. Casey Foundation, a leading national private nonprofit child welfare organization, has published resources and proposed solutions to improve the lives of American children and families, including more than 407,000 children in foster care as of 2020 (www.aecf.org/topics/foster-care). There exists, however, no shortage of headlines and articles bemoaning the shortcomings and failures of foster care. See, for example, Jane Coaston, "The All-Too-Common Tragedy of Foster Care, *NYT*, December 18, 2021, and Josh Gupta-Kagan, "America's Hidden Foster Care System," *Stanford Law Review* 72 (April 2020): 841–912.

76. *NCJC 1904*, 130–31. Even today, states with the most group homes are most likely to use them instead of foster families. Teresa Wiltz, "Finding Foster Families for Teens Is a Challenge in Many States," accessed October 3, 2022, www.pewtrusts.org/en/research-and-analysis/blogs/stateline/2019/06/20/finding-foster-families-for-teens-is-a-challenge-in-many-states.

77. Although Touro Infirmary was built in 1852 with funds from Judah Touro, it served patients of all religions. Touro Synagogue and Temple Sinai moved to new buildings on St. Charles Avenue in 1909 and 1928.

78. The author's description of the High Holy Days from a Reform perspective was inspired by Rabbi David Ellenson's essay, "Faith, Doubt, and Meaning in the Machzor," in Goldberg et al., eds., *Mishkan Hanefesh*, xxii–xxiv.

EPILOGUE

1. "Jewish Fund Drive to Bring Remodeling of Old Building," *T-P*, March 15, 1953.

2. "Center Pool Dedication to Be Today," *T-P*, August 30, 1953.

3. "Jewish Children's Home Alumni Gather," *T-P*, January 24, 1960.

4. "Orphan Alumni," DP, January 5, 1891; HB 1: 402, 822, 823; Louis H. Yarrut, "An Alumnus Writes," Century of Progress in Child Care (Jewish Children's Home, 1955); email from Louis Y. Fishman, November 30, 2018.

5. "Address by Judge Louis H. Yarrut at Homecoming Banquet, Jewish Children's Home, Roosevelt Hotel, January 23, 1960," TSC-JCH, box 41, folder 5.

6. Jewish Children's Home Alumni Reunion Newsletter, 1960, TSC-JCH, box 41, folder 11.

7. Hilda Crystal White to Joe Samuels, November 15, 1959, TSC-JCH, box 41, folder 11.

8. HB 3: 1470; HB 2: 821, 822.

9. AR 1863: 11.

10. HB 3: 1586–1588; Ellis Hart interviews; Lillie Oppenheim Hart interview.

11. Emails from Ned Goldberg and Mark Rubin, October 12, 2021.

12. Emails from Ned Goldberg and Mark Rubin, October 12, 2021.

13. Emails from Ned Goldberg and Mark Rubin, October 12, 2021.

14. Email from Harvey M. Stone, January 15, 2021.

15. Shanker interview.

16. B'nai B'rith District 7 ended direct financial support of JCRS in 1992, following a national decision to discontinue regional support through district service funds, and dissolved a few years later following a national reorganization. In addition to ongoing modest support from individual chapters, national B'nai B'rith later designated JCRS as a disaster relief organization and, starting with Hurricanes Katrina and Rita in 2005, has made grants to JCRS after floods and hurricanes. Email from Ned Goldberg, September 29, 2022; "B'nai B'rith Cuts Funding," *The Jewish Child*, fall 1992.

17. Email from Mark Rubin, August 18, 2022.

18. "New Orleans school integration," accessed September 27, 2022, crdl.usg.edu/events /new_orleans_integration/; Konigsmark, *Isidore Newman School*, 133.

19. Isidore Newman School website, accessed August 21, 2022, www.newmanschool.org.

20. Isidore Newman School articles of incorporation, article IV (as amended April 14, 1999).

BIBLIOGRAPHY

ARCHIVAL AND MANUSCRIPT COLLECTIONS

Early in this project, I discovered two things about the Home's records. First, no survey of Home children had previously been conducted. Second, with rare and incomplete exceptions, the children's case files no longer exist. Instead, I used the following sources of information.

From the Home's founding to its closing, administrators chronologically recorded all admissions in a series of three large leather-bound volumes. Titled "Biography" and maintained by JCRS in Metairie, Louisiana, each volume contains a uniquely numbered page per child (and prior to 1880, per widow). Employing varying degrees of consistency, completeness, and legibility, the handwritten entries in these registry books capture basic data including name, parents' names, nativity, "whence received," and dates of birth, admission, and discharge. Occasionally, the registries also contain information about the children's lives after discharge.

To fill in gaps and reconcile inconsistencies, I looked to the Home's annual reports and to the board's minutes. Annual reports (cited in notes as "AR"), which exist for almost all years prior to 1922, provide a separate, printed, and publicly disseminated source for some of the above data fields. The most comprehensive and publicly available collection of the Home's annual reports is maintained by Tulane University Library's Special Collections, Jewish Children's Home Collection, No. 180. Board meeting minute books (cited in notes as "BMM") are maintained in three locations: from 1855 through 1939 (vols. 1–14) at the American Jewish Archives in Cincinnati, Ohio, along with two volumes of annual meeting minutes ("AMM") covering 1854–1908; from 1940 through 1944 (vols. 15–17) at Tulane; and subsequent years at JCRS. Starting in 1922, to save money and reach a wider audience, the board discontinued its annual reports and instead, through 1933, published the *Golden City Messenger,* a monthly or bi-monthly newsletter, bound volumes of which are maintained at Tulane and JCRS.

ADDITIONAL ARCHIVAL AND MANUSCRIPT COLLECTIONS

American Jewish Archives, Cincinnati
> Association for the Relief of Jewish Widows and Orphans, SC-8870.
> B'nai B'rith District Grand Lodge No. 7, MS-180.
> Rabbi Isaac L. Leucht Papers, MS-596.

Baker Library Harvard Business School
> R. G. Dun & Co. Credit Reports, Louisiana vols.

Center for Jewish History, New York
> William F. Rosenblum Papers, P-327.

Howard Gottlieb Archival Research Center, Boston University
> Hilda Crystal White Papers.

Institute for Southern Jewish Life
> Interviews of Home Alumni.

Isidore Newman School Archives, New Orleans
> Including commencement programs, *Pioneer* literary magazine, and photographs.

Jewish Children's Regional Service
> Interviews, correspondence, and memorabilia of Home alumni and staff.

New Orleans Public Library, Louisiana Division.
> Friends of the Cabildo Oral History Collection.
> Property Tax Records.
> Scrapbook Collection.

Tulane University Library Special Collections, New Orleans
> Jewish Children's Home, LaRC-180.
> Touro Synagogue, LaRC-224.

Tulane University Southeastern Architectural Archive
> Thomas Sully Office Records, SEAA-008.

INTERVIEWS (YEARS IN HOME)

Akchin, Don (son of alumnus David Akchin, 1933–42). By author, June 7, 2018.

Anderson, Lydia Hartman (daughter of alumnus Sam Hartman, 1928–34). By author, March 11, 2018.

Andres, Amelia Cristol (daughter of alumna Hattie Szafir Cristol, 1889–93). By author, February 8, 2018.

Augustson, Revana (niece of alumnus Leon Clausner, 1903–9). By author, December 4, 2014.

Balkan, Gertrude (student counselor, 1938–42). By ISJL, March 21, 2004.

Beerman, Ralph (alumnus, 1924–30). By Marc Beerman (son), February 1, 1998.

———. By ISJL, 2004.

Bernstein, Joseph, and Rudolph Bernstein (alumni, 1896–1907). By JCRS, October 24, 1983.

Berry, Clara Jean Pulitzer (daughter of alumnus Jacob Pulitzer, 1912–16). By author, June 8, 2018.

Bihari, Joe (alumnus, 1931–43). By Steven L. Isoardi, UCLA, March 1995.

———. By John Broven, 2000, 2004, and 2013.

Block, Linda Freedman (granddaughter of alumna Goldie Berger Knobler, 1916–22). By author, June 9, 2020.

Blume, Nettie Cohen (daughter of alumnus Harry Cohen, 1936–44). By author, July 29, 2019.

Braslau, David (son of alumna Lena Kantrovich, 1904–11). By author, 2017.

Brier, Sharon Albert (daughter of alumnus Louis Albert, 1928–31). By author, March 9, 2018.

Brody, Sam (alumnus, 1936–46). By Al Stein, ISJL, March 20, 2004.

———. By author, January 30, 2018.

Brooks, Susan (granddaughter of alumna Rose Helen Jacobs, 1906–14). By author, September 13, 2021.

Buckman, Daniel (Newman alumnus class of 1947). By author, January 20, 2017.

Burka, Morris, Jr. (son of alumnus Morris Burka Sr., 1902–6). By JCRS, December 17, 2004.

Cahn, Adele Karp (alumna, 1923–35). By author, March 9, 2016; June 26, 2012.

Calman, Camille (descendant of alumnus Nathan Goldstein, 1859–64). By author, July 26, 2017.

Clairfield, Mildred Foreman (alumna, 1919–29). By Ned Goldberg, JCRS, June 15, 2004.

Cohen, Doris (widow of alumnus Harry Cohen, 1936–44). By author, July 19, 2019.

Cohn, Samuel (student counselor, 1938–41). By JCRS, 2003, and December 17, 2004.

Crosby, Liz (granddaughter of Superintendent Leon Volmer, 1911–26). By author, October 7, 2015.

Davis, David B., II (grandson of alumnus David Davis, 1877–88). By author, July 31, 2018.

Eisner, Bettye Sawl (Sawilowsky) (alumna, 1940–46). By author, December 29, 2021.

Elsas, Inge Friedlander (girls' supervisor, 1941–46). By Ned Goldberg, JCRS, January 7, 2004.

Embry, Britt (son of alumna Sally Miller, 1918–33). By author, January 7, 2019.

Fieldsmith, Wayne (son of alumnus Hugo Fielschmidt, 1910–25). By author, February 21, 2017.

Flanigan, Kristin (great-granddaughter of Superintendent Michel Heymann). By author, 2016.

Foreman, Earl (alumnus, 1919–29). By Ned Goldberg, JCRS, 2004.

Fox, Albert (alumnus, 1924–34). By JCRS, 1983, December 5, 2003.

———. By Al Stein, ISJL, 2003, 2004.

Freedman, Betty Knobler (daughter of alumna Goldie Berger Knobler, 1916–22). By author, March 11, 2018.

Freedman, Sam (alumnus, 1928–34). By JCRS, September 21, 1983.

Friedman, Herbert (alumnus, 1939–46). By JCRS, November 14, 1984.

Garonzik, Allan (son of alumna Ida Beerman Garonzik, 1924–32). By author, March 8, 2018.

Gayner, Emanuel (Ginsberg) (alumnus, 1923–36). By JCRS, September 3, 1983.

Gerson, Fanny (Mashinka) Maas (alumna, 1920–32). By Ned Goldberg, JCRS, November 15, 2003.

Gilberstadt, Lucille Pierce (alumna, 1935–43). By Al Stein, ISJL, March 19, 2004.

Goldstein, Hirsch (alumnus, 1907–19). By JCRS, September 6, 1983.

Golman, Susan Szafir (descendant of alumnus Edmund Szafir, 1889–93). By author, March 7, 2018.

Gorden, Jennie (alumna, 1913–22). By JCRS, 1983.

Gordon, Melvin (son of alumnus Donald Gordon, 1924–40). By author, May 22, 2019.

Greenwald, Leslie H. (grandson of alumni Leslie Greenwald, Judith Korn, Lillian Neuberger, Henry Hirsch, and Bertha Seligman, 1890s). By author, November 2, 2016.

Gubin, Jill (daughter of alumna Louise Fielschmidt, 1908–20). By author, January 2017.

Hart, Carol (alumnus, 1927–43, and board president). ISJL, March 19, 2004.

Hart, Ellis (alumnus, 1927–33). By ISJL, 2004, March 21, 2007.

———. By author, July 17, 2017.

Hart, Lillie Oppenheim (parent of alumni). By Carol Hart (son), 1970.

Hartman, Ben (grandson of alumnus Lee Hartman, 1928–34). By author, May 25, 2017.

Harvith, Beulah Blondheim (alumna, 1914–29). By Charles Harvith (son), 1994.

Haymon, Helen Gold (alumna, 1920–36). By JCRS, November 6, 1983; October 19, 2003.

Hirschhorn, Marilyn (daughter of alumna Annie Schneider Pilsk, 1914–24). By author, February 4, 2016.

Holt, Jackie Skalka (daughter of alumnus Morris Skalka, 1936–44). By author, December 13, 2016.

Hornikel, Fannie Weil Cohn (Newman alumna, 1923). By Dorothy Schlesinger, Friends of the Cabildo Oral History Program, August 27, 1989.

Jacoby, Jessica (daughter of staff member Claude Jacoby, 1940–41). By author, November 17, 2016.

Kahn, Catherine Cahn (archivist/historian and Newman alumna 1948). By ISJL, 2004.

Kern, Clifford H., III (great-great-grandson of widow Babette Schwartz, 1855–65). By author, March 26, 2019.

Klafert, Bena Lachoff (alumna, 1941–46). By Al Stein, ISJL, March 21, 2004.

———. By author, January 22, 2017.

Knobler, Goldie Berger (alumna, 1916–22). By JCRS, July 27, 1984.

Koltun, Sam (alumnus). By Helen Haymon, JCRS, October 11, 1983.

Kovner, Zalmon Harry (alumnus, 1928–42). By Ned Goldberg, JCRS, November 15, 2003.

———. By author, March 12, 2018.

Lashman, Deb (granddaughter of Superintendent L. Edward Lashman, 1926–29). By author, February 17, 2020.

Levin, Ralph (nephew of Nurse Anna Kamin, 1930s–1946). By Al Stein, ISJL, March 20, 2004.

Levine, Hyman "Herc" M. (alumnus, 1933–42). By JCRS, 1983, 2004.

Levitan, Sam (alumnus, 1927–36). By JCRS, 1983, 2004.

———. By author, September 25, 2017.

Likes, Julie (granddaughter of alumna Fannie Block, 1904–16). By author, August 26, 2017.

Limerick, Hannah Golden (alumna, 1935–42). By author, March 12, 2018.

Loeb, Rayna (great-niece of alumnus Abraham Miller and siblings, 1892–1904). By author, January 24, 2020.

Loewenthal, Carolyn Goldstein (great-niece of alumnus Harry Goldstein and siblings, 1906–12). By author, November 23, 2020.

Marsalis, Ellis (attended Gilbert Academy, 1948–49). By author, June 18, 2018.

McCrory, John (grandson of alumnus Archie Kronenberg, 1914–25). By author, May 24, 2019.

Meadow, Rose Sherman (alumna, 1925–40). By Ned Goldberg, JCRS, December 5, 2003.

———. By Al Stein, ISJL, 2004.

Mehlman, Joan (daughter of alumnus Murdock Mendelsohn, 1912–19). By author, November 10, 2019.

Milgrom, Jeff (son of alumna Shirley (Sawilowsky) Sawl Zenovich, 1940–46). By author, December 18, 2021.

Miller, Susan Katz (great-granddaughter of alumna Sarah Adler Rosenfelder, 1867–76). By author, February 19, 2020.

Milner, Lilyan Golden (alumna, 1935–40). By author, May 11, 2018; December 11, 2019.

Neiman, Harriet Elisabeth (daughter of alumna Miriam Tannenbaum, 1918–24). By author, October 26, 2019.

Pailet, Ethel Rosenbaum (alumna, 1921–25), By JCRS, 1983.

Pfeifer, Janet Loeb (alumna, 1930–35). By JCRS, 1983.

———. By unidentified interviewer, 1999.

Phelps, Kathleen (great-granddaughter of alumnus Adolph Phelps, 1884–98). By author, March 11, 2019.

Pilsk, Ann Schneider (alumna, 1914–24). By JCRS, November 30, 1983.

Plotkin, Mark (son of alumnus George Plotkin, 1921–30). By author, April 21, 2021.

Portnoy, Robert (son of alumna Dorothy Rosenbaum Portnoy, 1921–29). By author, August 27, 2020.

Raden, Irene (daughter of alumna Bryna Tannenbaum, 1918–24). By author, March 7, 2018.

Rose, Jonathan (descendant of alumnus Henry Ber Kaufman, 1855–58). By author, June 29, 2020.

Rosenberg, Morris (alumnus, 1916–22). By JCRS, April 26, 1984.

Rothstein, Bessie (Mashinka) Maas (alumna, 1920–34). By Ned Goldberg, JCRS, August 28, 2003.

Salky, Steve (descendant of alumnus Louise Fielschmidt, 1908–20). By author, February 15, 2017.

Samuels, Alvin "Pat" (alumnus, 1929–42), JCRS, August 28, 2003.

———. By author, March 10, 2018.

Samuels, Jeanne (widow of alumnus Joe Samuels, 1929–36). By author, March 10, 2018.

Samuels, Joe, and Alvin "Pat" Samuels (alumni). By JCRS, August 28, 2003.

Saparow, Susan Ladner (daughter of alumnus David Ladner, 1928–37). By author, October 7, 2021.

Sawl, Steve (son of alumnus Jack Sawilowsky, 1940–46). By author, April 4, 2022.

Scherck Morrison, Ann (great-granddaughter of President Isaac Scherck). By author, December 3, 2019.

Schlesinger, Ben, and Joseph Schlesinger (great-nephew and great-great-nephew of alumni Frishman siblings, 1881–91). By author, November 19, 2019.

Schneider, Jennie Ogden (alumna, 1940–46). By JCRS, December 3, 2004; April 18, 2005.

———, and Sara Ogden Sweet (alumnae, 1940–46). By family, 2009.

Schwertley, Rob (descendant of alumna Rachel Goldstein, 1868–71). By author, April 26, 2018.

Seltman, Sharon (daughter of alumna Jacqueline Behr, 1933–40). By author, December 10, 2020.

Shanker, Ben (alumnus, 1929–41). By author, May 10, 2016.

Simon, Ruby (alumna, 1910–17). By JCRS, July 27, 1983.

Singer, Mika (daughter of alumna Rachel/Ray Crystal, 1920–28). By author, March 1, 2019.

Sizeler, Helen Lubow (alumna, 1915–32). By Dorothy Schlesinger, Friends of the Cabildo Oral History Program, August 18, 1982.

Skalka, Morris (alumnus, 1936–44). By Al Stein, ISJL, March 19, 2004.

Skalka, Paulette (widow of alumnus Morris Skalka, 1936–44). By author, February 9, 2017.

Smith, Bessie Weinberg (alumna, 1919–33). By JCRS, October 25, 1983.

Smith, Kay (daughter of alumnus Leroy Swartzkopf, 1911–18). By author, January 5, 2017.

Smith, Lillian Hofstetter Pulitzer (alumna, 1927–38). By JCRS, 1983.

———. By ISJL, November 12, 2004.

Stahl, Joseph B. (attended Home's summer camp, 1940s). By author, April 2, 2021.

Stifft, Celeste (daughter of alumnus Nathan Stifft, 1869–79), and Sidney Friedman (Celeste's nephew). By Ned Goldberg, JCRS, 2004.

Stone, Edward (grandson of alumnus Edgar Goldberg, 1884–91). By author, March 7, 2018.

Strickland, Dale Caplan (granddaughter of alumnus Harry Caplan, 1896–1905). By author, July 3, 2020.

Sweet, Sara Ogden (alumna, 1940–46). By author, December 3, 2018.

Testa, Mitchell (son of alumnus Jack Testa, 1920–35). By author, March 9, 2018.

Testa, Peggy (daughter of alumnus David Testa, 1920–34). By author, March 21, 2018.

Tobias, Max (son of alumni Max Tobias, 1905–18, and Mildred Gordon, 1924–31). By author, October 2, 2019.

Tobias, Mildred Gordon (alumna, 1924–31). By JCRS, August 17, 1983.

Wade, Roberta (granddaughter of alumnus Morris Menges, 1856–61). By author, February 12, 2016.

Waldauer, Celeste Stifft, and Sidney Friedman (daughter and great-nephew of alumnus Nathan Stifft, 1869–79). By Ned Goldberg, JCRS, 2004.

Washofsky, Sonia Packman (alumna, 1941–46). By author, January 21, 2017.

Whitehead, James M. (alumnus, 1935–46). By Al Stein, ISJL, March 19, 2004.

Wizig, Debbie (daughter of alumna Bessie Mashinka Rothstein, 1920–34). By author, March 10, 2018.

Wolff, Harvey, and Calvin Wolff (grandsons of alumnus Isadore Moritz, 1884–91). By author, March 7, 2018.

Wolff, Marsha Albert (daughter of alumnus Louis Albert, 1928–31). By author, March 7, 2018.

Yasni, Rosalie Gorden (alumna, 1913–27). By JCRS, July 16, 1984.

Zenovich, Shirley (Sawilowsky) Sawl (alumna, 1940–46). By author, December 28, 2021.

GOVERNMENT REPORTS AND CONFERENCE PROCEEDINGS

National Conference of Charities and Correction. Proceedings, 1894–1903.

National Conference of Jewish Charities. Proceedings, 1902–10.

National Conference of Jewish Social Service. Proceedings, 1935.

Report of the [U.S.] *Commissioner of Education for 1884–1885.* Washington, DC, 1886.

Reports of the Boards of Commissioners of McDonogh School Fund, et al. New Orleans: L. Graham & Sons, 1896.

U.S. Bureau of Labor Statistics. "One hundred years of price change: the Consumer Price Index and the American Inflation experience." *Monthly Labor Review,* April 2014, 1–29.

U.S. Census Bureau. *Benevolent Institutions, 1904.* Washington, DC, 1905.

———. *Benevolent Institutions, 1910.* Washington, DC, 1913.

———. *Children Under Institutional Care, 1923.* Washington, DC, 1927.

———. *Children Under Institutional Care and in Foster Homes, 1933.* Washington, DC, 1935.

U.S. Children's Bureau. *Handbook for the Use of Boards of Directors, Superintendents, and Staffs of Institutions for Dependent Children.* Washington, DC, 1927.

———. The Work of Child-Placing Agencies. Washington, DC, 1927.

U.S. Dept. of Education, National Center for Education Statistics. *120 Years of American Education: A Statistical Portrait.* Washington, DC, 1993.

U.S. Dept. of Health, Education, and Welfare. *100 Years of Marriage and Divorce Statistics, United States, 1867–1967.* Publication No. 74–1902. Washington, DC: December 1973.

———. *The Story of the White House Conferences on Children and Youth.* Washington, DC, 1967.

U.S. Dept. of the Interior, Bureau of Education. *Report of the U.S. Commissioner of Education for 1884–1885.* Washington, D.C., 1886.

White House Conference on the Care of Dependent Children. Proceedings. Washington, DC, 1909.

OTHER WORKS CITED (EXCLUDING NEWSPAPER AND BRIEF MAGAZINE ARTICLES)

Adler, Cyrus, ed. "David Einhorn," *Jewish Encyclopedia* 5. New York: Funk & Wagnalls, 1903, 78–79.

———. "West Virginia," *Jewish Encyclopedia* 12. New York: Funk and Wagnalls, 1906, 510.

Alexander, Daniel B. "Congregation Gates of Prayer: 150 Years of Service to the Jewish Community." Metairie, LA: Congregation Gates of Prayer, 2001.

"Allowances." *Encyclopedia of Children and Childhood in History and Society.* Accessed August 16, 2021, www.encyclopedia.com.

Ambrose, Stephen. "New Orleans in the Second World War." January 15, 1992. Accessed July 29, 2022, www.nationalww2museum.org/war/articles/new-orleans-second-world-war.

Andrus, Olive P. "Isidore Newman School and the Manual Training Movement." MA thesis, Tulane University, 1938.

Ashkenazi, Elliott. *The Business of Jews in Louisiana, 1840–1875*. Tuscaloosa: University of Alabama Press, 1988.

———. *The Civil War Diary of Clara Solomon: Growing Up in New Orleans, 1861–1862*. Baton Rouge: Louisiana State University Press, 1995.

Ashton, Diane. *Rebecca Gratz: Women and Judaism in Antebellum America*. Detroit: Wayne State University Press, 1997.

Baker, Mark. "The Voice of the Deserted Jewish Woman, 1867–1870." *Jewish Social Studies* 2, no. 1 (Autumn 1995): 98–123.

Barbeck, Hugo. *History of Jews in Nuremberg and Fuerth*. Accessed December 29, 2021, www.rijo.homepage.t-online.de/pdf/EN_FU_JU_barbeck.pdf.

Bardes, John. "The New Orleans Streetcar Protests of 1867." April 28, 2018. Accessed June 30, 2022, werehistory.org/the-new-orleans-streetcar-protests-of-1867/.

Batt, William J. "Michel Heymann, Memorial Service." *Proceedings of the Annual Congress of the American Prison Association* (1909), 146–49.

Bauer, Nicholas. "The Kindergarten Movement in New Orleans." *Kindergarten Review* 18, no. 7 (March 1908): 385–86.

Bauman, Mark K. *Jewish American Chronology*. Santa Barbara, CA: Greenwood, 2011.

———. *A New Vision of Southern Jewish History: Studies in Institution Building, Leadership, Interaction, and Mobility*. Tuscaloosa: University of Alabama Press, 2019.

Berenson, Anna. "A Study of the Jewish Children's Home." MA thesis, Tulane University, 1933.

Berman, Jeremiah. "The Trend in Jewish Religious Observance in Mid–Nineteenth Century America." *American Jewish Historical Society* 37 (1947): 31–53, 41.

Bernard, Jacqueline. *The Children You Gave Us: A History of 150 Years of Service to Children, Jewish Child Care Association of New York*. New York: Bloch Pub. Co., 1967.

Besmann, Wendy. "The 'Typical Home Kid Overachievers': Instilling a Success Ethic in the Jewish Children's Home in New Orleans." *Southern Jewish History* 5 (2008): 121–59.

Biographical and Historical Memoirs of Louisiana. Vol. 2. Chicago: Goodspeed Pub. Co., 1892.

Biographical and Historical Memoirs of Mississippi. Vol. 1. Chicago: Goodspeed Pub. Co., 1891.

"Biographical Sketches of Jewish Communal Workers in the United States." *American Jewish Year Book* 7 (1905): 32–118.

Bishir, Catherine W. "William A. Freret." *North Carolina Architects and Builders: A Biographical Dictionary.* 2009. Accessed June 22, 2021, ncarchitects.lib.ncsu.edu/people/P000417.

Blokker, Laura Ewen. *Education in Louisiana.* Louisiana Dept. of Culture, Recreation, and Tourism, 2012.

Bogen, Hyman. *The Luckiest Orphans: A History of the Hebrew Orphan Asylum of New York.* Champaign: University of Illinois Press, 1962.

Broven, John. *Record Makers and Breakers: Voices of the Independent Rock 'n' Roll Pioneers,* Urbana: University of Illinois Press, 2009.

Bureau of Jewish Social Research. "Statistics of Jews." *American Jewish Year Book* 23 (1921): 279–99.

Bynum, Victoria. *Unruly Women: Politics of Social and Sexual Control in the Old South.* Chapel Hill: University of North Carolina Press, 1992,

Campanella, Richard. "From Landmark to Parking Lot: The Original Temple Sinai Endured for 105 Years." *Preservation in Print,* October 2018.

———. *Geographies of New Orleans: Urban Fabrics Before the Storm.* Lafayette: Center for Louisiana Studies, University of Louisiana at Lafayette, 2006.

Campbell, Jacqueline G. "'The Unmeaning Twaddle about Order 28': Benjamin F. Butler and Confederate Women in Occupied New Orleans, 1862." *Journal of the Civil War Era* 2, no. 1 (March 2012); 11–30.

Cahan, Emily D. *Past Caring: A History of U.S. Preschool Care and Education for the Poor, 1820–1965.* New York: National Center for Children in Poverty, 1989.

Capers, "Confederates and Yankees in Occupied New Orleans, 1862–1865." *Journal of Southern History* 30, no. 4 (November 1964): 405–26.

Carrigan, JoAnn. *The Saffron Scourge: A History of Yellow Fever in Louisiana, 1796–1905.* Lafayette: University of Louisiana, 2015.

Casso, Evans J. *Lorenzo: The History of the Casso Family.* Gretna, LA: Pelican Pub., 1998.

Chatelain, Neil. "The Persistence of the Mardi Gras Spirit in Civil War New Orleans." February 16, 2021. Accessed June 28, 2022, emergingcivilwar.com/2021/02/16/the-persistence-of-the-mardi-gras-spirit-in-civil-war-new-orleans.

Chetty, Raj, et al. "Social Capital I: measurement and associations with economic mobility." *Nature* 608 (2022): 108–21.

———. "Social Capital II: determinants of economic connectedness." *Nature* 608 (2022): 122–34.

Clement, Priscilla Ferguson. "Children and Charity: Orphanages in New Orleans, 1817–1914." *Louisiana History* 27, no. 4 (Autumn 1986): 337–51.

Cocca, Carolyn. *Jailbait: The Politics of Statutory Rape.* Albany: State University of New York Press, 2004.

Conway, Edward S. "The Origins of the Jewish Orphanage." *Transactions & Miscellanies* 22 (1968–69): 53–66.

Crenson, Matthew. *Building the Invisible Orphanage: A Prehistory of the American Welfare System*. Cambridge, MA: Harvard University Press, 2001.

Curet, Jourdan. "All Rape Is Not Created Equal." *Louisiana Law Review* 79, no. 2 (Winter 2018): 479–517.

Dedication of the Home for Jewish Widows and Orphans of New Orleans, January 8, 1856. New Orleans: Sherman, Wharton & Co. Printers, 1856.

Dollinger, Marc. *Quest for Inclusion: Jews and Liberalism in Modern America*. Princeton, NJ: Princeton University Press, 2000.

Doneson, Jules. *Deeds of Love: A History of the Jewish Foster Home and Orphan Asylum of Philadelphia, America's First Jewish Orphanage*. New York: Vantage Press, 1996.

Downs, Susan W., and Michael W. Sherraden. "The Orphan Asylum in the Nineteenth Century." *Social Service Review* 57, no. 2 (June 1983): 272–90.

Doyle, Elizabeth Joan. "Civilian Life in Occupied New Orleans, 1862–1865." PhD diss., Louisiana State University, 1955.

Duff, R. B. "The Playground Movement in the United States and its Influence." MA thesis, Indiana University, 1910.

Dye, Charles M. "Woodward and Manual Training: Early Reform in American Secondary Schools." *American Secondary Education* 4, no. 3 (June 1974): 20–22.

Edwards, Rebecca. "The Depression of 1893." Vassar College, 2000. Accessed October 20, 2021, projects.vassar.edu/1896/depression.html.

Elzas, Barnett A. *The Reformed Society of Israelites of Charleston, S.C.* New York: Bloch Pub. Co., 1916.

Evans, Eli N. *The Provincials*. Chapel Hill: University of North Carolina Press, 2005.

Ferris, Marcie Cohen. *Matzoh Ball Gumbo: Culinary Tales of the Jewish South*. Chapel Hill: University of North Carolina Press, 2005.

Firestone, Reuven. "Why Jews Don't Proselytize." *Renovatio*, Spring 2019. Accessed July 3, 2021, renovatio.zaytuna.edu/article/why-jews-dont-proselytize.

Fleischman, Samuel M. *The History of the Jewish Foster Home and Orphan Asylum of Philadelphia, 1855–1905*. Philadelphia: Board of Managers, 1905.

Focke, Jaap. "Jewish Orphanages in Dutch Society." Accessed December 29, 2021, www.degruyter.com/document/doi/10.1515/9789048553877-004/html?lang=en.

Ford, Emily, and Barry Stiefel. *The Jews of New Orleans and the Mississippi Delta*. Charleston, SC: History Press, 2012.

Frankel, B. "Notizen." *Monatsschrift für Geschichte und Wissenschaft des Judentums* 8 (1859): 227–32.

Friedman, Joel W. "The Legal, Political, and Religious Legacy of an Extended Jewish Family." *Southern Jewish History* 18 (2015): 63–99.

Friedman, Reena Sigman. "'Send Me My Husband Who Lives in New York City': Husband Desertion in the American Jewish Immigrant Community, 1900–1926." *Jewish Social Studies* 44, no. 1 (Winter 1982): 1–18.

———. *These Are Our Children: Jewish Orphanages in the United States, 1880–1925.* Hanover, NH: Brandeis University Press, 1994.

Fussell, Elizabeth. "Constructing New Orleans, Constructing Race." *Journal of American History* 94, no. 3 (December 2007): 846–55.

Gerome, John. "Battle of New Orleans once was national holiday." *Bryan Times* (OH), January 4, 2005.

Ginsburg, Harry L. "Institutional Intake." *Proceedings, National Conference of Jewish Social Service,* 1935, 134–35.

Goldberg, Rabbi Edwin, et al., eds. *Mishkan Hanefesh: Machzor for the Days of Awe—Rosh Hashanah.* New York: Central Conference of American Rabbis, 2015.

Goldin, Claudia. "How America Graduated from High School: 1910 to 1960." National Bureau of Economic Research, Working Paper no. 4762 (June 1994).

Goodkind, S. B. "Maurice Stern." *Eminent Jews of America.* Toledo, OH: American Hebrew Biographical Co., 1918, 294–95.

Greenwald, Erin M. *Purchased Lives: New Orleans and the Domestic Slave Trade, 1808–1865.* New Orleans: Historic New Orleans Collection, 2015.

Gutek, Gerald L. *An Historical Introduction to American Education.* 3rd ed. Long Grove, IL: Waveland Press, 2013.

Hacsi, Timothy. *Second Home: Orphan Asylums and Poor Families in America.* Cambridge, MA: Harvard University Press, 1997.

Hagy, James William. *This Happy Land: The Jews of Colonial and Antebellum Charleston.* Tuscaloosa: University of Alabama Press, 1993.

Hanger, Kimberly S. *A Medley of Cultures: Louisiana History at the Cabildo,* chap. 2, 34. Accessed June 21, 2021. www.crt.state.la.us/louisiana-state-museum/publications/a-medley-of-cultures/index.

Hansan, John E. "National Conference of Charities and Correction (1874–1917): Forerunner of the National Conference of Social Welfare." Accessed December 5, 2022, www.socialwelfare.library.vcu.edu/organizations/national-conference-of-charities-and-correction-the-beginning/.

Hanson, Margaret. "The New Orleans Normal Kindergarten Training School." *Kindergarten Review* 18, no. 7 (March 1908).

Haven, Caroline T. "The Relation of Kindergarten to Manual Training." *Proceedings and Addresses, National Educational Association, 1892.* Washington, DC: National Educational Association, 1893.

Heleniak, Roman. "Local Reaction to the Great Depression in New Orleans, 1929–1933." *Louisiana History* 10, no. 4 (Autumn 1969): 289–306.

Heller, Max. *Jubilee Souvenir of Temple Sinai, 1872–1922.* New Orleans, 1922.

Hemard, Ned. "New Orleans Nostalgia: Celebrating Victory." New Orleans Bar Association. Accessed July 3, 2021, www.neworleansbar.org/uploads/files/Celebrating%20Victory%20overs%203_11-12.pdf.

Hennick, Louis, and E. Harper Charlton. *The Streetcars of New Orleans.* Gretna, LA: Jackson Square Press, 1975.

Heymann, Michel. "Reminiscences of a Kindergarten Friend." *Kindergarten Magazine* 16, no. 1 (September 1901): 282–83.

Higgenbotham, Gary. "A. J. Heinemann: A Colorful Figure in Local Baseball Lore." Society for American Baseball Research. Accessed Jan. 30, 2023, https://www.sabrneworleans.com/publications/garyhigginbotham/index.html.

Hildreth, Peggy Bassett. "Early Red Cross: The Howard Association of New Orleans." *Louisiana History* 20, no. 1 (Winter 1979): 49–75.

History of the Jews of Louisiana. New Orleans: Jewish Historical Pub. Co., 1905.

Humphreys, Margaret. *Yellow Fever and the South.* Baltimore: Johns Hopkins University Press, 1992.

Hurwitz, David Lyon. "How Lucky We Were." *American Jewish History* 87, no. 1 (March 1999): 29–59.

Imber, Michael. "The First World War, Sex Education, and the American Social Hygiene Association's Campaign Against Venereal Disease." *Journal of Educational Administration and History* 16, no. 1 (1984): 47–56.

Jacobs, Joseph. "The Federation Movement in American Jewish Philanthropy." *American Jewish Year Book* 17 (1915): 159–98.

Johnson, Thomas Cary. *Life and Letters of Benjamin M. Palmer.* Richmond, VA: Presbyterian Publication Committee, 1906.

Jones, Mina Irma. "The Jewish Community in New Orleans: A Study of Social Organization." MA thesis, Tulane University,1925.

Jones, Wallace L., Jr. "A History of Compulsory School Attendance and Visiting Teacher Services in Louisiana." PhD diss., Louisiana State University, 1967.

Jumonville, Florence M. "Nameless Graves: The Touro Infirmary Cemetery in New Orleans, 1888–1908." *Southern Jewish History* 19 (2016): 29–73, 34.

Kelley, Laura D. "Erin's Enterprise: Immigration by Appropriation, The Irish in Antebellum New Orleans." PhD diss., Tulane University, 2004.

Kendall, John Smith. *History of New Orleans.* Vol. 1. Chicago: Lewis Pub. Co., 1922.

Klein, Gerda. *A Passion for Sharing: The Life of Edith Rosenwald Stern.* New York: Rossel Books, 1984.

Kobrin, Rebecca. "Teaching Profession in the United States." Shalvi/Hyman Encyclopedia of Jewish Women. Accessed June 23, 2022, jwa.org/encyclopedia/article/teaching-profession-in-united-states.

Konigsmark, Anne Rochell. *Isidore Newman School: One Hundred Years.* New Orleans: Isidore Newman School, 2004.

Korn, Bertram. *American Jewry and the Civil War.* Philadelphia: Jewish Publication Society, 1951.

———. *The Early Jews of New Orleans.* Waltham, MA: American Jewish Historical Society, 1969.

———. "Jews and Negro Slavery in the Old South, 1789–1865: Address of the President." *American Jewish Historical Society* 50, no. 3 (March 1961): 151–201.

Kotzin, Daniel P. *Judah L. Magnes: An American Jewish Nonconformist.* Syracuse, NY: Syracuse University Press, 2010.

Lachoff, Irwin. "Rabbi Bernard Illowy: Counter Reformer." *Southern Jewish History* 5 (2002): 43–67.

———. "Reform in Mid Nineteenth-Century Jewish New Orleans." *Louisiana History* 60, no. 2 (Spring 2019): 171–98.

———, and Catherine C. Kahn. *The Jewish Community of New Orleans.* Charleston, SC: Arcadia Pub., 2005.

Langston, Scott M. "James K. Gutheim as Southern Reform Rabbi, Community Leader, and Symbol." *Southern Jewish History* 5 (2002): 69–102.

Leatham, Karen Trahan. "Ida Weis Friend." Shalvi/Hyman Encyclopedia of Jewish Women. Accessed May 23, 2023, jwa.org/encyclopedia/article/friend_ida_weis.

LeMaster, Carolyn Gray. *Corner of the Tapestry: A History of the Jewish Experience in Arkansas, 1820s–1990s.* Fayetteville: University of Arkansas Press, 1994.

Light, Caroline. *That Pride of Race and Character: The Roots of Jewish Benevolence in the Jim Crow South.* New York: New York University Press, 2014.

Light, Jennifer S. *States of Childhood: From the Junior Republic to the American Republic, 1895–1945.* Cambridge, MA: MIT Press, 2020.

Lindley, Tom. *Opening Doors.* Oklahoma City: Full Circle Press, 2016.

Lord, Alexandra M. *Condom Nation: The U.S. Government's Sex Education Campaign from World War I to the Internet.* Baltimore: Johns Hopkins University Press, 2010.

Lorge, Michael M., and Gary P. Zola, eds. *A Place of Our Own: The Rise of Reform Jewish Camping.* Tuscaloosa: University of Alabama Press, 2006.

Louisiana Educational Society. *Constitution and Bylaws.* New Orleans: T. H. Thomason, Printer, 1884.

Lundberg, Emma Octavia. *Unto the Least of the These: Social Services for Children.* New York: Appleton-Century-Crofts, Inc., 1947.

MacKenzie, Constance. "Free Kindergartens." *Social Welfare History Project,* July 1886. socialwelfare.library.vcu.edu/programs/education/kindergartens-a-history-1886/.

Magner, Joseph. *The Story of the Jewish Orphans Home of New Orleans.* New Orleans: J. G. Hauser, 1906.

Malone, Bobbie. "As Told to Memoirs: Ruth and Rosalie, Two Tales of Jewish New Orleans." *Southern Jewish History* 1 (1998): 121–33.

———. "New Orleans Uptown Jewish Immigrants." *Louisiana History* 32, no. 3 (Summer 1991): 239–78.

———. *Rabbi Max Heller: Reformer, Zionist, Southerner, 1860–1929.* Tuscaloosa: University of Alabama Press, 1997.

Marcus, Jacob Rader. *United States Jewry, 1776–1985.* Vol. 2: *The Germanic Period.* Detroit: Wayne State University Press, 1991.

Mariano, Allie. "The 1884 Cotton Expo and New Orleans' First Case of World's Fair Fever." Nola.com, July 7, 2021. Accessed July 6, 2022, www.nola.com/300/article_21fc06f9 -a1f5-56f8-8440-dee682805dfe.html.

Marten, James. *The Children's Civil War.* Chapel Hill: University of North Carolina Press, 1998.

Martinez, Raymond. *The Story of the River Front at New Orleans.* New Orleans: Pelican Pub., 1948.

Mayer, Anna B., with Alfred J. Kahn. *Day Care as a Social Instrument: A Policy Paper.* New York: Columbia University School of Social Work, 1965.

Mayer, Susan L. "Amelia Greenwald and Regina Kaplan: Jewish Nursing Pioneers." *Southern Jewish History* 1 (1998): 83–108.

McEvoy, Thomas J. *The Science of Education,* 2d ed. Brooklyn, NY: T. J. McEvoy, 1911.

McKenzie, Richard B. *Home Away from Home: The Forgotten History of Orphanages.* New York: Encounter Books, 2009.

Mehrlander, Andrea. *The Germans of Charleston, Richmond and New Orleans During the Civil War Period, 1850–1870.* Berlin: Walter de Gruyter, 2011.

Mills-Nichol, Carol. *Louisiana's Jewish Immigrants from the Bas-Rhin, Alsace, France.* Santa Maria, CA: Janaway Pub., 2014.

Mintz, Steven. *Huck's Raft: A History of American Childhood.* Cambridge, MA: Harvard University Press, 2004.

Monaco, Chris. "Moses E. Levy of Florida: A Jewish Abolitionist Abroad." *American Jewish History* 86, no. 4 (December 1998): 377–96.

Nightingale, Florence. *Notes on Nursing for the Labouring Classes.* London: Harrison, 1876.

Olmsted, Frederick Law. *A Journey in the Seaboard Slave States: With Remarks on Their Economy.* New York: Dix and Edwards, 1858.

O'Neill, Aaron. "Child Mortality in the United States 1800–2020." March 19, 2021. Accessed January 24, 2022, www.statista.com/statistics/1041693/united-states-all -time-child-mortality-rate/.

Ophir, Natan. "Where does the blessing of 'shehechiyanu' come from?" Accessed June 22, 2021, www.jewishvaluesonline.org/512.

Otis, Olive. "New Orleans Notes: The Jewish Home." *Louisiana Review,* August 28, 1889.

Parton, James. *General Butler in New Orleans: History of the Administration of the Department of the Gulf in the Year 1862.* 16th ed. Boston: Fields, Osgood, & Co., 1871.

Pelger, Erin K. "Lives Through the Looking Glass: The Diaries of Three Nineteenth Century American Women." MA thesis, University of Montana, 1999.

Polster, Gary Edward. *Inside Looking Out: The Cleveland Jewish Orphan Asylum, 1868–1924.* Kent, OH: Kent State University Press, 1990.

Pugh, Robert G. *Juvenile Laws of Louisiana: History and Development.* Baton Rouge: Louisiana Youth Commission, 1957.

Pulitzer, Samuel C. *Dreams Can Come True: The Inspiring Story of Samuel C. Pulitzer.* New York: Advisions, 1989.

Purdon, Eric. *Black Company: The Story of Subchaser 1264.* Annapolis, MD: Naval Institute Press, 1972.

Ramey, Jessica B. *Child Care in Black and White: Working Parents and the History of Orphanages.* Urbana: University of Illinois Press, 2012.

Reed, Germaine A. "Race Legislation in Louisiana, 1864–1920." *Louisiana History* 6, no. 4 (1965): 379–92.

Reeves, Richard, and Coura Fall. "Seven Key Takeaways from Chetty's New Research on Friendship and Economic Mobility." Brookings.com. Accessed August 21, 2022, www.brookings.edu/blog/up-front/2022/08/02/7-key-takeaways-from-chettys-new-research-on-friendship-and-economic-mobility/.

Reinders, Robert C. *End of An Era: New Orleans, 1850–1860.* Gretna, LA: Firebird Press, 1989.

Robinson, William L. *The Diary of a Samaritan: By a Member of the Howard Association of New Orleans.* New York: Harper & Brothers, 1860.

Rogers, J. David. "History of the New Orleans Flood Protection System." New Orleans Levee Systems, May 17, 2006. Accessed June 21, 2021, biotech.law.lsu.edu/katrina/ILIT/report/CH_4.pdf.

Rogoff, Leonard. "Is the Jew White? The Racial Place of the Southern Jew." *American Jewish History* 85, no. 3 (1997): 195–230.

Roland, Charles P. "Louisiana and Secession." *Louisiana History* 19, no. 4 (Autumn 1978): 389–99.

Rosen, Robert N. *The Jewish Confederates.* Chapel Hill: University of South Carolina Press, 2000.

Rosenbaum, Fred. *Cosmopolitans: A Social and Cultural History of the Jews of the San Francisco Bay Area.* Berkeley: University of California Press, 2011.

Rosenwaike, Ira. "Eleazar Block—His Family and Career," *American Jewish Archives Journal* 31 (November 1979): 142–49.

Rothman, David J. *The Discovery of the Asylum: Social Order and Disorder in the New Republic.* Boston: Little, Brown and Co., 1971.

Roumillat, Shelene C. "The Glorious Eighth of January." *64 Parishes*, January 2015. Accessed October 15, 2021, 64parishes.org/glorious-eighth-january.

Rowland, Dunbar. *Mississippi: Comprising Sketches of Counties, Towns, Events, Institutions and Persons*. Vol. 3. Atlanta: Southern Historical Pub. Assn., 1907.

Sarna, Jonathan D. "The Cult of Synthesis in American Jewish Culture." *Jewish Social Studies* 5, nos. 1–2 (Autumn 1998): 52–79.

———, and Adam D. Mendelsohn, eds. *Jews and the Civil War: A Reader*. New York: New York University Press, 2010.

———, and Benjamin Shapell. *Lincoln and the Jews*. New York: St. Martin's Press, 2015.

Schafer, Judith Kelleher. *Brothels, Depravity, and Abandoned Women: Illegal Sex in Antebellum New Orleans*. Baton Rouge: Louisiana State University Press, 2009.

Shansky, Carol L. *The Hebrew Orphan Asylum Band of New York City, 1874–1894*. Newcastle Upon Tyne, UK: Cambridge Scholars Pub., 2016.

Sharlitt, Michael. *As I Remember: The Home in My Heart*. Shaker Heights, OH, 1959.

Shpall, Leo. "Rabbi James Koppel Guttheim [sic]." *Louisiana Historical Quarterly* 22, no. 1 (January 1939): 166–80.

Simons, Howard. *Jewish Times: Voices of the American Jewish Experience*. Boston: Houghton Mifflin Harcourt, 1988.

Sinclair, M. B. W. "Seduction and the Myth of the Ideal Woman." *Minnesota Journal of Law & Inequality* 5, no. 1 (March 1987): 33–102.

Singer, Jenny. "The 10 Best, Most Classic Jewish Jokes." *Forward*, April 4, 2019. Accessed June 20, 2021, forward.com/schmooze/421730/the-10-best-most-classic-jewish-jokes/.

Somers, Dale A. "War and Play: The Civil War in New Orleans." *Mississippi Quarterly* 26, no. 1 (Winter 1972–73): 3–28.

Sperber, Haim. "Agunot, 1851–1914: An Introduction," *Annales de démographie historique* 136, no. 2 (2018): 107–35.

Sribnick, Ethan, and Sara Johnsen. "Mother's Pensions: The Historical Perspective." *Uncensored: American Family Experiences with Poverty and Homelessness* 3, no. 3 (Fall 2012): 29–32.

Staples, J. Erin. "Yellow Fever: 100 Years of Discovery." *Journal of the American Medical Association* 300, no. 8 (2008): 960–62.

Stein, Herman D. "Jewish Social Work in the United States, 1654–1954." *American Jewish Year Book* 57 (1956): 1–98.

Stern, Walter C. *Race and Education in New Orleans: Creating the Segregated City, 1764–1960*. Baton Rouge: Louisiana State University Press, 2018.

Stolp-Smith, Michael. "New Orleans Massacre (1866)." April 7, 2011. Accessed June 30, 2022, www.blackpast.org/african-american-history/new-orleans-massacre-1866/.

Stone, Bryan Edward. "Edgar Goldberg and the Texas Jewish Herald." *Southern Jewish History* 7 (2004): 71–108.

Swierenga, Robert P. *The Forerunners: Dutch Jewry in the North American Diaspora.* Detroit: Wayne State University Press, 1994.

Teller, Chester Jacob. "Some Child Caring Ideals." *Philadelphia Jewish Exponent,* February 3, 1911.

Telushkin, Joseph. *Jewish Literacy: The Most Important Things to Know About the Jewish Religion, Its People, and Its History.* New York: William Morrow, 1991.

Thompson, Brian C. "Journeys of an Immigrant Violinist: Jacques Oliveira in Civil War–Era New York and New Orleans." *Journal of the Society for American Music* 6, no. 1 (2012): 51–82.

Tobias, Thomas J. *The Hebrew Orphan Society of Charleston, S.C.: An Historical Sketch.* Charleston, SC: Hebrew Orphan Society, 1957.

Trestman, Marlene. *Fair Labor Lawyer: The Remarkable Life of New Deal Attorney and Supreme Court Advocate Bessie Margolin.* Baton Rouge: Louisiana State University Press, 2016.

———. *Online Supplement* to *Most Fortunate Unfortunates: The Jewish Orphans' Home of New Orleans.* 2023. marlenetrestman.com.

Trevathan, Bradford Ward. "The Hebrew Orphans' Home of Atlanta, 1889–1930." BA thesis, Emory University, 1984.

Tuchinda, Nicole. "The Imperative for Trauma-Responsive Special Education." *New York University Law Review* 95, no. 3 (June 2020): 766–836.

Tyler, Pamela. *New Orleans Women and the Poydras Home.* Baton Rouge: Louisiana State University Press, 2016.

United Federation of Teachers. "Considering Trauma in Special Education Evaluations." July 2021. Accessed July 13, 2022, www.uft.org/sites/default/files/attachments /considering-trauma-in-special-education-evaluations-and-iep-development _SOPM.pdf.

Vandal, Gilles. "Curing the Insane in New Orleans: 'The Temporary Insane Asylum,' 1852–1882." *Louisiana History* 46, no. 2 (Spring 2005): 155–84, 181.

Van Zante, Gary A. *New Orleans 1867: Photographs by Theodore Lilienthal.* London: Merrell Publishers Ltd., 2008.

Vigil, Francisco DePaula G. *Escandalo Dado Al Mundo en Asunto Mortara.* Lima, Peru: Nacional de M.N. Corpancho, 1859.

Voorsanger, Jacob. *The Chronicles of Emanu-El.* San Francisco, CA: G. Spaulding & Co., 1900.

Weiner, Deborah R. "A Conflict of Interests." *JMORE Baltimore Jewish Living,* December 2017, 82–84.

Westerink, Diane. "The Manual Training Movement." Accessed September 15, 2022, www3.nd.edu/~rbarger/www7/manualtr.html.

White, Hilda. *Wild Decembers: A Biographical Portrait of the Brontës.* New York: E. P. Dutton, 1957.

Who's Who in California, 1928–1929. San Francisco: Who's Who Pub., 1929.

Wilhelm, Cornelia. *The Independent Orders of B'nai B'rith and True Sisters: Pioneers of a New Jewish Identity.* Detroit: Wayne State University Press, 2011.

Wilson, James. "The Irish Angel of New Orleans." May, 28, 2021. Accessed January 16, 2022, www.irishcentral.com/roots/history/irish-angel-new-orleans-leitrim-orphanages-louisiana.

Wilson, Samuel, Jr., ed. *Queen of the South: New Orleans, 1853–1863—The Journal of Thomas K. Wharton.* New Orleans: Historic New Orleans Collection, 1999.

Winegarten, Ruth, and Cathy Schecter. *Deep in the Heart: The Lives and Legends of Texas Jews.* Austin: Eakin Press, 1990.

Wisner, Elizabeth. "The Howard Association of New Orleans." *Social Science Review* 41, no. 4 (December 1967): 411–18.

Wyckoff, G. P. "Louisiana Notes." *Journal of Social Forces* 1, no. 4 (May 1923): 409–11.

Wyman, Brendan. "Jewish Contributions to Marshall, Texas." *Texas Historian,* September 2002, 7–10.

Yarrut, Louis H. "The Reflections of a Jew at a Catholic Retreat." *The Claverite,* March–April 1954, 17–20.

Young Men's Business League. *New Orleans of 1894: Its Advantages, Its Prospects, Its Conditions.* New Orleans: L. Graham & Son, 1894.

Zmora, Nurith. *Orphanages Reconsidered: Child Care Institutions in Progressive Era Baltimore.* Philadelphia: Temple University Press, 1994.

Zola, Gary P. "James Koppel Gutheim." *American National Biography,* 1999. Accessed June 19, 2021, doi.org/10.1093/anb/9780198606697.article.0801796.

———. "Southern Rabbis and the Founding of the First National Association of Rabbis." *American Jewish History* 85, no. 4 (December 1997): 353–72.

INDEX

Note: Page numbers in *italics* refer to illustrations; those followed by "n" indicate endnotes.

Child Welfare League of America, 195–205, 216, 219–20, 232–36

citizenship, 152, 154

Civil War, 48–57, 64–65

class consciousness, 200

Clausner, Leon, 123, 177

Cleveland Jewish Orphan Asylum/Home (CJOA/CJOH; later Bellefaire): admissions age, minimum, 34, 299n98; B'nai B'rith and, 70–71, 109, 250n4, 277n24; creation of, 54; discipline at, 68; Eastern Europeans immigrants and, 113–14; female directors, 184; foster care, resistance to, 240; Ginsburg at, 208; Lashman and, 193–94, 200; male control of, 62; move to suburban campus, 199; name change, 188; population, 3; rabbinical training and, 98; Schoenberg and, 75; Sharlitt at, 152; shoemaking shop, 91; Sunshine City program, 193; transfers to, 223; wards transferred to, 238

clothing: expenditures on, 120, 229; formal, 52–53, 294n56; individual, 107–8, 199, 212; Matron DePass and, 29; name tags on, 202–3; uniforms, 58, 106; yard clothes vs. school clothes, 167

clubs, 153, 171–72, 175, 193, 212–13

Cohen, Fannie, 119, 122

Cohen, Harry, 302n48

Cohn, Alice, 254n76

Cohn, Joe, 163

Cohn, Joseph, 14, 19, 254n67

Cohn, Samuel K., 216, 246

Communal Hebrew School, 202, 294n53

Community Chest of New Orleans, 197, 218–19, 293n27

Conference of Southern Rabbis, 79, 84, 108

Congregation Dispersed of Judah: breakaway from Gates of Mercy, 9, 13; Civil War and, 49–50; founders from, 16, 254n67; merger with Gates of Mercy, 84

Congregation Gates of Mercy: about, 9; break away to Dispersed of Judah, 9, 13; cemetery, 62–63; founders from, 16, 254n67; Gutheim at, 7, 9, 59; Illowy at,

50–51, 58–59; merger with Dispersed of Judah, 84

Congregation Gates of Prayer: Bergman at, 166; classroom provided by, 61; education at, 226; formation of, 9; founders not from, 16; Lazar Schwartz and, 54; Silber at, 176; wards worshipping at, 201–2

Congregation Kahl Montgomery, Mobile, 56

Congregation Temime Derech, 36–37

Conn, Hattie, 77

Cortissez, Mr., 76

cottage plan, 115, 199, 216

Council of Jewish Federations and Welfare Funds, 232

counselors, student, 183, 215–16, 230

Craighead, Edwin B., 115–16

Crystal, Anna (later Cook), 160

Crystal, Rachel (later Singer), 144

Crystal, Sam, 187

cultural performances, 173

Dan B., 118

Danziger, Alfred, 293n27

DaSilva, Benjamin, 16, 50, 52, 254n64

Davis, David, 99, 274n87

day care, 231

Day in the Jewish Orphans' Home, A (film), 174

deaths of wards, 39, 62–63, 68–69

Dehougne, Sybil Bianchini, 112

Delgado Central Trades School, 161, 201, 230

dental clinic, 155

DePass, Ann, 25–26, 28–30, 32, 40, 42, 52, 58, 257n2

Deutsch, Eberhard P., 194

Deutsch, Hermann B., 194

DeYoung, Mr. and Mrs., 30–31

Dick, George, 189

Dick, Gladys, 189

disabilities, children with, 39–40

discharge practices, 40–45, 220–21, 260n102

discipline: apprenticeships and, 43–44; Ginsburg and, 208, 211; Golden City and, 154, 167, 169, 199, 203–4, 286n28; Heymann and, 111–12; Volmer and, 167–70